W9-CSX-091

INTRODUCTION TO CRITICAL READING

Introduction to CRITICAL READING

Tom Barnwell

Leah McCraney

UNIVERSITY OF ALABAMA AT BIRMINGHAM

Harcourt Brace Jovanovich College Publishers
Fort Worth   Philadelphia   San Diego
New York   Orlando   Austin   San Antonio
Toronto   Montreal   London   Sydney   Tokyo

Editor-in-Chief   Ted Buchholz
Publisher   Charlyce Jones Owen
Acquisitions Editor   Charlyce Jones Owen
Project Editor   Michele Tomiak
Production Manager   Kathleen Ferguson
Design Supervisor   Vicki McAlindon Horton
Copy Editor   Ann Burns Moyer
Text Design   Rita Naughton
Cover Design   Rhonda Campbell

Library of Congress Cataloging-in-Publication Data

Barnwell, Thomas.
   Introduction to critical reading / Thomas Barnwell, Leah McCraney. —Student ed.
      p. cm.
   ISBN 0-03-030372-9 : $14.00
   1. College readers.   I. McCraney, Leah.   II. Title.
PE1122.B36   1990
428.6—dc20   89-19760
                                                                                        CIP

ISBN 0-03-030372-9

Requests for permission to make copies of any part of the work should be mailed to: Permissions Department, Harcourt Brace Jovanovich, Publishers, 8th Floor, Orlando, Florida 32887.

Address editorial correspondence to: 301 Commerce Street, Suite 3700, Fort Worth, TX 76102.

Address orders to: 6277 Sea Harbor Drive, Orlando, FL 32887 1-800-782-4479, or 1-800-433-0001 (in Florida).

Printed in the United States of America

      3   085   9 8 7 6 5 4

Harcourt Brace Jovanovich, Inc.
The Dryden Press
Saunders College Publishing

Literary and photographic credits appear on page 281.

For Lindy, Dot, and Britt
and
In memory of Frank, Linnie, Mamie, and Tim

Preface
To the Teacher

Introduction to Critical Reading is an anthology of poems, short stories, essays, and college textbook chapters. *Teaching Critical Reading* is a manual that invites teachers into an exciting approach toward developmental reading and contains suggestions for the use of the Anthology in teaching reading improvement generally and critical thinking specifically. The Anthology is different from other developmental reading texts both in its rationale and in its content. Thus, we would first like to explain the rationale for the Anthology and second, the role and content of the teacher's manual.

We were guided in our selection of pieces for the Anthology by two questions:

1. What will a student be required to read in college?
2. What materials are best suited for encouraging critical thinking?

We thus selected for each genre a range of representative college-level materials that encourage active involvement. Some of the selections in the Anthology are relatively easy, and some are difficult or esoteric. While our selections are not based on a "readability" formula, we generally avoided pieces that, for example, contain extensive literary allusions or demonstrate problems of style. We avoided these pieces not because we think that "developmental" students cannot handle them, but rather because such pieces require more time than our primary purposes allow. We feel that our students *will* be able to handle such materials later when they encounter them, in context, in the regular college curriculum. Some pieces in the Anthology present problems we generally tried to avoid, but we found these pieces to be workable, and even more, exciting.

The selections were also made with "critical thinking/critical reading" in mind. "Critical thinking" is a term that, unfortunately, has passed into the mindlessness of our jargon and has as many meanings as there are people who use it. A detailed discussion of critical thinking is included in the introductory essay of the teacher's manual. We need say here only that the heart of critical thinking is an active, personal involvement, and that students who become actively involved in a piece of writing will eventually come to terms with that piece. This does not mean that students will understand every scrap of information in a piece or recognize every inference that could be made. But active involvement, of necessity, stems from a desire to know, and most college students, regardless of their "developmental" status, can discern the essential message of a piece if they want to "know." We thus selected pieces that invite student involvement and therefore provide a foundation for developing critical thinking.

To eliminate some problems of comprehension and provide the best possible opportunity for active involvement, we include in the Anthology the following aids:

1. Definitions of "hard" words that are not defined in context;
2. Explanatory notes on allusions to literature, history, art, and so on;
3. A glossary that includes definitions and examples of common literary and rhetorical devices.

The Anthology does not include questions on the content of the pieces. The teacher's manual shows that part of our system is to encourage student questions, student-generated criteria. Questions that come from editors invite a mechanical investigation of what the editors think important; such an investigation limits the possibilities of a piece of writing and limits student thinking to only those points addressed by the questions. There is a need, of course, for some "teacher" questions, teacher-generated criteria. We hope that the teacher's manual provides such criteria, not only for evaluating the content of a piece but also for developing critical thinking. Our suggested questions in the manual, however, are not meant to limit the teacher's approach but to suggest typical questions that can accomplish specific goals.

The "apparatus" of our approach, then, is the teacher's manual. We do not include any "apparatus" in the Anthology for students because

1. Students are not likely to pay much attention to editorial statements;
2. Students become better readers by reading, not by being told how to read;
3. Almost anything one might say about how an adult should read, how "good" readers read, and what a reader should "get out" of a piece of writing is frequently negated by the great variety of effective reading styles and by the possibility of varying meanings that different readers might interpret from a text;
4. The things an individual college teacher might say about the reading process or about a "good" college reader are likely to be far more suitable for that teacher's particular students than a textbook apparatus that applies totally to no group of students.

A manual for teachers, therefore, seems to us a far better investment than "suggestions," "tips," and discussions intended for students. The manual contains suggestions, intended primarily for classroom use, for every piece in the Anthology. The entire contents of the manual are as follows:

1. An introductory essay, providing teachers with our rationale for the Anthology, explaining in detail what we consider to be the nature of critical thinking, and providing general guidelines for helping students develop critical thinking;
2. A discussion of each selection in the Anthology. This discussion both elucidates content and points out issues that teachers may want to explore in class discussion;
3. Specific suggestions for each piece contained in the Anthology. These suggestions are aimed at getting students meaningfully involved in the content of a piece and encouraging the development of critical thinking. For poetry, we provide ten step-by-step exercises involving nineteen poems; these exercises show the range of techniques we have found useful. Other poems have been included specifically for comparative

studies of important issues (eight poems, four lessons), and our suggestions focus on the ways different poets treat the same issue. The remaining poems are included because they team so well with other poems, short stories, and essays in the Anthology, and our suggestions focus on the possibilities for extended studies. We provide for all the pieces from the other three genres (fiction, essays, and textbook chapters) step-by-step exercises for classroom use.

This Anthology and teacher's manual stem from the practices of teachers in our developmental reading program and the exciting results of those practices. The approach we recommend not only results in measurable improvements but also avoids treating in a condescending manner students whose egos are already fragile. Our approach, we feel, is humane as well as practical and exciting. If we had to describe our approach in a sentence, we would quote the motto of Scripps Howard newspapers: "Give light and the people will find their own way." The light we hope to give is the practice of *critical thinking*, a tool that is needed regardless of the directions our students may take.

Acknowledgments

A host of people helped us with this book. We especially thank Thomas Brown, Chairman of the Department of English, and Betty Jean Duff, Director of Academic Services, University of Alabama at Birmingham, for their professional support throughout the process and for their unfailing friendship. We especially thank also Charlyce Jones Owen at Holt for her assistance in leading us through the process and for her gentle "editorialness," which always allowed us much freedom in charting our course.

For various types of assistance and kindnesses we thank sincerely the following: Bert Andrews, Susan Blair, Henny and Milton Bordwin, Marlene Brown, Jason Burnett, Stella Cocoris, Robby Cox, Tim Douglas, Barbara Enlow, Paula Fulton, Delores Gallo, Al Gardner, Travis Gordon, John Haggerty, Barbara Hill, Helen Jackson, Susan Labaschin, Pat Lisella, Randy McCraney, Mark Myers, Malka Moskowits, Rose Norman, Iris and Colm O'Dunlaing, Jane Patton, Terry Proctor, Candace Ridington, Beebe and Dave Roberts, Melissa Tate, Reuben Triplett, and John Walker. We are also very grateful for the advice and assistance of our reviewers: Samuel Bellman, California State Polytechnic University, Pomona; Susan Blair, Jefferson State Junior College; Beth Camp, Linn-Benton Community College; Lenore Lerner, Westchester Community College; Donna McKusick, Essex Community College; and Eileen Schwartz, Purdue University at Calumet. For their help in the production of our book and especially in editing the manuscript, we are very grateful to Michele Tomiak and Ruth Steinberg at Holt.

Finally, we thank our students, who have shown us the value of reaching beyond one's grasp.

To the Student

The readings in this book were selected for a number of reasons. First, they are all excellent pieces of writing and worthy to be included in a college anthology. Second, they comprise a representative sample of four common types of writing—poetry, fiction, essays, and textbook chapters. Third, they are exciting and thought-provoking.

This third reason is of utmost importance to our philosophy and purposes in this book. We believe that meaningful learning occurs when one is actively involved in the learning process, when one finds something in the process that is of personal importance. The majority of readings in this book offer ideas that are likely to be of importance to most readers. Literature in particular offers a field of universal ideas—after all, the essence of literature is life—and this is one reason we include so much literature.

As you work with these readings, we encourage you to examine your values and the values of others. The Socratic position is that the unexamined life is not worth living. This position suggests that one must value one's own thinking and judgment; it is grounded in the belief that examining—questioning—is the foundation for being free.

Contents

POETRY

FICTION

ESSAYS

TEXTBOOK CHAPTERS

1

POETRY

Lot's Wife

Kristine Batey

    While Lot, the conscience of a nation,
    struggles with the Lord,
    she struggles with the housework.
    The City of Sin is where
5   she raises the children.
    Ba'al or Adonai—
    Whoever is God—
    the bread must still be made
    and the doorsills swept.

10   The Lord may kill the children tomorrow,
    but today they must be bathed and fed.
    Well and good to condemn your neighbor's religion;
    but weren't they there
    when the baby was born,
15   and when the well collapsed?
    While her husband communes with God,
    she tucks the children into bed.
    In the morning when he tells her of judgement,
    she puts down the lamp she is cleaning
20   and calmly begins to pack.
    In between bundling up the children
    and deciding what will go,
    she runs for a moment
    to say goodbye to the herd,
25   gently patting each soft head
    with tears in her eyes for the animals that will not understand.
    She smiles blindly to the woman
    who held her hand at childbed.
    It is easy for eyes that have always turned to heaven
30   not to look back;
    those that have been—by necessity—drawn to earth
    cannot forget that life is lived from day to day.
    Good, to a God, and good in human terms
    are two different things?
35   On the breast of the hill, she chooses to be human,
    and turns, in farewell—
    and never regrets
    the sacrifice.

NOTES

Ba'al or Adonai (l.6): Ba'al was the name given to several non-Hebrew gods by the people of Lot's time; Adonai is one of the names for the Hebrew god.
communes (l.16): communicates
at childbed (l.28): at childbirth

Genesis 19:12–26

1   The two angels said to Lot, "Have you anyone else here, sons-in-law, sons or daughters, or any who belong to you in the city? Get them out of this place, because we are going to destroy it. The outcry against it has been so great that the Lord has sent us to destroy it." So Lot went out and spoke to his intended sons-in-law. He said, "Be quick and leave this place; the Lord is going to destroy the city." But they did not take him seriously.

2   As soon as it was dawn, the angels urged Lot to go, saying, "Be quick, take your wife and your two daughters who are here, or you will be swept away when the city is punished." When he lingered, they took him by the hand, with his wife and his daughters, and, because the Lord had spared him, led him on until he was outside the city. When they had brought them out, they said, "Flee for your lives; do not look back and do not stop anywhere in the Plain. Flee to the hills or you will be swept away." Lot replied, "No, sirs. You have shown your servant favour and you have added to your unfailing care for me by saving my life, but I cannot escape to the hills; I shall be overtaken by the disaster, and die. Look, here is a town, only a small place, near enough for me to reach quickly. Let me escape to it—it is very small—and save my life." He said to him, "I grant your request: I will not overthrow this town you speak of. But flee there quickly, because I can do nothing until you are there." That is why the place is called Zoar. The sun had risen over the land as Lot entered Zoar; and then the Lord rained down fire and brimstone from the skies on Sodom and Gomorrah. He overthrew those cities and destroyed all the Plain, with everyone living there and everything growing in the ground. But Lot's wife, behind him, looked back, and she turned into a pillar of salt.

NOTES

two angels (par. 1): messengers sent by God
Zoar (par. 2): The word means "small."

Richard Cory

E. A. Robinson

Whenever Richard Cory went down town,
We people on the pavement looked at him;
He was a gentleman from sole to crown,
Clean favored, and imperially slim.

5   And he was always quietly arrayed,
And he was always human when he talked;
But still he fluttered pulses when he said,
"Good-morning," and he glittered when he walked.

And he was rich—yes, richer than a king—
10   And admirably schooled in every grace:
In fine, we thought that he was everything
To make us wish that we were in his place.

So on we worked, and waited for the light,
And went without the meat, and cursed the bread;
15   And Richard Cory, one calm summer night,
Went home and put a bullet through his head.

NOTES

imperially (l. 4): royally
arrayed (l. 5): finely dressed
In fine (l. 11): in short or in summary

The Road Not Taken

Robert Frost

Two roads diverged in a yellow wood,
And sorry I could not travel both
And be one traveler, long I stood
And looked down one as far as I could
5   To where it bent in the undergrowth;

Then took the other, as just as fair,
And having perhaps the better claim,
Because it was grassy and wanted wear;
Though as for that, the passing there
10   Had worn them really about the same,

And both that morning equally lay
In leaves no step had trodden black.
Oh, I kept the first for another day!
Yet knowing how way leads on to way,
15   I doubted if I should ever come back.

I shall be telling this with a sigh
Somewhere ages and ages hence:
Two roads diverged in a wood, and I—
I took the one less traveled by,
20   And that has made all the difference.

NOTES

Two roads diverged (l. 1): The road became two roads that went in different directions.
undergrowth (l. 5): plants or bushes growing beneath trees
wanted wear (l. 8): lacked or needed wear
trodden (l. 12): crushed
hence (l. 17): from this time

Mother to Son

Langston Hughes

Well, son, I'll tell you:
Life for me ain't been no crystal stair.
It's had tacks in it,
And splinters,
5   And boards torn up,
And places with no carpet on the floor—
Bare.
But all the time
I'se been a-climbin' on,
10 And reachin' landin's
And turnin' corners,
And sometimes goin' in the dark
Where there ain't been no light.
So, boy, don't you turn back.
15 Don't you set down on the steps
'Cause you finds it kinder hard.
Don't you fall now—
For I'se still goin', honey,
I'se still climbin',
20 And life for me ain't been no crystal stair.

Those Winter Sundays

Robert Hayden

Sundays too my father got up early
and put his clothes on in the blueblack cold,
then with cracked hands that ached
from labor in the weekday weather made
5   banked fires blaze. No one ever thanked him.

I'd wake and hear the cold splintering, breaking.
When the rooms were warm, he'd call,
and slowly I would rise and dress,
fearing the chronic angers of that house,

10 Speaking indifferently to him,
who had driven out the cold
and polished my good shoes as well.
What did I know, what did I know
of love's austere and lonely offices?

NOTES

banked fires (l. 5): fires that have been smothered with ashes in order to save hot coals for a later time
chronic (l. 9): frequently occurring
austere (l. 14): marked by self-denial or self-discipline

I, Too

Langston Hughes

I, too, sing America.

I am the darker brother.
They send me to eat in the kitchen
When company comes,
5 But I laugh,
And eat well,
And grow strong.

Tomorrow,
I'll sit at the table
10 When company comes.
Nobody'll dare
Say to me,
"Eat in the kitchen,"
Then.

15 Besides,
They'll see how beautiful I am
And be ashamed—

I, too, am America.

Harlem

Langston Hughes

What happens to a dream deferred?

Does it dry up
like a raisin in the sun?
Or fester like a sore—
5 And then run?
Does it stink like rotten meat?
Or crust and sugar over—
like a syrupy sweet?

Maybe it just sags
10   like a heavy load.

Or does it explode?

NOTES

Harlem (title): a predominantly black area of New York City
deferred (l. 1): postponed or put off
fester (l. 4): and *run* (l.5): "Fester" refers to the swelling of inflamed tissue; when the tissue opens, pus is released or "runs."
crust and sugar over . . . (ll. 7–8): Certain sweets (like jelly), after a period of time, will form a crust of sugar.

Channel Firing

Thomas Hardy

That night your great guns, unawares,
Shook all our coffins as we lay,
And broke the chancel window-squares,
We thought it was the Judgment-day

5   And sat upright. While drearisome
Arose the howl of wakened hounds:
The mouse let fall the altar-crumb,
The worms drew back into the mounds,

The glebe cow drooled. Till God called, "No;
10   It's gunnery practice out at sea
Just as before you went below;
The world is as it used to be:

"All nations striving strong to make
Red war yet redder. Mad as hatters
15   They do no more for Christes sake
Than you who are helpless in such matters.

"That it is not the judgment-hour
For some of them's a blessed thing,
For if it were they'd have to scour
20   Hell's floor for so much threatening. . . .

"Ha, ha. It will be warmer when
I blow the trumpet (if indeed
I ever do; for you are men,
And rest eternal sorely need)."

25   So down we lay again. "I wonder,
Will the world ever saner be,"
Said one, "than when He sent us under
In our indifferent century!"

And many a skeleton shook his head.
30   "Instead of preaching forty year,"

My neighbor Parson Thirdly said,
"I wish I had stuck to pipes and beer."

Again the guns disturbed the hour,
Roaring their readiness to avenge,
35 As far inland as Stourton Tower,
And Camelot, and starlit Stonehenge.

NOTES

Channel Firing (title): The channel referred to is the English Channel; the firing is the gunnery practice of British ships in preparation for war. World War I began four months after this poem was written.
unawares (l. 1): unexpectedly
chancel (l. 3): the part of a church containing the altar
Judgment-day (l. 4): the day of God's judgment of man. Another reference to Judgment-day is "blow the trumpet" (l. 22), a signal that Judgment-day has begun.
drearisome (l. 5): sadly
altar-crumb (l. 7): the crumb of bread left from communion
glebe (l. 9): a plot of land providing income for a parish church
Mad as hatters (l. 14): a phrase made popular by Lewis Carroll in *Alice's Adventures in Wonderland.* The idea that hatters are mad or insane probably comes from the behavior of hatters who used the chemical mercurous nitrate in making hats; exposure to this chemical can cause a nervous disorder known as St. Vitus's Dance.
Christes (l. 15): Christ's
scour ((l. 19): to clean by vigorous scrubbing
sorely (l. 24): desperately
avenge (l. 34): to get revenge
Stourton Tower (l. 35): a memorial erected to commemorate King Alfred's defeat of the Danes in A.D. 879
Camelot (l. 36): the legendary location of King Arthur's court
Stonehenge (l. 36): a circle formed of large stones, probably a place of worship for an ancient people

Dulce et Decorum Est

Wilfred Owen

Bent double, like old beggers under sacks,
Knock-kneed, coughing like hags, we cursed through sludge,
Till on the haunting flares we turned our backs,
And towards our distant rest began to trudge.
5 Men marched asleep. Many had lost their boots,
But limped on, blood-shod. All went lame, all blind;
Drunk with fatigue; deaf even to the hoots
Of Five-Nines dropping softly behind.

Gas! GAS! Quick, boys!—An ecstasy of fumbling,
10 Fitting the clumsy helmets just in time,
But someone still was yelling out and stumbling
And flound'ring like a man in fire or lime.—
Dim through the misty panes and thick green light,
As under a green sea, I saw him drowning.

15   In all my dreams before my helpless sight
     He plunges at me, guttering, choking, drowning.

     If in some smothering dreams, you too could pace
     Behind the wagon that we flung him in,
     And watch the white eyes writhing in his face,
20   His hanging face, like a devil's sick of sin,
     If you could hear, at every jolt, the blood
     Come gargling from the froth-corrupted lungs,
     Obscene as cancer, bitter as the cud
     Of vile, incurable sores on innocent tongues—
25   My friend, you would not tell with such high zest
     To children ardent for some desperate glory,
     The old lie: *Dulce et decorum est*
     Pro patria mori.

NOTES

Dulce et Decorum Est (title): a quotation from Horace (Roman poet). The entire statement is given in the last two lines and means "It is sweet and fitting to die for one's country." The action referred to in the poem occurs in World War I, in which Wilfred Owen died a week before the fighting ended.

flares (l. 3): devices containing an explosive material that lights the sky
blood-shod (l. 6): "Shod" literally means wearing shoes.
Five-Nines (l. 8): exploding shells of poisonous gas
ecstasy (l. 9): furious activity
flound'ring (l. 12): floundering: struggling
lime (l. 12): an acid-like chemical
guttering (l. 16): harsh sounds made deep in the throat
writhing (l. 19): twisting in pain
froth-corrupted (l. 22): filled with foam
cud (l. 23): literally, something that is chewed; a wad
vile (l. 24): repulsive
zest (l. 25): great enthusiasm
ardent (l. 26): full of desire

Hope Is the Thing with Feathers

Emily Dickinson

     "Hope" is the thing with feathers—
     That perches in the soul—
     And sings the tune without the words—
     And never stops—at all—

5   And sweetest—in the Gale—is heard—
     And sore must be the storm—
     That could abash the little Bird
     That kept so many warm—

I've heard it in the chillest land—
10 And on the strangest Sea—
Yet, never, in Extremity,
It asked a crumb—of Me.

NOTES

Gale (l. 5): storm
sore (l. 6): severe
abash (l. 7): destroy
Extremity (l. 11): extreme need

Hope Is a Strange Invention

Emily Dickinson

Hope is a strange invention—
A Patent of the Heart—
In unremitting action
Yet never wearing out—

5 Of this electric Adjunct
Not anything is known
But its unique momentum
Embellish all we own—

NOTES

Patent (l. 2): Literally, a patent is the granting of exclusive right to an invention.
unremitting (l. 3): constant
Adjunct (l. 5): something added or someone who assists someone else
momentum (l. 7): force that keeps something moving
Embellish (l. 8): makes beautiful

Hope Is a Subtle Glutton

Emily Dickinson

Hope is a subtle Glutton—
He feeds upon the Fair—
And yet—inspected closely
What Abstinence is there—

5 His is the Halcyon Table—
That never seats but One—

And whatsoever is consumed
The same amount remain—

NOTES

subtle (l. 1): not readily noticeable
Glutton (l. 1): Literally, a glutton is one who frequently eats to excess.
Abstinence l. 4): literally, refraining from eating, drinking, etc.
Halcyon (l. 5): peaceful, calm

Four Poems from
Spoon River Anthology

Edgar Lee Masters

MINERVA JONES

I AM Minerva, the village poetess,
Hooted at, jeered at by the Yahoos of the street
For my heavy body, cock-eye, and rolling walk,
And all the more when "Butch" Weldy
5   Captured me after a brutal hunt.
He left me to my fate with Doctor Meyers;
And I sank into death, growing numb from the feet up,
Like one stepping deeper and deeper into a stream of ice.
Will some one go to the village newspaper,
10   And gather into a book the verses I wrote?—
I thirsted so for love!
I hungered so for life!

NOTES

Spoon River Anthology: A collection of poems about the citizens of Spoon River, a community invented by the poet; each poem is an epitaph, an inscription on the tomb in memory of the person buried there.
Yahoos (l. 2): coarse, rude persons

"INDIGNATION" JONES

YOU would not believe, would you,
That I came from good Welsh stock?
That I was purer blooded than the white trash here?
And of more direct lineage than the New Englanders
5   And Virginians of Spoon River?
You would not believe that I had been to school
And read some books.
You saw me only as a run-down man,
With matted hair and beard

10   And ragged clothes.
Sometimes a man's life turns into a cancer
From being bruised and continually bruised,
And swells into a purplish mass,
Like growths on stalks of corn.
15   Here was I, a carpenter, mired in a bog of life
Into which I walked, thinking it was a meadow,
With a slattern for a wife, and poor Minerva, my daughter,
Whom you tormented and drove to death.
So I crept, crept, like a snail through the days
20   Of my life.
No more you hear my footsteps in the morning,
Resounding on the hollow sidewalk,
Going to the grocery store for a little corn meal
And a nickel's worth of bacon.

NOTES

Welsh (l. 2): descended from a native of Wales, an area in southwest Great Britain
trash (l. 3): worthless people
lineage (l. 4): line of descent from ancestors
mired (l. 15): stuck
bog (l. 15): literally, a swamp-like area
slattern (l. 17): an untidy or immoral woman

DOCTOR MEYERS

NO other man, unless it was Doc Hill,
Did more for people in this town than I.
And all the weak, the halt, the improvident
And those who could not pay flocked to me.
5   I was good-hearted, easy Doctor Meyers.
I was healthy, happy, in comfortable fortune,
Blest with a congenial mate, my children raised,
All wedded, doing well in the world.
And then one night, Minerva, the poetess,
10   Came to me in her trouble, crying.
I tried to help her out—she died—
They indicted me, the newspapers disgraced me,
My wife perished of a broken heart.
And pneumonia finished me.

NOTES

halt (l. 3): crippled
improvident (l. 3): those who do not prepare for the future
congenial (l. 7): pleasant and harmonious
indicted (l. 12): to be charged with a crime by a jury

MRS. MEYERS

HE protested all his life long
The newspapers lied about him villainously;

That he was not at fault for Minerva's fall,
But only tried to help her.
5   Poor soul so sunk in sin he could not see
That even trying to help her, as he called it,
He had broken the law human and divine.
Passers by, an ancient admonition to you:
If your ways would be ways of pleasantness,
10   And all your pathways peace,
Love God and keep his commandments.

NOTES

villainously (1. 2): viciously
divine (1. 7): relating to God
admonition (1. 8): warning

Musee des Beaux Arts

W. H. Auden

About suffering they were never wrong,
The Old Masters: how well they understood
Its human position; how it takes place
While someone else is eating or opening a window
    or just walking dully along;
5   How, when the aged are reverently, passionately waiting
For the miraculous birth, there always must be
Children who did not specially want it to happen, skating
On a pond at the edge of the wood:
They never forgot
10   That even the dreadful martyrdom must run its course
Anyhow in a corner, some untidy spot
Where the dogs go on with their doggy life and the torturer's
    horse
Scratches its innocent behind on a tree.

In Brueghel's *Icarus*, for instance: how everything turns away
15   Quite leisurely from the disaster; the plowman may
Have heard the splash, the forsaken cry,
But for him it was not an important failure; the sun shone
As it had to on the white legs disappearing into the green
Water; and the expensive delicate ship that must have seen
20   Something amazing, a boy falling out of the sky,
Had somewhere to get to and sailed calmly on.

NOTES

Musee des Beaux Arts (title): Museum of Fine Arts. The "Old Masters" referred to in line
2 are great painters of the Renaissance; one of the Old Masters was Brueghel (1. 14),
whose great painting *Icarus* is discussed in the last stanza of the poem and is reproduced
on page 15. The painting is based on a story from Greek mythology about Icarus, who
tried to fly with wings made of feathers and wax. According to the story, he flew too close

Pieter Bruegel, the Elder, Landscape with the Fall of Icarus

to the sun, causing the wax to melt and the wings to fall apart. Icarus fell into the ocean and drowned.

reverently (1. 5): with great respect
miraculous birth (1. 6): afterlife
martyrdom (1. 10): suffering death for a worthwhile cause, especially a religious cause

The Accident

Willie Morris

One afternoon in late August, as the summer's sun streamed into the car and made little jumping shadows on the windows, I sat gazing out at the tenement-dwellers, who were themselves looking out of their windows from the gray crumbling buildings along the tracks of upper Manhattan. As we crossed into the Bronx, the train unexpectedly slowed down for a few miles. Suddenly from out of my window I saw a large crowd near the tracks, held back by two policemen. Then, on the other side, from my window, I saw a sight I will never be able to forget: a little boy almost severed in halves, lying at an incredible angle near the track. The ground was covered with blood, and the boy's eyes were opened wide, strained and disbelieving in his sudden oblivion. A policeman stood next to him, his arms folded, staring straight ahead at the windows of our train. In the orange glow of late afternoon the policeman, the crowd, the corpse of the boy were for a brief moment immobile, motionless, a small tableau to violence and death in the city. Behind me, in the next row of seats, there was a game of bridge. I heard one of the four men say as he looked at the sight, "God, that's horrible." Another said, in a whisper, "Terrible, terrible." There was a momentary silence, punctuated only by the clicking of the wheels on the track. Then, after a pause, I heard the first man say: "Two hearts."

NOTES

Manhattan and *the Bronx:* areas of New York City
oblivion: loss of consciousness
tableau to: picture of
Two hearts: a bid in the game of bridge

Mr. Flood's Party

E. A. Robinson

Old Eben Flood, climbing alone one night
Over the hill between the town below
And the forsaken upland hermitage
That held as much as he should ever know
5   On earth again of home, paused warily.

The road was his with not a native near;
And Eben, having leisure, said aloud,
For no man else in Tilbury Town to hear:

"Well, Mr. Flood, we have the harvest moon
10 Again, and we may not have many more;
The bird is on the wing, the poet says,
And you and I have said it here before.
Drink to the bird." He raised up to the light
The jug that he had gone so far to fill,
15 And answered huskily: "Well, Mr. Flood,
Since you propose it, I believe I will."

Alone, as if enduring to the end
A valiant armor of scarred hopes outworn,
He stood there in the middle of the road
20 Like Roland's ghost winding a silent horn.
Below him, in the town among the trees,
Where friends of other days had honored him,
A phantom salutation of the dead
Rang thinly till old Eben's eyes were dim.

25 Then, as a mother lays her sleeping child
Down tenderly, fearing it may awake,
He set the jug down slowly at his feet
With trembling care, knowing that most things break;
And only when assured that on firm earth
30 It stood, as the uncertain lives of men
Assuredly did not, he paced away,
And with his hand extended paused again:

"Well, Mr. Flood, we have not met like this
In a long time; and many a change has come
35 To both of us, I fear, since last it was
We had a drop together. Welcome home!"
Convivially returning with himself,
Again he raised the jug up to the light;
And with an acquiescent quaver said:
40 "Well, Mr. Flood, if you insist, I might.

"Only a very little, Mr. Flood—
For auld lang syne. No more, sir; that will do."
So, for the time, apparently it did,
And Eben evidently thought so too;
45 For soon amid the silver loneliness
Of night he lifted up his voice and sang,
Secure, with only two moons listening,
Until the whole harmonious landscape rang—

"For auld lang syne." The weary throat gave out,
50 The last word wavered; and the song being done,
He raised again the jug regretfully
And shook his head, and was again alone.
There was not much that was ahead of him,
And there was nothing in the town below—
Where strangers would have shut the many doors
That many friends had opened long ago.

NOTES

forsaken (l. 3): deserted
hermitage (l. 3): a secluded or remote place of residence
warily (l. 5): cautiously
Tilbury Town (l. 8): a town invented by Robinson
The bird is on the wing (l. 11): a reference to *The Rubaiyat of Omar Khayyam*. The bird is the bird of time, and thus the sense of the line is that time is flying.
valiant (l. 18): proud, courageous
Like Roland's ghost . . . (l. 20): a reference to an event recorded in *Chanson de Roland*. When the battle of Roncevilles became hopeless, Roland called Charlemagne for help by blowing a horn and then died.
phantom (l. 23): literally, a ghost or spirit
salutation (l. 23): greeting
convivially (l. 37): sociably
acquiescent (l. 39): consenting
quaver (l. 39): a trembling, as of the voice
auld lang syne (l. 42): a toasting song that celebrates the past (literally, "old long ago")
wavered (l. 50): was sung weakly

The Groundhog

Richard Eberhart

In June, amid the golden fields,
I saw a groundhog lying dead.
Dead lay he; my senses shook,
And mind outshot our naked frailty.
5   There lowly in the vigorous summer
His form began its senseless change,
And made my senses waver dim
Seeing nature ferocious in him.
Inspecting close his maggots' might
10   And seething cauldron of his being,
Half with loathing, half with a strange love,
I poked him with an angry stick.
The fever arose, became a flame
And Vigour circumscribed the skies,
15   Immense energy in the sun,
And through my frame a sunless trembling.
My stick had done nor good nor harm.
Then stood I silent in the day
Watching the object, as before;
20   And kept my reverence for knowledge
Trying for control, to be still,
To quell the passion of the blood;
Until I had bent down on my knees
Praying for joy in the sight of decay.
25   And so I left; and I returned
In Autumn strict of eye, to see
The sap gone out of the groundhog,
But the bony sodden hulk remained.
But the year had lost its meaning,

30 And in intellectual chains
  I lost both love and loathing,
  Mured up in the wall of wisdom.
  Another summer took the fields again
  Massive and burning, full of life,
35 But when I chanced upon the spot
  There was only a little hair left,
  And bones bleaching in the sunlight
  Beautiful as architecture;
  I watched them like a geometer,
40 And cut a walking stick from a birch.
  It has been three years, now.
  There is no sign of the groundhog.
  I stood there in the whirling summer,
  My hand capped a withered heart.
45 And thought of China and of Greece,
  Of Alexander in his tent;
  Of Montaigne in his tower,
  Of Saint Theresa in her wild lament.

NOTES

outshot (l. 4): literally, shot beyond; here, realized
frailty (l. 4): weakness
vigorous (l. 5): full of life, strength, or activity
waver dim (l. 7): weaken
seething (l. 10): churning
cauldron (l. 10): (caldron) literally, a large boiling pot; here, something in which there is great activity
loathing (l. 11): extreme disgust
Vigour (l. 14): energy
circumscribed (l. 14): marked off, as one would a boundary
reverence (l. 20): great respect
quell (l. 22): to quiet or to control
sodden (l. 28): dull or without expression
intellectual (l. 30): relating to "reason" or "logic," as opposed to the "emotions"
Mured (l. 32): (immured) enclosed or imprisoned by something
geometer (l. 39): someone who is a specialist in geometry, but also someone who is interested in the shapes and forms of things
withered (l. 44): shrunken
China and *Greece* (l. 45): These two countries had at one time the greatest civilizations in the world.
Alexander (l. 46): Greek military leader (fourth century B.C.)
Montaigne (l. 47): French essayist (1533–1592), whose study was in a small tower
Saint Theresa (l. 48): Catholic saint (1515–1582), who often experienced a combination of love and pain
lament (l. 48): the expression of sorrow or grief

Ozymandias

Percy Bysshe Shelley

I met a traveler from an antique land
Who said: Two vast and trunkless legs of stone
Stand in the desert . . . Near them, on the sand,
Half sunk, a shattered visage lies, whose frown,
5 And wrinkled lip, and sneer of cold command,
Tell that its sculptor well those passions read
Which yet survive, stamped on these lifeless things,
The hand that mocked them, and the heart that fed;
And on the pedestal these words appear:
10 "My name is Ozymandias, king of kings:
Look on my works, ye Mighty, and despair!"
Nothing beside remains. Round the decay
Of that colossal wreck, boundless and bare
The lone and level sands stretch far away.

NOTES

Ozymandias (title): the Greek name for Ramses II, who ruled Egypt 1292–1225 B.C.
antique land (l. 1): ancient civilization
visage (l. 4): face
yet (l. 7): still
mocked (l. 8): recreated. The "hand" is the hand of the sculptor; the "heart" is the heart
of Ozymandias.
pedestal (l. 9): the base of the statue
colossal (l. 13): referring to colossus, a gigantic statue

When I Heard the Learn'd Astronomer

Walt Whitman

When I heard the learn'd astronomer,
When the proofs, the figures, were ranged in columns before me,
When I was shown the charts and diagrams, to add, divide, and measure them,
When I sitting heard the astronomer where he lectured with much applause
      in the lecture-room,
5 How soon unaccountable I became tired and sick,
Till rising and gliding out I wander'd off by myself,
In the mystical moist night-air, and from time to time,
Look'd up in perfect silence at the stars.

NOTES

Learn'd (title): learned, that is, highly educated
unaccountable (l.5): without any clear explanation
mystical (l.7): having a spiritual quality

Eleven

Archibald MacLeish

And summer mornings the mute child, rebellious,
Stupid, hating the words the meanings, hating
The Think now, Think, the Oh but Think! would leave
On tiptoe the three chairs on the verandah
5   And crossing tree by tree the empty lawn
Push back the shed door and upon the sill
Stand pressing out the sunlight from his eyes
And enter and with outstretched fingers feel
The grindstone and behind it the bare wall
10   And turn and in the corner on the cool
Hard earth sit listening. And one by one,
Out of the dazzled shadow in the room,
The shapes would gather, the brown plowshare, spades,
Mattocks, the polished helves of picks, a scythe
15   Hung from the rafters, shovels, slender tines
Glinting across the curve of sickles—shapes
Older than men were, the wise tools, the iron
Friendly with earth. And sit there, quiet, breathing
The harsh dry smell of withered bulbs, the faint
20   Odor of dung, the silence. And outside
Beyond the half-shut door the blind leaves
And the corn moving. And at noon would come,
Up from the garden, his hard crooked hands,
Gentle with earth, his knees still earth-stained, smelling
25   Of sun, of summer, the old gardener, like
A priest, like an interpreter, and bend
Over his baskets.
                              And they would not speak:
They would say nothing. And the child would sit there
30   Happy as though he had no name, as though
He had been no one: like a leaf, a stem,
Like a root growing—

NOTES

mute (l. 1): silent or unwilling to speak
verandah (l. 4): porch
sill (l. 6): the base of a doorway
plowshare (l. 13): the metal part of a plow that cuts the earth
Mattocks (l. 14): kinds of picks
helves (l. 14): tool handles
scythe (l. 14): a tool with a long, curved blade and long handle
tines (l. 15): sharp, projecting points or prongs
sickles (l. 16): tools with curved blades and short handles
dung (l. 20): manure, used for fertilizer
interpreter (l. 26): one who sees the hidden meanings of things

My Mother

Robert Mezey

My mother writes from Trenton,
a comedian to the bone
but underneath, serious
and all heart. "Honey," she says,
5   "be a mensch and Mary too,
its no good to worry, you
are doing the best you can
your dad and everyone
thinks you turned out very well
10 as long as you pay your bills
nobody can say a word
you can tell them to drop dead
so save a dollar it can't
hurt—remember Frank you went
15 to high school with? he still lives
with his wife's mother, his wife
works while he writes his books and
did he ever sell a one
the four kids run around naked
20 36 and he's never had,
you'll forgive my expression
even a pot to piss in
or a window to throw it,
such a smart boy he couldn't
25 read the footprints on the wall
honey you think you know all
the answers you don't, please try
to put some money away
believe me it wouldn't hurt
30 artist shmartist life's too short
for that kind of, forgive me,
horseshit, I know what you want
better than you, all that counts
is to make a good living
35 and the best of everything,
as Sholem Aleichem said
he was a great writer did
you ever read his books dear,
you should make what he makes a year
40 anyway he says some place
Poverty is no disgrace
but its no honor either
that's what I say,
                        love,
                            Mother"

NOTES

mensch (l. 5): Yiddish for "a good person"; Yiddish is a combination of Hebrew, German, and Eastern European languages.
artist shmartist (l. 30): "Shmartist" is an invented word to rhyme with "artist"; such word plays are used to make something or someone seem unimportant (in this case, artists).
Sholem Aleichem (l. 36): pen name of Solmon Rabinowitz (1859–1916), famous humorist

nobody loses all the time

e.e. cummings

nobody loses all the time

i had an uncle named
Sol who was a born failure and
nearly everybody said he should have gone
5   into vaudeville perhaps because my Uncle Sol could
sing McCann He Was A Diver on Xmas Eve like Hell Itself which
may or may not account for the fact that my Uncle

Sol indulged in that possibly most inexcusable
of all to use a highfalootin phrase
10   luxuries that is or to
wit farming and be
it needlessly
added

my Uncle Sol's farm
15   failed because the chickens
ate the vegetables so
my Uncle Sol had a
chicken farm till the
skunks ate the chickens when

20   my Uncle Sol
had a skunk farm but
the skunks caught cold and
died and so
my Uncle Sol imitated the
25   skunks in a subtle manner

or by drowning himself in the watertank
but somebody who'd given my Uncle Sol a Victor
Victrola and records while he lived presented to
him upon the auspicious occasion of his decease a
30   scrumptious not to mention splendiferous funeral with
tall boys in black gloves and flowers and everything and

i remember we all cried like the Missouri
when my Uncle Sol's coffin lurched because
somebody pressed a button
35   (and down went
my Uncle
Sol

and started a worm farm)

NOTES

vaudeville (l. 5): a form of entertainment popular in the United States during the late nineteenth and early twentieth centuries, consisting of short performances by singers, comedians, jugglers, etc.
highfalootin (l. 9): (highfalutin) fancy
subtle (l. 25): not obvious and/or skillful
Victor Victrola (ll. 27–28): an early record player
auspicious occasion (l. 29): an occasion that shows signs of success
scrumptious (l. 30): very pleasing
splendiferous (l. 30): splendid
Missouri (l. 32): the Missouri River
lurched (l. 33): moved suddenly

Growing Old

Matthew Arnold

What is it to grow old?
Is it to lose the glory of the form,
The luster of the eye?
Is it for beauty to forego her wreath?
5   —Yes, but not this alone.

Is it to feel our strength—
Not our bloom only, but our strength—decay?
Is it to feel each limb
Grow stiffer, every function less exact,
10   Each nerve more loosely strung?

Yes, this, and more; but not
Ah, 'tis not what in youth we dreamed 'twould be!
'Tis not to have our life
Mellowed and softened as with sunset glow,
15   A golden day's decline.

'Tis not to see the world
As from a height, with rapt prophetic eyes,
And heart profoundly stirred;
And weep, and feel the fullness of the past,
20   The years that are no more.

It is to spend long days
And not once feel that we were ever young;
It is to add, immured
In the hot prison of the present, month
25 To month with weary pain.

It is to suffer this,
And feel but half, and feebly, what we feel.
Deep in our hidden heart
Festers the dull remembrance of a change,
30 But no emotion—none.

It is—last stage of all—
When we are frozen up within, and quite
The phantom of ourselves,
To hear the world applaud the hollow ghost
35 Which blamed the living man.

NOTES

forego (l. 4): give up
wreath (l. 4): award; the ancient Greeks and Romans crowned winners with wreaths.
'tis (l. 12): it is
'twould (l. 12): it would
rapt (l. 17): enraptured, that is, wholly absorbed
prophetic (l. 17): wise, foreseeing
profoundly (l. 18): deeply
immured (l. 23): confined
Festers (l. 29): literally, swells painfully (like a sore)
phantom (l. 33): shadow

The Bean Eaters

Gwendolyn Brooks

They eat beans mostly, this old yellow pair.
Dinner is a casual affair.
Plain chipware on a plain and creaking wood,
Tin flatware.

5 Two who are Mostly Good.
Two who have lived their day,
But keep on putting on their clothes
And putting things away.
And remembering . . .
10 Remembering, with twinklings and twinges,
As they lean over the beans in their rented back room that is full of
  beads and receipts and dolls and clothes, tobacco crumbs, vases
  and fringes.

Cherrylog Road

James Dickey

Off Highway 106
At Cherrylog Road I entered
The '34 Ford without wheels,
Smothered in kudzu,
5   With a seat pulled out to run
Corn whiskey down from the hills,

And then from the other side
Crept into an Essex
With a rumble seat of red leather
10   And then out again, aboard
A blue Chevrolet, releasing
The rust from its other color.

Reared up on three building blocks.
None had the same body heat;
15   I changed with them inward, toward
The weedy heart of the junkyard,
For I knew that Doris Holbrook
Would escape from her father at noon

And would come from the farm
20   To seek parts owned by the sun
Among the abandoned chassis,
Sitting in each in turn
As I did, leaning forward
As in a wild stock-car race

25   In the parking lot of the dead.
Time after time, I climbed in
And out the other side, like
An envoy or movie star
Met at the station by crickets.
30   A radiator cap raised its head,

Become a real toad or a kingsnake,
As I neared the hub of the yard,
Passing through many states,
Many lives, to reach
35   Some grandmother's long Pierce-Arrow
Sending platters of blindness forth

From its nickel hubcaps
And spilling its tender upholstery
On sleepy roaches,
40   The glass panel in between
Lady and colored driver
Not all the way broken out,

The back-seat phone
Still on its hook.
45 I got in as though to exclaim,
"Let us go to the orphan asylum,
John; I have some old toys
For children who say their prayers."

I popped with sweat as I thought
50 I heard Doris Holbrook scrape
Like a mouse in the southern-state sun
That was eating the paint in blisters
From a hundred car tops and hoods.
She was tapping like code,

55 Loosening the screws,
Carrying off headlights,
Sparkplugs, bumpers,
Cracked mirrors and gear-knobs,
Getting ready, already,
60 To go back with something to show

Other than her lips' new trembling
I would hold to me soon, soon,
Where I sat in the ripped back seat
Talking over the interphone,
65 Praying for Doris Holbrook
To come from her father's farm

And to get back there
With no trace of me on her face
To be seen by her red-haired father
70 Who would change, in the squalling barn,
Her back's pale skin with a strop,
Then lay for me

In a bootlegger's roasting car
With a string-triggered 12-gauge shotgun
75 To blast the breath from the air.
Not cut by the jagged windshields,
Through the acres of wrecks she came
With a wrench in her hand,

Through dust where the blacksnake dies
80 Of boredom, and the beetle knows
The compost has no more life.
Someone outside would have seen
The oldest car's door inexplicably
Close from within:

85 I held her and held her and held her,
Convoyed at terrific speed
By the stalled, dreaming traffic around us,
So the blacksnake, stiff
With inaction, curved back
90 Into life, and hunted the mouse

With deadly overexcitement,
The beetles reclaimed their field
As we clung, glued together,

With the hooks of the seat springs
95   Working through to catch us red-handed
Amidst the gray breathless batting

That burst from the seat at our backs.
We left by separate doors
Into the changed, other bodies
100   Of cars, she down Cherrylog Road
And I to my motorcycle
Parked like a soul in the junkyard

Restored, a bicycle fleshed
With power, and tore off
105   Up Highway 106, continually
Drunk on the wind in my mouth,
Wringing the handlebar for speed,
Wild to be wreckage forever.

NOTES

kudzu (l. 4): a climbing plant, common in southern states
rumble seat (l. 9): an exterior, folding seat in the back of a car
chassis (l. 21): car bodies
envoy (l. 28): representative of a government
strop (l. 71): leather strap used for sharpening straight razors
compost (l. 81): manure
inexplicably (l. 83): mysteriously
Convoyed (l. 86): accompanied
batting (l. 96): padding

In a Prominent Bar in Secaucus One Day

X. J. Kennedy

To the tune of "The Old Orange Flute" or
the tune of "Sweet Betsy from Pike"

In a prominent bar in Secaucus one day
Rose a lady in skunk with a topheavy sway,
Raised a knobby red finger—all turned from their beer—
While with eyes bright as snowcrust she sang high and clear:

5   "Now who of you'd think from an eyeload of me
That I once was a lady as proud as could be?
Oh I'd never sit down by a tumbledown drunk
If it wasn't, my dears, for the high cost of junk.

"All the gents used to swear that the white of my calf
10   Beat the down of a swan by a length and a half.
In the kerchief of linen I caught to my nose
Ah, there never fell snot, but a little gold rose.

"I had seven gold teeth and a toothpick of gold,
My Virginia cheroot was a leaf of it rolled

15 And I'd light it each time with a thousand in cash—
Why the bums used to fight if I flicked them an ash.

"Once the toast of the Biltmore, the belle of the Taft,
I would drink bottle beer at the Drake, never draft,
And dine at the Astor on Salisbury steak
20 With a clean tablecloth for each bite I did take.

"In a car like the Roxy I'd roll to the track,
A steel-guitar trio, a bar in the back,
And the wheels made no noise, they turned over so fast,
Still it took you ten minutes to see me go past.

25 "When the horses bowed down to me that I might choose,
I bet on them all, for I hated to lose.
Now I'm saddled each night for my butter and eggs
And the broken threads race down the backs of my legs.

"Let you hold in mind, girls, that your beauty must pass
30 Like a lovely white clover that rusts with its grass.
Keep your bottoms off barstools and marry you young
Or be left—an old barrel with many a bung.

"For when time takes you out for a spin in his car
You'll be hard-pressed to stop him from going too far
35 And be left by the roadside, for all your good deeds,
Two toadstools for tits and a face full of weeds."

All the house raised a cheer, but the man at the bar
Made a phonecall and up pulled a red patrol car
And she blew us a kiss as they copped her away
40 From that prominent bar in Secaucus, N.J.

NOTES

Prominent (title): well-known
junk (l. 8): narcotics
down (l. 10): soft feathers
length and a half (l. 10): literally, a term used in horse racing to indicate the distance between horses; "length" refers to the length of a horse.
cheroot (l. 14): a cigar
Biltmore, Taft, Drake, Astor (ll. 17–19): expensive hotels in New York City
Roxy (l. 21): theatre in New York City
bung (l. 32): hole

Barbie Doll

Marge Piercy

This girlchild was born as usual
and presented dolls that did pee-pee
and miniature GE stoves and irons
and wee lipsticks the color of cherry candy.
5 Then in the magic of puberty, a classmate said:
You have a great big nose and fat legs.

She was healthy, tested intelligent,
possessed strong arms and back,
abundant sexual drive and manual dexterity.
10   She went to and fro apologizing.
Everyone saw a fat nose on thick legs.

She was advised to play coy,
exhorted to come on hearty,
exercise, diet, smile and wheedle.
15   Her good nature wore out
like a fan belt.
So she cut off her nose and legs
and offered them up.

In the casket displayed on satin she lay
20   with the undertaker's cosmetics painted on,
a turned-up putty nose,
dressed in a pink and white nightie.
Doesn't she look pretty? everyone said.
Consummation at last.
25   To every woman a happy ending.

NOTES

dexterity (l. 9): skillfulness
coy (l. 12): pretended shyness or "cuteness"
exhorted (l. 13): strongly urged or advised
wheedle (l. 14): to influence by flattery
Consummation (l. 24): completion or fulfillment of a goal

Mending Wall

Robert Frost

Something there is that doesn't love a wall,
That sends the frozen-ground-swell under it,
And spills the upper boulders in the sun;
And makes gaps even two can pass abreast.
5   The work of hunters is another thing:
I have come after them and made repair
Where they have left not one stone on a stone,
But they would have the rabbit out of hiding,
To please the yelping dogs. The gaps I mean,
10   No one has seen them made or heard them made,
But at spring mending-time we find them there.
I let my neighbor know beyond the hill;
And on a day we meet to walk the line
And set the wall between us once again.
15   We keep the wall between us as we go.
To each the boulders that have fallen to each.
And some are loaves and some so nearly balls
We have to use a spell to make them balance:
"Stay where you are until our backs are turned!"
20   We wear our fingers rough with handling them.
Oh, just another kind of outdoor game,

Stone Wall, Concord, Massachusetts

One on a side. It comes to little more:
There where it is we do not need the wall:
He is all pine and I am apple orchard.
25 My apple trees will never get across
And eat the cones under his pines, I tell him.
He only says, "Good fences make good neighbors."
Spring is the mischief in me, and I wonder
If I could put a notion in his head:
30 "*Why* do they make good neighbors? Isn't it
Where there are cows? But here there are no cows.
Before I built a wall I'd ask to know
What I was walling in or walling out,
And to whom I was like to give offense.
35 Something there is that doesn't love a wall,
That wants it down." I could say "Elves" to him,
But it's not elves exactly, and I'd rather
He said it for himself. I see him there
Bringing a stone grasped firmly by the top
40 In each hand, like an old-stone savage armed.
He moves in darkness as it seems to me,
Not of woods only and the shade of trees.
He will not go behind his father's saying,
And he likes having thought of it so well
45 He says again, "Good fences make good neighbors."

NOTES

frozen-ground-swell (l. 2): When the earth freezes, it expands or "swells."
boulders (l. 3): large stones
abreast (l. 4): side by side
yelping (l. 9): barking
spell (l. 18): a magic power
Spring is the mischief in me (l. 28): Spring makes me mischievous.
old-stone savage (l. 40): suggesting the image of a stone-age man or "cave man"
go behind (l. 43): dispute, abandon

Ithaca

Constantine Cavafis

When you start on your journey to Ithaca,
then pray that the road is long,
full of adventure, full of knowledge.
Do not fear the Lestrygonians
5   and the Cyclopes and the angry Poseidon.
You will never meet such as these on your path,
if your thoughts remain lofty, if a fine
emotion touches your body and your spirit.
You will never meet the Lestrygonians,
10 the Cyclopes and the fierce Poseidon,
if you do not carry them within your soul,
if your soul does not raise them up before you.

Then pray that the road is long.
That the summer mornings are many,

15   that you will enter ports seen for the first time
with such pleasure, with such joy!
Stop at the Phoenician markets,
and purchase fine merchandise,
mother-of-pearl and corals, amber and ebony,

20   and pleasurable perfumes of all kinds,
buy as many pleasurable perfumes as you can;
visit hosts of Egyptian cities,
to learn and learn from those who have knowledge.
Always keep Ithaca fixed in your mind.

25   To arrive there is your ultimate goal.
But do not hurry the voyage at all.
It is better to let it last for long years;
and even to anchor at the isle when you are old,
rich with all that you have gained on the way,

30   not expecting that Ithaca will offer you riches.

Ithaca has given you the beautiful voyage.
Without her you would never have taken the road.
But she has nothing more to give you.

And if you find her poor, Ithaca has not defrauded you.

35   With the great wisdom you have gained, with so much experience,
you must surely have understood by then what Ithacas mean.

NOTES

Ithaca (title): the island home of Odysseus, hero of Homer's *Odyssey*. Odysseus fought
for ten years in the Trojan War, the subject of Homer's *Iliad*. Odysseus spent ten years after the war trying to get home to Ithaca, and his adventures are the subject of the *Odyssey*.
Some of his adventures involve the Lestrygonians (l. 4), who were cannibals; the Cyclopes (l. 5), one-eyed monsters; and Poseidon (l. 5), the god of the sea and Odysseus' chief
enemy.
lofty (l. 7): noble
Phoenician (l. 17): of ancient Phoenicia, an area on the eastern Mediterranean coast
defrauded (l. 34): deceived or cheated

The Undead

Richard Wilbur

Even as children they were late sleepers,
Preferring their dreams, even when quick with monsters,
To the world with all its breakable toys,
Its compacts with the dying;

5   From the stretched arms of withered trees
They turned, fearing contagion of the mortal,
And even under the plums of summer
Drifted like winter moons.

Secret, unfriendly, pale, possessed
10   Of the one wish, the thirst for mere survival,

They came, as all extremists do
   In time, to a sort of grandeur:

   Now, to their Balkan battlements
Above the vulgar town of their first lives,
15   They rise at the moon's rising. Strange
     That their utter self-concern

   Should, in the end, have left them selfless:
Mirrors fail to perceive them as they float
   Through the great hall and up the staircase;
20   Nor are the cobwebs broken.

   Into the pallid night emerging,
Wrapped in their flapping capes, routinely maddened
   By a wolf's cry, they stand for a moment
     Stoking the mind's eye

25   With lewd thoughts of the pressed flowers
And bric-a-brac of rooms with something to lose,—
   Of love-dismembered dolls, and children
     Buried in quilted sleep.

   Then they are off in a negative frenzy,
30   Their black shapes cropped into sudden bats
   That swarm, burst, and are gone. Thinking
     Of a thrush cold in the leaves

   Who has sung his few summers truly,
Or an old scholar resting his eyes at last,
35   We cannot be much impressed with vampires,
     Colorful though they are;

   Nevertheless, their pain is real,
And requires our pity. Think how sad it must be
   To thirst always for a scorned elixir,
40   The salt quotidian blood,

   Which, if mistrusted, has no savor;
To prey on life forever and not possess it,
   As rock-hollows, tide after tide,
     Glassily strand the sea.

NOTES

Vampires, beings who are neither alive nor dead, are called "the undead" by Wilbur. He mentions a number of qualities and activities associated with vampires: they rise with the moon (l. 15); they cast no reflection in mirrors and pass through cobwebs without disturbing them (ll. 18–20); they wear capes (l. 22); they are "maddened by a wolf's cry" (ll. 22–23); they can turn into bats (l. 30); they exist by consuming blood (l. 40).

quick (l. 2): full of or alive with
compacts (l. 4): agreements or rules governing conduct
withered (l. 5): shrivelled
contagion (l. 6): corruption through contact
mortal (l. 6): that which dies
mere (l. 10): simple
Balkan battlements (l. 13): Vampires are said to occupy an area of Eastern Europe known as the Balkans; "battlements" are structures on a castle usually used for defense.
vulgar (l. 14): ordinary
pallid (l. 21): dull, colorless
maddened (l. 22): made insane

Stoking (l. 24): filling up
lewd (l. 25): evil
bric-a-brac (l. 26): a collection of small, decorative items or souvenirs
dismembered (l. 27): missing an arm or leg
frenzy (l. 29): wild or furious activity
cropped (l. 30): trimmed
thrush (l. 32): a song bird
scorned (l. 39): forbidden
elixir (l. 39): something that prolongs life
quotidian (l. 40): common or ordinary
savor (l. 41): appeal
strand (l. 44): to leave in an undesirable place

The Unknown Citizen

W. H. Auden

(To JS/07/M/378
This Marble Monument
Is Erected by the State)

He was found by the Bureau of Statistics to be
One against whom there was no official complaint,
And all the reports on his conduct agree
That, in the modern sense of an old-fashioned word, he was a saint,
5   For in everything he did he served the Greater Community.
Except for the War till the day he retired
He worked in a factory and never got fired
But satisfied his employers, Fudge Motors Inc.
Yet he wasn't a scab or odd in his views,
10   For his union reports that he paid his dues,
(Our report on his Union shows it was sound)
And our Social Psychology workers found
That he was popular with his mates and liked a drink.
The Press are convinced that he bought a paper every day
15   And that his reactions to advertisements were normal in every way.
Policies taken out in his name prove that he was fully insured,
And his Health-card shows he was once in hospital but left it cured.
Both Producers Research and High-Grade Living declare
He was fully sensible to the advantages of the Installment Plan
20   And had everything necessary to the Modern Man,
A phonograph, a radio, a car and a frigidaire.
Our researchers into Public Opinion are content
That he held the proper opinions for the time of year;
When there was peace, he was for peace; when there was war, he went.
25   He was married and added five children to the population,
Which our Eugenist says was the right number for a parent of his
        generation.
And our teachers report that he never interfered with their education.

Was he free? Was he happy? The question is absurd:
Had anything been wrong, we should certainly have heard.

NOTES

scab (l. 9): a worker who will not join a labor union or who takes a striker's job
Installment Plan (l. 19): a plan in which goods are paid for over a period of time
frigidaire (l. 21): a refrigerator
Eugenist (l. 26): an expert on the production of healthy offspring
absurd: (l. 28): ridiculous

Mr. Z

M. Carl Holman

Taught early that his mother's skin was the sign of error,
He dressed and spoke the perfect part of honor;
Won scholarships, attended the best schools,
Disclaimed kinship with jazz and spirituals;
5   Chose prudent, raceless views for each situation,
Or when he could not cleanly skirt dissension,
Faced up to the dilemma, firmly seized
Whatever ground was Anglo-Saxonized.
In diet, too, his practice was exemplary:
10 Of pork in its profane forms he was wary;
Expert in vintage wines, sauces and salads,
His palate shrank from cornbread, yams and collards.

He was as careful whom he chose to kiss:
His bride had somewhere lost her Jewishness,
15 But kept her blue eyes; an Episcopalian
Prelate proclaimed them matched chameleon.
Choosing the right addresses, here, abroad,
They shunned those places where they might be barred;
Even less anxious to be asked to dine
20 Where hosts catered to kosher accent or exotic skin.
And so he climbed, unclogged by ethnic weights,
An airborne plant, flourishing without roots.
Not one false note was struck—until he died:
His subtly grieving widow could have flayed
25 The obit writers, ringing crude changes on a clumsy phrase:
"One of the most distinguished members of his race."

NOTES

Disclaimed (l. 4): refused to claim
prudent (l. 5): wise, reasonable
skirt dissension (l. 6): avoid disagreement
dilemma (l. 7): a complex problem
Anglo-Saxonized (l. 8): dominated by Anglo-Saxon thinking, that is, "white" thinking
exemplary (l. 9): worth imitating
profane (l. 10): crude, coarse
wary (l. 10): cautious
vintage (l. 11): fine
palate (l. 12): taste buds
shrank from (l. 12): rejected

Prelate (l. 16): a high-ranking church official, such as a bishop
chameleon (l. 16): literally, a lizard with the ability to change its color
shunned (l. 18): avoided
barred (l. 18): not allowed to enter
catered to (l. 20): provided what was needed or desired
kosher (l. 20): literally, approved by Jewish law
exotic (l. 20): strange, different
unclogged (l. 21): freed from a difficulty
ethnic (l. 21): relating to a group of people that have certain characteristics in common, such as race, language, religion, etc.
subtly (l. 24): quietly, unobviously
flayed (l. 24): literally, to strip off the skin (as by lashing with a whip)
obit (l. 25): short for obituary, a notice of a person's death, usually with a short account of the person's life
ringing . . . changes (l. 25): running through the possible variations
distinguished (l. 26): outstanding

Bells for John Whiteside's Daughter

John Crowe Ransom

There was such speed in her little body,
And such lightness in her footfall,
It is no wonder her brown study
Astonishes us all.

5 Her wars were bruited in our high window.
We looked among orchard trees and beyond
Where she took arms against her shadow,
Or harried unto the pond

The lazy geese, like a snow cloud
10 Dripping their snow on the green grass,
Tricking and stopping, sleepy and proud,
Who cried in goose, Alas,

For the tireless heart within the little
Lady with rod that made them rise
15 From their noon apple-dreams and scuttle
Goose-fashion under the skies!

But now go the bells, and we are ready,
In one house we are sternly stopped
To say we are vexed at her brown study,
20 Lying so primly propped.

NOTES

brown study (l. 3): literally, a state of serious involvement in thought: here, an understated description of the death pose
bruited (l. 5): well-known
harried (l. 8): forced
scuttle (l. 15): run with a quick, shuffling motion
vexed (l. 19): distressed, puzzled

2

FICTION

The Lottery

Shirley Jackson

1   The morning of June 27th was clear and sunny, with the fresh warmth of a full-summer day; the flowers were blossoming profusely and the grass was richly green. The people of the village began to gather in the square, between the post office and the bank, around ten o'clock; in some towns there were so many people that the lottery took two days and had to be started on June 26th, but in this village, where there were only about three hundred people, the whole lottery took less than two hours, so it could begin at ten o'clock in the morning and still be through in time to allow the villagers to get home for noon dinner.

2   The children assembled first, of course. School was recently over for the summer, and the feeling of liberty sat uneasily on most of them; they tended to gather together quietly for a while before they broke into boisterous play, and their talk was still of the classroom and the teacher, of books and reprimands. Bobby Martin had already stuffed his pockets full of stones, and the other boys soon followed his example, selecting the smoothest and roundest stones; Bobby and Harry Jones and Dickie Delacroix—the villagers pronounced this name "Dellacroy"—eventually made a great pile of stones in one corner of the square and guarded it against the raids of the other boys. The girls stood aside, talking among themselves, looking over their shoulders at the boys, and the very small children rolled in the dust or clung to the hands of their older brothers or sisters.

3   Soon the men began to gather, surveying their own children, speaking of planting and rain, tractors and taxes. They stood together, away from the pile of stones in the corner, and their jokes were quiet and they smiled rather than laughed. The women, wearing faded house dresses and sweaters, came shortly after their menfolk. They greeted one another and exchanged bits of gossip as they went to join their husbands. Soon the women, standing by their husbands, began to call to their children, and the children came reluctantly, having to be called four or five times. Bobby Martin ducked under his mother's grasping hand and ran, laughing, back to the pile of stones. His father spoke up sharply, and Bobby came quickly and took his place between his father and his oldest brother.

4   The lottery was conducted—as were the square dances, the teenage club, the Halloween program—by Mr. Summers, who had time and energy to devote to civic activities. He was a round-faced, jovial man and he ran the coal business, and people were sorry for him, because he had no children and his wife was a scold. When he arrived in the square, carrying the black wooden box, there was a murmur of conversation among the villagers, and he waved and called, "Little late today, folks." The postmaster, Mr. Graves, followed him, carrying a three-legged stool, and the stool was put in the center of the square and Mr. Summers set the black box down on it. The villagers kept their distance, leaving a space between themselves and the stool, and when Mr. Summers said, "Some of you fellows want to give me a hand?" there was a hesitation before two men, Mr.

profusely (par. 1): in great quantity
boisterous (par. 2): noisy, rough
jovial (par. 4): jolly

Martin and his oldest son, Baxter, came forward to hold the box steady on the stool while Mr. Summers stirred up the papers inside it.

5   The original paraphernalia for the lottery had been lost long ago, and the black box now resting on the stool had been put into use even before Old Man Warner, the oldest man in town, was born. Mr. Summers spoke frequently to the villagers about making a new box, but no one liked to upset even as much tradition as was represented by the black box. There was a story that the present box had been made with some of the box that had preceded it, the one that had been constructed when the first people settled down to make a village here. Every year, after the lottery, Mr. Summers began talking again about a new box, but every year the subject was allowed to fade off without anything's being done. The black box grew shabbier each year; by now it was no longer completely black but splintered badly along one side to show the original wood color, and in some places faded or stained.

6   Mr. Martin and his oldest son, Baxter, held the black box securely on the stool until Mr. Summers had stirred the papers thoroughly with his hand. Because so much of the ritual had been forgotten or discarded, Mr. Summers had been successful in having slips of paper substituted for the chips of wood that had been used for generations. Chips of wood, Mr. Summers had argued, had been all very well when the village was tiny, but now that the population was more than three hundred and likely to keep on growing, it was necessary to use something that would fit more easily into the black box. The night before the lottery, Mr. Summers and Mr. Graves made up the slips of paper and put them in the box, and it was taken to the safe of Mr. Summers' coal company and locked up until Mr. Summers was ready to take it to the square next morning. The rest of the year, the box was put away, sometimes one place, sometimes another; it had spent one year in Mr. Graves's barn and another year underfoot in the post office, and sometimes it was set on a shelf in the Martin grocery and left there.

7   There was a great deal of fussing to be done before Mr. Summers declared the lottery open. There were the lists to make up—of heads of families, heads of households in each family, members of each household in each family. There was the proper swearing-in of Mr. Summers by the postmaster, as the official of the lottery; at one time, some people remembered, there had been a recital of some sort, performed by the official of the lottery, a perfunctory, tuneless chant that had been rattled off duly each year; some people believed that the official of the lottery used to stand just so when he said or sang it, others believed that he was supposed to walk among the people, but years and years ago this part of the ritual had been allowed to lapse. There had been, also, a ritual salute, which the official of the lottery had had to use in addressing each person who came up to draw from the box, but this also had changed with time, until now it was felt necessary only for the official to speak to each person approaching. Mr. Summers was very good at all this; in his clean white shirt and blue jeans, with one hand resting carelessly on the black box. He seemed very proper and important as he talked interminably to Mr. Graves and the Martins.

8   Just as Mr. Summers finally left off talking and turned to the assembled villagers, Mrs. Hutchinson came hurriedly along the path to the square, her sweater thrown over her shoulders, and slid into place in the back of the crowd. "Clean forgot what day it was," she said to Mrs. Delacroix, who stood next to her, and they both laughed softly. "Thought my old man was out back stacking wood," Mrs. Hutchinson went on, "and then I looked out the window and the kids were gone, and then I remembered it was the twenty-seventh and came a-

paraphernalia (par. 5): the articles or equipment used in some activity

perfunctory (par. 7): done automatically or with little personal interest

interminably (par. 7): endlessly

running." She dried her hands on her apron, and Mrs. Delacroix said, "You're in time, though. They're still talking away up there."

9   Mrs. Hutchinson craned her neck to see through the crowd and found her husband and children standing near the front. She tapped Mrs. Delacroix on the arm as a farewell and began to make her way through the crowd. The people separated good-humoredly to let her through; two or three people said, in voices just loud enough to be heard across the crowd, "Here comes your Missus, Hutchinson," and "Bill, she made it after all." Mrs. Hutchinson reached her husband, and Mr. Summers, who had been waiting, said cheerfully, "Thought we were going to have to get on without you, Tessie." Mrs. Hutchinson said, grinning, "Wouldn't have me leave m'dishes in the sink, now, would you, Joe?" and soft laughter ran through the crowd as the people stirred back into position after Mrs. Hutchinson's arrival. "Well, now," Mr. Summers said soberly, "guess we better get started, get this over with, so's we can go back to work. Anybody ain't here?"

10   "Dunbar," several people said. "Dunbar, Dunbar."

11   Mr. Summers consulted his list. "Clyde Dunbar," he said. "That's right. He's broke his leg, hasn't he? Who's drawing for him?"

12   "Me, I guess," a woman said, and Mr. Summers turned to look at her. "Wife draws for her husband," Mr. Summers said. "Don't you have a grown boy to do it for you, Janey?" Although Mr. Summers and everyone else in the village knew the answer perfectly well, it was the business of the official of the lottery to ask such questions formally. Mr. Summers waited with an expression of polite interest while Mrs. Dunbar answered.

13   "Horace's not but sixteen yet," Mrs. Dunbar said regretfully. "Guess I gotta fill in for the old man this year."

14   "Right," Mr. Summers said. He made a note on the list he was holding. Then he asked, "Watson boy drawing this year?"

15   A tall boy in the crowd raised his hand. "Here," he said. "I'm drawing for m'mother and me." He blinked his eyes nervously and ducked his head as several voices in the crowd said things like "Good fellow, Jack," and "Glad to see your mother's got a man to do it."

16   "Well," Mr. Summers said, "guess that's everyone. Old Man Warner make it?"

17   "Here," a voice said, and Mr. Summers nodded.

18   A sudden hush fell on the crowd as Mr. Summers cleared his throat and looked at the list. "All ready?" he said. "Now, I'll read the names—heads of families first—and the men come up and take a paper out of the box. Keep the paper folded in your hand without looking at it until everyone has had a turn. Everything clear?"

19   The people had done it so many times that they only half listened to the directions; most of them were quiet, wetting their lips, not looking around. Then Mr. Summers raised one hand high and said, "Adams." A man disengaged himself from the crowd and came forward. "Hi, Steve," Mr. Summers said, and Mr. Adams said, "Hi, Joe." They grinned at one another humorlessly and nervously. Then Mr. Adams reached into the black box and took out a folded paper. He held it firmly by one corner as he turned and went hastily back to his place in the crowd, where he stood a little apart from his family, not looking down at his hand.

20   "Allen," Mr. Summers said. "Anderson . . . . Bentham."

21   "Seems like there's no time at all between lotteries any more," Mrs. Delacroix said to Mrs. Graves in the back row. "Seems like we got through with the last one only last week."

22   "Time sure goes fast," Mrs. Graves said.

23 "Clark . . . . Delacroix."

24 "There goes my old man," Mrs. Delacroix said. She held her breath while her husband went forward.

25 "Dunbar," Mr. Summers said, and Mrs. Dunbar went steadily to the box while one of the women said, "Go on, Janey," and another said, "There she goes."

26 "We're next," Mrs. Graves said. She watched while Mr. Graves came around from the side of the box, greeted Mr. Summers gravely, and selected a slip of paper from the box. By now, all through the crowd there were men holding the small folded papers in their large hands, turning them over and over nervously. Mrs. Dunbar and her two sons stood together, Mrs. Dunbar holding the slip of paper.

27 "Harburt . . . . Hutchinson."

28 "Get up there, Bill," Mrs. Hutchinson said, and the people near her laughed.

29 "Jones."

30 "They do say," Mr. Adams said to Old Man Warner, who stood next to him, "that over in the north village they're talking of giving up the lottery."

31 Old Man Warner snorted. "Pack of crazy fools," he said. "Listening to the young folks, nothing's good enough for them. Next thing you know, they'll be wanting to go back to living in caves, nobody work any more, live *that* way for a while. Used to be a saying about 'Lottery in June, corn be heavy soon.' First thing you know, we'd all be eating stewed chickweed and acorns. There's *always* been a lottery," he added petulantly. "Bad enough to see young Joe Summers up there joking with everybody."

32 "Some places have already quit lotteries," Mrs. Adams said.

33 "Nothing but trouble in *that*," Old Man Warner said stoutly. "Pack of young fools."

34 "Martin." And Bobby Martin watched his father go forward. "Overdyke . . . . Percy."

35 "I wish they'd hurry," Mrs. Dunbar said to her older son. "I wish they'd hurry."

36 "They're almost through," her son said.

37 "You get ready to run tell Dad," Mrs. Dunbar said.

38 Mr. Summers called his own name and then stepped forward precisely and selected a slip from the box. Then he called, "Warner."

39 "Seventy-seventh year I been in the lottery," Old Man Warner said as he went through the crowd. "Seventy-seventh time."

40 "Watson." The tall boy came awkwardly through the crowd. Someone said, "Don't be nervous, Jack," and Mr. Summers said, "Take your time, son."

41 "Zanini."

42 After that, there was a long pause, a breathless pause, until Mr. Summers, holding his slip of paper in the air, said, "All right, fellows." For a minute, no one moved, and then all the slips of paper were opened. Suddenly, all the women began to speak at once, saying, "Who is it?," "Who's got it?," "Is it the Dunbars?," "Is it the Watson's?" Then the voices began to say, "It's Hutchinson. It's Bill," "Bill Hutchinson's got it."

43 "Go tell your father," Mrs. Dunbar said to her older son.

44 People began to look around to see the Hutchinsons. Bill Hutchinson was standing quiet, staring down at the paper in his hand. Suddenly, Tessie Hutchinson shouted to Mr. Summers, "You didn't give him time enough to take any paper he wanted. I saw you. It wasn't fair."

petulantly (par. 31): with irritation

45   "Be a good sport, Tessie," Mrs. Delacroix called, and Mrs. Graves said, "All of us took the same chance."

46   "Shut up, Tessie," Bill Hutchinson said.

47   "Well, everyone," Mr. Summers said, "that was done pretty fast, and now we've got to be hurrying a little more to get done in time." He consulted his next list. "Bill," he said, "you draw for the Hutchinson family. You got any other households in the Hutchinsons?"

48   "There's Don and Eva," Mrs. Hutchinson yelled. "Make *them* take their chance!"

49   "Daughters draw with their husbands' families, Tessie," Mr. Summers said gently. "You know that as well as anyone else."

50   "It wasn't *fair*," Tessie said.

51   "I guess not, Joe," Bill Hutchinson said regretfully. "My daughter draws with her husband's family, that's only fair. And I've got no other family except the kids."

52   "Then, as far as drawing for families is concerned, it's you," Mr. Summers said in explanation, "and as far as drawing for households is concerned, that's you, too. Right?"

53   "Right," Bill Hutchinson said.

54   "How many kids, Bill?" Mr. Summers asked formally.

55   "Three," Bill Hutchinson said. "There's Bill, Jr., and Nancy, and little Dave. And Tessie and me."

56   "All right, then," Mr. Summers said. "Harry, you got their tickets back?"

57   Mr. Graves nodded and held up the slips of paper. "Put them in the box, then," Mr. Summers directed. "Take Bill's and put it in."

58   "I think we ought to start over," Mrs. Hutchinson said, as quietly as she could. "I tell you it wasn't *fair*. You didn't give him time enough to choose. *Every*body saw that."

59   Mr. Graves had selected the five slips and put them in the box, and he dropped all the papers but those onto the ground, where the breeze caught them and lifted them off.

60   "Listen, everybody," Mrs. Hutchinson was saying to the people around her.

61   "Ready, Bill?" Mr. Summers asked, and Bill Hutchinson, with one quick glance around at his wife and children, nodded.

62   "Remember," Mr. Summers said, "take the slips and keep them folded until each person has taken one. Harry, you help little Dave." Mr. Graves took the hand of the little boy, who came willingly with him up to the box. "Take a paper out of the box, Davy," Mr. Summers said. Davy put his hand into the box and laughed. "Take just *one* paper," Mr. Summers said. "Harry, you hold it for him." Mr. Graves took the child's hand and removed the folded paper from the tight fist and held it while little Dave stood next to him and looked up at him wonderingly.

63   "Nancy next," Mr. Summers said. Nancy was twelve, and her school friends breathed heavily as she went forward, switching her skirt, and took a slip daintily from the box. "Bill, Jr.," Mr. Summers said, and Billy, his face red and his feet over-large, nearly knocked the box over as he got a paper out. "Tessie," Mr. Summers said. She hesitated for a minute, looking around defiantly, and then set her lips and went up to the box. She snatched a paper out and held it behind her.

64   "Bill," Mr. Summers said, and Bill Hutchinson reached into the box and felt around, bringing his hand out at last with the slip of paper in it.

65   The crowd was quiet. A girl whispered, "I hope it's not Nancy," and the sound of the whisper reached the edges of the crowd.

defiantly (par. 63): with challenge or resistance

66   "It's not the way it used to be," Old Man Warner said clearly. "People ain't the way they used to be."

67   "All right," Mr. Summers said. "Open the papers. Harry, you open little Dave's."

68   Mr. Graves opened the slip of paper and there was a general sigh through the crowd as he held it up and everyone could see that it was blank. Nancy and Bill, Jr., opened theirs at the same time, and both beamed and laughed, turning around to the crowd and holding their slips of paper above their heads.

69   "Tessie," Mr. Summers said. There was a pause, and then Mr. Summers looked at Bill Hutchinson, and Bill unfolded his paper and showed it. It was blank.

70   "It's Tessie," Mr. Summers said, and his voice was hushed. "Show us her paper, Bill."

71   Bill Hutchinson went over to his wife and forced the slip of paper out of her hand. It had a black spot on it, the black spot Mr. Summers had made the night before with the heavy pencil in the coal-company office. Bill Hutchinson held it up, and there was a stir in the crowd.

72   "All right, folks," Mr. Summers said. "Let's finish quickly."

73   Although the villagers had forgotten the ritual and lost the original black box, they still remembered to use stones. The pile of stones the boys had made earlier was ready; there were stones on the ground with the blowing scraps of paper that had come out of the box. Mrs. Delacroix selected a stone so large she had to pick it up with both hands and turned to Mrs. Dunbar. "Come on," she said. "Hurry up."

74   Mrs. Dunbar had small stones in both hands, and she said, gasping for breath, "I can't run at all. You'll have to go ahead and I'll catch up with you."

75   The children had stones already, and someone gave little Davy Hutchinson a few pebbles.

76   Tessie Hutchinson was in the center of a cleared space by now, and she held her hands out desperately as the villagers moved in on her. "It isn't fair," she said. A stone hit her on the side of the head.

77   Old Man Warner was saying, "Come on, come on, everyone." Steve Adams was in the front of the crowd of villagers, with Mrs. Graves beside him.

78   "It isn't fair, it isn't right," Mrs. Hutchinson screamed, and then they were upon her.

Birthday Party

Katharine Brush

1   They were a couple in their late thirties, and they looked unmistakably married. They sat on the banquette opposite us in a little narrow restaurant, having dinner. The man had a round, self-satisfied face, with glasses on it; the woman was fadingly pretty, in a big hat. There was nothing conspicuous about them, nothing particularly noticeable, until the end of their meal, when it suddenly became obvious that this was an Occasion—in fact, the husband's birthday, and the wife had planned a little surprise for him.

2   It arrived, in the form of a small but glossy birthday cake, with one pink candle burning in the center. The headwaiter brought it in and placed it before the husband, and meanwhile the violin-and-piano orchestra played "Happy

banquette (par. 1): an upholstered bench along a wall

Birthday to You" and the wife beamed with shy pride over her little surprise, and such few people as there were in the restaurant tried to help out with a pattering of applause. It became clear at once that help was needed, because the husband was not pleased. Instead he was hotly embarrassed, and indignant at his wife for embarrassing him.

3   You looked at him and saw this and you thought, "Oh, now don't *be* like that!" But he was like that, and as soon as the little cake had been deposited on the table, and the orchestra had finished the birthday piece, and the general attention had shifted from the man and woman, I saw him say something to her under his breath—some punishing thing, quick and curt and unkind. I couldn't bear to look at the woman then, so I stared at my plate and waited for quite a long time. Not long enough, though. She was still crying when I finally glanced over there again. Crying quietly and heartbrokenly and hopelessly, all to herself, under the gay big brim of her best hat.

The Catbird Seat

James Thurber

1   Mr. Martin bought the pack of Camels on Monday night in the most crowded cigar store on Broadway. It was theater time and seven or eight men were buying cigarettes. The clerk didn't even glance at Mr. Martin, who put the pack in his overcoat pocket and went out. If any of the staff at F & S had seen him buy the cigarettes, they would have been astonished, for it was generally known that Mr. Martin did not smoke, and never had. No one saw him.

2   It was just a week to the day since Mr. Martin had decided to rub out Mrs. Ulgine Barrows. The term "rub out" pleased him because it suggested nothing more than the correction of an error—in this case an error of Mr. Fitweiler. Mr. Martin had spent each night of the past week working out his plan and examining it. As he walked home now he went over it again. For the hundredth time he resented the element of imprecision, the margin of guesswork that entered into the business. The project as he had worked it out was casual and bold, the risks were considerable. Something might go wrong anywhere along the line. And therein lay the cunning of his scheme. No one would ever see in it the cautious, painstaking hand of Erwin Martin, head of the filing department at F & S, of whom Mr. Fitweiler had once said, "Man is fallible but Martin isn't." No one would see his hand, that is, unless it were caught in the act.

3   Sitting in this apartment, drinking a glass of milk, Mr. Martin reviewed his case against Mrs. Ulgine Barrows, as he had every night for seven nights. He began at the beginning. Her quacking voice and braying laugh had first profaned the halls of F & S on March 7, 1941 (Mr. Martin had a head for dates). Old Roberts, the personnel chief, had introduced her as the newly appointed special advisor to the president of the firm, Mr. Fitweiler. The woman had appalled Mr. Martin instantly, but he hadn't shown it. He had given her his dry hand, a look

cunning (par. 2): cleverness

fallible (par. 2): capable of making mistakes

braying (par. 3): loud, harsh

profaned (par. 3): corrupted, spoiled

appalled (par. 3): shocked

of studious concentration, and a faint smile. "Well," she had said, looking at the paper on his desk, "are you lifting the oxcart out of the ditch?" As Mr. Martin recalled that moment, over his milk, he squirmed slightly. He must keep his mind on her crimes as a special adviser, not on her peccadillos as a personality. This he found difficult to do, in spite of entering an objection and sustaining it. The faults of the woman as a woman kept chattering on in his mind like an unruly witness. She had, for almost two years now, baited him. In the halls, in the elevator, even in his own office, into which she romped now and then like a circus horse, she was constantly shouting these silly questions at him. "Are you lifting the oxcart out of the ditch? Are you tearing up the pea patch? Are you hollering down the rain barrel? Are you scraping around the bottom of the pickle barrel? Are you sitting in the catbird seat?"

4   It was Joey Hart, one of Mr. Martin's two assistants, who had explained what the gibberish meant. "She must be a Dodger fan," he had said. "Red Barber announces the Dodger games over the radio and he uses those expressions—picked 'em up down South." Joey had gone on to explain one or two. "Tearing up the pea patch" meant going on a rampage; "Sitting in the catbird seat" meant sitting pretty, like a batter with three balls and no strikes on him. Mr. Martin dismissed all this with an effort. It had been annoying, it had driven him near to distraction, but he was too solid a man to be moved to murder by anything so childish. It was fortunate, he reflected as he passed on to the important charges against Mrs. Barrows, that he had stood up under it so well. He had maintained always an outward appearance of polite tolerance. "Why, I even believe you like the woman," Miss Paird, his other assistant, had once said to him. He had simply smiled.

5   A gavel rapped in Mr. Martin's mind and the case proper was resumed. Mrs. Ulgine Barrows stood charged with willful, blatant, and persistent attempts to destroy the efficiency and system of F & S. It was competent, material, and relevant to review her advent and rise to power. Mr. Martin had got the story from Miss Paird, who seemed always able to find things out. According to her, Mrs. Barrows had met Mr. Fitweiler at a party, where she had rescued him from the embraces of a powerfully built drunken man who had mistaken the president of F & S for a famous retired Middle Western football coach. She had led him to a sofa and somehow worked upon him a monstrous magic. The aging gentleman had jumped to the conclusion there and then that this was a woman of singular attainments, equipped to bring out the best in him and in the firm. A week later he had introduced her into F & S as his special adviser. On that day confusion got its foot in the door. After Miss Tyson, Mr. Brundage, and Mr. Bartlett had been fired and Mr. Munson had taken his hat and stalked out, mailing in his resignation later, old Roberts had been emboldened to speak to Mr. Fitweiler. He mentioned that Mr. Munson's department had been "a little disrupted" and hadn't they perhaps better resume the old system there? Mr. Fitweiler had said certainly not. He had the greatest faith in Mrs. Barrow's ideas. "They require a little seasoning, a little seasoning, is all," he had added. Mr. Roberts had given it up. Mr. Martin reviewed in detail all the changes wrought

peccadillos (par. 3): small faults

baited (par. 3): aggravated

gibberish (par. 4): nonsense

distraction (par. 4): great emotional disturbance

blatant (par.5): obvious

had been emboldened (par. 5): became brave enough

wrought (par. 5): brought about

by Mrs. Barrows. She had begun chipping at the cornices of the firm's edifice and now she was swinging at the foundation stones with a pickaxe.

6   Mr. Martin came now, in his summing up, to the afternoon of Monday, November 2, 1942—just one week ago. On that day, at 3 P.M., Mrs. Barrows had bounced into his office. "Boo!" she had yelled. "Are you scraping around the bottom of the pickle barrel?" Mr. Martin had looked at her from under his green eyeshade, saying nothing. She had begun to wander about the office, taking it in with her great, popping eyes. "Do you really need *all* these filing cabinets?" she had demanded suddenly. Mr. Martin's heart had jumped. "Each of these files," he had said, keeping his voice even, "plays an indispensable part in the system of F & S." She had brayed at him, "Well, don't tear up the pea patch!" and gone to the door. From there she had bawled, "But you sure have got a lot of fine scrap in here!" Mr. Martin could no longer doubt that the finger was on his beloved department. Her pickaxe was on the upswing, poised for the first blow. It had not come yet; he had received no blue memo from the enchanted Mr. Fitweiler bearing nonsensical instructions deriving from the obscene woman. But there was no doubt in Mr. Martin's mind that one would be forthcoming. He must act quickly. Already a precious week had gone by. Mr. Martin stood up in his living room, still holding his milk glass. "Gentlemen of the jury," he said to himself, "I demand the death penalty for this horrible person."

7   The next day Mr. Martin followed his routine, as usual. He polished his glasses more often and once sharpened an already sharp pencil, but not even Miss Paird noticed. Only once did he catch sight of his victim; she swept past him in the hall with a patronizing "Hi!" At five-thirty he walked home, as usual, and had a glass of milk, as usual. He had never drunk anything stronger in his life—unless you could count ginger ale. The late Sam Schlosser, the S of F & S, had praised Mr. Martin at a staff meeting several years before for his temperate habits. "Our most efficient worker neither drinks nor smokes," he had said. "The results speak for themselves," Mr. Fitweiler had sat by, nodding approval.

8   Mr. Martin was still thinking about that red-letter day as he walked over to the Schrafft's on Fifth Avenue near Forty-sixth Street. He got there, as he always did, at eight o'clock. He finished his dinner and the financial page of the *Sun* at a quarter to nine, as he always did. It was his custom after dinner to take a walk. This time he walked down Fifth Avenue at a casual pace. His gloved hands felt moist and warm, his forehead cold. He transferred the Camels from his overcoat to a jacket pocket. He wondered, as he did so, if they did not represent an unnecessary note of strain. Mrs. Barrows smoked only Luckies. It was his idea to puff a few puffs on a Camel (after the rubbing-out), stub it out in the ashtray holding her lipstick-stained Luckies and thus drag a small red herring across the trail. Perhaps it was not a good idea. It would take time. He might even choke, too loudly.

9   Mr. Martin had never seen the house on West Twelfth Street where Mrs. Barrows lived, but he had a clear enough picture of it. Fortunately, she had bragged to everybody about her ducky first-floor apartment in the perfectly dar-

cornices (par. 5): molding around the top of a building

edifice (par. 5): a large building

patronizing (par. 7): assuming a superior attitude

drag a small red herring across the trail (par. 8): Red herring (a fish) is dragged across the trail of hunted animals to overpower their scent and, thus, throw the dogs off course; "red herring" has become a common expression meaning something intended to confuse or distract.

ling three-story red-brick. There would be no doorman or other attendants; just the tenants of the second and third floors. As he walked along, Mr. Martin realized that he would get there before nine-thirty. He had considered walking north on Fifth Avenue from Schrafft's to a point from which it would take him until ten o'clock to reach the house. At that hour people were less likely to be coming in or going out. But the procedure would have made an awkward loop in the straight thread of his casualness, and he had abandoned it. It was impossible to figure when people would be entering or leaving the house, anyway. There was a great risk at any hour. If he ran into anybody, he would simply have to place the rubbing-out of Ulgine Barrows in the inactive file forever. The same thing would hold true if there were someone in her apartment. In that case he would just say that he had been passing by, recognized her charming house and thought to drop in.

10   It was eighteen minutes after nine when Mr. Martin turned into Twelfth Street. A man passed him, and a man and a woman talking. There was no one within fifty paces when he came to the house, halfway down the block. He was up the steps and in the small vestibule in no time, pressing the bell under the card that said "Mrs. Ulgine Barrows." When the clicking in the lock started, he jumped forward against the door. He got inside fast, closing the door behind him. A bulb in a lantern hung from the hall ceiling on a chain seemed to give a monstrously bright light. There was nobody on the stair, which went up ahead of him along the left wall. A door opened down the hall in the wall on the right. He went toward it swiftly, on tiptoe.

11   "Well, for God's sake, look who's here!" bawled Mrs. Barrows, and her braying laugh rang out like the report of a shotgun. He rushed past her like a football tackle, bumping her. "Hey, quit shoving!" she said, closing the door behind him. They were in her living room, which seemed to Mr. Martin to be lighted by a hundred lamps. "What's after you?" she said. "You're as jumpy as a goat." He found he was unable to speak. His heart was wheezing in his throat. "I—yes," he finally brought out. She was jabbering and laughing as she started to help him off with his coat. "No, no," he said. "I'll put it here." He took it off and put it on a chair near the door. "Your hat and gloves, too," she said. "You're in a lady's house." He put his hat on top of the coat. Mrs. Barrows seemed larger than he had thought. He kept his gloves on. "I was passing by," he said. "I recognized—is there anyone here?" She laughed louder than ever. 'No," she said, "we're all alone. You're as white as a sheet, you funny man. Whatever *has* come over you? I'll mix you a toddy." She started toward a door across the room. "Scotch-and-soda be all right? But say, you don't drink do you?" She turned and gave him her amused look. Mr. Martin pulled himself together. "Scotch-and-soda will be all right," he heard himself say. He could hear her laughing in the kitchen.

12   Mr. Martin looked quickly around the living room for the weapon. He had counted on finding one there. There were andirons and a poker and something in a corner that looked like an Indian club. None of them would do. It couldn't be that way. He began to pace around. He came to a desk. On it lay a metal paper knife with an ornate handle. Would it be sharp enough? He reached for it and knocked over a small brass jar. Stamps spilled out of it and it fell to the floor with a clatter. "Hey," Mrs. Barrows yelled from the kitchen, "are you tearing up the pea patch?" Mr. Martin gave a strange laugh. Picking up the knife, he tried its point against his left wrist. It was blunt. It wouldn't do.

report (par. 11): sound

andirons (par. 12): metal supports that hold up logs in a fireplace

13   When Mrs. Barrows reappeared, carrying two highballs, Mr. Martin, standing there with his gloves on, became acutely conscious of the fantasy he had wrought. Cigarettes in his pocket, a drink prepared for him—it was all too grossly improbable. It was more than that; it was impossible. Somewhere in the back of his mind a vague idea stirred, sprouted. "For heaven's sake, take off those gloves," said Mrs. Barrows. "I always wear them in the house," said Mr. Martin. The idea began to bloom, strange and wonderful. She put the glasses on a coffee table in front of a sofa and sat on the sofa. "Come over here, you odd little man," she said. Mr. Martin went over and sat beside her. It was difficult getting a cigarette out of the pack of Camels, but he managed it. She held a match for him, laughing. "Well," she said, handing him his drink, "this is perfectly marvelous. You with a drink and a cigarette."

14   Mr. Martin puffed, not too awkwardly, and took a gulp of the highball. "I drink and smoke all the time," he said. He clinked his glass against hers. "Here's nuts to that old windbag, Fitweiler," he said, and gulped again. The stuff tasted awful, but he made no grimace. "Really, Mr. Martin," she said, her voice and posture changing, "you are insulting our employer." Mrs. Barrows was now all special adviser to the president. "I am preparing a bomb," said Mr. Martin, "which will blow the old goat higher than hell." He had only had a little of the drink, which was not strong. It couldn't be that. "Do you take dope or something?" Mrs. Barrows asked coldly. "Heroin," said Mr. Martin. "I'll be coked to the gills when I bump that old buzzard off." "Mr. Martin!" she shouted, getting to her feet. "That will be all of that. You must go at once." Mr. Martin took another swallow of his drink. He tapped his cigarette out in the ashtray and put the pack of Camels on the coffee table. Then he got up. She stood glaring at him. He walked over and put on his hat and coat. "Not a word about this," he said, and laid an index finger against his lips. All Mrs. Barrows could bring out was "Really!" Mr. Martin put his hand on the doorknob. "I'm sitting in the catbird seat," he said. He stuck his tongue out at her and left. Nobody saw him go.

15   Mr. Martin got to his apartment, walking, well before eleven. No one saw him go in. He had two glasses of milk after brushing his teeth, and he felt elated. It wasn't tipsiness, because he hadn't been tipsy. Anyway, the walk had worked off all effects of the whisky. He got in bed and read a magazine for a while. He was asleep before midnight.

16   Mr. Martin got to the office at eight-thirty the next morning, as usual. At a quarter to nine, Ulgine Barrows, who had never before arrived at work before ten, swept into his office. "I'm reporting to Mr. Fitweiler now!" she shouted. "If he turns you over to the police, it's no more than you deserve!" Mr. Martin gave her a look of shocked surprise. "I beg your pardon?" he said. Mrs. Barrows snorted and bounced out of the room, leaving Miss Paird and Joey Hart staring after her. "What's the matter with that old devil now?" asked Miss Paird. "I have no idea," said Mr. Martin, resuming his work. The other two looked at him and then at each other. Miss Paird got up and went out. She walked slowly past the closed door of Mr. Fitweiler's office. Mrs. Barrows was yelling inside, but she was not braying. Miss Paird could not hear what the woman was saying. She went back to her desk.

17   Forty-five minutes later, Mrs. Barrows left the president's office and went into her own, shutting the door. It wasn't until half an hour later that Mr. Fitweiler sent for Mr. Martin. The head of the filing department, neat, quiet, attentive, stood in front of the old man's desk. Mr. Fitweiler was pale and nervous. He took his glasses off and twiddled them. He made a small, bruffing sound in his throat. "Martin," he said, "you have been with us more than twenty years."

elated (par. 15): in high spirits

"Twenty-two, sir," said Mr. Martin. "In that time," pursued the president, "your work and your—uh—manner have been exemplary." "I trust so, sir," said Mr. Martin. "I have understood, Martin," said Mr. Fitweiler, "that you have never taken a drink or smoked." "That is correct, sir," said Mr. Martin. "Ah, yes." Mr. Fitweiler polished his glasses. "You may describe what you did after leaving the office yesterday, Martin," he said. Mr. Martin allowed less than a second for his bewildered pause. "Certainly, sir," he said. "I walked home. Then I went to Schrafft's for dinner. Afterward I walked home again. I went to bed early, sir, and read a magazine for a while. I was asleep before eleven." "Ah, yes," said Mr. Fitweiler again. He was silent for a moment, searching for the proper words to say to the head of the filing department. "Mrs. Barrows," he said finally, "Mrs. Barrows has worked hard, Martin, very hard. It grieves me to report that she has suffered a severe breakdown. It has taken the form of a persecution complex accompanied by distressing hallucinations." "I am very sorry, sir," said Mr. Martin. "Mrs. Barrows is under the delusion," continued Mr. Fitweiler, "that you visited her last evening and behaved yourself in an—uh—unseemly manner." He raised his hand to silence Mr. Martin's little pained outcry. "It is the nature of these psychological diseases," Mr. Fitweiler said, "to fix upon the least likely and most innocent party as the—uh—source of persecution. These matters are not for the lay mind to grasp, Martin. I've just had my psychiatrist, Dr. Fitch, on the phone. He would not, of course, commit himself, but he made enough generalizations to substantiate my suspicions. I suggested to Mrs. Barrows when she had completed her—uh—story to me this morning, that she visit Dr. Fitch, for I suspected a condition at once. She flew, I regret to say, into a rage, and demanded—uh—requested that I call you on the carpet. You may not know, Martin, but Mrs. Barrows had planned a reorganization of your department—subject to my approval, of course, subject to my approval. This brought you, rather than anyone else, to her mind—but again that is a phenomenon for Dr. Fitch and not for us. So, Martin, I am afraid Mrs. Barrows' usefulness here is at an end." "I am dreadfully sorry, sir," said Mr. Martin.

18   It was at this point that the door to the office blew open with the suddenness of a gas-main explosion and Mrs. Barrows catapulted through it. "Is the little rat denying it?" she screamed. "He can't get away with that!" Mr. Martin got up and moved discreetly to a point beside Mr. Fitweiler's chair. "You drank and smoked at my apartment," she bawled at Mr. Martin, "and you know it! You called Mr. Fitweiler an old windbag and said you were going to blow him up when you got coked to the gills on your heroin!" She stopped yelling to catch her breath and a new glint came into her popping eyes. "If you weren't such a drab, ordinary little man," she said, "I'd think you'd planned it all. Sticking your tongue out at me, saying you were sitting in the catbird seat, because you thought no one would believe me when I told it! My God, it's really too perfect!" She brayed loudly and hysterically, and the fury was on her again. She glared at Mr. Fitweiler. "Can't you see how he has tricked us, you old fool! Can't you see his little game?" But Mr. Fitweiler had been surreptitiously pressing all the buttons under the top of his desk and employees of F & S began pouring into the room. "Stockton," said Mr. Fitweiler, "you and Fishbein will take Mrs. Barrows to her home. Mrs. Powell, you will go with them." Stockton, who had played a little football in high school, blocked Mrs. Barrows as she made for Mr. Martin. It took him and Fishbein together to force her out of the door into the hall,

persecution complex (par. 17): a feeling that one is being singled out for unjust treatment

delusion (par. 17): false belief

phenomenon (par. 17): unusual occurrence

surreptitiously (par. 18): secretly

crowded with stenographers and office boys. She was still screaming imprecations at Mr. Martin, tangled and contradictory imprecations. The hubbub finally died out down the corridor.

19   "I regret that this had happened," said Mr. Fitweiler. "I shall ask you to dismiss it from your mind, Martin." "Yes, sir," said Mr. Martin, anticipating his chief's "That will be all" by moving to the door. "I will dismiss it." He went out and shut the door, and his step was light and quick in the hall. When he entered his department he had slowed down to his customary gait, and he walked quietly across the room to the W20 file, wearing a look of studious concentration.

stenographers (par. 18): someone skilled in shorthand

imprecations (par. 18): curses

gait (par. 19): manner of walking

The Man Who Was Almost a Man

Richard Wright

1   Dave struck out across the fields, looking homeward through paling light. Whut's the use talkin wid em niggers in the field? Anyhow, his mother was putting supper on the table. Them niggers can't understan nothing. One of these days he was going to get a gun and practice shooting, then they couldn't talk to him as though he were a little boy. He slowed, looking at the ground. Shucks, Ah ain scareda them even ef they are biggern me! Aw, Ah know whut Ahma do. Ahm going by ol Joe's sto n git that Sears Roebuck catlog n look at them guns. Mebbe Ma will lemme buy one when she gits mah pay from ol man Hawkins. Ahma beg her gimme some money. Ahm ol ernough to hava gun. Ahm seventeen. Almost a man. He strode, feeling his long loose-jointed limbs. Shucks, a man oughta hava little gun aftah he done worked hard all day.

2   He came in sight of Joe's store. A yellow lantern glowed on the front porch. He mounted steps and went through the screen door, hearing it bang behind him. There was a strong smell of coal oil and mackerel fish. He felt very confident until he saw fat Joe walk in through the rear door, then his courage began to ooze.

3   "Howdy, Dave! Whutcha want?"

4   "How yuh, Mistah Joe? Aw, Ah don wanna buy nothing. Ah jus wanted t see ef yuhd lemme look at tha catlog erwhile."

5   "Sure! You wanna see it here?"

6   "Nawsuh. Ah wans t take it home wid me. Ah'll bring it back termorrow when Ah come in from the fiels."

In this story, the characters' speeches and thoughts are written in dialect. This means that words are spelled the way they would be pronounced by the characters. For example, "I" would be pronounced "Ah," so it is spelled "Ah." In other instances, *d*'s, *t*'s and *g*'s are left off the end of words because they would not be pronounced ("understan[d]"; "jus[t]"; "puttin[g]"). Some words are run together, as they would be in speech: "bigger than" becomes "bigbern"; "let me," "lemme"; "what do you," "whutcha"; etc.

7   "You plannin on buying something?"

8   "Yessuh."

9   "Your ma lettin you have your own money now?

10   "Shucks. Mistah Joe. Ahm gittin t be a man like anybody else!"

11   Joe laughed and wiped his greasy white face with a red bandanna.

12   "Whut you plannin on buyin?"

13   Dave looked at the floor, scratched his head, scratched his thigh, and smiled. Then he looked up shyly.

14   "Ah'll tell yuh, Mistah Joe, ef yuh promise yuh won't tell."

15   "I promise."

16   "Waal, Ahma buy a gun."

17   "A gun? Whut you want with a gun?"

18   "Ah wanna keep it."

19   "You ain't nothing but a boy. You don't need a gun."

20   "Aw, lemme have the catlog, Mistah Joe. Ah'll bring it back."

21   Joe walked through the rear door. Dave was elated. He looked around at barrels of sugar and flour. He heard Joe coming back. He craned his neck to see if he were bringing the book. Yeah, he's got it. Gawddog, he's got it!

22   "Here, but be sure you bring it back. It's the only one I got."

23   "Sho, Mistah Joe."

24   "Say, if you wanna buy a gun, why don't you buy one from me? I gotta gun to sell."

25   "Will it shoot."

26   "Sure it'll shoot."

27   "Whut kind is it?"

28   "Oh, it's kinda old . . . a left-hand Wheeler. A pistol. A big one."

29   "Is it got bullets in it?"

30   "It's loaded."

31   "Kin Ah see it?"

32   "Where's your money?"

33   "Whut yuh wan fer it?"

34   "I'll let you have it for two dollars."

35   "Just two dollahs? Shucks, Ah could buy tha when Ah git mah pay."

36   "I'll have it here when you want it."

37   "Awright, suh. Ah be in fer it."

38   He went through the door, hearing it slam again behind him. Ahma git some money from Ma n buy me a gun! Only two dollahs! He tucked the thick catalogue under his arm and hurried.

39   "Where yuh been, boy?" His mother held a steaming dish of black-eyed peas.

40   "Aw, Ma, Ah jus stopped down the road t talk wid the boys."

41   "Yuh know bettah t keep suppah waitin."

42   He sat down, resting the catalogue on the edge of the table.

43   "Yuh git up from there and git to the well n wash yoself! Ah ain feedin no hogs in mah house!"

44   She grabbed his shoulder and pushed him. He stumbled out of the room, then came back to get the catalogue.

45   "Whut this?"

46   "Aw, Ma, it's jusa catlog."

47   "Who yuh git it from?"

bandanna (par. 11): handkerchief

elated (par. 21): thrilled

craned (par. 21): stretched

48   "From Joe, down at the sto."

49   "Waal, thas good. We kin use it in the outhouse."

50   "Naw, Ma." He grabbed for it. "Gimme ma catlog, Ma."

51   She held onto it and glared at him.

52   "Quit hollerin at me! Whut's wrong wid yuh? Yuh crazy?"

53   "But Ma, please. It ain mine! It's Joe's! He tol me t bring it back t im termorrow."

54   She gave up the book. He stumbled down the back steps, hugging the thick book under his arm. When he had splashed water on his face and hands, he groped back to the kitchen and fumbled in a corner for the towel. He bumped into a chair; it clattered to the floor. The catalogue sprawled at his feet. When he had dried his eyes he snatched up the book and held it again under his arm. His mother stood watching him.

55   "Now, ef yuh gonner act a fool over that ol book, Ah'll take it n burn it up."

56   "Naw, Ma, please."

57   "Waal, set down n be still!"

58   He sat down and drew the oil lamp close. He thumbed page after page, unaware of the food his mother set on the table. His father came in. Then his small brother.

59   "Whutcha got there, Dave?" his father asked.

60   "Jusa catlog," he answered, not looking up.

61   "Yeah, here they is!" His eyes glowed at blue-and-black revolvers. He glanced up, feeling sudden guilt. His father was watching him. He eased the book under the table and rested it on his knees. After the blessing was asked, he ate. He scooped up peas and swallowed fat meat without chewing. Buttermilk helped to wash it down. He did not want to mention money before his father. He would do much better by cornering his mother when she was alone. He looked at his father uneasily out of the edge of his eye.

62   "Boy, how come yuh don quit foolin wid tha book n eat yo suppah?"

63   "Yessuh."

64   "How you n ol man Hawkins gittin erlong?"

65   "Suh?"

66   "Can't yuh hear? Why don yuh lissen? Ah ast yu how wuz yuh n ol man Hawkins gittin erlong?"

67   "Oh, swell, Pa. Ah plows mo lan than anybody over there."

68   "Waal, yuh oughta keep yo mind on whut yuh doin."

69   "Yessuh."

70   He poured his plate full of molasses and sopped it up slowly with a chunk of cornbread. When his father and brother had left the kitchen, he still sat and looked again at the guns in the catalogue, longing to muster courage enough to present his case to his mother. Lawd, ef Ah only had tha pretty one! He could almost feel the slickness of the weapon with his fingers. If he had a gun like that he would polish it and keep it shining so it would never rust. N Ah'd keep it loaded, by Gawd!

71   "Ma?" His voice was hesitant.

72   "Hunh?"

73   "Ol man Hawkins give yuh mah money yit?"

74   "Yeah, but ain no usa yuh thinking bout throwin nona it erway. Ahm keepin tha money sos yuh kin have cloes t go to school this winter."

glared (par. 51): looked angrily

groped (par. 54): felt his way

muster (par. 70): gather, work up

75   He rose and went to her side with the open catalogue in his palms. She was washing dishes, her head bent low over a pan. Shyly he raised the book. When he spoke, his voice was husky, faint.

76   "Ma, Gawd knows Ah wans one of these."

77   "One of whut?" she asked, not raising her eyes.

78   "One of these," he said again, not daring even to point. She glanced up at the page, then at him with wide eyes.

79   "Nigger, is yuh gone plumb crazy?"

80   "Aw, Ma—"

81   "Git outta here! Don yuh talk t me bout no gun! Yuh a fool!"

82   "Ma, Ah kin buy one for two dollahs."

83   "Not ef Ah knows it, yuh ain!"

84   "But yuh promised me one—"

85   "Ah don care whut Ah promised! Yuh ain nothing but a boy yit!"

86   "Ma, ef yuh lemme buy one Ah'll *never* ast yuh fer nothing no mo."

87   "Ah tol yuh t git outta here! Yuh ain gonna toucha penny of tha money fer no gun! Thas how come Ah has Mistah Hawkins t pay yo wages t me, cause Ah knows yuh ain got no sense."

88   "But, Ma, we needa gun. Pa ain got no gun. We needa gun in the house. Yuh kin never tell whut might happen."

89   "Now don yuh try to maka fool outta me, boy! If we did hava gun, yuh wouldn't have it!"

90   He laid the catalogue down and slipped his arm around her waist.

91   "Aw, Ma, Ah done worked hard alla summer n ain ast yuh fer nothin, is Ah, now?"

92   "Thas whut yuh spose t do!"

93   "But Ma, Ah wans a gun. Yuh kin lemme have two dollahs outta mah money. Please, Ma. I kin give it to Pa . . . Please, Ma! Ah loves yuh, Ma."

94   When she spoke her voice came soft and low.

95   "Whut yu wan wida gun, Dave? Yuh don need no gun. You'll git in trouble. N ef yo pa jus thought Ah let yuh have money t buy a gun he'd hava fit."

96   "Ah'll hide it, Ma. It ain but two dollahs."

97   "Lawd, chil, whut's wrong wid yuh?"

98   "Ain nothin wrong, Ma. Ahm almos a man now. Ah wans a gun."

99   "Who gonna sell yuh a gun?"

100   "Ol Joe at the sto."

101   "N it don cos but two dollahs?"

102   "Thas all, Ma. Jus two dollahs. Please, Ma."

103   She was stacking the plates away; her hands moved slowly, reflectively. Dave kept an anxious silence. Finally, she turned to him.

104   "Ah'll let yuh git tha gun ef yuh promise me one thing."

105   "Whut's tha, Ma?"

106   "Yuh bring it straight back t me, yuh hear? It be fer Pa."

107   "Yessum! Lemme go now, Ma."

108   She stooped, turned slightly to one side, raised the hem of her dress, rolled down the top of her stocking, and came up with a slender wad of bills.

109   "Here," she said. "Lawd knows yuh don need no gun. But yer pa does. Yuh bring it right back t me, yuh hear? Ahma put it up. Now ef yuh don, Ahma have yuh pa lick yuh so hard yuh won fergit it."

110   "Yessum."

111   He took the money, ran down the steps, and across the yard.

112   "Dave! Yuuuuuh Daaaaave!"

113   He heard, but he was not going to stop now. "Naw, Lawd!"

reflectively (par. 103): thoughtfully

114   The first movement he made the following morning was to reach under his pillow for the gun. In the gray light of dawn he held it loosely, feeling a sense of power. Could kill a man with a gun like this. Kill anybody, black or white. And if he were holding his gun in his hand, nobody could run over him; they would have to respect him. It was a big gun, with a long barrel and a heavy handle. He raised and lowered it in his hand, marveling at its weight.

115   He had not come straight home with it as his mother had asked; instead he had stayed out in the fields, holding the weapon in his hand, aiming it now and then at some imaginary foe. But he had not fired it; he had been afraid that his father might hear. Also he was not sure he knew how to fire it.

116   To avoid surrendering the pistol he had not come into the house until he knew that they were all asleep. When his mother had tiptoed to his bedside late that night and demanded the gun, he had first played possum; then he had told her that the gun was hidden outdoors, that he would bring it to her in the morning. Now he lay turning it slowly in his hands. He broke it, took out the cartridges, felt them, and then put them back.

117   He slid out of bed, got a long strip of old flannel from a trunk, wrapped the gun in it, and tied it to his naked thigh while it was still loaded. He did not go in to breakfast. Even though it was not yet daylight, he started for Jim Hawkins' plantation. Just as the sun was rising he reached the barns where the mules and plows were kept.

118   "Hey! That you, Dave?"

119   He turned. Jim Hawkins stood eyeing him suspiciously.

120   "What're yuh doing here so early?"

121   "Ah didn't know Ah wuz gittin up so early, Mistah Hawkins. Ah wuz fixin t hitch up ol Jenny n take her t the fiels."

122   "Good. Since you're so early, how about plowing that stretch down by the woods?"

123   "Suits me, Mistah Hawkins."

124   "O.K. Go to it!"

125   He hitched Jenny to a plow and started across the fields. Hot dog! This was just what he wanted. If he could get down by the woods, he could shoot his gun and nobody would hear. He walked behind the plow, hearing the traces creaking, feeling the gun tied tight to his thigh.

126   When he reached the woods, he plowed two whole rows before he decided to take out the gun. Finally, he stopped, looked in all directions, then untied the gun and held it in his hand. He turned to the mule and smiled.

127   "Know whut this is, Jenny? Naw, yuh wouldn know! Yuhs jusa ol mule! Anyhow, this is a gun, n it kin shoot, by Gawd!"

128   He held the gun at arm's length. Whut t hell, Ahma shoot this thing! He looked at Jenny again.

129   "Lissen here, Jenny! When Ah pull this ol trigger, Ah don wan yuh to run n acka fool now!"

130   Jenny stood with head down, her short ears pricked straight. Dave walked off about twenty feet, held the gun out from him at arm's length, and turned his head. Hell, he told himself. Ah ain afraid. The gun felt loose in his fingers; he waved it wildly for a moment. Then he shut his eyes and tightened his forefinger. Bloom! A report half deafened him and he thought his right hand was torn from his arm. He heard Jenny whinnying and galloping over the field, and he found himself on his knees squeezing his fingers hard between his legs. He

played possum (par. 116): pretended to be asleep

broke (par. 116): opened

traces (par. 125): straps that connect a work animal to a wagon, plow, etc.

report (par. 130): sound of a gunshot

hand was numb; he jammed it into his mouth trying to warm it, trying to stop the pain. The gun lay at his feet. He did not quite know what had happened. He stood up and stared at the gun as though it were a living thing. He gritted his teeth and kicked the gun. Yuh almos broke mah arm! He turned to look for Jenny; she was far over the fields tossing her head and kicking wildly.

131 "Hol on there, ol mule!"

132 When he caught up with her she stood trembling, walling her big white eyes at him. The plow was far away; the traces had broken. Then Dave stopped short, looking, not believing. Jenny was bleeding. Her left side was red and wet with blood. He went closer. Lawd, have mercy! Wondah did Ah shoot this mule? He grabbed for Jenny's mane. She flinched, snorted, whirled, tossing her head.

133 "Hol on now! Hol on."

134 The he saw the hole in Jenny's side, right between the ribs. It was round, wet, red. A crimson stream streaked down the front leg, flowing fast. Good Gawd! Ah wuzn't shootin at tha mule. He felt panic. He knew he had to stop that blood, or Jenny would bleed to death. He had never seen so much blood in all his life. He chased the mule for half a mile, trying to catch her. Finally she stopped, breathing hard, stumpy tail half arched. He caught her mane and led her back to where the plough and gun lay. Then he stooped and grabbed handfuls of damp black earth and tried to plug the bullet hole. Jenny shuddered, whinnied, and broke from him.

135 "Hol on! Hol on now!"

136 He tried to plug it again, but blood came anyhow. His fingers were hot and sticky. He rubbed dirt into his palms, trying to dry them. Then again he attempted to plug the bullet hole, but Jenny shied away, kicking her heels high. He stood helpless. He had to do something. He ran at Jenny; she dodged him. He watched a red stream of blood flowing down Jenny's leg and form a bright pool at her feet.

137 "Jenny . . . Jenny," he called weakly.

138 His lips trembled. She's bleeding t death! He looked in the direction of home, wanting to go back, wanting to get help. But he saw the pistol lying in the damp black clay. He had a queer feeling that if he only did something, this would not be; Jenny would not be there bleeding to death.

139 When he went to her this time, she did not move. She stood with sleepy, dreamy eyes; and when he touched her she gave a low-pitched whinny and knelt to the ground, her front knees slopping in blood.

140 "Jenny . . . Jenny . . ." he whispered.

141 For a long time she held her neck erect; then her head sank, slowly. Her ribs swelled with a mighty heave and she went over.

142 Dave's stomach felt empty, very empty. He picked up the gun and held it gingerly between his thumb and forefinger. He buried it at the foot of a tree. He took a stick and tried to cover the pool of blood with dirt—but what was the use? There was Jenny lying with her mouth open and her eyes walled and glassy. He could not tell Jim Hawkins he had shot his mule. But he had to tell something. Yeah, Ah'll tell em Jenny started gittin wil n fell on the joint of the plow. . . . But that would hardly happen to a mule. He walked across the field slowly, head down.

143 It was sunset. Two of Jim Hawkins' men were over near the edge of the woods digging a hole in which to bury Jenny. Dave was surrounded by a knot

walling (par. 132): rolling

shied (par. 136): moved fearfully

gingerly (par. 142): carefully

of people, all of whom were looking down at the dead mule.

144   "I don't see how in the world it happened," said Jim Hawkins for the tenth time.

145   The crowd parted and Dave's mother, father, and small brother pushed into the center.

146   "Where Dave?" his mother called.

147   "There he is," said Jim Hawkins.

148   His mother grabbed him.

149   "Whut happened, Dave? Whut yuh done?"

150   "Nothin."

151   "C mon, boy, talk," his father said.

152   "Dave took a deep breath and told the story he knew nobody believed.

153   "Waal," he drawled. "Ah brung ol Jenny down here sos Ah could do mah plowin. Ah plowed bout two rows, just like yuh see." He stopped and pointed at the long rows of upturned earth. "Then somethin musta been wrong wid ol Jenny. She wouldn ack right a-tall. She started snortin n kickin her heels. Ah tried t hol her, but she pulled erway, rearin n goin in. Then when the point of the plow was stickin up in the air, she swung erroun n twisted herself back on it. . . She stuck herself n started to bleed. N fo Ah could do anything, she wuz dead."

154   "Did you ever hear of anything like that in all your life?" asked Jim Hawkins.

155   There were white and black standing in the crowd. They murmured. Dave's mother came close to him and looked hard into his face. "Tell the truth, Dave," she said.

156   "Looks like a bullet hole to me," said one man.

157   "Dave, whut yuh do wid the gun?" his mother asked.

158   The crowd surged in, looking at him. He jammed his hands into his pockets, shook his head slowly from left to right, and backed away. His eyes were wide and painful.

159   "Did he hava gun?" asked Jim Hawkins.

160   "By Gawd, Ah tol him tha wuz a gun wound," said a man, slapping his thigh.

161   His father caught his shoulders and shook him till his teeth rattled.

162   "Tell whut happened, yuh rascal! Tell whut . . ."

163   Dave looked at Jenny's stiff legs and began to cry.

164   "Whut yuh do wid tha gun?" his mother asked.

165   "Whut wuz he doin wida gun?" his father asked.

166   "Come on and tell the truth," said Hawkins. "Ain't nobody going to hurt you. . ."

167   His mother crowded close to him.

168   "Did yuh shoot tha mule, Dave?"

169   Dave cried, seeing blurred white and black faces.

170   "Ahh ddinn gggo tt sshooot hher . . . Ah ssswear ffo Gawd Ahh ddin. . . . Ah wuz a-tryin to sssee ef the old gggun would sshoot—"

171   "Where yuh git the gun from?" his father asked.

172   "Ah got it from Joe, at the sto."

173   "Where yuh git the money?"

174   "Ma give it t me."

175   "He kept worryin me, Bob. Ah had t. Ah tol im t bring the gun right back t me . . . It was fer yuh, the gun."

176   "But how yuh happen to shoot that mule?" asked Jim Hawkins.

177   "Ah wuzn shootin at the mule, Mistah Hawkins. The gun jumped when Ah pulled the trigger . . . N for Ah knowed anythin Jenny was there a-bleedin."

178   Somebody in the crowd laughed. Jim Hawkins walked close to Dave and looked into his face.

179   "Well, looks like you have bought a mule, Dave."

180   "Ah swear to Gawd, Ah didn go t kill the mule, Mistah Hawkins!"

181   "But you killed her!"

182   All the crowd was laughing now. They stood on tiptoe and poked heads over one another's shoulders.

183   "Well, boy, looks like yuh done bought a dead mule! Hahaha!"

184   "Ain tha ershame."

185   "Hohohohoho."

186   Dave stood, head down, twisting his feet in the dirt.

187   "Well, you needn't worry about it, Bob," said Jim Hawkins to Dave's father. "Just let the boy keep on working and pay me two dollars a month."

188   "Whut yuh wan fer yo mule, Mistah Hawkins?"

189   Jim Hawkins screwed up his eyes.

190   "Fifty dollars."

191   "Whut yuh do wid tha gun?" Dave's father demanded.

192   Dave said nothing.

193   "Yuh wan me t take a tree n beat yuh till yuh talk!"

194   "Nawsuh!"

195   "Whut yuh do wid it?"

196   "Ah throwed it erway."

197   "Where?"

198   "Ah . . . Ah throwed it in the creek."

199   "Waal, c mon home. N firs thing in the mawnin git to tha creekn fin tha gun."

200   "Yessuh."

201   "Whut yuh pay fer it?"

202   "Two dollahs."

203   "Take tha gun n git yu money back n carry it t Mistah Hawkins, yuh hear? N don fergit Ahma lam you black bottom good fer this! Now march yosef on home, suh!"

204   Dave turned and walked slowly. He heard people laughing. Dave glared, his eyes welling with tears. Hot anger bubbled in him. Then he swallowed and stumbled on.

205   That night Dave did not sleep. He was glad that he had gotten out of killing the mule so easily, but he was hurt. Something hot seemed to turn over inside him each time he remembered how they had laughed. He tossed on his bed, feeling his hard pillow. N Pa says he's gonna beat me . . . He remembered other beatings, and his back quivered. Naw, naw. Ah sho don wan im t beat me tha way no mo. Dam em all! Nobody ever gave him anything. All he did was work. They treat me like a mule, n then they beat me. He gritted his teeth. N Ma ha t tell on me.

206   Well, if he had to, he would take old man Hawkins that two dollars. But that meant selling th gun. And he wanted to keep that gun. Fifty dollars for a dead mule.

207   He turned over, thinking how he had fired the gun. He had an itch to fire it again. Ef other men kin shoota gun, by Gawd, Ah kin! He was still, listening. Mebbe they all sleepin now. The house was still. He heard the soft breathing of his brother. Yes, now! He would go down and get that gun and see if he could fire it! He eased out of bed and slipped into overalls.

208   The moon was bright. He ran almost all the way to the edge of the woods. He stumbled over the ground, looking for the spot where he had buried the gun. Yeah, here it is. Like a hungry dog scratching for a bone, he pawed it up. He puffed his black cheeks and blew dirt from the trigger and barrel. He broke it and found four cartridges unshot. He looked around; the fields were filled with silence and moonlight. He clutched the gun stiff and hard in his fingers. But, as

soon as he wanted to pull the trigger, he shut his eyes and turned his head. Naw, Ah can't shoot wid mah eyes closed n mah head turned. With effort he held his eyes open; then he squeezed. *Blooooom!* He was stiff, not breathing. The gun was still in his hands. Dammit, he'd done it! He fired again. *Blooooom!* He smiled. *Blooooom! Blooooom! Click, Click.* There! It was empty. If anybody could shoot a gun, he could. He put the gun into his hip pocket and started across the fields.

209   When he reached the top of a ridge he stood straight and proud in the moonlight, looking at Jim Hawkins' big white house, feeling the gun sagging in his pocket. Lawd, ef Ah had just one mo bullet Ah'd taka shot at tha house. Ah'd like t scare ol man Hawkins jusa little . . . Jusa enough t let im know Dave Saunders is a man.

210   To his left the road curved, running to the tracks of the Illinois Central. He jerked his head, listening. From far off came a faint *hoooof-hoooof; hoooof-hoooof; hoooof-hoooof* . . . . He stood rigid. Two dollahs a mont. Les see now . . . Tha means it'll take bout two years. Shucks! Ah'll be dam!

211   He started down the road, toward the tracks. Here she comes, erroun the ben . . . C mon, yuh slow poke! C mon! He had his hand on his gun; something quivered in his stomach. Then the train thundered past, the gray and brown box cars rumbling and clinking. He gripped the gun tightly; then he jerked his hand out of his pocket. Ah betcha Bill wouldn't do it! Ah-betcha . . . The cars slid past, steel grinding upon steel. Ahm ridin yuh ternight, so hep me Gawd! He was hot all over. He hesitated just a moment; then he grabbed, pulled atop of a car, and lay flat. He felt his pocket; the gun was still there. Ahead the long rails were glinting in the moonlight, stretching away, away to somewhere, somewhere where he could be a man . . .

quivered (par. 211): trembled

glinting (par. 211): shining

Why I Live at the P.O.

Eudora Welty

1   I was getting along fine with Mama, Papa-Daddy and Uncle Rondo until my sister Stella-Rondo just separated from her husband and came back home again. Mr. Whitaker! Of course I went with Mr. Whitaker first, when he first appeared here in China Grove, taking "Pose Yourself" photos, and Stella-Rondo broke us up. Told him I was one-sided. Bigger on one side than the other, which is a deliberate, calculated falsehood: I'm the same. Stella-Rondo is exactly twelve months to the day younger than I am and for that reason she's spoiled.

2   She's always had anything in the world she wanted and then she'd throw it away. Papa-Daddy gave her this gorgeous Add-a-Pearl necklace when she was eight years old and she threw it away playing baseball when she was nine, with only two pearls.

3   So as soon as she got married and moved away from home the first thing she did was separate! From Mr. Whitaker! This photographer with the popeyes she said she trusted. Came home from one of those towns up in Illinois and to our complete surprise brought this child of two.

calculated (par. 1): planned

4   Mama said she like to made her drop dead for a second. "Here you had this marvelous blonde child and never so much as wrote your mother a word about it," says Mama. "I'm thoroughly ashamed of you." But of course she wasn't.

5   Stella-Rondo just calmly takes off this *hat*, I wish you could see it. She says, "Why Mama, Shirley-T.'s adopted, I can prove it."

6   "How?" says Mama, but all I says was, "H'm!" There I was over the hot stove, trying to stretch two chickens over five people and a completely unexpected child into the bargain, without one moment's notice.

7   "What do you mean—'H'm'?" says Stella-Rondo, and Mama says, "I heard that, Sister."

8   I said that oh, I didn't mean a thing, only that whoever Shirley-T. was, she was the spit-image of Papa-Daddy if he'd cut off his beard, which of course he'd never do in the world. Papa-Daddy's Mama's papa and sulks.

9   Stella-Rondo got furious! She said, "Sister, I don't need to tell you you got a lot of nerve and always did have and I'll thank you to make up no future reference to my adopted child whatsoever."

10   "Very well," I said. "Very well, very well. Of course I noticed at once she looks like Mr. Whitaker's side too. That frown. She looks like a cross between Mr. Whitaker and Papa-Daddy."

11   "Well, all I can say is she isn't."

12   "She looks exactly like Shirley Temple to me," says Mama, but Shirley-T. just ran away from her.

13   So the first thing Stella-Rondo did at the table was turn Papa-Daddy against me.

14   "Papa-Daddy," she says. He was trying to cut up his meat. "Papa-Daddy!" I was taken completely by surprise. Papa-Daddy is about a million years old and's got this long-long beard. "Papa-Daddy, Sister says she fails to understand why you don't cut off your beard."

15   So Papa-Daddy l-a-y-s down his knife and fork! He's real rich. Mama says he is, he says he isn't. So he says, "Have I heard correctly? You don't understand why I don't cut off my beard?"

16   "Why," I says, "Papa-Daddy, of course I understand, I did not say any such of a thing, the idea!"

17   He says, "Hussy!"

18   I says, "Papa-Daddy, you know I wouldn't any more want you to cut off your beard than the man in the moon. It was the farthest thing from my mind! Stella-Rondo sat there and made that up while she was eating breast of chicken."

19   But he says, "So the postmistress fails to understand why I don't cut off my beard. Which job I got you through my influence with the government. 'Bird's nest'—is that what you call it?"

20   Not that it isn't the next smallest P.O. in the entire state of Mississippi.

21   I says, "Oh, Papa-Daddy," I says, "I didn't say any such thing, I never dreamed it was a bird's nest, I have always been grateful though this is the next to smallest P.O. in the state of Mississippi, and I do not enjoy being referred to as a hussy by my own grandfather."

22   But Stella-Rondo says, "Yes, you did say it too. Anybody in the world could of heard you, that had ears."

23   "Stop right there," says Mama, looking at *me*.

24   So I pulled my napkin straight back through the napkin ring and left the table.

25   As soon as I was out of the room Mama says, "Call her back, or she'll starve to death," but Papa-Daddy says, "This is the beard I started growing on

the Coast when I was fifteen years old." He would of gone on till nightfall if Shirley T. hadn't lost the Milky Way she ate in Cairo.

26   So Papa-Daddy says, "I am going out and lie in the hammock, and you can all sit here and remember my words: I'll never cut off my beard as long as I live, even one inch, and I don't appreciate it in you at all." Passed right by me in the hall and went straight out and got in the hammock.

27   It would be a holiday. It wasn't five minutes before Uncle Rondo suddenly appeared in the hall in one of Stella-Rondo's flesh-colored kimonos, all cut on the bias, like something Mr. Whitaker probably thought was gorgeous.

28   "Uncle Rondo!" I says. "I didn't know who that was! Where are you going?"

29   "Sister," he says, "get out of my way, I'm poisoned."

30   "If you're poisoned stay away from Papa-Daddy," I says. "Keep out of the hammock. Papa-Daddy will certainly beat you on the head if you come within forty miles of him. He thinks I deliberately said he ought to cut off his beard after he got me the P.O., and I've told him and told him and told him, and he acts like he just don't hear me. Papa-Daddy must of gone stone deaf."

31   "He picked a fine day to do it then," says Uncle Rondo, and before you could say "Jack Robinson" flew out in the yard.

32   What he'd really done, he'd drunk another bottle of that prescription. He does it every single Fourth of July as sure as shooting, and it's horribly expensive. Then he falls over in the hammock and snores. So he insisted on zigzagging right on out to the hammock, looking like a half-wit.

33   Papa-Daddy woke up with this horrible yell and right there without moving an inch he tried to turn Uncle Rondo against me. I heard every word he said. Oh, he told Uncle Rondo I didn't learn to read till I was eight years old and he didn't see how in the world I ever got the mail put up at the P.O., much less read it all, and he said if Uncle Rondo could only fathom the lengths he had gone to to get me that job! And he said on the other hand he thought Stella-Rondo had a brilliant mind and deserved credit for getting out of town. All the time he was just lying there swinging as pretty as you please and looping out his beard, and poor Uncle Rondo was *pleading* with him to slow down the hammock, it was making him dizzy as a witch to watch it. But that's what Papa-Daddy likes about a hammock. So Uncle Rondo was too dizzy to get turned against me for the time being. He's Mama's only brother and is a good case of a one-track mind. Ask anybody. A certified pharmacist.

34   Just then I heard Stella-Rondo raising the upstairs window. While she was married she got this peculiar idea that it's cooler with the windows shut and locked. So she has to raise the window before she can make a soul hear her outdoors.

35   So she raises the window and says, *"Oh!"* You would have thought she was mortally wounded.

36   Uncle Rondo and Papa-Daddy didn't even look up, but kept right on with what they were doing. I had to laugh.

37   I flew up the stairs and threw the door open! I says, "What in the wide world's the matter, Stella-Rondo? You mortally wounded?"

38   "No," she says, "I am not mortally wounded but I wish you would do me the favor of looking out that window there and telling me what you see."

39   So I shade my eyes and look out the window.

Cairo (par. 25): city in Illinois

kimonos (par. 27): loose Japanese robes

cut on the bias (par. 27): The material is cut so that the pattern runs diagonally.

fathom the lengths (par. 33): understand the amount of trouble

40   "I see the front yard," I says.

41   "Don't you see any human beings?" she says.

42   "I see Uncle Rondo trying to run Papa-Daddy out of the hammock," I says. "Nothing more. Naturally, it's so suffocating-hot in the house, with all the windows shut and locked, everybody who cares to stay in their right mind will have to go out and get in the hammock before the Fourth of July is over."

43   "Don't you notice anything different about Uncle Rondo?" asks Stella-Rondo.

44   "Why no, except he's got on some terrible-looking flesh-colored contraption I wouldn't be found dead in, is all I can see," I says.

45   "Never mind, you won't be found dead in it, because it happens to be part of my trousseau, and Mr. Whitaker took several dozen photographs of me in it," says Stella-Rondo. "What on earth could Uncle Rondo *mean* by wearing part of my trousseau out in broad open daylight without saying so much as 'Kiss my foot,' *knowing* I only got home this morning after my separation and hung my negligee up on the bathroom door, just as nervous as I could be?"

46   "I'm sure I don't know, and what do you expect me to do about it?" I says. "Jump out the window?"

47   "No, I expect nothing of the kind. I simply declare that Uncle Rondo looks like a fool in it, that's all," she says. "It makes me sick to my stomach."

48   "Well, he looks as good as he can," I says. "As good as anybody in reason could." I stood up for Uncle Rondo, please remember. And I said to Stella-Rondo, "I think I would do well not to criticize so freely if I were you and came home with a two-year-old child I had never said a word about, and no explanation whatever about my separation."

49   "I asked you the instant I entered this house not to refer one more time to my adopted child, and you gave me your word of honor you would not," was all Stella-Rondo would say, and started pulling out every one of her eyebrows with some cheap Kress tweezers.

50   So I merely slammed the door behind me and went down and made some green-tomato pickle. Somebody had to do it. Of course Mama had turned both the Negroes loose; she always said no earthly power could hold one anyway on the Fourth of July, so she wouldn't even try. It turned out that Jaypan fell in the lake and came within a very narrow limit of drowning.

51   So Mama trots in. Lifts up the lid and says, "H'm! Not very good for your Uncle Rondo in his precarious condition, I must say. Or poor little adopted Shirley-T. Shame on you!"

52   That made me tired. I says, "Well, Stella-Rondo had better thank her lucky stars it was her instead of me came trotting in with that very peculiar-looking child. Now if it had been me that trotted in from Illinois and brought a peculiar-looking child of two, I shudder to think of the reception I'd of got, much less controlled the diet of an entire family."

53   "But you must remember, Sister, that you were never married to Mr. Whitaker in the first place and didn't go up to Illinois to live," says Mama, shaking a spoon in my face. "If you had I would of been just as overjoyed to see you and your little adopted girl as I was to see Stella-Rondo when you wound up with your separation and came on back home."

54   "You would not," I says.

55   "Don't contradict me, I would," says Mama.

56   But I said she couldn't convince me though she talked till she was blue in

contraption (par. 44): literally, a gadget

trousseau (par. 45): collection of goods given a bride

Kress (par. 49): the name of a chain of variety stores

the face. Then I said, "Besides, you know as well as I do that that child is not adopted."

57 "She most certainly is adopted," says Mama, stiff as a poker.

58 I says, "Why, Mama, Stella-Rondo had her just as sure as anything in this world, and just too stuck up to admit it."

59 "Why, Sister," said Mama. "Here I thought we were going to have a pleasant Fourth of July, and you start right out not believing a word your own baby sister tells you!"

60 "Just like Cousin Annie Flo. Went to her grave denying the facts of life," I reminded Mama.

61 "I told you if you ever mentioned Annie Flo's name I'd slap your face," says Mama, and slaps my face.

62 "All right, you wait and see," I says.

63 "I," says Mama, "*I* prefer to take my children's word for anything when it's humanly possible." You ought to see Mama, she weighs two hundred pounds and has real tiny feet.

64 Just then something perfectly horrible occurred to me.

65 "Mama," I say, "can that child talk?" I simply had to whisper! "Mama, I wonder if that child can be—you know—in any way? Do you realize," I says, "that she hasn't spoken one single, solitary word to a human being up to this minute? This is the way she looks," I says, and I looked like this.

66 Well, Mama and I just stood there and stared at each other. It was horrible!

67 "I remember well that Joe Whitaker frequently drank like a fish," says Mama. "I believed to my soul he drank *chemicals*." And without another word she marches to the foot of the stairs and calls Stella-Rondo.

68 "Stella-Rondo? O-o-o-o-o! Stella-Rondo!"

69 "What?" says Stella-Rondo from upstairs. Not even the grace to get up off the bed.

70 "Can that child of yours talk?" asks Mama.

71 Stella-Rondo says, "Can she what?"

72 "Talk! Talk!" says Mama. "Burdyburdyburdyburdy!"

73 So Stella-Rondo yells back, "Who says she can't talk?"

74 "Sister says so," says Mama.

75 "You didn't have to tell me, I know whose word of honor don't mean a thing in this house," says Stella-Rondo.

76 And in a minute the loudest Yankee voice I ever heard in my life yells out, "OE'm Pop-OE the Sailor-r-r Ma-a-an!" and then somebody jumps up and down in the upstairs hall. In another second the house would of fallen down.

77 "Not only talks, she can tap-dance!" calls Stella-Rondo. "Which is more than some people I won't name can do."

78 "Why, the little precious darling thing!" Mama says, so surprised. "Just as smart as she can be!" Starts talking baby talk right there. Then she turns on me. "Sister, you ought to be thoroughly ashamed! Run upstairs this instant and apologize to Stella-Rondo and Shirley-T."

79 "Apologize for what?" I says. "I merely wondered if the child was normal, that's all. Now that she's proved she is, why, I have nothing further to say."

80 But Mama just turned her on her heel and flew out, furious. She ran right upstairs and hugged the baby. She believed it was adopted. Stella-Rondo hadn't done a thing but turn her against me from upstairs while I stood there helpless over the hot stove. So that made Mama, Papa-Daddy and the baby all on Stella-Rondo's side.

81 Next, Uncle Rondo.

the grace (par. 69): the politeness

"OE'm Pop-OE . . . Ma-a-an!" (par. 76): "I'm Popeye the Sailor Man."

82   I must say that Uncle Rondo has been marvelous to me at various times in the past and I was completely unprepared to be made to jump out of my skin, the way it turned out. Once Stella-Rondo did something perfectly horrible to him—broke a chain letter from Flanders Fields—and he took the radio back he had given her and gave it to me. Stella-Rondo was furious! For six months we all had to call her Stella instead of Stella-Rondo, or she wouldn't answer. I always thought Uncle Rondo had all the brains of the entire family. Another time he sent me to Mammoth Cave, with all expenses paid.

83   But this would be the day he was drinking that prescription, the Fourth of July.

84   So at supper Stella-Rondo speaks up and says she thinks Uncle Rondo ought to try to eat a little something. So finally Uncle Rondo said he would try a little cold biscuits and ketchup, but that was all. So *she* brought it to him.

85   "Do you think it wise to disport with ketchup in Stella-Rondo's flesh-colored kimono?" I says. Trying to be considerate! If Stella-Rondo couldn't watch out for her trousseau, somebody had to.

86   "Any objections?" asks Uncle Rondo, just about to pour out all the ketchup.

87   "Don't mind what she says, Uncle Rondo," says Stella-Rondo, "Sister has been devoting this solid afternoon to sneering out my bedroom window at the way you look."

88   "What's that?" says Uncle Rondo. Uncle Rondo has got the most terrible temper in the world. Anything is liable to make him tear the house down if it comes at the wrong time.

89   So Stella-Rondo says, "Sister says 'Uncle Rondo certainly does look like a fool in that pink kimono!' "

90   Do you remember who it was really said that?

91   Uncle Rondo spills out all the ketchup and jumps out of his chair and tears off the kimono and throws it down on the dirty floor and puts his foot on it. It had to be sent all the way to Jackson to the cleaners and re-pleated.

92   "So that's your opinion of your Uncle Rondo, is it?" he says. "I look like a fool, do I? Well, that's the last straw. A whole day in this house with nothing to do, and then to hear you come out with a remark like that behind my back!"

93   "I didn't say any such of a thing, Uncle Rondo," I says, "and I'm not saying who did either. Why, I think you look all right. Just try to take care of yourself and not talk and eat at the same time," I says. "I think you better go lie down."

94   "Lie down my foot," says Uncle Rondo. I ought to of known by that he was fixing to do something perfectly horrible.

95   So he didn't do anything that night in the precarious state he was in—just played Casino with Mama and Stella-Rondo and Shirley-T. and gave Shirley T. a nickel with a head on both sides. It tickled her nearly to death, and she called him "Papa." But at 6:30 a.m. the next morning, he threw a whole five-cent package of some unsold one-inch firecrackers from the store as hard as he could into my bedroom and they everyone went off. Not one bad one in the string. Anybody else, there'd be one that wouldn't go off.

Flanders Field (par. 82): World War I cemetery in Belgium for American dead

Mammoth Cave (par. 82): In Kentucky, the location of the world's largest caves

disport (par. 85): play

precarious (par. 95): unstable

Casino (par. 95): a card game

susceptible (par. 96): sensitive

96   Well, I'm just terribly susceptible to noise of any kind, the doctor has always told me I was the most sensitive person he had ever seen in his whole life, and I was simply prostrated. I couldn't eat! People tell me they heard it as far as the cemetery, and old Aunt Jep Patterson, that had been holding her own so good, thought it was Judgment Day and she was going to meet her whole family. It's usually so quiet here.

97   And I'll tell you it didn't take me any longer than a minute to make up my mind what to do. There I was with the whole entire house on Stella-Rondo's side and turned against me. If I have anything at all I have pride.

98   So I just decided I'd go straight down to the P.O. There's plenty of room there in the back, I says to myself.

99   Well! I made no bones about letting the family catch on to what I was up to. I didn't try to conceal it.

100   The first thing they knew, I marched in where they were all playing Old Maid and pulled the electric oscillating fan out by the plug, and everything got real hot. Next I snatched the pillow I'd done the needle-point on right off the davenport from behind Papa-Daddy. He went "Ugh!" I beat Stella-Rondo up the stairs and finally found my charm bracelet in her bureau drawer under a picture of Nelson Eddy.

101   "So that's the way the land lies," says Uncle Rondo. There he was, piecing on the ham. "Well, Sister, I'll be glad to donate my army cot if you got any place to set it up, providing you'll leave right this minute and let me get some peace." Uncle Rondo was in France.

102   "Thank you kindly for the cot and 'peace' is hardly the word I would select if I had to resort to firecrackers at 6:30 a.m. in a young girl's bedroom," I says back to him. And as to where I intend to go, you seem to forget my position as postmistress of China Grove, Mississippi," I says. "I've always got the P.O."

103   Well, that made them all sit up and take notice.

104   I went out front and started digging up some four-o'clocks to plant around the P.O.

105   "Ah-ah-ah!" says Mama, raising the window. "Those happen to be my four-o'clocks. Everything planted in that star is mine. I've never known you to make anything grow in your life."

106   "Very well," I says. "But I take the fern. Even you, Mama, can't stand there and deny that I'm the one watered that fern. And I happen to know where I can send in a box top and get a packet of one thousand mixed seeds, no two the same kind free."

107   "Oh, where?" Mama wants to know.

108   But I says, "Too late. You 'tend to your house, and I'll 'tend to mine. You hear things like that all the time if you know how to listen to the radio. Perfectly marvelous offers. Get anything you want free."

109   So I hope to tell you I marched in and got that radio, and they could of all bit a nail in two, especially Stella-Rondo, that it used to belong to, and she well knew she couldn't get it back, I'd sue for it like a shot. And I very politely took the sewing machine motor I helped pay the most on to give Mama for Christmas back in 1929, and a good big calendar, with the first-aid remedies on it. The thermometer and the Hawaiian ukulele certainly were rightfully mine, and I stood

prostrated (par. 96): overcome

davenport (par. 100): sofa

Nelson Eddy (par. 100): a famous singer and actor (1901–1967)

piecing (par. 101): nibbling

four-o'clocks (par. 104): a common type of flower

ukulele (par. 109): small stringed instrument, like a guitar

on the stepladder and got all my watermelon-rind preserves and every fruit and vegetable I'd put up, every jar. Then I began to pull the tacks out of the bluebird wall vases on the archway to the dining room.

110   "Who told you you could have those, Miss Priss?" says Mama, fanning as hard as she could.

111   "I bought 'em and I'll keep track of 'em, I says. "I'll tack 'em up one on each side of the post-office window, and you can see 'em when you come to ask me for your mail, if you're so dead to see 'em."

112   "Not I! I'll never darken the door to that post office again if I live to be a hundred," Mama says. "Ungrateful child! After all the money we spent on you at the Normal."

113   "Me either," says Stella-Rondo. "You can just let my mail lie there and *rot*, for all I care. I'll never come and relieve you of a single, solitary piece."

114   "I should worry," I says. "And who you think's going to sit down and write you all those big fat letters and postcards, by the way? Mr. Whitaker? Just because he was the only man ever dropped down in China Grove and you got him—unfairly—is he going to sit down and write you a lengthy correspondence after you come home giving no rhyme nor reason whatsoever for your separation and no explanation for the presence of that child? I may not have your brilliant mind, but I fail to see it."

115   So Mama says, "Sister, I've told you a thousand times that Stella-Rondo simply got homesick, and this child is far too big to be hers," and she says, "Now, why don't you just sit down and play Casino?"

116   Then Shirley-T. sticks out her tongue at me in this perfectly horrible way. She has no more manners than the man in the moon. I told her she was going to cross her eyes like that some day and they'd stick.

117   "It's too late to stop me now," I says. "You should have tried that yesterday. I'm going to the P.O. and the only way you can possibly see me is to visit me there."

118   So Papa-Daddy says, "You'll never catch me setting foot in that post office, even if I should take a notion into my head to write a letter some place." He says, "I won't have you reachin' out of that little old window with a pair of shears and cuttin' off any beard of mine. I'm too smart for you!"

119   "We all are," says Stella-Rondo.

120   But I said, "If you're so smart, where's Mr. Whitaker?"

121   So Uncle Rondo says, "I'll thank you from now on to stop reading all the orders I get on postcards and telling everybody in China Grove what you think is the matter with them," but I says, "I draw my own conclusions and will continue in the future to draw them." I says, "If people want to write their inmost secrets on penny postcards, there's nothing in the wide world you can do about it, Uncle Rondo."

122   "And if you think we'll ever *write* another postcard you're sadly mistaken," says Mama.

123   "Cutting off your nose to spite your face then," I says. "But if you're all determined to have no more to do with the U.S. mail, think of this: What will Stella-Rondo do now, if she wants to tell Mr. Whitaker to come after her?"

124   "Wah!" says Stella-Rondo. I knew she'd cry. She had a conniption fit right there in the kitchen.

125   "It will be interesting to see how long she holds out," I says. "And now— I am leaving."

126   "Good-bye," says Uncle Rondo.

the Normal (par. 112): Normal school, a two-year college for training teachers

conniption fit (par. 124): an outburst of anger or hysteria

127   "Oh, I declare," says Mama, "to think that a family of mine should quarrel on the Fourth of July, or the day after, over Stella-Rondo leaving old Mr. Whitaker and having the sweetest little adopted child! It looks like we'd all be glad!"

128   "Wah!" says Stella-Rondo, and has a fresh conniption fit.

129   "*He* left *her*—you mark my words," I says, "That's Mr. Whitaker. I know Mr. Whitaker. After all, I knew him first. I said from the beginning he'd up and leave her. I foretold every single thing that's happened.

130   "Where did he go?" asks Mama.

131   "Probably to the North Pole, if he knows what's good for him," I says.

132   But Stella-Rondo just bawled and wouldn't say another word. She flew to her room and slammed the door.

133   "Now look what you've gone and done, Sister," says Mama. "You go and apologize."

134   "I haven't got time, I'm leaving," I says.

135   "Well, what are you waiting around for?" asks Uncle Rondo.

136   So I just picked up the kitchen clock and marched off, without saying "Kiss my foot" or anything, and never did tell Stella-Rondo good-bye.

137   There was a girl going along on a little wagon right in front.

138   "Girl," I says, "come help me haul these things down the hill, I'm going to live in the post office."

139   Took her nine trips in her express wagon. Uncle Rondo came out on the porch and threw her a nickel.

140   And that's the last I've laid eyes on any of my family or my family laid eyes on me for five solid days and nights. Stella-Rondo may be telling the most horrible tales in the world about Mr. Whitaker, but I haven't heard them. As I tell everybody, I draw my own conclusions.

141   But oh, I like it here. It's ideal, as I've been saying. You see, I've got everything cater-cornered, the way I like it. Hear the radio? All the war news. Radio, sewing machine, book ends, ironing board and that great big piano lamp—peace, that's what I like. Butter-bean vines planted all along the front where the strings are.

142   Of course, there's not much mail. My family are naturally the main people in China Grove, and if they prefer to vanish from the face of the earth, for all the mail they get or the mail they write, why, I'm not going to open my mouth. Some of the folks here in town are taking up for me and some turned against me. I know which is which. There are always people who will quit buying stamps just to get on the right side of Papa-Daddy.

143   But here I am, and here I'll stay, I want the world to know I'm happy.

144   And if Stella-Rondo should come to me this minute, on bended knees, and *attempt* to explain the incidents of her life with Mr. Whitaker, I'd simply put my fingers in both my ears and refuse to listen.

cater-cornered (par. 141): positioned diagonally

Everyday Use

for your grandmama

Alice Walker

1   I will wait for her in the yard that Maggie and I made so clean and wavy yesterday afternoon. A yard like this is more comfortable than most people know. It is not just a yard. It is like an extended living room. When the hard clay is swept clean as a floor and the fine sand around the edges lined with tiny, irregular grooves anyone can come and sit and look up into the elm tree and wait for the breezes that never come inside the house.

2   Maggie will be nervous until after her sister goes: she will stand hopelessly in corners homely and ashamed of the burn scars down her arms and legs, eyeing her sister with a mixture of envy and awe. She thinks her sister has held life always in the palm of one hand, that "no" is a word the world never learned to say to her.

3   You've no doubt seen those TV shows where the child who has "made it" is confronted, as a surprise, by her own mother and father, tottering in weakly from backstage. (A pleasant surprise, of course: What would they do if parent and child came on the show only to curse out and insult each other?) On TV mother and child embrace and smile into each other's faces. Sometimes the mother and father weep, the child wraps them in her arms and leans across the table to tell how she would not have made it without their help. I have seen these programs.

4   Sometimes I dream a dream in which Dee and I are suddenly brought together on a TV program of this sort. Out of a dark and soft-seated limousine I am ushered into a bright room filled with many people. There I meet a smiling, gray, sporty man like Johnny Carson who shakes my hand and tells me what a fine girl I have. Then we are on the stage and Dee is embracing me with tears in her eyes. She pins on my dress a large orchid, even though she has told me once that she thinks orchids are tacky flowers.

5   In real life I am a large, big-boned woman with rough, man-working hands. In the winter I wear flannel nightgowns to bed and overalls during the day. I can kill and clean a hog as mercilessly as a man. My fat keeps me hot in zero weather. I can work outside all day, breaking ice to get water for washing; I can eat pork liver cooked over the open fire minutes after it comes steaming from the hog. One winter I knocked a bull calf straight in the brain between the eyes with a sledge hammer and had the meat hung up to chill before nightfall. But of course all this does not show on television. I am the way my daughter would want me to be; a hundred pounds lighter, my skin like an uncooked barley pancake. My hair glistens in the hot bright lights. Johnny Carson has much to do to keep up with my quick and witty tongue.

6   But that is a mistake. I know even before I wake up. Who ever knew a

---

awe (par. 2): a combination of fear and wonder

confronted (par. 3): brought face to face

tottering (par. 3): walking unsteadily

glistens (par. 5): shines

Johnson with a quick tongue? Who can even imagine me looking a strange white man in the eye? It seems to me I have talked to them always with one foot raised in flight, with my head turned in whichever way is farthest from them. Dee, though. She would always look anyone in the eye. Hesitation was no part of her nature.

7   "How do I look, Mama?" Maggie says, showing just enough of her thin body enveloped in pink shirt and red blouse for me to know she's there, almost hidden by the door.

8   "Come out into the yard," I say.

9   Have you ever seen a lame animal, perhaps a dog run over by some careless person rich enough to own a car, sidle up to someone who is ignorant enough to be kind to him? That is the way my Maggie walks. She has been like this, chin on chest, eyes on ground, feet in shuffle, ever since the fire that burned the other house to the ground.

10   Dee is lighter than Maggie, with nicer hair and a fuller figure. She's a woman now, though sometimes I forget. How long ago was it that the other house burned? Ten, twelve years? Sometimes I can still hear the flames and feel Maggie's arms sticking to me, her hair smoking and her dress falling off her in little black papery flakes. Her eyes seemed stretched open, blazed open by the flames reflected in them. And Dee. I see her standing off under the sweet gum tree she used to dig gum out of; a look of concentration on her face as she watched the last dingy gray board of the house fall in toward the red-hot brick chimney. Why don't you do a dance around the ashes? I'd wanted to ask her. She had hated the house that much.

11   I used to think she hated Maggie, too. But that was before we raised the money, the church and me, to send her to Augusta to school. She used to read to us without pity; forcing words, lies, other folks' habits, whole lives upon us two, sitting trapped and ignorant underneath her voice. She washed us in a river of make-believe, burned us with a lot of knowledge we didn't necessarily need to know. Pressed us to her with the serious way she read, to shove us away at just the moment, like dimwits, we seemed about to understand.

12   Dee wanted nice things. A yellow organdy dress to wear to her graduation from high school; black pumps to match a green suit she'd made from an old suit somebody gave me. She was determined to stare down any disaster in her efforts. He eyelids would not flicker for minutes at a time. Often I fought off the temptation to shake her. At sixteen she had a style of her own: and knew what style was.

13   I never had an education myself. After second grade the school was closed down. Don't ask me why: in 1927 colored asked fewer questions than they do now. Sometimes Maggie reads to me. She stumbles along good-naturedly but can't see well. She knows she is not bright. Like good looks and money, quickness passed her by. She will marry John Thomas (who has mossy teeth in an earnest face) and then I'll be free to sit here and I guess just sing church songs to myself. Although I never was a good singer. Never could carry a tune. I was always better at a man's job. I used to love to milk till I was hooked in the side in '49. Cows are soothing and slow and don't bother you, unless you try to milk them the wrong way.

sidle up (par. 9): to move sideways toward something

Augusta (par. 11): city in Georgia

organdy (par. 12): a type of fabric

mossy (par. 13): dark and coated

earnest (par. 13): sincere

hooked (par. 13): struck by the horns of a cow

14   I have deliberately turned my back on the house. It is three rooms, just like the one that burned, except the roof is tin; they don't make shingle roofs any more. There are no real windows, just some holes cut in the sides, like the port-holes in a ship, but not round and not square, with rawhide holding the shutters up on the outside. This house is in a pasture, too, like the other one. No doubt when Dee sees it she will want to tear it down. She wrote me once that no matter where we "choose" to live, she will manage to come see us. But she will never bring her friends. Maggie and I thought about this and Maggie asked me, "Mama, when did Dee ever *have* any friends?"

15   She had a few. Furtive boys in pink shirts hanging about on washday after school. Nervous girls who never laughed. Impressed with her they worshipped the well-turned phrase, the cute shape, the scalding humor that erupted like bubbles in lye. She read to them.

16   When she was courting Jimmy T she didn't have much time to pay to us, but turned all her faultfinding power on him. He *flew* to marry a cheap gal from a family of ignorant flashy people. She hardly had time to recompose herself.

17   When she comes I will meet—but there they are!

18   Maggie attempts to make a dash for the house, in her shuffling way, but I stay her with my hand. "Come back here," I say. And she stops and tries to dig a well in the sand with her toe.

19   It is hard to see them clearly through the strong sun. But even the first glimpse of leg out of the car tells me it is Dee. Her feet were always neat-looking, as if God himself had shaped them with a certain style. From the other side of the car comes a short, stocky man. Hair is all over his head a foot long and hang-ing from his chin like a kinky mule tail. I hear Maggie suck in her breath. "Uhn-nnh," is what it sounds like. Like when you see the wriggling end of a snake just in front of your foot on the road. "Uhnnnh."

20   Dee next. A dress down to the ground, in this hot weather. A dress so loud it hurts my eyes. There are yellows and oranges enough to throw back the light of the sun. I feel my whole face warming from the heat waves it throws out. Ear-rings gold, too, and hanging down to her shoulders. Bracelets dangling and making noises when she moves her arm up to shake the folds of the dress out of her armpits. The dress is loose and flows, and as she walks closer, I like it. I hear Maggie go "Uhnnnh" again. It is her sister's hair. It stands straight up like the wool on a sheep. It is black as night and around the edges are two long pigtails that rope about like small lizards disappearing behind her ears.

21   "Wa-su-zo-Tean-o!" she says, coming on in that gliding way the dress makes her move. The short stocky fellow with the hair to his navel is all grinning and he follows up with "Asalamalakim, my mother and sister!" He moves to hug Maggie but she falls back, right up against the back of my chair. I feel her trembling there and when I look up I see the perspiration falling off her chin.

22   "Don't get up," says Dee. Since I am stout it takes something of a push. You can see me trying to move a second or two before I make it. She turns, showing white heels through her sandals, and goes back to the car. Out she

shingle roofs (par. 14): here, roofs with wooden shingles

furtive (par. 15): sly, sneaky

well-turned phrase (par. 15): clever statement

lye (par. 15): a chemical that bubbles when mixed with a liquid

courting (par. 16): dating

recompose (par. 16): return to a calm state

stay (par. 18): stop

stout (par. 22): heavy

peeks next with a Polaroid. She stoops down quickly and lines up picture after picture of me sitting there in front of the house with Maggie cowering behind me. She never takes a shot without making sure the house is included. When a cow comes nibbling around the edge of the yard she snaps it and me and Maggie *and* the house. Then she puts the Polaroid in the back seat of the car, and comes up and kisses me on the forehead.

23   Meanwhile Asalamalakim is going through the motions with Maggie's hand. Maggie's hand is as limp as a fish, and probably as cold, despite the sweat, and she keeps trying to pull it back. It looks like Asalamalakim wants to shake hands but wants to do it fancy. Or maybe he don't know how people shake hands. Anyhow, he soon gives up on Maggie.

24   "Well," I say. "Dee."

25   "No, Mama," she says. "Not 'Dee,' Wangero Leewanika Kemanjo!"

26   "What happened to 'Dee'?" I wanted to know.

27   "She's dead," Wangero said. "I couldn't bear it any longer being named after the people who oppress me."

28   "You know as well as me you was named after your aunt Dicie," I said. Dicie is my sister. She is named Dee. We called her "Big Dee" after Dee was born.

29   "But who was *she* named after?" asked Wangero.

30   "I guess after Grandma Dee," I said.

31   "And who was she named after?" asked Wangero.

32   "Her mother," I said, and saw Wangero was getting tired. "That's about as far back as I can trace it," I said. Though, in fact, I probably could have carried it back beyond the Civil War through the branches.

33   "Well," said Asalamalakim, "there you are."

34   "Uhnnnh," I heard Maggie say.

35   "There I was not," I said, "before 'Dicie' cropped up in our family, so why should I try to trace it that far back?"

36   He just stood there grinning, looking down on me like somebody inspecting a Model A car. Every once in a while he and Wangero sent eye signals over my head.

37   "How do you pronounce this name?" I asked.

38   "You don't have to call me by it if you don't want to," said Wangero.

39   "Why shouldn't I?" I asked. "If that's what you want us to call you, We'll call you."

40   "I know it might sound awkward at first," said Wangero.

41   "I'll get used to it," I said. "Ream it out again."

42   Well, soon we got the name out of the way. Asalamalakim had a name twice as long and three times as hard. After I tripped over it two or three times he told me to just call him Hakim-a-barber. I wanted to ask him was he a barber, but I didn't really think he was, so I didn't ask.

43   "You must belong to those beef-cattle peoples down the road," I said. They said "Asalamalakim" when they met you, too, but they didn't shake hands. Always too busy: feeding the cattle, fixing the fences, putting up salt-lick shelters, throwing down hay. When the white folks poisoned some of the herd the men stayed up all night with rifles in their hands. I walked a mile and a half just to see the sight.

cowering (par. 22): shrinking away, as in fear

oppress (par. 27): burden, persecute

branches (par. 32): that is, the branches of a "family tree"

Model A (par. 36): a Ford car produced from 1927–1931

ream it out again (par. 41): repeat it

salt-lick (par. 43): a block of salt that cows lick

44   Hakim-a-barber said, "I accept some of their doctrines, but farming and raising cattle is not my style." (They didn't tell me, and I didn't ask, whether Wangero [Dee] had really gone and married him.)

45   We sat down to eat and right away he said he didn't eat collards and pork was unclean. Wangero, though, went on through the chitlins and corn bread, the greens and everything else. She talked a blue streak over the sweet potatoes. Everything delighted her. Even the fact that we still used the benches her daddy made for the table when we couldn't afford to buy chairs.

46   "Oh, Mama!" she cried. Then turned to Hakim-a-barber. "I never knew how lovely these benches are. You can feel the rump prints," she said, running her hands underneath her and along the bench. Then she gave a sigh and her hand closed over Grandma Dee's butter dish. "That's it!" she said. "I knew there was something I wanted to ask you if I could have." She jumped up from the table and went over in the corner where the churn stood, the milk in it clabber by now. She looked at the churn and looked at it.

47   "This churn top is what I need," she said. "Didn't Uncle Buddy whittle it out of a tree you all used to have?"

48   "Yes," I said.

49   "Uh huh," she said happily. "And I want the dasher, too."

50   "Uncle Buddy whittle that, too?" asked the barber.

51   Dee (Wangero) looked up at me.

52   "Aunt Dee's first husband whittled the dash," said Maggie so low you almost couldn't hear her. "His name was Henry, but they called him Stash."

53   "Maggie's brain is like an elephant's," Wangero said, laughing. "I can use the churn top as a centerpiece for the alcove table," she said, sliding a plate over the churn, "and I'll think of something artistic to do with the dasher."

54   When she finished wrapping the dasher the handle stuck out. I took it for a moment in my hands. You didn't even have to look close to see where hands pushing the dasher up and down to make butter had left a kind of sink in the wood. In fact, there were a lot of small sinks; you could see where thumbs and fingers had sunk into the wood. It was beautiful light yellow wood, from a tree that grew in the yard where Big Dee and Stash had lived.

55   After dinner Dee (Wangero) went to the trunk at the foot of my bed and started rifling through it. Maggie hung back in the kitchen over the dishpan. Out came Wangero with two quilts. They had been pieced by Grandma Dee and then Big Dee and me had hung them on the quilt frames on the front porch and quilted them. One was in the Lone Star pattern. The other was Walk Around the Mountain. In both of them were scraps of dresses Grandma Dee had worn fifty and more years ago. Bits and pieces of Grandpa Jarrell's Paisley shirts. And one teeny faded blue piece, about the size of a penny matchbox, that was from Great Grandpa Ezra's uniform that he wore in the Civil War.

56   "Mama," Wangero said sweet as a bird. "Can I have these old quilts?"

57   I heard something fall in the kitchen, and a minute later the kitchen door slammed.

58   "Why don't you take one or two of the others?" I asked. "These old things

doctrines (par. 44): principles by which one lives

chitlins (par. 45): hog intestines

churn (par. 46): a container in which milk is placed and allowed to sour and thicken ("clabber," par. 46); a "dasher" (par. 49) is moved up and down in the churn to separate the butter from the milk

alcove (par. 53): an area separated from the main part of a room

rifling (par. 55): rummaging, plundering

pieced (par. 55): put together

was just done by me and Big Dee from some tops your grandma pieced before she died."

59   "No," said Wangero. "I don't want those. They are stitched around the borders by machine."

60   "That'll make them last better," I said.

61   "That's not the point," said Wangero. "These are all pieces of dresses Grandma used to wear. She did all this stitching by hand. Imagine!" She held the quilts securely in her arms, stroking them.

62   "Some of the pieces, like those lavender ones, come from old clothes her mother handed down to her," I said, moving up to touch the quilts. Dee (Wangero) moved back just enough so that I couldn't reach the quilts. They already belonged to her.

63   "Imagine!" she breathed again, clutching them closely to her bosom.

64   "The truth is," I said, "I promised to give them quilts to Maggie, for when she marries John Thomas."

65   She gasped like a bee had stung her.

66   "Maggie can't appreciate these quilts!" she said. "She'd probably be backward enough to put them to everyday use."

67   "I reckon she would," I said. "God knows I been saving 'em for long enough with nobody using 'em. I hope she will!" I didn't want to bring up how I had offered Dee (Wangero) a quilt when she went away to college. Then she had told me they were old-fashioned, out of style.

68   "But they're *priceless!*" she was saying now, furiously; for she has a temper. "Maggie would put them on the bed and in five years they'd be in rags. Less than that!"

69   "She can always make some more," I said. "Maggie knows how to quilt."

70   Dee (Wangero) looked at me with hatred. "You just will not understand. The point is these quilts, *these* quilts!"

71   "Well," I said, stumped. "What would *you* do with them?"

72   "Hang them," she said. As if that was the only thing you *could* do with quilts.

73   Maggie by now was standing in the door. I could almost hear the sound her feet made as they scraped over each other.

74   "She can have them, Mama," she said, like somebody used to never winning anything, or having anything reserved for her. "I can 'member Grandma Dee without the quilts."

75   I looked at her hard. She had filled her bottom lip with checkerberry snuff and it gave her face a kind of dopey, hangdog look. It was Grandma Dee and Big Dee who taught her how to quilt herself. She stood there with her scarred hands hidden in the folds of her skirt. She looked at her sister with something like fear but she wasn't mad at her. This was Maggie's portion. This was the way she knew God to work.

76   When I looked at her like that something hit me in the top of my head and ran down to the soles of my feet. Just like when I'm in church and the spirit of God touches me and I get happy and shout. I did something I never had done before: hugged Maggie to me, then dragged her on into the room, snatched the quilts out of Miss Wangero's hands and dumped them into Maggie's lap. Maggie just sat there on my bed with her mouth open.

77   "Take one or two of the others," I said to Dee.

78   But she turned without a word and went out to Hakim-a-barber.

79   "You just don't understand," she said, as Maggie and I came out to the car.

backward (par. 66): ignorant

snuff (par. 75): ground tobacco that is inhaled or placed inside the lip or cheek

hangdog (par. 75): defeated

80   "What don't I understand?" I wanted to know.

81   "Your heritage," she said. And then she turned to Maggie, kissed her, and said, "You ought to try to make something of yourself, too, Maggie. It's really a new day for us. But from the way you and Mama still live you'd never know it."

82   She put on some sunglasses that hid everything above the tip of her nose and her chin.

83   Maggie smiled; maybe at the sunglasses. But a real smile, not scared. After we watched the car dust settle I asked Maggie to bring me a dip of snuff. And then the two of us sat there just enjoying, until it was time to go in the house and go to bed.

I Stand Here Ironing

Tillie Olsen

1   I stand here ironing, and what you asked me moves tormented back and forth with the iron.

2   "I wish you would manage the time to come in and talk with me about your daughter. I'm sure you can help me understand her. She's a youngster who needs help and whom I'm deeply interested in helping."

3   "Who needs help. . . ." Even if I came, what good would it do? You think because I am her mother I have a key, or that in some way you could use me as a key? She has lived for nineteen years. There is all that life that has happened outside of me, beyond me.

4   And when is there time to remember, to sift, to weigh, to estimate, to total? I will start and there will be an interruption and I will have to gather it all together again. Or I will become engulfed with all I did or did not do, with what should have been and what cannot be helped.

5   She was a beautiful baby. The first and only one of our five that was beautiful at birth. You do not guess how new and uneasy her tenancy in her now-loveliness. You did not know her all those years she was thought homely, or see her poring over her baby pictures, making me tell her over and over how beautiful she had been—and would be, I would tell her—and was now, to the seeing eye. But the seeing eyes were few or non-existent. Including mine.

6   I nursed her. They feel that's important nowadays. I nursed all the children, but with her, with all the fierce rigidity of first motherhood, I did like the books then said. Though her cries battered me to trembling and my breasts ached with swollenness, I waited till the clock decreed.

7   Why do I put that first? I do not even know if it matters, or if it explains anything.

8   She was a beautiful baby. She blew shining bubbles of sound. She loved motion, loved light, loved color and music and textures. She would lie on the floor in her blue overalls patting the surface so hard in ecstasy her hands and feet would blur. She was a miracle to me, but when she was eight months old I had to leave her daytimes with the woman downstairs to whom she was no mir-

engulfed (par. 4): overwhelmed

tenancy (par. 5): occupancy

ecstasy (par. 8): great joy

acle at all, for I worked or looked for work and for Emily's father, who "could no longer endure" (he wrote in his good-bye note) "sharing want with us."

9   I was nineteen. It was the pre-relief, pre-WPA world of the depression. I would start running as soon as I got off the streetcar, running up the stairs, the place smelling sour, and awake or asleep to startle awake, when she saw me she would break into a clogged weeping that could not be comforted, a weeping I can hear yet.

10   After a while I found a job hashing at night so I could be with her days, and it was better. But it came to where I had to bring her to his family and leave her.

11   It took a long time to raise the money for her fare back. Then she got chicken pox and I had to wait longer. When she finally came, I hardly knew her, walking quick and nervous like her father, looking like her father, thin, and dressed in a shoddy red that yellowed her skin and glared at the pockmarks. All the baby loveliness gone.

12   She was two. Old enough for nursery school they said, and I did not know then what I know now—the fatigue of the long day, and the lacerations of group life in the kinds of nurseries that are only parking places for children.

13   Except that it would have made no difference if I had known. It was the only place there was. It was the only way we could be together, the only way I could hold a job.

14   And even without knowing, I knew. I knew the teacher that was evil because all these years it has curdled into my memory, the little boy hunched in the corner, her rasp, "why aren't you outside, because Alvin hits you? that's no reason, go out, scaredy." I knew Emily hated it even if she did not clutch and implore "don't go Mommy" like the other children, mornings.

15   She always had a reason why we should stay home. Momma, you look sick, Momma. I feel sick. Momma, the teachers aren't there today, they're sick. Momma, we can't go, there was a fire there last night. Momma, it's a holiday today, no school, they told me.

16   But never a direct protest, never rebellion. I think of our others in their three-, four-year-oldness—the explosions, the tempers, the denunciations, the demands—and I feel suddenly ill. I put the iron down. What in me demanded that goodness in her? And what was the cost, the cost to her of such goodness?

17   The old man living in the back once said in his gentle way: "You should smile at Emily more when you look at her." What *was* in my face when I looked at her? I loved her. There were all the acts of love.

18   It was only with others I remembered what he said, and it was the face of joy, and not of care or tightness or worry I turned to them—too late for Emily. She does not smile easily, let alone almost always as her brothers and sisters do. Her face is closed and sombre, but when she wants, how fluid. You must have

pre-relief (par. 9): before welfare

pre-WPA (par. 9): before Work Projects Administration, a government program that provided jobs during the 1930's

the depression (par. 9): a time of terrible economic conditions, beginning with the great Stock Market crash in 1929 and lasting until about 1940

hashing (par. 10): cooking

shoddy (par. 11): cheap

lacerations (par. 12): literally, wounds

curdled (par. 14): literally, thickened and soured

rasp (par. 14): harsh voice

denunciations (par. 16): accusations

sombre (par. 18): serious

fluid (par. 18): full of expression

seen it in her pantomimes, you spoke of her rare gift for comedy on the stage that rouses a laughter out of the audience so dear they applaud and applaud and do not want to let her go.

19   Where does it come from, that comedy? There was none of it in her when she came back to me that second time, after I had had to send her away again. She had a new daddy now to learn to love, and I think perhaps it was a better time.

20   Except when we left her alone nights, telling ourselves she was old enough.

21   "Can't you go some other time, Mommy, like tomorrow?" she would ask. "Will it be just a little while you'll be gone? Do you promise?"

22   The time we came back, the front door open, the clock on the floor in the hall. She rigid awake. "It wasn't just a little while. I didn't cry. Three times I called you, just three times, and then I ran downstairs to open the door so you could come faster. The clock talked loud. I threw it away, it scared me what it talked."

23   She said the clock talked loud again that night I went to the hospital to have Susan. She was delirious with the fever that comes before red measles, but she was fully conscious all the week I was gone and the week after we were home when she could not come near the new baby or me.

24   She did not get well. She stayed skeleton thin, not wanting to eat, and night after night she had nightmares. She would call for me, and I would rouse from exhaustion to sleepily call back: "You're all right, darling, go to sleep, it's just a dream," and if she still called, in a sterner voice, "now go to sleep, Emily, there's nothing to hurt you." Twice, only twice, when I had to get up for Susan anyhow, I went in to sit with her.

25   Now when it is too late (as if she would let me hold and comfort her like I do the others) I get up and go to her at once at her moan or restless stirring. "Are you awake, Emily? Can I get you something?" And the answer is always the same: "No, I'm all right, go back to sleep, Mother."

26   They persuaded me at the clinic to send her away to a convalescent home in the country where "she can have the kind of food and care you can't manage for her, and you'll be free to concentrate on the new baby." They still send children to that place. I see pictures on the society page of sleek young women planning affairs to raise money for it, or dancing at the affairs, or decorating Easter eggs or filling Christmas stockings for the children.

27   They never have a picture of the children so I do not know if the girls still wear those gigantic red bows and the ravaged looks on the every other Sunday when parents can come to visit "unless otherwise notified"—as we were notified the first six weeks.

28   Oh it is a handsome place, green lawns and tall trees and fluted flower beds. High up on the balconies of each cottage the children stand, the girls in their red bows and the white dresses, the boys in white suits and giant red ties. The parents stand below shrieking up to be heard and the children shriek down to be heard, and between them the invisible wall "Not To Be Contaminated by Parental Germs or Physical Affection."

29   There was a tiny girl who always stood hand in hand with Emily. Her par-

pantomimes (par. 18): acting in which the performer communicates by movements rather than by speech

delirious (par. 23): mentally unbalanced

rouse (par. 24): wake up

sleek (par. 26): slender and graceful

ravaged (par. 27): defeated

ents never came. One visit she was gone. "They moved her to Rose Cottage," Emily shouted in explanation. "They don't like you to love anybody here."

30   She wrote once a week, the labored writing of a seven-year-old. "I am fine. How is the baby. If I write my letter nicly I will have a star. Love." There never was a star. We wrote every other day, letters she could never hold or keep but only hear read—once. "We simply do not have room for children to keep any personal possessions," they patiently explained when we pieced one Sunday's shrieking together to plead how much it would mean to Emily, who loved so to keep things, to be allowed to keep her letters and cards.

31   Each visit she looked frailer. "She isn't eating," they told us.

32   (They had runny eggs for breakfast or mush with lumps, Emily said later, I'd hold it in my mouth and not swallow. Nothing ever tasted good, just when they had chicken.)

33   It took us eight months to get her released home, and only the fact that she gained back so little of her seven lost pounds convinced the social worker.

34   I used to try to hold and love her after she came back, but her body would stay stiff, and after a while she'd push away. She ate little. Food sickened her, and I think much of life too. Oh she had physical lightness and brightness, twinkling by on skates, bouncing like a ball up and down up and down over the jump rope, skimming over the hill; but these were momentary.

35   She fretted about her appearance, thin and dark and foreign-looking at a time when every little girl was supposed to look or thought she should look a chubby blonde replica of Shirley Temple. The doorbell sometimes rang for her, but no one seemed to come and play in the house or be a best friend. Maybe because we moved so much.

36   There was a boy she loved painfully through two school semesters. Months later she told me how she had taken pennies from my purse to buy him candy. "Licorice was his favorite and I brought him some every day, but he still liked Jennifer better'n me. Why, Mommy?" The kind of question for which there is no answer.

37   School was a worry to her. She was not glib or quick in a world where glibness and quickness were easily confused with ability to learn. To her overworked and exasperated teachers she was an overconscientious "slow learner" who kept trying to catch up and was absent entirely too often.

38   I let her be absent, though sometimes the illness was imaginary. How different from my now-strictness about attendance with the others. I wasn't working. We had a new baby, I was home anyhow. Sometimes, after Susan grew old enough, I would keep her home from school, too, to have them all together.

39   Mostly Emily had asthma, and her breathing, harsh and labored, would fill the house with a curiously tranquil sound. I would bring the two old dresser mirrors and her boxes of collections to her bed. She would select beads and single earrings, bottle tops and shells, dried flowers and pebbles, old postcards and scraps, all sorts of oddments; then she and Susan would play Kingdom, setting up landscapes and furniture, peopling them with action.

labored (par. 30): showing much effort

mush (par. 32): boiled cornmeal

fretted (par. 35): worried

replica (par. 35): copy

glib (par. 37): quick with words

exasperated (par. 37): frustrated

overconscientious (par. 37): overly dedicated

tranquil (par. 39): peaceful

40   Those were the only times of peaceful companionship between her and Susan. I have edged away from it, that poisonous feeling between them, that terrible balancing of hurts and needs I had to do between the two, and did so badly, those earlier years.

41   Oh there are conflicts between the others too, each one human, needing, demanding, hurting, taking—but only between Emily and Susan, no Emily toward Susan that corroding resentment. It seems so obvious on the surface, yet it is not obvious. Susan, the second child, Susan, golden- and curly-haired and chubby, quick and articulate and assured, everything in appearance and manner Emily was not; Susan, not able to resist Emily's precious things, losing or sometimes clumsily breaking them: Susan telling jokes and riddles to company for applause while Emily sat silent (to say to me later: that was *my* riddle, Mother. I told it to Susan); Susan, who for all the five years' difference in age was just a year behind Emily in developing physically.

42   I am glad for that slow physical development that widened the difference between her and her contemporaries, though she suffered over it. She was too vulnerable for that terrible world of youthful competition, of preening and parading, of constant measuring of yourself against every other, of envy, "If I had that copper hair," "If I had that skin. . . ." She tormented herself enough about not looking like the others, there was enough of the unsureness, the having to be conscious of words before you speak, the constant caring—what are they thinking of me? without having it all magnified by the merciless physical drives.

43   Ronnie is calling. He is wet and I change him. It is rare there is such a cry now. That time of motherhood is almost behind me when the ear is not one's own but must always be racked and listening for the child cry, the child call. We sit for a while and I hold him, looking out over the city spread in charcoal with its soft aisles of light. *"Shoogily,"* he breathes and curls closer. I carry him back to bed, asleep. *Shoogily.* A funny word, a family word, inherited from Emily, invented by her to say: *comfort.*

44   In this and other ways she leaves her seal, I say aloud. And startle at my saying it. What do I mean? What did I start to gather together, to try and make coherent? I was at the terrible, growing years. War years. I do not remember them well. I was working, there were four smaller ones now, there was not time for her. She had to help be a mother, and housekeeper, and shopper. She had to set her seal. Mornings of crisis and near hysteria trying to get lunches packed, hair combed, coats and shoes found, everyone to school or Child Care on time, the baby ready for transportation. And always the paper scribbled on by a smaller one, the book looked at by Susan then mislaid, the homework not done. Running out to that huge school where she was one, she was lost, she was a drop; suffering over the unpreparedness, stammering and unsure in her classes.

45   There was so little time left at night after the kids were bedded down. She would struggle over books, always eating (it was those years she developed her enormous appetite that is legendary in our family) and I would be ironing, or preparing food for the next day, or writing V-mail to Bill, or tending the baby.

corroding (par. 41): destructive

articulate (par. 41): good with words

vulnerable (par. 42): defenseless

preening (par. 42): primping

racked (par. 43): strained

coherent (par. 44): understandable

hysteria (par. 44): panic

V-mail (par. 45): Victory mail—the name given to mail sent to soldiers during World War II

Sometimes, to make me laugh, or out of her despair, she would imitate happenings or types at school.

46   I think I said once: "Why don't you do something like this in the school amateur show?" One morning she phoned me at work, hardly understandable through the weeping: "Mother, I did it. I won, I won; they gave me first prize; they clapped and clapped and wouldn't let me go."

47   Now suddenly she was Somebody, and as imprisoned in her difference as she had been in anonymity.

48   She began to be asked to perform at other high schools, even in colleges, then at city and statewide affairs. The first one we went to, I only recognized her that first moment when thin, shy, she almost drowned herself into the curtains. Then: Was this Emily? The control, the command, the convulsing and deadly clowning, the spell, then the roaring, stamping audience, unwilling to let this rare and precious laughter out of their lives.

49   Afterwards: You ought to do something about her with a gift like that—but without money or knowing how, what does one do? We have left it all to her, and the gift has as often eddied inside, clogged and clotted, as been used and growing.

50   She is coming. She runs up the stairs two at a time with her light graceful step, and I know she is happy tonight. Whatever it was that occasioned your call did not happen today.

51   "Aren't you ever going to finish the ironing, Mother? Whistler painted his mother in a rocker. I'd have to paint mine standing over an ironing board." This is one of her communicative nights and she tells me everything and nothing as she fixes herself a plate of food out of the icebox.

52   She is so lovely. Why did you want me to come in at all? Why were you concerned? She will find her way.

53   She starts up the stairs to bed. "Don't get me up with the rest in the morning." "But I thought you were having midterms." "Oh, those," she comes back in, kisses me, and says lightly, "in a couple of years when we'll all be atom-dead they won't matter a bit."

54   She has said it before. She *believes* it. But because I have been dredging the past, and all that compounds a human being is so heavy and meaningful in me, I cannot endure it tonight.

55   I will never total it all. I will never come in to say: She was a child seldom smiled at. Her father left me before she was a year old. I had to work her first six years when there was work, or I sent her home and to his relatives. There were years she had care she hated. She was dark and thin and foreign-looking in a world where the prestige went to blondeness and curly hair and dimples, she was slow where glibness was prized. She was a child of anxious, not proud, love. We were poor and could not afford for her the soil of easy growth. I was a young mother, I was a distracted mother. There were the other children pushing up, demanding. Her younger sister seemed all that she was not. There were years she did not want me to touch her. She kept too much in herself, her life

anonymity (par. 47): state of being unknown

convulsing (par. 48): laughable

occasioned (par. 50): caused

Whistler (par. 51): James Abbot Whistler (1834–1903), American painter

icebox (par. 51): refrigerator

dredging (par. 54): examining

anxious (par. 55): nervous, worried

distracted (par. 55): distressed

was such she had to keep too much in herself. My wisdom came too late. She has much to her and probably little will come of it. She is a child of her age, of depression, of war, of fear.

56   Let her be. So all that is in her will not bloom—but in how many does it? There is still enough left to live by. Only help her to know—help make it so there is cause for her to know—that she is more than this dress on the ironing board, helpless before the iron.

He

Katherine Anne Porter

1   Life was very hard for the Whipples. It was hard to feed all the hungry mouths, it was hard to keep the children in flannels during the winter, short as it was: "God knows what would become of us if we lived north," they would say: keeping them decently clean was hard. "It looks like our luck won't never let up on us," said Mr. Whipple, but Mrs. Whipple was all for taking what was sent and calling it good, anyhow when the neighbors were in earshot. "Don't ever let a soul hear us complain," she kept saying to her husband. She couldn't stand to be pitied. "No, not if it comes to it that we have to live in a wagon and pick cotton around the country," she said, "nobody's going to get a chance to look down on us."

2   Mrs. Whipple loved her second son, the simple-minded one, better than she loved the other two children put together. She was forever saying so, and when she talked with certain of her neighbors, she would even throw in her husband and her mother for good measure.

3   "You needn't keep on saying it around," said Mr. Whipple, "you'll make people think nobody else has any feelings about Him but you."

4   "It's natural for a mother," Mrs. Whipple would remind him. "You know yourself it's more natural for a mother to be that way. People don't expect so much of fathers, some way."

5   This didn't keep the neighbors from talking plainly among themselves. "A Lord's pure mercy if He should die," they said. "It's the sins of the fathers," they agreed among themselves. "There's bad blood and bad doings somewhere, you can bet on that." This behind the Whipples' backs. To their faces everybody said, "He's not so bad off. He'll be all right yet. Look how He grows!"

6   Mrs. Whipple hated to talk about it, she tried to keep her mind off it, but every time anybody set foot in the house, the subject always came up, and she had to talk about Him first before she could get on to anything else. It seemed to ease her mind. "I wouldn't have anything happen to Him for all the world, but it just looks like I can't keep Him out of mischief. He's so strong and active, He's always into everything; He was like that since He could walk. It's actually funny sometimes, the way He can do anything; it's laughable to see Him up to His tricks. Emly has more accidents; I'm forever tying up her bruises, and Adna can't fall a foot without cracking a bone. But He can do anything and not get a scratch. The preacher said such a nice thing once when he was here. He said, and I'll remember it to my dying day, 'The innocent walk with God—that's why

flannels (par. 1): underwear

tying up (par. 6): bandaging

He don't get hurt.' " Whenever Mrs. Whipple repeated these words, she always felt a warm pool spread in her breast, and the tears would fill her eyes, and then she could talk about something else.

7   He did grow and He never got hurt. A plank blew off the chicken house and struck Him on the head and He never seemed to know it. He had learned a few words, and after this He forgot them. He didn't whine for food as the other children did, but waited until it was given Him; He ate squatting in the corner, smacking and mumbling. Rolls of fat covered Him like an overcoat, and He could carry twice as much wood and water as Adna. Emly had a cold in the head most of the time—"she takes that after me," said Mrs. Whipple—so in bad weather they gave her the extra blanket off His cot. He never seemed to mind the cold.

8   Just the same, Mrs. Whipple's life was a torment for fear something might happen to Him. He climbed the peach trees much better than Adna and went skittering along the branches like a monkey, just a regular monkey. "Oh, Mrs. Whipple, you hadn't ought to let Him do that. He'll lose His balance sometime. He can't rightly know what He's doing."

9   Mrs. Whipple almost screamed out at the neighbor. "He *does* know what He's doing! He's as able as any other child! Come down out of there, you!" When He finally reached the ground she could hardly keep her hands off Him for acting like that before people, a grin all over His face and her worried sick about Him all the time.

10   "It's the neighbors," said Mrs. Whipple to her husband. "Oh, I do mortally wish they would keep out of our business. I can't afford to let Him do anything for fear they'll come nosing around about it. Look at the bees, now. Adna can't handle them, they sting him up so; I haven't got time to do everything, and now I don't dare let Him. But if He gets a sting He don't really mind."

11   "It's just because He ain't got sense enough to be scared of anything," said Mr. Whipple.

12   "You ought to be ashamed of yourself," said Mrs. Whipple, "talking that way about you own child. Who's to take up for Him if we don't, I'd like to know? He sees a lot that goes on, He listens to things all the time. And anything I tell Him to do He does it. Don't never let anybody hear you say such things. They'd think you favored the other children over Him."

13   "Well, now I don't, and you know it, and what's the use of getting all worked up about it? You always think the worst of everything. Just let Him alone, He'll get along somehow. He gets plenty to eat and wear, don't He?" Mr. Whipple suddenly felt tired out. "Anyhow, it can't be helped now."

14   Mrs. Whipple felt tired too, she complained in a tired voice. "What's done can't never be undone, I know that as good as anybody; but He's my child, and I'm not going to have people say anything. I get sick of people coming around saying things all the time."

15   In the early fall Mrs. Whipple got a letter from her brother saying he and his wife and two children were coming over for a little visit next Sunday week. "Put the big pot in the little one," he wrote at the end. Mrs. Whipple read this part out loud twice, she was so pleased. Her brother was a great one for saying funny things. "We'll just show him that's no joke," she said, "we'll just butcher one of the sucking pigs."

16   "It's a waste and I don't hold with waste the way we are now," said Mr. Whipple. "That pig'll be worth money by Christmas."

17   "It's a shame and a pity we can't have a decent meal's vittles once in a

skittering (par. 8): moving lightly

mortally (par. 10): seriously

vittles (par. 17): food

while when my own family comes to see us," said Mrs. Whipple. "I'd hate for his wife to go back and say there wasn't a thing in the house to eat. My God, it's better than buying up a great chance of meat in town. There's where you'd spend the money!"

18   "All right, do it yourself then," said Mr. Whipple. "Christamighty, no wonder we can't get ahead!"

19   The question was how to get the little pig away from his ma, a great fighter, worse than a Jersey cow. Adna wouldn't try it: "That sow'd rip my insides out all over the pen." "All right, old fraidy," said Mrs. Whipple, "*He's* not scared. Watch *Him* do it." And she laughed as though it was all a good joke and gave Him a little push towards the pen. He sneaked up and snatched the pig right away from the teat and galloped back and was over the fence with the sow raging at His heels. The little black squirming thing was screeching like a baby in a tantrum, stiffening its back and stretching its mouth to the ears. Mrs. Whipple took the pig with her face stiff and sliced its throat with one stroke. When He saw the blood He gave a great jolting breath and ran away. "But He'll forget and eat plenty, just the same," thought Mrs. Whipple. Whenever she was thinking, her lips moved making words. "He'd eat it all if I didn't stop Him. He'd eat up every mouthful from the other two if I'd let Him."

20   She felt badly about it. He was ten years old now and a third again as large as Adna, who was going on fourteen. "It's a shame, a shame," she kept saying under her breath, "and Adna with so much brains!"

21   She kept on feeling badly about all sorts of things. In the first place it was the man's work to butcher; the sight of the pig scraped pink and naked made her sick. He was too fat and soft and pitiful-looking. It was simply a shame the way things had to happen. By the time she had finished it up, she almost wished her brother would stay at home.

22   Early Sunday morning Mrs. Whipple dropped everything to get Him all cleaned up. In an Hour he was dirty again, with crawling under fences after a possum, and straddling along the rafters of the barn looking for eggs in the hayloft. "My Lord, look at you now after all my trying! And here's Adna and Emly staying so quiet. I get tired trying to keep you decent. Get off that shirt and put on another, people will say I don't half dress you!" And she boxed Him on the ears, hard. He blinked and blinked and rubbed His head, and His face hurt Mrs. Whipple's feelings. Her knees began to tremble, she had to sit down while she buttoned His shirt. "I'm just all gone before the days starts."

23   The brother came with his plump healthy wife and two great roaring hungry boys. They had a grand dinner, with the pig roasted to a crackling in the middle of the table, full of dressing, a pickled peach in his mouth and plenty of gravy for the sweet potatoes.

24   "This looks like prosperity all right," said the brother; "you're going to have to roll me home like I was a barrel when I'm done."

25   Everybody laughed out loud; it was fine to hear them laughing all at once around the table. Mrs. Whipple felt warm and good about it. "Oh, we've got six

chance of meat (par. 17): an amount of meat

sow (par. 19): female pig

teat (par. 19): tit

tantrum (par. 19): fit of anger

jolting (par. 19): jerking

crackling (par. 23): crisp

dressing (par. 23): stuffing

prosperity (par. 24): financial success

more of these; I say it's as little as we can do when you come to see us so seldom."

26 He wouldn't come into the dining room, and Mrs. Whipple passed it off very well. "He's timider than my other two," she said, "He'll just have to get used to you. There isn't everybody He'll make up with, you know how it is with children, even cousins." Nobody said anything out of the way.

27 "Just like my Alfy here," said the brother's wife. "I sometimes got to lick him to make him shake hands with his own grandmammy."

28 So that was over, and Mrs. Whipple loaded up a big plate for Him first, before everybody. "I always say He ain't to be slighted, no matter who else goes without," she said, and carried it to Him herself.

29 "He can chin Himself on the top of the door," said Emly, helping along.

30 "That's fine. He's getting along fine," said the brother.

31 They went away after supper. Mrs. Whipple rounded up the dishes, and sent the children to bed and sat down and unlaced her shoes. "You see?" she said to Mr. Whipple. "That's the way my whole family is. Nice and considerate about everything. No out-of-the-way remarks—they *have* got refinement. I get awfully sick of people's remarks. Wasn't that pig good?"

32 Mr. Whipple said, "Yes, we're out three hundred pounds of pork, that's all. It's easy to be polite when you come to eat. Who knows what they had in their minds all along?"

33 "Yes, that's like you," said Mrs. Whipple. "I don't expect anything else from you. You'll be telling me next that my own brother will be saying around that we made Him eat in the kitchen! Oh, my God!" She rocked her head in her hands, a hard pain started in the very middle of her forehead. "Now it's all spoiled, and everything was so nice and easy. All right, you don't like them and you never did—all right, they'll not come here again soon, never you mind! But they *can't* say He wasn't dressed every lick as good as Adna—oh, honest, sometimes I wish I was dead!"

34 "I wish you'd let up," said Mr. Whipple. "It's bad enough as it is."

35 It was a hard winter. It seemed to Mrs. Whipple that they hadn't ever known anything but hard times, and now to cap it all a winter like this. The crops were about half of what they had a right to expect; after the cotton was in it didn't do much more than cover the grocery bill. They swapped off one of the plow horses, and got cheated, for the new one died of the heaves. Mrs. Whipple kept thinking all the time it was terrible to have a man you couldn't depend on not to get cheated. They cut down on everything, but Mrs. Whipple kept saying there are things you can't cut down on, and they cost money. It took a lot of warm clothes for Adna and Emly, who walked four miles to school during the three-months session. "He sets around the fire a lot, He won't need so much," said Mr. Whipple. "That's so," said Mrs. Whipple, "and when He does the outdoor chores He can wear your tarpaullion coat. I can't do no better, that's all."

36 In February He was taken sick, and lay curled up under His blanket looking very blue in the face and acting as if He would choke. Mr. and Mrs. Whipple did everything they could for Him for two days, and then they were scared and sent for the doctor. The doctor told them they must keep Him warm and give Him plenty of milk and eggs. "He isn't as stout as He looks, I'm afraid," said the

lick (par. 27): whip

slighted (par. 28): uncared for

refinement (par. 31): good manners

tarpaullion coat (par. 35): a waterproof overcoat

stout (par. 36): strong, healthy

doctor. "You've got to watch them when they're like that. You must put more cover onto Him, too."

37   "I just took off His big blanket to wash," said Mrs. Whipple, ashamed. "I can't stand dirt."

38   "Well, you'd better put it back on the minute it's dry," said the doctor, "or He'll have pneumonia."

39   Mr. and Mrs. Whipple took a blanket off their own bed and put His cot in by the fire. "They can't say we didn't do everything for Him," she said, "even to sleeping cold ourselves on His account."

40   When the winter broke He seemed to be well again, but He walked as if His feet hurt Him. He was able to run a cotton planter during the season.

41   "I got it all fixed up with Jim Ferguson about breeding the cow next time," said Mr. Whipple. "I'll pasture the bull this summer and give Jim some fodder in the fall. That's better than paying out money when you haven't got it."

42   "I hope you didn't say such a thing before Jim Ferguson," said Mrs. Whipple. "You oughtn't to let him know we're so down as all that."

43   "Godamighty, that ain't saying we're down. A man is got to look ahead sometimes. He can lead the bull over today. I need Adna on the place."

44   At first Mrs. Whipple felt easy in her mind about sending Him for the bull. Adna was too jumpy and couldn't be trusted. You've got to be steady around animals. After He was gone she started thinking, and after a while she could hardly bear it any longer. She stood in the lane and watched for Him. It was nearly three miles to go and a hot day, but He oughtn't to be so long about it. She shaded her eyes and stared until colored bubbles floated in her eyeballs. It was just like everything else in life, she must always worry and never know a moment's peace about anything. After a long time she saw Him turn into the side lane, limping. He came on very slowly, leading the big bulk of an animal by a ring in the nose, twirling a little stick in His hand, never looking back or sideways, but coming on like a sleepwalker with His eyes half shut.

45   Mrs. Whipple was scared sick of bulls; she had heard awful stories about how they followed on quietly enough, and then suddenly pitched on with a bellow and pawed and gored a body to pieces. Any second now that black monster would come down on Him, my God, He'd never have sense enough to run.

46   She mustn't make a sound nor a move; she mustn't get the bull started. The bull heaved his head aside and horned the air at a fly. Her voice burst out of her in a shriek, and she screamed at Him to come on, for God's sake. He didn't seem to hear her clamor, but kept on twirling His switch and limping on, and the bull lumbered along behind him as gently as a calf. Mrs. Whipple stopped calling and ran towards the house, praying under her breath: "Lord, don't let anything happen to Him. Lord, you *know* people will say we oughtn't to have sent Him. You *know* they'll say we didn't take care of Him. Oh, get Him home, safe home, safe home, and I'll look out for Him better! Amen."

47   She watched from the window while He led the beast in, and tied him up in the barn. It was no use trying to keep up, Mrs. Whipple couldn't bear another thing. She sat down and rocked and cried with her apron over her head.

48   From year to year the Whipples were growing poorer and poorer. The place just seemed to run down of itself, no matter how hard they worked.

fodder (par. 41): the stalks of corn, wheat, etc. used to feed farm animals

ring in the nose (par. 44): a ring placed through the nose of a farm animal as a means of controlling the animal

pitched (par. 45): dived, plunged

bellow (par. 45): roar

clamor (par. 46): loud outcry

"We're losing our hold," said Mrs. Whipple. "Why can't we do like other people and watch for our best chances? They'll be calling us poor white trash next."

49   "When I get to be sixteen I'm going to leave," said Adna. "I'm going to get a job in Powell's grocery store. There's money in that. No more farm for me."

50   "I'm going to be a schoolteacher," said Emly. "But I've got to finish the eighth grade, anyhow. Then I can live in town. I don't see any chances here."

51   "Emly takes after my family," said Mrs. Whipple. "Ambitious every last one of them, and they don't take second place for anybody."

52   When fall came Emly got a chance to wait on table in the railroad eating-house in the town near by, and it seemed such a shame not to take it when the wages were good and she could get her food too, that Mrs. Whipple decided to let her take it, and not bother with school until the next session. "You've got plenty of time," she said. "You're young and smart as a whip."

53   With Adna gone too, Mr. Whipple tried to run the farm with just Him to help. He seemed to get along fine, doing His work and part of Adna's without noticing it. They did well enough until Christmas time, when one morning He slipped on the ice coming up from the barn. Instead of getting up He thrashed round and round, and when Mr. Whipple got to Him, He was having some sort of fit.

54   They brought Him inside and tried to make Him sit up, but He blubbered and rolled, so they put Him to bed and Mr. Whipple rode to town for the doctor. All the way there and back he worried about where the money was to come from: it sure did look like he had about all the troubles he could carry.

55   From then on He stayed in bed. His legs swelled up double their size, and the fits kept coming back. After four months the doctor said, "It's no use, I think you'd better put Him in the County Home for treatment right away. I'll see about it for you. He'll have good care there and be off your hands."

56   "We don't begrudge Him any care, and I won't let Him out of my sight," said Mrs. Whipple. "I won't have it said I sent my sick child off among strangers."

57   "I know how you feel," said the doctor. "You can't tell me anything about that, Mrs. Whipple. I've got a boy of my own. But you'd better listen to me. I can't do anything more for Him, that's the truth."

58   Mr. and Mrs. Whipple talked it over a long time that night after they went to bed. "It's just charity," said Mrs. Whipple, "that's what we've come to, charity! I certainly never looked for this."

59   "We pay taxes to help support the place just like everybody else," said Mr. Whipple, "and I don't call that taking charity. I think it would be fine to have Him where He'd get the best of everything . . . and besides, I can't keep up with these doctor bills any longer."

60   "Maybe that's why the doctor wants us to send Him—he's scared he won't get his money," said Mrs. Whipple.

61   "Don't talk like that," said Mr. Whipple, feeling pretty sick, "or we won't be able to send Him."

62   "Oh, but we won't keep Him there long," said Mrs. Whipple. "Soon's He's better, we'll bring Him right back home."

63   "The doctor has told you and told you time and again He can't ever get better, and you might as well stop talking," said Mr. Whipple.

64   "Doctors don't know everything," said Mrs. Whipple, feeling almost happy. "But anyhow in the summer Emly can come home for a vacation, and Adna can get down for Sundays: we'll all work together and get on our feet again, and the children will feel they've got a place to come to."

65   All at once she saw it full summer again, with the garden going fine, and

begrudge (par. 56): resent giving

new white roller shades up all over the house, and Adna and Emly home, so full of life, all of them happy together. Oh, it could happen, things would ease up on them.

66   They didn't talk before Him much, but they never knew just how much He understood. Finally the doctor set the day and a neighbor who owned a double-seated carryall offered to drive them over. The hospital would have sent an ambulance, but Mrs. Whipple couldn't stand to see Him going away looking so sick as all that. They wrapped Him in blankets, and the neighbor and Mr. Whipple lifted Him into the back seat of the carryall beside Mrs. Whipple, who had on her black shirt waist. She couldn't stand to go looking like charity.

67   "You'll be all right, I guess I'll stay behind," said Mr. Whipple. "It don't look like everybody ought to leave the place at once."

68   "Besides, it ain't as if He was going to stay forever," said Mrs. Whipple to the neighbor. "This is only for a little while."

69   They started away, Mrs. Whipple holding to the edges of the blankets to keep Him from sagging sideways. He sat there blinking and blinking. He worked His hands out and began rubbing His nose with His knuckles, and then with the end of the blanket. Mrs. Whipple couldn't believe what she saw; He was scrubbing away big tears that rolled out of the corners of His eyes. He sniveled and made a gulping noise. Mrs. Whipple kept saying, "Oh, honey, you don't feel so bad, do you? You don't feel so bad, do you?" for He seemed to be accusing her of something. Maybe He remembered that time she boxed His ears, maybe He had been scared that day with the bull, maybe He had slept cold and couldn't tell her about it; maybe He knew they were sending Him away for good and all because they were too poor to keep Him. Whatever it was, Mrs. Whipple couldn't bear to think of it. She began to cry, frightfully, and wrapped her arms tight around Him. His head rolled on her shoulder: she had loved Him as much as she possibly could, there were Adna and Emly who had to be thought of too, there was nothing she could do to make up to Him for His life. Oh what a mortal pity He was ever born.

70   They came in sight of the hospital, with the neighbor driving very fast, not daring to look behind him.

The Kugelmass Episode

Woody Allen

1   Kugelmass, a professor of humanities at City College, was unhappily married for the second time. Daphne Kugelmass was an oaf. He also had two dull sons by his first wife, Flo, and was up to his neck in alimony and child support.

2   "Did I know it would turn out so badly?" Kugelmass whined to his analyst one day. "Daphne had promise. Who suspected she'd let herself go and swell up like a beach ball? Plus she had a few bucks, which is not in itself a healthy reason to marry a person, but it doesn't hurt, with the kind of operating nut I have. You see my point?"

Kugelmass (title): in Yiddish, a "kugel" is a noodle pudding; Yiddish is a combination of Hebrew, German, and Eastern European languages.

oaf (par. 1): a stupid person

analyst (par. 2): a psychiatrist or psychologist

operating nut (par. 2): expenses

3   Kugelmass was bald and as hairy as a bear, but he had soul.

4   "I need to meet a new woman," he went on. "I need to have an affair. I may not look the part, but I'm a man who needs romance. I need softness, I need flirtation. I'm not getting younger, so before it's too late I want to make love in Venice, trade quips at '21,' and exchange coy glances over red wine and candlelight. You see what I'm saying?"

5   Dr. Mandel shifted in his chair and said, "An affair will solve nothing. You're so unrealistic. Your problems run much deeper."

6   "And also this affair must be discreet," Kugelmass continued. "I can't afford a second divorce. Daphne would really sock it to me."

7   "Mr. Kugelmass—"

8   "But it can't be anyone at City College, because Daphne also works there. Not that anyone on the faculty at C.C.N.Y. is any great shakes, but some of those coeds . . ."

9   "Mr. Kugelmass—"

10   "Help me. I had a dream last night. I was skipping through a meadow holding a picnic basket and the basket was marked 'Options.' And then I saw there was a hole in the basket."

11   "Mr. Kugelmass, the worst thing you could do is act out. You must simply express your feelings here, and together we'll analyze them. You have been in treatment long enough to know there is no overnight cure. After all, I'm an analyst, not a magician."

12   "Then perhaps what I need is a magician," Kugelmass said, rising from his chair. And with that he terminated his therapy.

13   A couple of weeks later, while Kugelmass and Daphne were moping around in their apartment one night like two pieces of old furniture, the phone rang.

14   "I'll get it," Kugelmass said. "Hello."

15   "Kugelmass?" a voice said. "Kugelmass, this is Persky."

16   "Who?"

17   "Persky. Or should I say The Great Persky?"

18   "Pardon me?"

19   "I hear you're looking all over town for a magician to bring a little exotica into your life? Yes or no?"

20   "Sh-h-h," Kugelmass whispered. "Don't hang up. Where are you calling from, Persky?"

21   Early the following afternoon, Kugelmass climbed three flights of stairs in a broken-down apartment house in the Bushwick section of Brooklyn. Peering through the darkness of the hall, he found the door he was looking for and pressed the bell. I'm going to regret this, he thought to himself.

22   Seconds later, he was greeted by a short, thin, waxy-looking man.

quips (par. 4): clever remarks

"21" (par. 4): nightclub in New York City

coy (par. 4): teasing

discreet (par. 6): secret

C.C.N.Y. (par. 8): City College of New York

act out (par. 11): that is, to carry out

terminated (par. 12): ended

exotica (par. 19): something exciting and different

Brooklyn (par. 21): a section of New York City

23   *"You're* Persky the Great?" Kugelmass said.

24   "The Great Persky. You want a tea?"

25   "No, I want romance. I want music. I want love and beauty."

26   "But not tea, eh? Amazing. O.K., sit down."

27   Persky went to the back room, and Kugelmass heard the sounds of boxes and furniture being moved around. Persky reappeared, pushing before him a large object on squeaky roller-skate wheels. He removed some old silk handkerchiefs that were lying on its top and blew away a bit of dust. It was a cheap-looking Chinese cabinet, badly lacquered.

28   "Persky," Kugelmass said, "what's your scam?"

29   "Pay attention," Persky said. "This is some beautiful effect. I developed it for a Knights of Pythias date last year, but the booking fell through. Get into the cabinet."

30   "Why, so you can stick it full of swords or something?"

31   "You see any swords?"

32   Kugelmass made a face and, grunting, climbed into the cabinet. He couldn't help noticing a couple of ugly rhinestones glued onto the raw plywood just in front of his face. "If this is a joke," he said.

33   "Some joke. Now, here's the point. If I throw any novel into this cabinet with you, shut the doors, and tap it three times, you will find yourself projected into that book."

34   Kugelmass made a grimace of disbelief.

35   "It's the emess," Persky said. "My hand to God. Not just a novel, either. A short story, a play, a poem. You can meet any of the women created by the world's best writers. Whoever you dreamed of. You could carry on all you like with a real winner. Then when you've had enough you give a yell, and I'll see you're back there in a split second."

36   "Persky, are you some kind of outpatient?"

37   "I'm telling you it's on the level," Persky said.

38   Kugelmass remained skeptical. "What are you telling me—that this cheesy homemade box can take me on a ride like you're describing?"

39   "For a double sawbuck."

40   Kugelmass reached for his wallet. "I'll believe this when I see it," he said.

41   Persky tucked the bills in his pants pocket and turned toward his bookcase. "So who do you want to meet? Sister Carrie? Hester Prynne? Ophelia? Maybe someone by Saul Bellow? Hey, what about Temple Drake? Although for a man your age she'd be a workout."

42   "French. I want to have an affair with a French lover."

lacquered (par. 27): covered with a high-glass coating (lacquer)

scam (par. 28): a "con" game

Knights of Pythias (par. 29): a men's charitable organization

grimace (par. 34): a facial expression

emess (par. 35): Yiddish for "truth"

skeptical (par. 38): doubtful

double sawbuck (par. 39): twenty dollars

Sister Carrie (par. 41): a character in the novel *Sister Carrie* by Theodore Dreiser (1871–1945)

Hester Prynne (par. 41): a character in the novel *The Scarlet Letter* by Nathaniel Hawthorne

Ophelia (par. 41): a character in the play *Hamlet* by Shakespeare (1564–1616)

Saul Bellow (par. 41): an American novelist (b. 1925)

Temple Drake (par. 41): a character in the novel *Sanctuary* by William Faulkner (1897–1962)

43   "Nana?"

44   "I don't want to have to pay for it."

45   "What about Natasha in 'War and Peace'?"

46   "I said French. I know! What about Emma Bovary? That sounds to me perfect."

47   "You got it, Kugelmass. Give me a holler when you've had enough." Persky tossed in a paperback copy of Flaubert's novel.

48   "You sure this is safe?" Kugelmass asked as Persky began shutting the cabinet doors.

49   "Safe. Is anything safe in this crazy world?" Persky rapped three times on the cabinet and flung open the doors.

50   Kugelmass was gone. At the same moment, he appeared in the bedroom of Charles and Emma Bovary's house at Yonville. Before him was a beautiful woman, standing alone with her back turned to him as she folded some linen. I can't believe this, thought Kugelmass, staring at the doctor's ravishing wife. This is uncanny. I'm here. It's her.

51   Emma turned in surprise. "Goodness, you startled me," she said.

52   "Who are you?" She spoke in the same fine English translation as the paperback.

53   It's simply devastating, he thought. Then, realizing that it was he whom she had addressed, he said, "Excuse me. I'm Sidney Kugelmass. I'm from City College. A professor of humanities. C.C.N.Y.? Uptown. I—oh, boy!"

54   Emma Bovary smiled flirtatiously and said, "Would you like a drink? A glass of wine, perhaps?"

55   She is beautiful, Kugelmass thought. What a contrast with the troglodyte who shared his bed! He felt a sudden impulse to take this vision into his arms and tell her she was the kind of woman he had dreamed of all his life.

56   "Yes, some wine," he said hoarsely. "White. No, red. No, white. Make it white."

57   "Charles is out for the day," Emma said, her voice full of playful implication.

58   After the wine, they went for a stroll in the lovely French countryside. "I've always dreamed that some mysterious stranger would appear and rescue me from the monotony of this crass rural existence," Emma said, clasping his hand. They passed a small church. "I love what you have on," she murmured. "I've never seen anything like it around here. It's so . . . so modern."

59   "It's called a leisure suit," he said romantically. "It was marked down." Suddenly he kissed her. For the next hour they reclined under a tree and whispered together and told each other deeply meaningful things with their eyes.

Nana (par. 43): a character in the novel *Nana* by Emile Zola (1840–1902)

Natasha in 'War and Peace' (par. 45): a novel by Leo Tolstoy (1828–1910)

Emma Bovary (par. 46): the main character in *Madame Bovary* by Gustave Flaubert (1821–1880); Emma's husband, Charles, is a doctor (par. 50), and they live in Yonville, France (par. 50); she has two lovers, Rodolphe (par. 71) and Leon (par. 78); Abbe Bournisien (par. 80) is her priest; Binet (par. 94) is the tax collector.

ravishing (par. 50): gorgeous, sexy

uncanny (par. 50): unbelievable

devastating (par. 53): amazing

troglodyte (par. 55): literally, a cave dweller

implication (par. 57): suggestion

monotony (par. 58): boredom

crass (par. 58): common, lacking "class"

Then Kugelmass sat up. He had just remembered he had to meet Daphne at Bloomingdale's. "I must go," he told her. "But don't worry, I'll be back."

60   "I hope so," Emma said.

61   He embraced her passionately, and the two walked back to the house. He held Emma's face cupped in his palms, kissed her again, and yelled, "O.K., Persky! I got to be at Bloomingdale's by three-thirty."

62   There was an audible pop, and Kugelmass was back in Brooklyn.

63   "So? Did I lie?" Persky asked triumphantly.

64   "Look, Persky, I'm right now late to meet the ball and chain at Lexington Avenue, but when can I go again? Tomorrow?"

65   "My pleasure. Just bring a twenty. And don't mention this to anybody."

66   "Yeah. I'm going to call Rupert Murdoch."

67   Kugelmass hailed a cab and sped off to the city. His heart danced on point. I am in love, he thought. I am the possessor of a wonderful secret. What he didn't realize was that at this very moment students in various classrooms across the country were saying to their teachers, "Who is this character on page 100? A bald Jew is kissing Madame Bovary?" A teacher in Sioux Falls, South Dakota, sighed and thought, Jesus, these kids, with their pot and acid. What goes through their minds!

68   Daphne Kugelmass was in the bathroom-accessories department at Bloomingdale's when Kugelmass arrived breathlessly. "Where've you been?" she snapped. "It's four-thirty."

69   "I got held up in traffic," Kugelmass said.

70   Kugelmass visited Persky the next day, and in a few minutes was again passed magically to Yonville. Emma couldn't hide her excitement at seeing him. The two spent hours together, laughing and talking abut their different backgrounds. Before Kugelmass left, they made love. "My God, I'm doing it with Madame Bovary! Kugelmass whispered to himself. "Me, who failed freshman English."

71   As the months passed, Kugelmass saw Persky many times and developed a close and passionate relationship with Emma Bovary. "Make sure and always get me into the book before page 120," Kugelmass said to the magician one day. "I always have to meet her before she hooks up with this Rodolphe character."

72   "Why?" Persky asked. "You can't beat his time?"

73   "Beat his time. He's landed gentry. Those guys have nothing better to do than flirt and ride horses. To me, he's one of those faces you see in the pages of *Women's Wear Daily*. With the Helmut Berger hairdo. But to her he's hot stuff."

74   "And her husband suspects nothing?"

75   "He's out of his depth. He's a lackluster little paramedic who's thrown in his lot with a jitterbug. He's ready to go to sleep by ten, and she's putting on her dancing shoes. Oh, well . . . See you later."

Bloomingdale's (par. 59): department store in New York City located on Lexington Avenue (par. 64)

audible (par. 62): loud enough to be heard

the ball and chain (par. 64): that is, his wife, Daphne; a ball and chain were once attached to prisoners to prevent them from escaping

Rupert Murdoch (par. 66): a newspaper publisher

landed gentry (par. 73): a landowner of high social position

Women's Wear Daily (par. 73): a fashion magazine

lackluster (par. 75): dull

thrown in his lot (par. 75): joined in

jitterbug (par. 75): Literally, the jitterbug is a dance done to fast music such as jazz.

76   And once again Kugelmass entered the cabinet and passed instantly to the Bovary estate at Yonville. "How you doing, cupcake?" he said to Emma.

77   "Oh, Kugelmass," Emma sighed. "What I have to put up with. Last night at dinner, Mr. Personality dropped off to sleep in the middle of the dessert course. I'm pouring my heart out about Maxim's and the ballet, and out of the blue I hear snoring."

78   "It's O.K., darling. I'm here now," Kugelmass said, embracing her. I've earned this, he thought, smelling Emma's French perfume and burying his nose in her hair. I've suffered enough. I've paid enough analysts. I've searched till I'm weary. She's young and nubile, and I'm here a few pages after Leon and just before Rodolphe. By showing up during the correct chapters, I've got the situation knocked.

79   Emma, to be sure, was just as happy as Kugelmass. She had been starved for excitement, and his tales of Broadway night life, of fast cars and Hollywood and TV stars, enthralled the young French beauty.

80   "Tell me again about O. J. Simpson," she implored that evening, as she and Kugelmass strolled past Abbe Bournisien's church.

81   "What can I say? The man is great. He sets all kinds of rushing records. Such moves. They can't touch him."

82   "And the Academy Awards?" Emma said wistfully. "I'd give anything to win one."

83   "First you've got to be nominated."

84   "I know. You explained it. But I'm convinced I can act. Of course, I'd want to take a class or two. With Strasberg maybe. Then, if I had the right agent—"

85   "We'll see, we'll see. I'll speak to Persky."

86   That night, safely returned to Persky's flat, Kugelmass brought up the idea of having Emma visit him in the big city.

87   "Let me think about it," Persky said. "Maybe I could work it. Stranger things have happened." Of course, neither of them could think of one.

88   "Where the hell do you go all the time?" Daphne Kugelmass barked at her husband as he returned home late that evening. "You got a chippie stashed somewhere?"

89   "Yeah, sure, I'm just the type," Kugelmass said wearily. "I was with Leonard Popkin. We were discussing Socialist agriculture in Poland. You know Popkin. He's a freak on the subject."

90   "Well, you've been very odd lately," Daphne said. "Distant. Just don't forget about my father's birthday. On Saturday?"

91   "Oh, sure, sure," Kugelmass said, heading for the bathroom.

92   "My whole family will be there. We can see the twins. And Cousin Hamish. You should be more polite to Cousin Hamish—he likes you."

93   "Right, the twins," Kugelmass said, closing the bathroom door and shutting out the sound of his wife's voice. He leaned against it and took a deep breath. In a few hours he told himself, he would be back in Yonville again, back with his beloved. And this time, if all went well, he would bring Emma back with him.

94   At three-fifteen the following afternoon, Persky worked his wizardry

Maxim's (par. 77): a restaurant in Paris

nubile (par. 78): ready for sex

Broadway (par. 79): theatre district in New York City

O. J. Simpson (par. 80): a football player

Strasberg (par. 84): Lee Strasberg (1901–1982), famous actor, acting teacher, and director

chippie (par. 88): prostitute

again. Kugelmass appeared before Emma, smiling and eager. The two spent a few hours at Yonville with Binet and then remounted the Bovary carriage. Following Persky's instructions, they held each other tightly, closed their eyes, and counted to ten. When they opened them, the carriage was just drawing up at the side door of the Plaza Hotel, where Kugelmass had optimistically reserved a suite earlier in the day.

95   "I love it! It's everything I dreamed it would be," Emma said as she swirled joyously around the bedroom, surveying the city from their window. "There's F. A. O. Schwarz. And there's Central Park, and the Sherry is which one? Oh, there—I see. It's too divine."

96   On the bed there were boxes from Halston and Saint Laurent. Emma unwrapped a package and held up a pair of black velvet pants against her perfect body.

97   "The slacks suit is by Ralph Lauren," Kugelmass said. "You'll look like a million bucks in it. Come on, sugar, give us a kiss."

98   "I've never been so happy!" Emma squealed as she stood before the mirror. "Let's go out on the town. I want to see 'Chorus Line' and the Guggenheim and this Jack Nicholson character you always talk about. Are any of his flicks showing?"

99   "I cannot get my mind around this," a Stanford professor said. "First a strange character named Kugelmass, and now she's gone from the book. Well, I guess the mark of a classic is that you can reread it a thousand times and always find something new."

100   The lovers passed a blissful weekend. Kugelmass had told Daphne he would be away at a symposium in Boston and would return Mondy. Savoring each moment, he and Emma went to the movies, had dinner in Chinatown, passed two hours at a discotheque, and went to bed with a TV movie. They slept till noon Sunday, visited SoHo, and ogled celebrities at Elaine's. They had caviar and champagne in their suite on Sunday night and talked until dawn. That morning, in the cab taking them to Persky's apartment, Kugelmass thought, It was hectic, but worth it. I can't bring her here too often, but now and then it will be a charming contrast with Yonville.

101   At Persky's, Emma climbed into the cabinet, arranged her new boxes of clothes neatly around her, and kissed Kugelmass fondly. "My place next time," she said with a wink. Persky rapped three times on the cabinet. Nothing happened.

102   "Hmm." Persky said, scratching his head. He rapped again, but still no magic. "Something must be wrong," he mumbled.

optimistically (par. 94): hopefully

F.A.O. Schwarz (par. 95): a toy store in New York City

the Sherry (par. 95): a hotel in New York City

Halston and Saint Laurent (par. 96): fashion designers

'Chorus Line' (par. 98): a Broadway musical

the Guggenheim (par. 98): an art museum

Jack Nicholson (par. 98): an actor

flicks (par. 98): movies

symposium (par. 100): convention

savoring (par. 100): enjoying

SoHo (par. 100): a popular district of New York City

ogled (par. 100): stared at

Elaine's (par. 100): a restaurant in New York City

103   "Persky you're joking!" Kugelmass cried. "How can it not work?"

104   "Relax, relax. Are you still in the box, Emma?"

105   "Yes."

106   Persky rapped again—harder this time.

107   "I'm still here, Persky."

108   "I know, darling. Sit tight."

109   "Persky, we *have* to get her back," Kugelmass whispered. "I'm a married man, and I have a class in three hours. I'm not prepared for anything more than a cautious affair at this point."

110   "I can't understand it," Persky muttered. "It's such a realiable little trick."

111   But he could do nothing. "It's going to take a little while," he said to Kugelmass. "I'm going to have to strip it down. I'll call you later."

112   Kugelmass bundled Emma into a cab and took her back to the Plaza. He barely made it to his class on time. He was on the phone all day, to Persky and to his mistress. The magician told him it might be several days before he got to the bottom of the trouble.

113   "How was the symposium?" Daphne asked him that night.

114   "Fine, fine," he said, lighting the filter end of a cigarette.

115   "What's wrong? You're as tense as a cat."

116   "Me? Ha, that's a laugh. I'm as calm as a summer night. I'm just going to take a walk." He eased out the door, hailed a cab, and flew to the Plaza.

117   "This is no good," Emma said. "Charles will miss me."

118   "Bear with me, sugar," Kugelmass said. He was pale and sweaty. He kissed her again, raced to the elevators, yelled at Persky over a pay phone in the Plaza lobby, and just made it home before midnight.

119   "According to Popkin, barley prices in Krakow have not been this stable since 1971," he said to Daphne, and smiled wanly as he climbed into bed.

120   The whole week went by like that. On Friday night, Kugelmass told Daphne there was another symposium he had to catch, this one in Syracuse. He hurried back to the Plaza, but the second weekend there was nothing like the first. "Get me back into the novel or marry me," Emma told Kugelmass. "Meanwhile, I want to get a job or go to class, because watching TV all day is the pits."

121   "Fine. We can use the money," Kugelmass said. "You consume twice your weight in room service."

122   "I met an Off Broadway producer in Central Park yesterday, and he said I might be right for a project he's doing," Emma said.

123   "Who is this clown?" Kugelmass asked.

124   "He's not a clown. He's sensitive and kind and cute. His name's Jeff Something-or-Other, and he's up for a Tony."

125   Later that afternoon, Kugelmass showed up at Persky's drunk.

126   "Relax," Persky told him. "You'll get a coronary."

127   "Relax. The man says relax. I've got a fictional character stashed in a hotel room, and I think my wife is having me tailed by a private shamus."

128   "O.K., O.K. We know there's a problem." Persky crawled under the cabinet and started banging on something with a wrench.

129   "I'm like a wild animal," Kugelmass went on. "I'm sneaking around town, and Emma and I have had it up to here with each other. Not to mention a hotel tab that reads like the defense budget."

Krakow (par. 119): city in Poland

Syracuse (par. 120): city in New York

Tony (par. 124): award given for excellence in theatre

shamus (par. 127) detective

130   "So what should I do? This is the world of magic," Persky said. "It's all nuance."

131   "Nuance, my foot. I'm pouring Dom Perignon and black eggs into this little mouse, plus her wardrobe, plus she's enrolled at the Neighborhood Playhouse and suddenly needs professional photos. Also, Persky, Professor Fivish Kopkind, who teaches Comp Lit and who has always been jealous of me, has identified me as the sporadically appearing character in the Flaubert book. He's threatened to go to Daphne. I see ruin and alimony jail. For adultery with Madame Bovary, my wife will reduce me to beggary."

132   "What do you want me to say? I'm working on it night and day. As far as your personal anxiety goes, that I can't help you with. I'm a magician, not an analyst."

133   By Sunday afternoon, Emma had locked herself in the bathroom and refused to respond to Kugelmass's entreaties. Kugelmass stared out the window at the Wollman Rink and contemplated suicide. Too bad this is a low floor, he thought, or I'd do it right now. Maybe if I ran away to Europe and started life over . . . Maybe I could sell the *International Herald Tribune,* like those young girls used to.

134   The phone rang. Kugelmass lifted it to his ear mechanically.

135   "Bring her over," Persky said. "I think I got the bugs out of it."

136   Kugelmass's heart leaped. "You're serious?" he said. "You got it licked?"

137   "It was something in the transmission. Go figure."

138   "Persky, you're a genius. We'll be there in a minute. Less than a minute."

139   Again the lovers hurried to the magician's apartment, and again Emma Bovary climbed into the cabinet with her boxes. This time there was no kiss. Persky shut the doors, took a deep breath, and tapped the box three times. There was the reassuring popping noise, and when Persky peered inside, the box was empty. Madame Bovary was back in her novel. Kugelmass heaved a great sigh of relief and pumped the magician's hand.

140   "It's over," he said. "I learned my lesson. I'll never cheat again, I swear it." He pumped Persky's hand again and made a mental note to send him a necktie.

141   Three weeks later, at the end of a beautiful spring afternoon, Persky answered his doorbell. It was Kugelmass, with a sheepish expression on his face.

142   "O.K., Kugelmass," the magician said. "Where to this time?"

143   "It's just this once," Kugelmass said. "The weather is so lovely, and I'm not getting any younger. Listen, you've read 'Portnoy's Complaint'? Remember The Monkey?"

144   "The price is now twenty-five dollars, because the cost of living is up, but I'll start you off with one freebie, due to all the trouble I caused you."

145   "You're good people," Kugelmass said, combing his few remaining hairs as he climbed into the cabinet again. "This'll work all right?"

nuance (par. 130): literally, a slight difference

Dom Perignon (par. 131): a brand of expensive champagne

black eggs (par. 131): caviar

Neighborhood Playhouse (par. 131): theatre in New York City

sporadically (par. 131): occasionally

entreaties (par. 133): pleas

Wollman Rink (par. 133): ice-skating rink in Central Park

International Herald Tribune (par. 133): an American newspaper published in France

sheepish (par. 141): timid, embarrassed

Portnoy's Complaint (par. 143): a novel by Philip Roth (b. 1933)

146   "I hope. But I haven't tried it much since all that unpleasantness."

147   "Sex and romance," Kugelmass said from inside the box. "What we go through for a pretty face."

148   Persky tossed in a copy of "Portnoy's Complaint" and rapped three times on the box. This time, instead of a popping noise there was a dull explosion, followed by a series of crackling noises and a shower of sparks. Persky leaped back, was seized by a heart attack, and dropped dead. The cabinet burst into flames, and eventually the entire house burned down.

149   Kugelmass, unaware of this catastrophe, had his own problems. He had not been thrust into "Portnoy's Complaint," or into any other novel, for that matter. He had been projected into an old textbook, "Remedial Spanish," and was running for his life over a barren, rocky terrain as the word *"tener"* ("to have")—a large and hairy irregular verb—raced after him on its spindly legs.

terrain (par. 149): ground

spindly (par. 149): long and skinny

Shiloh

Bobbie Ann Mason

1   Leroy Moffitt's wife, Norma Jean, is working on her pectorals. She lifts three-pound dumbbells to warm up, then progresses to a twenty-pound barbell. Standing with her legs apart, she reminds Leroy of Wonder Woman.

2   "I'd given anything if I could just get these muscles to where they're real hard," says Norma Jean. "Feel this arm. It's not as hard as the other one."

3   "That's 'cause you're right-handed," says Leroy, dodging as she swings the barbell in an arc.

4   "Do you think so?"

5   "Sure."

6   Leroy is a truckdriver. He injured his leg in a highway accident four months ago, and his physical therapy, which involves weights and a pulley, prompted Norma Jean to try building herself up. Now she is attending a body-building class. Leroy has been collecting temporary disability since his tractor-trailer jack-knifed in Missouri, badly twisting his left leg in its socket. He has a steel pin in his hip. He will probably not be able to drive his rig again. It sits in the backyard, like a gigantic bird that has flown home to roost. Leroy has been home in Kentucky for three months, and his leg is almost healed, but the accident frightened him and he does not want to drive any more long hauls. He is not sure what to do next. In the meantime, he makes things from craft kits. He started by building a miniature log cabin from notched Popsicle sticks. He varnished it and placed it on the TV set, where it remains. It reminds him of a rustic Nativity scene. Then he tried string art (sailing ships on black velvet), a macrame owl kit, a snap-together B-17 Flying Fortress, and a lamp made out of a model truck, with a light fixture screwed in the top of the cab. At first the kits were di-

Shiloh (title): a town in Tennessee where over twenty thousand soldiers died during a Civil War battle; the Confederate army was defeated and driven back to Corinth, Mississippi (par. 135).

pectorals (par. 1): chest muscles

jack-knifed (par. 6): twisted sideways

versions, something to kill time, but now he is thinking about building a full-scale log house from a kit. It would be considerably cheaper than building a regular house, and besides, Leroy has grown to appreciate how things are put together. He has begun to realize that in all the years he was on the road he never took time to examine anything. He was always flying past scenery.

7   "They won't let you build a log cabin in any of the new subdivisions," Norma Jean tells him.

8   "They will if I tell them it's for you," he says, teasing her. Ever since they were married, he has promised Norma Jean he would build her a new house one day. They have always rented, and the house they live in is small and non-descript. It does not even feel like a home, Leroy realizes now.

9   Norma Jean works at the Rexall drugstore, and she has acquired an amazing amount of information about cosmetics. When she explains to Leroy the three stages of complexion care, involving creams, toners, and moisturizers, he thinks happily of other petroleum products—axle grease, diesel fuel. This is a connection between him and Norma Jean. Since he has been home, he has felt unusually tender about his wife and guilty over his long absences. But he can't tell what she feels about him. Norma Jean has never complained about his traveling; she has never made hurt remarks, like calling his truck a "widow-maker." He is reasonably certain she has been faithful to him, but he wishes she could celebrate his permanent homecoming more happily. Norma Jean is often startled to find Leroy at home, and he thinks she seems a little disappointed about it. Perhaps it reminds her too much of the early days of their marriage, before he went on the road. They had a child who died as an infant, years ago. They never speak about their memories of Randy, which have almost faded, but now that Leroy is home all the time, they sometimes feel awkward around each other, and Leroy wonders if one of them should mention the child. He has the feeling that they are waking up out of a dream together—that they must create a new marriage, start afresh. They are lucky they are still married. Leroy has read that for most people losing a child destroys the marriage—or else he heard this on *Donahue*. He can't always remember where he learns things anymore.

10   At Christmas, Leroy bought an electric organ for Norma Jean. She used to play the piano when she was in high school. "It don't leave you," she told him once. "It's like riding a bicycle."

11   The new instrument had so many keys and buttons that she was bewildered by it at first. She touched the keys tentatively, pushed some buttons, then pecked out "Chopsticks." It came out in an amplified fox-trot rhythm, with marimba sounds.

12   "It's an orchestra!" she cried.

13   The organ had a pecan-look finish and eighteen preset chords, with optional flute, violin, trumpet, clarinet, and banjo accompaniments. Norma Jean mastered the organ almost immediately. At first she played Christmas songs. Then she bought *The Sixties Songbook* and learned every tune in it, adding variations to each with the rows of brightly colored buttons.

14   "I didn't like these old songs back then," she said. "But I have this crazy feeling I missed something."

startled (par. 9): surprised

bewildered (par. 11): confused

tentatively (par. 11): uncertainly

amplified (par. 11): to "amplify" sounds is to make them louder

fox-trot (par. 11): a ballroom dance with slow and fast steps

marimba (par. 11): a large xylophone—a musical instrument having wooden bars that are struck to produce sound

15   "You didn't miss a thing," said Leroy.

16   Leroy likes to lie on the couch and smoke a joint and listen to Norma Jean play "Can't Take My Eyes Off You" and "I'll Be Back." He is back again. After fifteen years on the road, he is finally settling down with the woman he loves. She is still pretty. Her skin is flawless. Her frosted curls resemble pencil trimmings.

17   Now that Leroy has come home to stay, he notices how much the town has changed. Subdivisions are spreading across western Kentucky like an oil slick. The sign at the edge of town says "Pop: 11,500"—only seven hundred more than it said twenty years before. Leroy can't figure out who is living in all the new houses. The farmers who used to gather around the courthouse square on Saturday afternoons to play checkers and spit tobacco juice have gone. It has been years since Leroy has thought about the farmers, and they have disappeared without his noticing.

18   Leroy meets a kid named Stevie Hamilton in the parking lot at the new shopping center. While they pretend to be strangers meeting over a stalled car, Stevie tosses an ounce of marijuana under the front seat of Leroy's car. Stevie is wearing orange jogging shoes and a T-shirt that says CHATTAHOOCHEE SUPER-RAT. His father is a prominent doctor who lives in one of the expensive subdivisions in a new white-columned brick house that looks like a funeral parlor. In the phone book under his name there is a separate number, with the listing "Teenagers."

19   "Where do you get this stuff?" asks Leroy. "From your pappy?"

20   "That's for me to know and you to find out," Stevie says. He is slit-eyed and skinny.

21   "What else you got?"

22   "What you interested in?"

23   "Nothing special. Just wondered."

24   Leroy used to take speed on the road. Now he has to go slowly. He needs to be mellow. He leans back against the car and says, "I'm aiming to build me a log house, soon as I get time. My wife, though, I don't think she likes the idea."

25   "Well, let me know when you want me again," Stevie says. He has a cigarette in his cupped palm, as though sheltering it from the wind. He takes a long drag, then stomps it on the asphalt and slouches away.

26   Stevie's father was two years ahead of Leroy in high school. Leroy is thirty-four. He married Norma Jean when they were both eighteen, and their child Randy was born a few months later, but he died at the age of four months and three days. He would be about Stevie's age now. Norma Jean and Leroy were at the drive-in, watching a double feature (*Dr. Strangelove* and *Lover Come Back*), and the baby was sleeping in the back seat. When the first movie ended, the baby was dead. It was the sudden infant death syndrome. Leroy remembers handing Randy to a nurse at the emergency room, as though he were offering her a large doll as a present. A dead baby feels like a sack of flour. "It just happens sometimes," said the doctor, in what Leroy always recalls as a nonchalant tone. Leroy can hardly remember the child anymore, but he still sees vividly a scene from *Dr. Strangelove* in which the President of the United States was talking in a folksy voice on the hot line to the Soviet premier about the bomber accidentally headed toward Russia. He was in the War Room, and the world map

a joint (par. 16): a marijuana cigarette

prominent (par. 18): well known

nonchalant (par. 26): unconcerned

folksy (par 26): friendly, personal

was lit up. Leroy remembers Norma Jean standing catatonically beside him in the hospital and himself thinking: Who is this strange girl? He had forgotten who she was. Now scientists are saying that crib death is caused by a virus. Nobody knows anything, Leroy thinks. The answers are always changing.

27   When Leroy gets home from the shopping center, Norma Jean's mother, Mabel Beasley, is there. Until this year, Leroy has not realized how much time she spends with Norma Jean. When she visits, she inspects the closets and then the plants, informing Norma Jean when a plant is droopy or yellow. Mabel calls the plants "flowers," although there are never any blooms. She always notices if Norma Jean's laundry is piling up. Mabel is a short, overweight woman whose tight, brown-dyed curls look more like a wig than the actual wig she sometimes wears. Today she has brought Norma Jean an off-white dust ruffle she made for the bed; Mabel works in a custom-upholstery shop.

28   "This is the tenth one I made this year," Mabel says. "I got started and couldn't stop."

29   "It's real pretty," says Norma Jean.

30   "Now we can hide things under the bed," says Leroy, who gets along with his mother-in-law primarily by joking with her. Mabel has never really forgiven him for disgracing her by getting Norma Jean pregnant. When the baby died, she said that fate was mocking her.

31   "What's that thing?" Mabel says to Leroy in a loud voice, pointing to a tangle of yarn on a piece of canvas.

32   Leroy holds it up for Mabel to see. "It's my needlepoint," he explains. "This is a *Star Trek* pillow cover."

33   "That's what a woman would do," says Mabel. "Great day in the morning!"

34   "All the big football players on TV do it," he says.

35   "Why, Leroy, you're always trying to fool me. I don't believe you for one minute. You don't know what to do with yourself—that's the whole trouble. Sewing!"

36   "I'm aiming to build us a log house," says Leroy. "Soon as my plans come."

37   "Like *heck* you are," says Norma Jean. She takes Leroy's needlepoint and shoves it into a drawer. "You have to find a job first. Nobody can afford to build now anyway."

38   Mabel straightens her girdle and says, "I still think before you get tied down y'all ought to take a little run to Shiloh."

39   "One of these days, Mama," Norma Jean says impatiently.

40   Mabel is talking about Shiloh, Tennessee. For the past few years, she has been urging Leroy and Norma Jean to visit the Civil War battleground there. Mabel went there on her honeymoon—the only real trip she ever took. Her husband died of perforated ulcer when Norma Jean was ten, but Mabel, who was accepted into the United Daughters of the Confederacy in 1975, is still preoccupied with going back to Shiloh.

41   "I've been to kingdom come and back in that truck out yonder," Leroy says to Mabel, "but we never yet set foot in that battleground. Ain't that something? How did I miss it?"

42   "It's not even that far," Mabel says.

43   After Mabel leaves, Norma Jean reads to Leroy from a list she has made.

catatonically (par. 26): motionless, stunned

mocking (par. 30): ridiculing

preoccupied with (par. 40): extremely interested in

kingdom come (par. 41): as far as one can travel

"Things you could do," she announces. "You could get a job as a guard at Union Carbide, where they'd let you set on a stool. You could get on at the lumberyard. You could do a little carpenter work, if you want to build so bad. You could—"

44   "I can't do something where I'd have to stand up all day."

45   "You ought to try standing up all day behind a cosmetics counter. It's amazing that I have strong feet, coming from two parents that never had strong feet at all." At the moment Norma Jean is holding on to the kitchen counter, raising her knees one at a time as she talks. She is wearing two pound ankle weights.

46   "Don't worry," says Leroy. "I'll do something."

47   "You could truck calves to slaughter for somebody. You wouldn't have to drive any big old truck for that."

48   "I'm going to build you this house," says Leroy. "I want to make you a real home."

49   "I don't want to live in any log cabin."

50   "It's not a cabin. It's a house."

51   "I don't care. It looks like a cabin."

52   "You and me together could lift those logs. It's just like lifting weights."

53   Norma Jean doesn't answer. Under her breath, she is counting. Now she is marching through the kitchen. She is doing goose steps.

54   Before his accident, when Leroy came home he used to stay in the house with Norma Jean, watching TV in bed and playing cards. She would cook fried chicken, picnic ham, chocolate pie—all his favorites. Now he is home alone much of the time. In the mornings, Norma Jean disappears, leaving a cooling place in the bed. She eats a cereal called Body Buddies, and she leaves the bowl on the table, with the soggy tan balls floating in a milk puddle. He sees things about Norma Jean that he never realized before. When she chops onions, she stares off into a corner, as if she can't bear to look. She puts on her house slippers almost precisely at nine o'clock every evening and nudges her jogging shoes under the couch. She saves bread heels for the birds. Leroy watches the birds at the feeder. He notices the peculiar way goldfinches fly past the window. They close their wings, then fall, then spread their wings to catch and lift themselves. He wonders if they close their eyes when they fall. Norma Jean closes her eyes when they are in bed. She wants the lights turned out. Even then, he is sure she closes her eyes.

55   He goes for long drives around town. He tends to drive a car rather carelessly. Power steering and an automatic shift make a car feel so small and inconsequential that his body is hardly involved in the driving process. His injured leg stretches out comfortably. Once or twice he has almost hit something, but even the prospect of an accident seems minor in a car. He cruises the new subdivisions, feeling like a criminal rehearsing for a robbery. Norma Jean is probably right about a log house being inappropriate here in the new subdivisions. All the houses look grand and complicated. They depress him.

56   One day when Leroy comes home from a drive he finds Norma Jean in tears. She is in the kitchen making a potato and mushroom-soup casserole, with grated-cheese topping. She is crying because her mother caught her smoking.

57   "I didn't hear her coming. I was standing here puffing away pretty as you please," Norma Jean says, wiping her eyes.

inconsequential (par. 55): unimportant, insignificant

prospect (par. 55): possibility

58   "I knew it would happen sooner or later," says Leroy, putting his arm around her.

59   "She don't know the meaning of the word 'knock,' " says Norma Jean. "It's a wonder she hadn't caught me years ago."

60   "Think of it this way," Leroy says. "What if she caught me with a joint?"

61   "You better not let her!" Norma Jean shrieks. "I'm warning you, Leroy Moffitt!"

62   "I'm just kidding. Here, play me a tune. That'll help you relax."

63   Norma Jean puts the casserole in the oven and sets the timer. Then she plays a ragtime tune, with horns and banjo, as Leroy lights up a joint and lies on the couch, laughing to himself about Mabel's catching him at it. He thinks of Stevie Hamilton—a doctor's son pushing grass. Everything is funny. The town seems crazy and small. He is reminded of Virgil Mathis, a boastful policeman Leroy used to shoot pool with. Virgil recently led a drug bust in a back room at a bowling alley, where he seized ten thousand dollars' worth of marijuana. The newspaper had a picture of him holding up the bags of grass and grinning widely. Right now, Leroy can imagine Virgil breaking down the door and arresting him with a lungful of smoke. Virgil would probably have been alerted to the scene because of all the racket Norma Jean is making. Now she sounds like a hard-rock band. Norma Jean is terrific. When she switches to a Latin-rhythm version of "Sunshine Superman," Leroy hums along. Norma Jean's foot goes up and down, up and down.

64   "Well, what do you think?" Leroy says, when Norma Jean pauses to search through her music.

65   "What do I think about what?"

66   His mind has gone blank. Then he says, "I'll sell my rig and build us a house." That wasn't what he wanted to say. He wanted to know what she thought—what she *really* thought—about them.

67   "Don't start in on that again," says Norma Jean. She begins playing "Who'll Be the Next in Line?"

68   Leroy used to tell hitchhikers his whole life story—about his travels, his hometown, the baby. He would end with a question: "Well, what do you think?" It was just a rhetorical question. In time, he had the feeling that he'd been telling the same story over and over to the same hitchhikers. He quit talking to hitchhikers when he realized how his voice sounded—whining and self-pitying, like some teenage-tragedy song. Now Leroy has the sudden impulse to tell Norma Jean about himself, as if he had just met her. They have known each other so long they have forgotten a lot about each other. They could become reacquainted. But when the oven timer goes off and she runs to the kitchen, he forgets why he wants to do this.

69   The next day, Mabel drops by. It is Saturday and Norma Jean is cleaning. Leroy is studying the plans of his log house, which have finally come in the mail. He has them spread out on the table—big sheets of stiff blue paper, with diagrams and numbers printed in white. While Norma Jean runs the vacuum, Mabel drinks coffee. She sets her coffee cup on a blueprint.

70   "I'm just waiting for time to pass," she says to Leroy, drumming her fingers on the table.

71   As soon as Norma Jean switches off the vacuum, Mabel says in a loud voice, "Did you hear about the datsun dog that killed the baby?"

72   Norma Jean says, "The word is 'dachshund.' "

pushing grass (par. 63): selling marijuana

rhetorical question (par. 68): a question that is not meant to be answered

impulse (par. 68): desire

73   "They put the dog on trial. It chewed the baby's legs off. The mother was in the next room all the time." She raises her voice. "They thought it was neglect."

74   Norma Jean is holding her ears. Leroy manages to open the refrigerator and get some Diet Pepsi to offer Mabel. Mabel still has some coffee and she waves away the Pepsi.

75   "Datsuns are like that," Mabel says. "They're jealous dogs. They'll tear a place to pieces if you don't keep an eye on them."

76   "You better watch out what you're saying, Mabel," says Leroy.

77   "Well, facts is facts."

78   Leroy looks out the window at his rig. It is like a huge piece of furniture gathering dust in the backyard. Pretty soon it will be an antique. He hears the vacuum cleaner. Norma Jean seems to be cleaning the living room rug again.

79   Later, she says to Leroy, "She just said that about the baby because she caught me smoking. She's trying to pay me back."

80   "What are you talking about?" Leroy says, nervously shuffling blueprints.

81   "You know good and well," Norma Jean says. She is sitting in a kitchen chair with her feet up and her arms wrapped around her knees. She looks small and helpless. She says, "The very idea, her bringing up a subject like that! Saying it was neglect."

82   "She didn't mean that," Leroy says.

83   "She might not have *thought* she meant it. She always says things like that. You don't know how she goes on."

84   "But she didn't really mean it. She was just talking."

85   Leroy opens a king-sized bottle of beer and pours it into two glasses, dividing it carefully. He hands a glass to Norma Jean, and she takes it from him mechanically. For a long time, they sit by the kitchen window watching the birds at the feeder.

86   Something is happening. Norma Jean is going to night school. She has graduated from her six-week body-building course and now she is taking an adult-education course in composition at Paducah Community College. She spends her evenings outlining paragraphs.

87   "First you have a topic sentence," she explains to Leroy. "Then you divide it up. Your secondary topic has to be connected to your primary topic."

88   To Leroy, this sounds intimidating. "I never was any good in English," he says.

89   "It makes a lot of sense."

90   "What are you doing this for, anyhow?"

91   She shrugs. "It's something to do." She stands up and lifts her dumbbells a few times.

92   "Driving a rig, nobody cared about my English."

93   "I'm not criticizing your English."

94   Norma Jean used to say, "If I lose ten minutes' sleep, I just drag all day." Now she stays up late, writing compositions. She got a B on her first paper—a how-to theme on soup-based casseroles. Recently Norma Jean has been cooking unusual foods—tacos, lasagna, Bombay chicken. She doesn't play the organ anymore, though her second paper was called "Why Music Is Important to Me." She sits at the kitchen table, concentrating on her outlines, while Leroy plays with his log house plans, practicing with a set of Lincoln Logs. The thought of getting a truckload of notched, numbered logs scares him, and he wants to be prepared. As he and Norma Jean work together at the kitchen table, Leroy has the hopeful thought that they are sharing something, but he knows he is a fool

intimidating (par. 88): threatening

to think this. Norma Jean is miles away. He knows he is going to lose her. Like Mabel, he is just waiting for time to pass.

95   One day, Mabel is there before Norma Jean gets home from work, and Leroy finds himself confiding in her. Mabel, he realizes, must know Norma Jean better than he does.

96   "I don't know what's got into that girl," Mabel says. "She used to go to bed with the chickens. Now you say she's up all hours. Plus her a-smoking. I like to died."

97   "I want to make her this beautiful home," Leroy says, indicating the Lincoln Logs. "I don't think she even wants it. Maybe she was happier with me gone."

98   "She don't know what to make of you, coming home like this."

99   "Is that it?"

100   Mabel takes the roof off his Lincoln Log cabin. "You couldn't get *me* in a log cabin," she says. "I was raised in one. It's no picnic, let me tell you."

101   "They're different now," says Leroy.

102   "I tell you what," Mabel says, smiling oddly at Leroy.

103   "What?"

104   "Take her on down to Shiloh. Y'all need to get out together, stir a little. Her brain's all balled up over them books."

105   Leroy can see traces of Norma Jean's features in her mother's face. Mabel's worn face has the texture of crinkled cotton, but suddenly she looks pretty. It occurs to Leroy that Mabel has been hinting all along that she wants them to take her with them to Shiloh.

106   "Let's all go to Shiloh," he says. "You and me and her. Come Sunday."

107   Mabel throws up her hands in protest. "Oh, no, not me. Young folks want to be by themselves."

108   When Norma Jean comes in with groceries, Leroy says excitedly, "Your mama here's been dying to go to Shiloh for thirty-five years. It's about time we went, don't you think?"

109   "I'm not going to butt in on anybody's second honeymoon," Mabel says.

110   "Who's going on a honeymoon, for Christ's sake?" Norma Jean says loudly.

111   "I never raised no daughter of mine to talk that-a-way," Mabel says.

112   "You ain't seen nothing yet," says Norma Jean. She starts putting away boxes and cans, slamming cabinet doors.

113   "There's a log cabin at Shiloh," Mabel says. "It was there during the battle. There's bullet holes in it."

114   "When are you going to *shut up* about Shiloh, Mama?" asks Norma Jean.

115   "I always thought Shiloh was the prettiest place, so full of history," Mabel goes on. "I just hoped y'all could see it once before I die, so you could tell me about it." Later, she whispers to Leroy, "You do what I said. A little change is what she needs."

116   "Your name means 'the king,' " Norma Jean says to Leroy that evening. He is trying to get her to go to Shiloh, and she is reading a book about another century.

117   "Well, I reckon I ought to be right proud."

118   "I guess so."

119   "Am I still king around here?"

120   Norma Jean flexes her biceps and feels them for hardness. "I'm not fooling around with anybody, if that's what you mean," she says.

confiding in (par. 95): talking privately to

biceps (par. 120): upper arm muscles

121   "Would you tell me if you were?"

122   "I don't know."

123   "What does *your* name mean?"

124   "It was Marilyn Monroe's real name."

125   "No kidding!"

126   "Norma comes from the Normans. They were invaders," she says. She closes her book and looks hard at Leroy. "I'll go to Shiloh with you if you'll stop staring at me."

127   On Sunday, Norma Jean packs a picnic and they go to Shiloh. To Leroy's relief, Mabel says she does not want to come with them. Norma Jean drives, and Leroy, sitting beside her, feels like some boring hitchhiker she has picked up. He tries some conversation, but she answers him in monosyllables. At Shiloh, she drives aimlessly through the park, past bluffs and trails and steep ravines. Shiloh is an immense place, and Leroy cannot see it as a battleground. It is not what he expected. He thought it would look like a golf course. Monuments are everywhere, showing through the thick clusters of trees. Norma Jean passes the log cabin Mabel mentioned. It is surrounded by tourists looking for bullet holes.

128   "That's not the kind of log house I've got in mind," says Leroy apologetically.

129   "I know *that*."

130   "This is a pretty place. Your mama was right."

131   "It's O.K.," says Norma Jean. "Well, we've seen it. I hope she's satisfied."

132   They burst out laughing together.

133   At the park museum, a movie on Shiloh is shown every half hour, but they decide that they don't want to see it. They buy a souvenir Confederate flag for Mabel, and then they find a picnic spot near the cemetery. Norma Jean has brought a picnic cooler, with pimiento sandwiches, soft drinks, and Yodels. Leroy eats a sandwich and then smokes a joint, hiding it behind the picnic cooler. Norma Jean has quit smoking altogether. She is picking cake crumbs from the cellophane wrapper, like a fussy bird.

134   Leroy says, "So the boys in gray ended up in Corinth. The Union soldiers zapped 'em finally, April 7, 1862."

135   They both know he doesn't know any history. He is just talking about some of the historical plaques they have read. He feels awkward, like a boy on a date with an older girl. They are still just making conversation.

136   "Corinth is where Mama eloped to," says Norma Jean.

137   They sit in silence and stare at the cemetery for the Union dead and, beyond, at a tall cluster of trees. Campers are parked nearby, bumper to bumper, and small children in bright clothing are cavorting and squealing. Norma Jean wads up the cake wrapper and squeezes it tightly in her hand. Without looking at Leroy, she says, "I want to leave you."

138   Leroy takes a bottle of Coke out of the cooler and flips off the cap. He holds the bottle poised near his mouth but cannot remember to take a drink. Finally he says, "No, you don't."

139   "Yes, I do."

Normans (par. 126): Scandinavian invaders of Normandy (in France); the French Normans later invaded England (in 1066).

monosyllables (par. 127): one-syllable sounds or words

aimlessly (par. 127): without purpose or direction

immense (par. 127): huge

the boys in gray (par. 134): Confederate soldiers

cavorting (par. 137): leaping, hopping, etc.

140   "I won't let you."

141   "You can't stop me."

142   "Don't do me that way."

143   Leroy knows Norma Jean will have her own way. "Didn't I promise to be home from now on?" he says.

144   "In some ways, a woman prefers a man who wanders," says Norma Jean. "That sounds crazy, I know."

145   "You're not crazy."

146   Leroy remembers to drink from his Coke. Then he says, "Yes, you *are* crazy. You and me could start all over again. Right back at the beginning."

147   "We *have* started all over again," says Norma Jean. "And this is how it turned out."

148   "What did I do wrong?"

149   "Nothing."

150   "Is this one of those women's lib things?" Leroy asks.

151   "Don't be funny."

152   The cemetery, a green slope dotted with white markers, looks like a subdivision site. Leroy is trying to comprehend that his marriage is breaking up, but for some reason he is wondering about white slabs in a graveyard.

153   "Everything was fine till Mama caught me smoking," says Norma Jean, standing up. "That set something off."

154   "What are you talking about?"

155   "She won't leave me alone—*you* won't leave me alone." Norma Jean seems to be crying, but she is looking away from him. "I feel eighteen again. I can't face that all over again." She starts walking away. "No, it *wasn't* fine. I don't know what I'm saying. Forget it."

156   Leroy takes a lungful of smoke and closes his eyes as Norma Jean's words sink in. He tries to focus on the fact that thirty-five hundred soldiers died on the grounds around him. He can only think of that war as a board game with plastic soldiers. Leroy almost smiles, as he compares the Confederates' daring attack on the Union camps and Virgil Mathis's raid on the bowling alley. General Grant, drunk and furious, shoved the Southerners back to Corinth, where Mabel and Jet Beasley were married years later, when Mabel was still thin and good-looking. The next day Mabel and Jet visited the battleground and then Norma Jean was born, and then she married Leroy and they had a baby, which they lost, and now Leroy and Norma Jean are here at the same battleground. Leroy knows he is leaving out a lot. He is leaving out the insides of history. History was always just names and dates to him. It occurs to him that building a house out of logs is similarly empty—too simple. And the real inner workings of a marriage, like most of history, have escaped him. Now he sees that building a log house is the dumbest idea he could have had. It was clumsy of him to think Norma Jean would want a log house. It was a crazy idea. He'll have to think of something else, quickly. He will wad the blueprints into tight balls and fling them into the lake. Then he'll get moving again. He opens his eyes. Norma Jean has moved away and is walking through the cemetery, following a serpentine brick path.

157   Leroy gets up to follow his wife, but his good leg is asleep and his bad leg still hurts him. Norma Jean is far away, walking rapidly toward the bluff by the river, and he tries to hobble toward her. Some children run past him, screaming noisily. Norma Jean has reached the bluff, and she is looking out over the Tennessee River. Now she turns toward Leroy and waves her arms. Is she beckoning to him? She seems to be doing an exercise for her chest muscles. The sky is unusually pale—the color of the dust ruffle Mabel made for their bed.

General Grant (par. 156): Commander of the Union Army

serpentine (par. 156): twisted, like a snake

A Rose for Emily

William Faulkner

I

1   When Miss Emily Grierson died, our whole town went to her funeral: the men through a sort of respectful affection for a fallen monument, the women mostly out of curiosity to see the inside of her house, which no one save an old man-servant—a combined gardener and cook—had seen in at least ten years.

2   It was a big, squarish frame house that had once been white, decorated with cupolas and spires and scrolled balconies in the heavily lightsome style of the seventies, set on what had once been our most select street. But garages and cotton gins had encroached and obliterated even the august names of that neighborhood; only Miss Emily's house was left, lifting its stubborn and coquettish decay above the cotton wagons and the gasoline pumps—an eyesore among eyesores. And now Miss Emily had gone to join the representatives of those august names where they lay in the cedar-bemused cemetery among the ranked and anonymous graves of Union and Confederate soldiers who fell at the battle of Jefferson.

3   Alive, Miss Emily had been a tradition, a duty, and a care; a sort of hereditary obligation upon the town, dating from that day in 1894 when Colonel Sartoris, the mayor—he who fathered the edict that no Negro woman should appear on the street without an apron—remitted her taxes, the dispensation dating from the death of her father on into perpetuity. Not that Miss Emily would have accepted charity. Colonel Sartoris invented an involved tale to the effect that Miss Emily's father had loaned money to the town, which the town, as a matter of business, preferred this way of repaying. Only a man of Colonel Sartoris' generation and thought could have invented it, and only a woman could have believed it.

4   When the next generation, with its more modern ideas, became mayors and aldermen, this arrangement created some little dissatisfaction. On the first of the year they mailed her a tax notice. February came, and there was no reply. They wrote her a formal letter, asking her to call at the sheriff's office at her convenience. A week later the mayor wrote her himself, offering to call or to send

cupolas (par. 2): a rounded structure forming part of the roof of a house

spires (par. 2): small steeples

scrolled balconies (par. 2): balconies with fancy designs or "scrollwork"

encroached (par. 2): moved in

obliterated (par 2): destroyed

august (par. 2): grand

coquettish (par. 2): Literally, a "coquette" is a flirtatious woman.

cedar-bemused (par. 2): overgrown with cedars

hereditary (par. 3): inherited

remitted (par. 3): cancelled

dispensation (par. 3): exemption

perpetuity (par. 3): eternity

his car for her, and received in reply a note on paper of an archaic shape, in a thin, flowing calligraphy in faded ink, to the effect that she no longer went out at all. The tax notice was also enclosed, without comment.

5   They called a special meeting of the Board of Aldermen. A deputation waited upon her, knocked at the door through which no visitor had passed since she ceased giving china-painting lessons eight or ten years earlier. They were admitted by the old Negro into a dim hall from which a stairway mounted into still more shadow. It smelled of dust and disuse—a close, dank smell. The Negro led them into the parlor. It was furnished in heavy, leather-covered furniture. When the Negro opened the blinds of one window, they could see that the leather was cracked; and when they sat down, a faint dust rose sluggishly about their thighs, spinning with slow motes in the single sun-ray. On a tarnished gilt easel before the fireplace stood a crayon portrait of Miss Emily's father.

6   They rose when she entered—a small, fat woman in black, with a thin gold chain descending to her waist and vanishing into her belt, leaning on an ebony cane with a tarnished gold head. Her skeleton was small and spare; perhaps that was why what would have been merely plumpness in another was obesity in her. She looked bloated, like a body long submerged in motionless water, and of that pallid hue. Her eyes, lost in the fatty ridges of her face, looked like two small pieces of coal pressed into a lump of dough as they moved from one face to another while the visitors stated their errand.

7   She did not ask them to sit. She just stood in the door and listened quietly until the spokesman came to a stumbling halt. Then they could hear the invisible watch ticking at the end of the gold chain.

8   Her voice was dry and cold. "I have no taxes in Jefferson. Colonel Sartoris explained it to me. Perhaps one of you can gain access to the city records and satisfy yourselves."

9   "But we have. We are the city authorities, Miss Emily. Didn't you get a notice from the sheriff, signed by him?"

10   "I received a paper, yes," Miss Emily said. "Perhaps he considers himself the sheriff . . . I have no taxes in Jefferson."

11   "But there is nothing on the books to show that, you see. We must go by the—"

12   "See Colonel Sartoris. I have no taxes in Jefferson."

13   "But, Miss Emily—"

14   "See Colonel Sartoris." (Colonel Sartoris had been dead almost ten years.) "I have no taxes in Jefferson. Tobe!" The Negro appeared. "Show these gentlemen out."

II

15   So she vanquished them, horse and foot, just as she had vanquished their fathers thirty years before about the smell. That was two years after her father's death and a short time after her sweetheart—the one we believed would marry

archaic (par. 4): old fashioned

calligraphy (par. 4): fancy writing

deputation (par. 5): a group of citizens that represents others

dank (par. 5): moldy

motes (par. 5): specks

gilt (par. 5): a gold coating

ebony (par. 6): a black wood

pallid hue (par. 6): pale color

vanquished (par. 15): defeated

her—had deserted her. After her father's death she went out very little; after her sweetheart went away, people hardly saw her at all. A few of the ladies had the temerity to call, but were not received, and the only sign of life about the place was the Negro man—a young man then—going in and out with a market basket.

16 'Just as if a man—any man—could keep a kitchen properly," the ladies said; so they were not surprised when the smell developed. It was another link between the gross, teeming world and the high and mighty Griersons.

17 A neighbor, a woman, complained to the mayor, Judge Stevens, eighty years old.

18 "But what will you have me to do about it, madam?" he said.

19 "Why, send her word to stop it," the woman said. "Isn't there a law?"

20 "I'm sure that won't be necessary," Judge Stevens said. "It's probably just a snake or a rat that nigger of hers killed in the yard. I'll speak to him about it."

21 The next day he received two more complaints, one from a man who came in diffident deprecation. "We really must do something about it, Judge. I'd be the last one in the world to bother Miss Emily, but we've got to do something." That night the Board of Aldermen met—three graybeards and one younger man, a member of the rising generation.

22 "It's simple enough," he said. "Send her word to have her place cleaned up. Give her a certain time to do it in, and if she don't . . ."

23 "Dammit, sir," Judge Stevens said, "will you accuse a lady to her face of smelling bad?"

24 So the next night, after midnight, four men crossed Miss Emily's lawn and slunk about the house like burglars, sniffing along the base of the brickwork and at the cellar openings while one of them performed a regular sowing motion with his hand out of a sack slung from his shoulder. They broke open the cellar door and sprinkled lime there, and in all the outbuildings. As they recrossed the lawn, a window that had been dark was lighted and Miss Emily sat in it, the light behind her, and her upright torso motionless as that of an idol. They crept quietly across the lawn and into the shadow of the locusts that lined the street. After a week or two the smell went away.

25 That was when people had begun to feel really sorry for her. People in our town, remembering how old lady Wyatt, her great-aunt, had gone completely crazy at last, believed that the Griersons held themselves a little too high for what they really were. None of the young men were quite good enough for Miss Emily and such. We had long thought of them as a tableau, Miss Emily a slender figure in white in the background, her father a spraddled silhouette in the foreground, his back to her and clutching a horsewhip, the two of them framed by the backflung front door. So when she got to be thirty and was still single, we were not pleased exactly, but vindicated; even with insanity in the family she wouldn't have turned down all of her chances if they had really materialized.

26 When her father died, it got about that the house was all that was left to

temerity (par. 15): nerve

teeming (par. 16): crowded

diffident (par. 21): hesitant

deprecation (par. 21): mild disapproval

torso (par. 24): upper body

tableau (par. 25): posed picture

spraddled (par. 25): spread out

silhouette (par. 25): literally, the outline of some figure

vindicated (par. 25): proven correct

materialized (par. 25): occurred

her, and in a way, people were glad. At last they could pity Miss Emily. Being left alone, and a pauper, she had become humanized. Now she too would know the old thrill and the old despair of a penny more or less.

27   The day after his death all the ladies prepared to call at the house and offer condolence and aid, as is our custom. Miss Emily met them at the door, dressed as usual and with no trace of grief on her face. She told them that her father was not dead. She did that for three days, with the ministers calling on her, and the doctors, trying to persuade her to let them dispose of the body. Just as they were about to resort to law and force, she broke down, and they buried her father quickly.

28   We did not say she was crazy then. We believed she had to do that. We remembered all the young men her father had driven away, and we knew that with nothing left, she would have to cling to that which had robbed her, as people will.

III

29   She was sick for a long time. When we saw her again, her hair was cut short, making her look like a girl, with a vague resemblance to those angels in colored church windows—sort of tragic and serene.

30   The town had just let the contracts for paving the sidewalks, and in the summer after her father's death they began the work. The construction company came with niggers and mules and machinery, and a foreman named Homer Barron, a Yankee—a big, dark, ready man, with a big voice and eyes lighter than his face. The little boys would follow in groups to hear him cuss the niggers, and the niggers singing in time to the rise and fall of picks. Pretty soon he knew everybody in town. Whenever you heard a lot of laughing anywhere about the square, Homer Barron would be in the center of the group. Presently, we began to see him and Miss Emily on Sunday afternoons driving in the yellow-wheeled buggy and the matched team of bays from the livery stable.

31   At first we were glad that Miss Emily would have an interest, because the ladies all said, "Of course a Grierson would not think seriously of a Northerner, a day laborer." But there were still others, older people, who said that even grief could not cause a real lady to forget *noblesse oblige*—without calling it *noblesse oblige*. They just said, "Poor Emily. Her kinsfolk should come to her." She had some kin in Alabama; but years ago her father had fallen out with them over the estate of old lady Wyatt, the crazy woman, and there was no communication between the two families. They had not even been represented at the funeral.

32   And as soon as the old people said, "Poor Emily," the whispering began. "Do you suppose it's really so?" they said to one another. "Of course it is. What else could . . ." This behind their hands; rustling of craned silk and satin behind jalousies closed upon the sun of Sunday afternoon as the thin, swift clop-clop-clop of the matched team passed: "Poor Emily."

33   She carried her head high enough—even when we believed that she was fallen. It was as if she demanded more than ever the recognition of her dignity as the last Grierson; as if it had wanted that touch of earthiness to reaffirm her

pauper (par. 26): a very poor person

condolence (par. 27): sympathy

serene (par. 29): peaceful

let (par. 30): issued

noblesse oblige (par. 31): literally, "nobility obligates"; the term refers to the obligation of a person of high standing to be honorable and generous.

jalousies (par. 32): blinds

reaffirm (par. 33): prove again

imperviousness. Like when she bought the rat poison, the arsenic. That was over a year after they had begun to say "Poor Emily," and while the two female cousins were visiting her.

34   "I want some poison," she said to the druggist. She was over thirty then, still a slight woman, though thinner than usual, with cold, haughty black eyes in a face the flesh of which was strained across the temples and about the eye-sockets as you imagine a lighthouse-keeper's face ought to look. "I want some poison," she said.

35   "Yes, Miss Emily. What kind? For rats and such? I'd recom—"

36   "I want the best you have. I don't care what kind."

37   The druggist named several. "They'll kill anything up to an elephant. But what you want is—"

38   "Arsenic," Miss Emily said. "Is that a good one?"

39   "Is . . . arsenic? Yes, ma'am. But what you want—"

40   "I want arsenic."

41   The druggist looked down at her. She looked back at him, erect, her face like a strained flag. "Why, of course," the druggist said. "If that's what you want. But the law requires you to tell what you are going to use it for."

42   Miss Emily just stared at him, her head tilted back in order to look him eye for eye, until he looked away and went and got the arsenic and wrapped it up. The Negro delivery boy brought her the package; the druggist didn't come back. When she opened the package at home there was written on the box, under the skull and bones: "For rats."

IV

43   So the next day we all said, "She will kill herself"; and we said it would be the best thing. When she had first begun to be seen with Homer Barron, we had said, "She will marry him." Then we said, "She will persuade him yet," because Homer himself had remarked—he liked men, and it was known that he drank with the younger men in the Elks' Club—that he was not a marrying man. Later we said, "Poor Emily" behind the jalousies as they passed on Sunday afternoon in the glittering buggy, Miss Emily with her head high and Homer Barron with his hat cocked and a cigar in his teeth, reins and whip in a yellow glove.

44   Then some of the ladies began to say that it was a disgrace to the town and a bad example to the young people. The men did not want to interfere, but at last the ladies forced the Baptist minister—Miss Emily's people were Episcopal—to call upon her. He would never divulge what happened during that interview, but he refused to go back again. The next Sunday they again drove about the streets, and the following day the minister's wife wrote to Miss Emily's relations in Alabama.

45   So she had blood-kin under her roof again and we sat back to watch developments. At first nothing happened. Then we were sure that they were to be married. We learned that Miss Emily had been to the jeweler's and ordered a man's toilet set in silver, with the letters H. B. on each piece. Two days later we learned that she had bought a complete outfit of men's clothing, including a nightshirt, and we said, "They are married." We were really glad. We were glad because the two female cousins were even more Grierson than Miss Emily had ever been.

46   So we were not surprised when Homer Barron—the streets had been finished some time since—was gone. We were a little disappointed that there was

imperviousness (par. 33): ability to be affected by nothing

divulge (par. 44): reveal

a man's toilet set (par. 45): personal items such as a hair brush, a razor, etc.

not a public blowing-off, but we believed that he had gone on to prepare for Miss Emily's coming, or to give her a chance to get rid of the cousins. (By that time it was a cabal, and we were all Miss Emily's allies to help circumvent the cousins.) Sure enough, after another week they departed. And, as we had expected all along, within three days Homer Barron was back in town. A neighbor saw the Negro man admit him at the kitchen door at dusk one evening.

47   And that was the last we saw of Homer Barron. And of Miss Emily for some time. The Negro man went in and out with the market basket, but the front door remained closed. Now and then we would see her at the window for a moment, as the men did that night when they sprinkled the lime, but for almost six months she did not appear on the streets. Then we knew that this was to be expected too; as if that quality of her father which had thwarted her woman's life so many times had been too virulent and too furious to die.

48   When we next saw Miss Emily, she had grown fat and her hair was turning gray. During the next few years it grew grayer and grayer until it attained an even pepper-and-salt iron-gray, when it ceased turning. Up to the day of her death at seventy-four it was still that vigorous iron-gray, like the hair of an active man.

49   From that time on her front door remained closed, save for a period of six or seven years, when she was about forty, during which she gave lessons in china-painting. She fitted up a studio in one of the downstairs rooms, where the daughters and granddaughters of Colonel Sartoris' contemporaries were sent to her with the same regularity and in the same spirit that they were sent to church on Sundays with a twenty-five-cent piece for the collection plate. Meanwhile her taxes had been remitted.

50   Then the newer generation became the backbone and the spirit of the town, and the painting pupils grew up and fell away and did not send their children to her with boxes of color and tedious brushes and pictures cut from the ladies' magazines. The front door closed upon the last one and remained closed for good. When the town got free postal delivery, Miss Emily alone refused to let them fasten the metal numbers above her door and attach a mailbox to it. She would not listen to them.

51   Daily, monthly, yearly we watched the Negro grow grayer and more stooped, going in and out with the market basket. Each December we sent her a tax notice, which would be returned by the post office a week later, unclaimed. Now and then we would see her in one of the downstairs windows—she had evidently shut up the top floor of the house—like the cavern torso of an idol in a niche, looking or not looking at us, we could never tell which. Thus she passed from generation to generation—dear, inescapable, impervious, tranquil, and perverse.

52   And so she died. Fell ill in the house filled with dust and shadows, with only a doddering Negro man to wait on her. We did not even know she was sick; we had long since given up trying to get any information from the Negro. He talked to no one, probably not even to her, for his voice had grown harsh and rusty, as if from disuse.

cabal (par. 46): a group of people united to bring about a certain result

circumvent (par. 46): outsmart

thwarted (par. 47): frustrated

virulent (par. 47): poisonous

tedious (par. 50): tiresome

niche (par. 51): literally, a recess in a wall in which a statue is usually placed

tranquil (par. 51): calm

perverse (par. 51): extremely strange

53   She died in one of the downstairs rooms, in a heavy walnut bed with a curtain, her gray head propped on a pillow yellow and moldy with age and lack of sunlight.

V

54   The Negro met the first of the ladies at the front door and let them in, with their hushed, sibilant voices and their quick, curious glances, and then he disappeared. He walked right through the house and out the back and was not seen again.

55   The two female cousins came at once. They held the funeral on the second day, with the town coming to look at Miss Emily beneath a mass of bought flowers, with the crayon face of her father musing profoundly above the bier and the ladies sibilant and macabre; and the very old men—some in their brushed Confederate uniforms—on the porch and the lawn, talking of Miss Emily as if she had been a contemporary of theirs, believing that they had danced with her and courted her perhaps, confusing time with its mathematical progression, as the old do, to whom all the past is not a diminishing road but, instead, a huge meadow which no winter ever quite touches, divided from them now by the narrow bottleneck of the most recent decade of years.

56   Already we knew that there was one room in that region above stairs which no one had seen in forty years, and which would have to be forced. They waited until Miss Emily was decently in the ground before they opened it.

57   The violence of breaking down the door seemed to fill this room with pervading dust. A thin, acrid pall as of the tomb seemed to lie everywhere upon this room decked and furnished as for a bridal: upon the valance curtains of faded rose color, upon the rose-shaded lights, upon the dressing table, upon the delicate array of crystal and the man's toilet things backed with tarnished silver, silver so tarnished that the monogram was obscured. Among them lay a collar and tie, as if they had just been removed, which lifted, left upon the surface a pale crescent in the dust. Upon a chair hung the suit, carefully folded; beneath it the two mute shoes and the discarded socks.

58   The man himself lay in the bed.

59   For a long while we just stood there, looking down at the profound and fleshless grin. The body had apparently once lain in the attitude of an embrace, but now the long sleep that outlasts love, that conquers even the grimace of love, had cuckolded him. What was left of him, rotted beneath what was left of the nightshirt, had become inextricable from the bed in which he lay; and upon him and upon the pillow beside him lay that even coating of the patient and biding dust.

60   Then we noticed that in the second pillow was the indentation of a head. One of us lifted something from it, and leaning forward, that faint and invisible dust dry and acrid in the nostrils, we saw a long strand of iron-gray hair.

sibilant (par. 54): hissing

bier (par. 55): a stand upon which a coffin is placed

macabre (par. 55): fascinated with death

a contemporary (par. 55): a person of approximately the same age

acrid (par. 57): harsh, irritating

pall (par. 57): atmosphere of gloom

profound (par. 59): difficult to understand

grimace (par. 59): a facial expression showing disapproval or disbelief

cuckolded (par. 59): Literally, a cuckold is a man whose wife is unfaithful to him.

inextricable (par. 59): inseparable

The Chrysanthemums

John Steinbeck

1   The high grey-flannel fog of winter closed off the Salinas Valley from the sky and from all the rest of the world. On every side it sat like a lid on the mountains and made of the great valley a closed pot. On the broad, level land floor the gang plows bit deep and left the black earth shining like metal where the shares had cut. On the foothill ranches across the Salinas River, the yellow stubble fields seemed to be bathed in pale cold sunshine, but there was no sunshine in the valley now in December. The thick willow scrub along the river flamed with sharp and positive yellow leaves.

2   It was a time of quiet and of waiting. The air was cold and tender. A light wind blew up from the southwest so that the farmers were mildly hopeful of a good rain before long; but fog and rain do not go together.

3   Across the river, on Henry Allen's foothill ranch there was little work to be done, for the hay was cut and stored and the orchards were plowed up to receive the rain deeply when it should come. The cattle on the higher slopes were becoming shaggy and rough-coated.

4   Elisa Allen, working in her flower garden, looked down across the yard and saw Henry, her husband, talking to two men in business suits. The three of them stood by the tractor shed, each man with one foot on the side of the little Fordson. They smoked cigarettes and studied the machine as they talked.

5   Elisa watched them for a moment and then went back to her work. She was thirty-five. Her face was lean and strong and her eyes were as clear as water. Her figure looked blocked and heavy in her gardening costume, a man's black hat pulled low down over her eyes, clodhopper shoes, a figured print dress almost completely covered by a big corduroy apron with four big pockets to hold the snips, the trowel and scratcher, the seeds and the knife she worked with. She wore heavy leather gloves to protect her hands while she worked.

6   She was cutting down the old year's chrysanthemum stalks with a pair of short and powerful scissors. She looked down toward the men by the tractor shed now and then. Her face was eager and mature and handsome; even her work with the scissors was over-eager, over-powerful. The chrysanthemum stems seemed too small and easy for her energy.

7   She brushed a cloud of hair out of her eyes with the back of her glove, and left a smudge of earth on the cheek in doing it. Behind her stood the neat white farm house with red geraniums close-banked around it as high as the windows. It was a hard-swept looking little house, with hard-polished windows, and a clean mud-mat on the front steps.

8   Elisa cast another glance toward the tractor shed. The strangers were getting into their Ford coupe. She took off a glove and put her strong fingers down into the forest of new green chrysanthemum sprouts that were growing around the old roots. She spread the leaves and looked down among the close-growing

gang plows (par. 1): plows that turn more than one furrow (row) at a time

clodhopper shoes (par. 5): large work shoes

snips, trowel, scratcher (par. 5): gardening tools

coupe (par. 8): a two-door automobile

stems. No aphids were there, no sowbugs or snails or cutworms. Her terrier fingers destroyed such pests before they could get started.

9   Elisa started at the sound of her husband's voice. He had come near quietly, and he leaned over the wire fence that protected her flower garden from cattle and dogs and chickens.

10   "At it again," he said. "You've got a strong new crop coming."

11   Elisa straightened her back and pulled on the gardening glove again. "Yes. They'll be strong this coming year." In her tone and on her face there was a little smugness.

12   "You've got a gift with things," Henry observed. "Some of those yellow chrysanthemums you had this year were ten inches across. I wish you'd work out in the orchard and raise some apples that big."

13   Her eyes sharpened. "Maybe I could do it, too. I've a gift with things, all right. My mother had it. She could stick anything in the ground and make it grow. She said it was having planters' hands that knew how to do it."

14   "Well, it sure works with flowers," he said.

15   "Henry, who were those men you were talking to?"

16   "Why, sure, that's what I came to tell you. They were from the Western Meat Company. I sold those thirty head of three-year-old steers. Got nearly my own price, too."

17   "Good," she said. "Good for you."

18   "And I thought," he continued, "I thought how it's Saturday afternoon, and we might go to Salinas for dinner at a restaurant, and then to a picture show—to celebrate, you see."

19   "Good," she repeated. "Oh, yes. That will be good."

20   Henry put on his joking tone. "There's fights tonight. How'd you like to go to the fights?"

21   "Oh, no," she said breathlessly. "No, I wouldn't like fights."

22   "Just fooling, Elisa. We'll go to a movie. Let's see. It's two now. I'm going to take Scotty and bring down those steers from the hill. It'll take us maybe two hours. We'll go in town about five and have dinner at the Cominos Hotel. Like that?"

23   "Of course, I'll like it. It's good to eat away from home."

24   "All right, then. I'll go get up a couple of horses."

25   She said, "I'll have plenty of time to transplant some of these sets, I guess."

26   She heard her husband calling Scotty down by the barn. And a little later she saw the two men ride up the pale yellow hillside in search of the steers.

27   There was a little square sandy bed kept for rooting the chrysanthemums. With her trowel she turned the soil over and over, and smoothed it and patted it firm. Then she dug ten parallel trenches to receive the sets. Back at the chrysanthemum bed she pulled out the little crisp shoots, trimmed off the leaves of each one with her scissors and laid it on a small orderly pile.

28   A squeak of wheels and plod of hoofs came from the road. Elisa looked up. The country road ran along the dense bank of willows and cottonwoods that bordered the river, and up this road came a curious vehicle, curiously drawn. It was an old spring-wagon, with a round canvas top on it like the cover of a prairie schooner. It was drawn by an old bay horse and a little grey-and-white burro. A big stubble-bearded man sat between the cover flaps and drove the crawling

aphids, sowbugs, snails, cutworms (par. 8): garden pests

terrier fingers (par. 8): fingers that work like a terrier's claws; a terrier is known for its digging ability.

smugness (par. 11): self-satisfaction

spring-wagon (par. 28): a farm wagon equipped with springs

prairie schooner (par. 28): a covered wagon

team. Underneath the wagon, between the hind wheels, a lean and rangy mongrel dog walked sedately. Words were painted on the canvas in clumsy, crooked letters. "Pots, pans, knives, sisors, lawn mores. Fixed." Two rows of articles and the triumphantly definitive "Fixed" below. The black paint had run down in little sharp points beneath each letter.

29   Elisa, squatting on the ground, watched to see the crazy, loose-jointed wagon pass by. But it didn't pass. It turned into the farm road in front of her house, crooked old wheels skirling and squeaking. The rangy dog darted from between the wheels and ran ahead. Instantly the two ranch shepherds flew out at him. Then all three stopped, and with stiff and quivering tails, with taut straight legs, with ambassadorial dignity, they slowly circled, sniffing daintily. The caravan pulled up to Elisa's wire fence and stopped. Now the newcomer dog, feeling outnumbered, lowered his tail and retired under the wagon with raised hackles and bared teeth.

30   The man on the wagon seat called out. "That's a bad dog in a fight when he gets started."

31   Elisa laughed. "I see he is. How soon does he generally get started?"

32   The man caught up her laughter and echoed it heartily. "Sometimes not for weeks and weeks," he said. He climbed stiffly down, over the wheel. The horse and the donkey drooped like unwatered flowers.

33   Elisa saw that he was a very big man. Although his hair and beard were greying, he did not look old. His worn black suit was wrinkled and spotted with grease. The laughter had disappeared from his face and eyes the moment his laughing voice ceased. His eyes were dark and they were full of the brooding that gets in the eyes of teamsters and of sailors. The calloused hands he rested on the wire fence were cracked, and every crack was a black line. He took off his battered hat.

34   "I'm off my general road, ma'am," he said. "Does this dirt road cut over across the river to the Los Angeles highway?"

35   Elisa stood up and shoved the thick scissors in her apron pocket. "Well, yes, it does, but it winds around and then fords the river. I don't think your team could pull through the sand."

36   He replied with some asperity, "It might surprise you what them beasts can pull through."

37   "When they get started?" she asked.

38   He smiled for a second. "Yes. When they get started."

39   "Well," said Elisa, "I think you'll save time if you go back to the Salinas road and pick up the highway there."

40   He drew a big finger down the chicken wire and made it sing. "I ain't in

rangy (par. 28): long-limbed

mongrel dog (par. 28): a mutt

sedately (par. 28): calmly

skirling (par. 29): making a high-pitched sound

quivering (par. 29): trembling

taut (par. 29): tight

caravan (par. 29): a travelling group

hackles (par. 29): hair on the neck and back of a dog

brooding (par. 33): serious

teamsters (par. 33): people who drive teams or trucks as an occupation

fords (par. 35): crosses

asperity (par. 36): harshness

any hurry, ma'am. I go from Seattle to San Diego and back every year. Takes all my time. About six months each way. I aim to follow nice weather."

41   Elisa took off her gloves and stuffed them in the apron pocket with the scissors. She touched the under edge of her man's hat, searching for fugitive hairs. "That sounds like a nice kind of a way to live," she said.

42   He leaned confidentially over the fence. "Maybe you noticed the writing on my wagon. I mend pots and sharpen knives and scissors. You got any of them things to do?"

43   "Oh, no," she said quickly. "Nothing like that." Her eyes hardened with resistance.

44   "Scissors is the worst thing," he explained. "Most people just ruin scissors trying to sharpen 'em, but I know how. I got a special tool. It's a little bobbit kind of thing, and patented. But it sure does the trick."

45   "No. My scissors are all sharp."

46   "All right, then. Take a pot," he continued earnestly, "a bent pot, or a pot with a hole. I can make it like new so you don't have to buy no new ones. That's a saving for you."

47   "No," she said shortly. "I tell you I have nothing like that for you to do."

48   His face fell to an exaggerated sadness. His voice took on a whining undertone. "I ain't had a thing to do today. Maybe I won't have no supper tonight. You see I'm off my regular road. I know folks on the highway clear from Seattle to San Diego. They save their things for me to sharpen up because they know I do it so good and save them money."

49   "I'm sorry," Elisa said irritably. "I haven't anything for you to do."

50   His eyes left her face and fell to searching the ground. They roamed about until they came to the chrysanthemum bed where she had been working. "What's them plants, ma'am?"

51   The irritation and resistance melted from Elisa's face. "Oh, those are chrysanthemums, giant whites and yellows. I raise them every year, bigger than anybody around here."

52   "Kind of a long-stemmed flower? Looks like a quick puff of colored smoke?" he asked.

53   "That's it. What a nice way to describe them."

54   "They smell kind of nasty till you get used to them," he said.

55   "It's a good bitter smell," she retorted, "not nasty at all."

56   He changed his tone quickly. "I like the smell myself."

57   "I had ten-inch blooms this year," she said.

58   The man leaned farther over the fence. "Look. I know a lady down the road a piece, has got the nicest garden you ever seen. Got nearly every kind of flower but no chrysanthemums. Last time I was mending a copper-bottom washtub for her (that's a hard job but I do it good), she said to me, 'If you ever run acrost some nice chrysanthemums I wish you'd try to get me a few seeds.' That's what she told me."

59   Elisa's eyes grew alert and eager. "She couldn't have known much about chrysanthemums. You can raise them from seed, but it's much easier to root the little sprouts you see there."

60   "Oh," he said. "I s'pose I can't take none to her, then."

61   "Why yes you can," Elisa cried. "I can put some in damp sand, and you can carry them right along with you. They'll take root in the pot if you keep them damp. And then she can transplant them."

62   "She'd sure like to have some, ma'am. You say they're nice ones?"

63   "Beautiful," she said. "Oh, beautiful." Her eyes shone. She tore off the battered hat and shook out her dark pretty hair. "I'll put them in a flower pot, and you can take them right with you. Come into the yard."

64   While the man came through the picket gate Elisa ran excitedly along the

geranium-bordered path to the back of the house. And she returned carrying a big red flower pot. The gloves were forgotten now. She kneeled on the ground by the starting bed and dug up the sandy soil with her fingers and scooped it into the bright new flower pot. Then she picked up the little pile of shoots she had prepared. With her strong fingers she pressed them into the sand and tamped around them with her knuckles. The man stood over her. "I'll tell you what to do," she said. "You remember so you can tell the lady."

65   "Yes, I'll try to remember."

66   "Well, look. These will take root in about a month. Then she must set them out, about a foot apart in good rich earth like this, see?" She lifted a handful of dark soil for him to look at. "They'll grow fast and tall. Now remember this. In July tell her to cut them down, about eight inches from the ground."

67   "Before they bloom?" he asked.

68   "Yes, before they bloom." Her face was tight with eagerness. "They'll grow right up again. About the last of September the buds will start."

69   She stopped and seemed perplexed. "It's the budding that takes the most care," she said hesitantly. "I don't know how to tell you." She looked deep into his eyes, searchingly. Her mouth opened a little, and she seemed to be listening. "I'll try to tell you," she said. "Did you ever hear of planting hands?"

70   "Can't say I have, ma'am."

71   "Well, I can only tell you what it feels like. It's when you're picking off the buds you don't want. Everything goes right down into your fingertips. You watch your fingers work. They do it themselves. You can feel how it is. They pick and pick the buds. They never make a mistake. They're with the plant. Do you see? Your fingers and the plant. You can feel that, right up your arm. They know. They never make a mistake. You can feel it. When you're like that you can't do anything wrong. Do you see that? Can you understand that?"

72   She was kneeling on the ground looking up at him. Her breast swelled passionately.

73   The man's eyes narrowed. He looked away self-consciously. "Maybe I know," he said. "Sometimes in the night in the wagon there—"

74   Elisa's voice grew husky. She broke in on him. "I've never lived as you do, but I know what you mean. When the night is dark—why, the stars are sharp-pointed, and there's a quiet. Why, you rise up and up! Every pointed star gets driven into your body. It's like that. Hot and sharp and—lovely."

75   Kneeling there, her hand went out toward his legs in the greasy black trousers. Her hesitant fingers almost touched the cloth. Then her hand dropped to the ground. She crouched low like a fawning dog.

76   He said, "It's nice, just like you say. Only when you don't have no dinner, it ain't."

77   She stood up then, very straight, and her face was ashamed. She held the flower pot out to him and placed it gently in his arms. "Here. Put it in your wagon, on the seat, where you can watch it. Maybe I can find something for you to do."

78   At the back of the house she dug in the can pile and found two old and battered aluminum saucepans. She carried them back and gave them to him. "Here, maybe you can fix these."

79   His manner changed. He became professional. "Good as new I can fix them." At the back of his wagon he set a little anvil, and out of an oily tool box dug a small machine hammer. Elisa came through the gate to watch him while he pounded out the dents in the kettles. His mouth grew sure and knowing. At a difficult part of the work he sucked his under-lip.

80   "You sleep right in the wagon?" Elisa asked.

fawning (par. 75): timid

81   "Right in the wagon, ma'am. Rain or shine I'm dry as a cow in there."

82   "It must be nice," she said. "It must be very nice. I wish women could do such things."

83   "It ain't the right kind of a life for a woman."

84   Her upper lip raised a little, showing her teeth. "How do you know? How can you tell?" she said.

85   "I don't know ma'am," he protested. "Of course I don't know. Now here's your kettles, done. You don't have to buy no new ones."

86   "How much?"

87   "Oh, fifty cents'll do. I keep my prices down and my work good. That's why I have all them satisfied customers up and down the highway."

88   Elisa brought him a fifty-cent piece from the house and dropped it in his hand. "You might be surprised to have a rival some time. I can sharpen scissors, too. And I can beat the dents out of little pots. I could show you what a woman might do."

89   He put his hammer back in the oily box and shoved the little anvil out of sight. "It would be a lonely life for a woman, ma'am, and a scarey life, too, with animals creeping under the wagon all night." He climbed over the single-tree, steadying himself with a hand on the burro's white rump. He settled himself in the seat, picked up the lines. "Thank you kindly, ma'am," he said. "I'll do like you told me; I'll go back and catch the Salinas road."

90   "Mind," she called, "if you're long in getting there, keep the sand damp."

91   "Sand, ma'am? . . . Sand? Oh, sure. You mean round the chrysanthemums. Sure I will." He clucked his tongue. The beasts leaned luxuriously into their collars. The mongrel dog took his place between the back wheels. The wagon turned and crawled out the entrance road and back the way it had come, along the river.

92   Elisa stood in front of her wire fence watching the slow progress of the caravan. Her shoulders were straight, her head thrown back, her eyes half-closed, so that the scene came vaguely into them. Her lips moved silently forming the words "Good-bye—good-bye." Then she whispered, "That's a bright direction. There's a glowing there." The sound of her whisper startled her. She shook herself free and looked about to see whether anyone had been listening. Only the dogs had heard. They lifted their heads toward her from their sleeping in the dust, and then stretched out their chins and settled asleep again. Elisa turned and ran hurriedly into the house.

93   In the kitchen she reached behind the stove and felt the water tank. It was full of hot water from the noonday cooking. In the bathroom she tore off her soiled clothes and flung them into the corner. And then she scrubbed herself with a little block of pumice, legs and thighs, loins and chest and arms, until her skin was scratched and red. When she had dried herself she stood in front of a mirror in her bedroom and looked at her body. She tightened her stomach and threw out her chest. She turned and looked over her shoulder at her back.

94   After a while she began to dress, slowly. She put on her newest underclothing and her nicest stockings and the dress which was the symbol of her prettiness. She worked carefully on her hair, pencilled her eyebrows and rouged her lips.

95   Before she was finished she heard the little thunder of hoofs and the shouts of Henry and his helper as they drove the red steers into the corral. She heard the gate bang shut and set herself for Henry's arrival.

96   His steps sounded on the porch. He entered the house calling "Elisa, where are you?"

pumice (par. 93): a rough, light-weight stone

rouged (par. 94): reddened

97   "In my room, dressing. I'm not ready. There's hot water for your bath. Hurry up. It's getting late."

98   When she heard him splashing in the tub, Elisa laid his dark suit on the bed, and shirt and socks and tie beside it. She stood his polished shoes on the floor beside the bed. Then she went to the porch and sat primly and stiffly down. She looked toward the river road where the willow-line was still yellow with frosted leaves so that under the high grey fog they seemed a thin band of sunshine. This was the only color in the grey afternoon. She sat unmoving for a long time. Her eyes blinked rarely.

99   Henry came banging out of the door, shoving his tie inside his vest as he came. Elisa stiffened and her face grew tight. Henry stopped short and looked at her. "Why—why, Elisa. You look so nice!"

100   "Nice? You think I look nice? What do you mean by 'nice'?"

101   Henry blundered on. "I don't know. I mean you look different, strong and happy."

102   "I am strong? Yes, strong. What do you mean 'strong'?"

103   He looked bewildered. "You're playing some kind of a game," he said helplessly. "It's a kind of a play. You look strong enough to break a calf over your knee, happy enough to eat it like watermelon."

104   For a second she lost her rigidity. "Henry! Don't talk like that. You didn't know what you said." She grew complete again. "I'm strong," she boasted. "I never knew before how strong."

105   Henry looked down toward the tractor shed, and when he brought his eyes back to her, they were his own again. "I'll get out the car. You can put on your coat while I'm starting."

106   Elisa went into the house. She heard him drive to the gate and idle down his motor, and then she took a long time to put on her hat. She pulled it here and pressed it there. When Henry turned the motor off she slipped into her coat and went out.

107   The little roadster bounced along on the dirt road by the river, raising the birds and driving the rabbits into the brush. Two cranes flapped heavily over the willow-line and dropped into the riverbed.

108   Far ahead on the road Elisa saw a dark speck. She knew.

109   She tried not to look as they passed it, but her eyes would not obey. She whispered to herself sadly. "He might have thrown them off the road. That wouldn't have been much trouble, not very much. But he kept the pot," she explained. "He had to keep the pot. That's why he couldn't get them off the road."

110   The roadster turned a bend and she saw the caravan ahead. She swung full around toward her husband so she could not see the little covered wagon and the mismatched team as the car passed them.

111   In a moment it was over. The thing was done. She did not look back. She said loudly, to be heard above the motor, "It will be good, tonight, a good dinner."

112   "Now you're changed again," Henry complained. He took one hand from the wheel and patted her knee. "I ought to take you in to dinner oftener. It would be good for both of us. We get so heavy out on the ranch."

113   "Henry," she asked, "could we have wine at dinner?"

114   "Sure we could. Say! That will be fine."

115   She was silent for a little while; then she said, "Henry, at those prize fights, do the men hurt each other very much?"

116   "Sometimes a little, not often. Why?"

117   "Well, I've read how they break noses, and blood runs down their chests. I've read how the fighting gloves get heavy and soggy with blood."

bewildered (par. 103): confused

118   He looked around at her. "What's the matter, Elisa? I didn't know you read things like that." He brought the car to a stop then turned to the right over the Salinas River bridge.

119   "Do any women ever go to the fights?" she asked.

120   "Oh, sure, some. What's the matter, Elisa? Do you want to go? I don't think you'd like it, but I'll take you if you really want to go."

121   She relaxed limply in the seat. "Oh, no. No. I don't want to go. I'm sure I don't." Her face was turned away from him. "It will be enough if we can have wine. It will be plenty." She turned up her coat collar so he could not see that she was crying weakly—like an old woman.

The Magic Barrel

Bernard Malamud

1   Not long ago there lived in uptown New York, in a small, almost meager room, though crowded with books, Leo Finkle, a rabbinical student in the Yeshivah University. Finkle, after six years of study, was to be ordained in June and had been advised by an acquaintance that he might find it easier to win himself a congregation if he were married. Since he had no present prospects of marriage, after two tormented days of turning it over in his mind, he called in Pinye Salzman, a marriage broker whose two-line advertisement he had read in the *Forward*.

2   The matchmaker appeared one night out of the dark fourth-floor hallway of the graystone rooming house where Finkle lived, grasping a black, strapped portfolio that had been worn thin with use. Salzman, who had been long in the business, was of slight but dignified build, wearing an old hat, and an overcoat too short and tight for him. He smelled frankly of fish, which he loved to eat, and although he was missing a few teeth, his presence was not displeasing, because of an amiable manner curiously contrasted with mournful eyes. His voice, his lips, his wisp of beard, his bony fingers were animated, but give him a moment of repose and his mild blue eyes revealed a depth of sadness, a characteristic that put Leo a little at ease although the situation, for him, was inherently tense.

3   He at once informed Salzman why he had asked him to come, explaining that his home was in Cleveland, and that but for his parents, who had married comparatively late in life, he was alone in the world. He had for six years devoted himself almost entirely to his studies, as a result of which, understand-

rabbinical student (par. 1): someone studying to be a rabbi, the leader of a Jewish congregation

ordained (par. 1): authorized as a rabbi

Forward (par. 1): a Yiddish language newspaper; Yiddish is a combination of Hebrew, German, and Eastern European languages.

portfolio (par. 2): briefcase

amiable (par. 2): friendly

animated (par. 2): lively

repose (par. 2): rest

inherently (par. 2): essentially

ably, he had found himself without time for a social life and the company of young women. Therefore he thought it the better part of trial and error—of embarrassing fumbling—to call in an experienced person to advise him on these matters. He remarked in passing that the function of the marriage broker was ancient and honorable, highly approved in the Jewish community, because it made practical the necessary without hindering joy. Moreover, his own parents had been brought together by a matchmaker. They had made, if not a financially profitable marriage—since neither had possessed any worldly goods to speak of—at least a successful one in the sense of their everlasting devotion to each other. Salzman listened in embarrassed surprise, sensing a sort of apology. Later, however, he experienced a glow of pride in his work, an emotion that had left him years ago, and he heartily approved of Finkle.

4   The two went to their business. Leo had led Salzman to the only clear place in the room, a table near a window that overlooked the lamp-lit city. He seated himself at the matchmaker's side but facing him, attempting by an act of will to suppress the unpleasant tickle in his throat. Salzman eagerly unstrapped his portfolio and removed a loose rubber band from a thin packet of much-handled cards. As he flipped through them, a gesture and sound that physically hurt Leo, the student pretended not to see and gazed steadfastly out the window. Although it was still February, winter was on its last legs, signs of which he had for the first time in years begun to notice. He now observed the round white moon, moving high in the sky through a cloud menagerie, and watched with half-open mouth as it penetrated a huge hen, and dropped out of her like an egg laying itself. Salzman, though pretending through eyeglasses he had just slipped on, to be engaged in scanning the writing on the cards, stole occasional glances at the young man's distinguished face, noting with pleasure the long, severe scholar's nose, brown eyes heavy with learning, sensitive yet ascetic lips, and a certain, almost hollow quality of the dark cheeks. He gazed around at the shelves upon shelves of books and let out a soft, contented sigh.

5   When Leo's eyes fell upon the cards, he counted six spread out in Salzman's hand.

6   "So few?" he asked in disappointment.

7   "You wouldn't believe me how much cards I got in my office," Salzman replied. "The drawers are already filled to the top, so I keep them now in a barrel, but is every girl good for a new rabbi?"

8   Leo blushed at this, regretting all he had revealed of himself in a curriculum vitae he had sent to Salzman. He had thought it best to acquaint him with his strict standards and specifications, but in having done so, felt he had told the marriage broker more than was absolutely necessary.

9   He hesitantly inquired, "Do you keep photographs of your clients on file?"

10   "First comes family, amount of dowry, also what kind promises," Salzman replied, unbuttoning his tight coat and settling himself in the chair. "After comes pictures, rabbi."

11   "Call me Mr. Finkle. I'm not yet a rabbi."

12   Salzman said he would, but instead called him doctor, which he changed to rabbi when Leo was not listening too attentively.

menagerie (par. 4): collection of animals

ascetic (par. 4): severe

curriculum vitae (par. 8): a list of career accomplishments

dowry (par. 10): money or property a woman brings to her husband in marriage

attentively (par. 12): carefully

13   Salzman adjusted his horn-rimmed spectacles, gently cleared his throat and read in an eager voice the contents of the top card:

14   "Sophie P. Twenty four years. Widow one year. No children. Educated high school and two years college. Father promises eight thousand dollars. Has wonderful wholesale business. Also real estate. On the mother's side comes teachers, also one actor. Well known on Second Avenue."

15   Leo gazed up in surprise. "Did you say a widow?"

16   "A widow don't mean spoiled, rabbi. She lived with her husband maybe four months. He was a sick boy she made a mistake to marry him."

17   "Marrying a widow has never entered my mind."

18   "This is because you have no experience. A widow, especially if she is young and healthy like this girl, is a wonderful person to marry. She will be thankful to you the rest of her life. Believe me, if I was looking now for a bride, I would marry a widow."

19   Leo reflected, then shook his head.

20   Salzman hunched his shoulders in an almost imperceptible gesture of disappointment. He placed the card down on the wooden table and began to read another:

21   "Lily H. High school teacher. Regular. Not a substitute. Has savings and new Dodge car. Lived in Paris one year. Father is successful dentist thirty-five years. Interested in professional man. Well Americanized family. Wonderful opportunity."

22   "I knew her personally," said Salzman. "I wish you could see this girl. She is a doll. Also very intelligent. All day you could talk to her about books and theyater and what not. She also knows current events."

23   "I don't believe you mentioned her age?"

24   "Her age?" Salzman said, raising his brows. "Her age is thirty-two years."

25   Leo said after a while, "I'm afraid that seems a little too old."

26   Salzman let out a laugh. "So how old are you, rabbi?"

27   "Twenty-seven."

28   "So what is the difference, tell me, between twenty-seven and thirty-two? My own wife is seven years older than me. So what did I suffer?—Nothing. If Rothschild's a daugher wants to marry you, would you say on account her age, no?"

29   "Yes," Leo said dryly.

30   Salzman shook off the no in the yes. "Five years don't mean a thing. I give you my word that when you will live with her for one week, you will forget her age. What does it mean five years—that she lived more and knows more than somebody who is younger? On this girl, God bless her, years are not wasted. Each one that it comes makes better the bargain."

31   "What subject does she teach in high school?"

32   "Languages. If you heard the way she speaks French, you will think it is music. I am in the business twenty-five years, and I recommend her with my whole heart. Believe me, I know what I'm talking, rabbi."

33   "What's on the next card?" Leo said abruptly.

spectacles (par. 13): eyeglasses

Second Avenue (par. 14): center of Jewish cultural life in New York City

reflected (par. 19): thought

imperceptible (par. 20): unnoticeable

Well Americanized (par. 21): The family has immigrated to America and has become much like other Americans.

theyater (par. 22): theater

Rothschild (par. 28): a wealthy family

34   Salzman reluctantly turned up the third card:

35   "Ruth K. Nineteen years. Honor student. Father offers thirteen thousand cash to the right bridegroom. He is a medical doctor. Stomach specialist with marvelous practice. Brother in law owns own garment business. Particular people."

36   Salzman looked as if he had read his trump card.

37   "Did you say nineteen?" Leo said with interest.

38   "On the dot."

39   "Is she attractive?" He blushed. "Pretty?"

40   Salzman kissed his finger tips. "A little doll. On this I give you my word. Let me call the father tonight and you will see what means pretty."

41   But Leo was troubled. "You're sure she's that young?"

42   "This I am positive. The father will show you the birth certificate."

43   "Are you positive there isn't something wrong with her?" Leo insisted.

44   "Who says there is wrong?"

45   "I don't understand why an American girl her age should go to a marriage broker."

46   A smile spread over Salzman's face.

47   "So for the same reason you went, she comes."

48   Leo flushed. "I am pressed for time."

49   Salzman, realizing he had been tactless, quickly explained, "The father came, not her. He wants she should have the best, so he looks around himself. When we will locate the right boy he will introduce him and encourage. This makes a better marriage than if a young girl without experience takes for herself. I don't have to tell you this."

50   "But don't you think this young girl believes in love?" Leo spoke uneasily.

51   Salzman was about to guffaw but caught himself and said soberly, "Love comes with the right person, not before."

52   Leo parted dry lips but did not speak. Noticing that Salzman had snatched a glance at the next card, he cleverly asked, "How is her health?"

53   "Perfect," Salzman said, breathing with difficulty. "Of course, she is a little lame on her right foot from an auto accident that it happened to her when she was twelve years, but nobody notices on account she is so brilliant and also beautiful."

54   Leo got up heavily and went to the window. He felt curiously bitter and upbraided himself for having called in the marriage broker. Finally, he shook his head.

55   "Why not?" Salzman persisted, the pitch of his voice rising.

56   "Because I detest stomach specialists."

57   "So what do you care what is his business? After you marry her do you need him? Who says he must come every Friday night in your house?"

58   Ashamed of the way the talk was going, Leo dismissed Salzman, who went home with heavy, melancholy eyes.

59   Though he had felt only relief at the marriage broker's departure, Leo was in low spirits the next day. He explained it as arising from Salzman's failure to produce a suitable bride for him. He did not care for his type of clientele. But when Leo found himself hesitating whether to seek out another matchmaker, one more polished than Pinye, he wondered if it could be—his protestations to

tactless (par. 49): insensitive, thoughtless

upbraided (par. 54): scolded

melancholy (par. 58): sad

protestations (par. 59): declarations, statements

the contrary, and although he honored his father and mother—that he did not, in essence, care for the matchmaking institution? This thought he quickly put out of mind yet found himself still upset. All day he ran around in the woods— missed an important appointment, forgot to give out his laundry, walked out of a Broadway cafeteria without paying and had to run back with the ticket in his hand; had even not recognized his landlady in the street when she passed with a friend and courteously called out, "A good evening to you, Doctor Finkle." By nightfall, however, he had regained sufficient calm to sink his nose into a book and there found peace from his thoughts.

60   Almost at once there came a knock on the door. Before Leo could say enter, Salzman, commercial cupid, was standing in the room. His face was gray and meager, his expression hungry, and he looked as if he would expire on his feet. Yet the marriage broker managed, by some trick of the muscles, to display a broad smile.

61   "So good evening. I am invited?"

62   Leo nodded, disturbed to see him again, yet unwilling to ask the man to leave.

63   Beaming still, Salzman laid his portfolio on the table. "Rabbi, I got for you tonight good news."

64   "I've asked you not to call me rabbi. I'm still a student."

65   "Your worries are finished. I have for you a first-class bride."

66   "Leave me in peace concerning this project." Leo pretended lack of interest.

67   "The world will dance at your wedding."

68   "Please, Mr. Salzman, no more."

69   "But first must come back my strength," Salzman said weakly. He fumbled with the portfolio straps and took out of the leather case an oily paper bag, from which he extracted a hard, seeded roll and a small, smoked white fish. With a quick motion of his hand he stripped the fish out of its skin and began ravenously to chew. "All day in a rush," he muttered.

70   Leo watched him eat.

71   "A sliced tomato you have maybe?" Salzman hesitantly inquired.

72   "No."

73   The marriage broker shut his eyes and ate. When he had finished he carefully cleaned up the crumbs and rolled up the remains of the fish, in the paper bag. His spectacled eyes roamed the room until he discovered, amid some piles of books, a one-burner gas stove. Lifting his hat he humbly asked, "A glass tea you got, rabbi?"

74   Conscience-stricken, Leo rose and brewed the tea. He served it with a chunk of lemon and two cubes of lump sugar, delighting Salzman.

75   After he had drunk his tea, Salzman's strength and good spirits were restored.

76   "So tell me, rabbi," he said amiably, "you considered more the three clients I mentioned yesterday?"

77   "There was no need to consider."

---

contrary (par. 59): opposite

cupid (par. 60): someone who encourages a love match; Cupid was the Roman god of love.

meager (par. 60): thin

expire (par. 60): die

ravenously (par. 69): hungrily

78   "Why not?"

79   "None of them suits me."

80   "What then suits you?"

81   Leo let it pass because he could only give a confused answer.

82   Without waiting for a reply, Salzman asked, "You remember this girl I talked to you—the high school teacher?"

83   "Age thirty-two?"

84   But, surprisingly, Salzman's face lit in a smile. "Age twenty-nine."

85   Leo shot him a look. "Reduced from thirty-two?"

86   "A mistake," Salzman avowed. "I talked today with the dentist. He took me to his safety deposit box and showed me the birth certificate. She was twenty-nine years last August. They made her a party in the mountains where she went for her vacation. When her father spoke to me the first time I forgot to write the age and I told you thirty-two, but now I remember this was a different client, a widow."

87   "The same one you told me about? I thought she was twenty-four?"

88   "A different. Am I responsible that the world is filled with widows?"

89   "No, but I'm not interested in them, nor for that matter, in school teachers."

90   Salzman pulled his clasped hands to his breast. Looking at the ceiling he devoutly exclaimed, "Yiddishe kinder, what can I say to somebody that he is not interested in high school teachers? So what then you are interested?"

91   Leo flushed but controlled himself.

92   "In what else will you be interested," Salzman went on, "if you not interested in this fine girl that she speaks four languages and has personally in the bank ten thousand dollars? Also her father guarantees further twelve thousand. Also she has a new car, wonderful clothes, talks on all subjects, and she will give you a first-class home and children. How near do we come in our life to paradise?"

93   "If she's so wonderful, why wasn't she married ten years ago?"

94   "Why?" Salzman with a heavy laugh. "—Why? Because she is *partikiler*. This is why. She wants the *best*."

95   Leo was silent, amused at how he had entangled himself. But Salzman had aroused his interest in Lily H., and he began seriously to consider calling on her. When the marriage broker observed how intently Leo's mind was at work on the facts he had supplied, he felt certain they would soon come to an agreement.

96   Late Saturday afternoon, conscious of Salzman, Leo Finkle walked with Lily Hirschorn along Riverside Drive. He walked briskly and erectly, wearing with distinction the black fedora he had that morning taken with trepidation out of the dusty hat box on his closet shelf, and the heavy black Saturday coat he had thoroughly whisked clean. Leo also owned a walking stick, a present from a distant relative, but quickly put temptation aside and did not use it. Lily, petite and not unpretty, had on something signifying the approach of spring. She was au courant, animatedly, with all sorts of subjects, and he weighed her words

devoutly (par. 90): religiously

Yiddishe kinder (par. 90): Jewish children

fedora (par. 96): hat

trepidation (par. 96): nervousness

Saturday coat (par. 96): coat worn on holy days; Saturday is the Jewish holy day of the week.

whisked (par. 96): brushed

and found her surprisingly sound—score another for Salzman, whom he uneasily sensed to be somewhere around, hiding perhaps high in a tree along the street, flashing the lady signals with a pocket mirror; or perhaps a cloven-hoofed Pan, piping nuptial ditties as he danced his invisible way before them, strewing wild buds on the walk and purple grapes in their path, symbolizing fruit of a union, though there was of course still none.

97   Lily startled Leo by remarking, "I was thinking of Mr. Salzman, a curious figure, wouldn't you say?"

98   Not certain what to answer, he nodded.

99   She bravely went on, blushing, "I for one am grateful for his introducing us. Aren't you?"

100   He courteously replied, "I am."

101   "I mean," she said with a little laugh—and it was all in good taste, or at least gave the effect of being not in bad—"do you mind that we came together so?"

102   He was not displeased with her honesty, recognizing that she meant to set the relationship aright, and understanding that it took a certain amount of experience in life, and courage, to want to do it quite that way. One had to have some sort of past to make that kind of beginning.

103   He said that he did not mind. Salzman's function was traditional and honorable—valuable for what it might achieve, which, he pointed out, was frequently nothing.

104   Lily agreed with a sigh. They walked on for a while and she said after a long silence, again with a nervous laugh, "Would you mind if I asked you something a little bit personal? Frankly, I find the subject fascinating." Although Leo shrugged, she went on half embarrassedly, "How was it you came to your calling? I mean was it a sudden passionate inspiration?"

105   Leo, after a time, slowly replied, "I was always interested in the Law."

106   "You saw revealed in it the presence of the Highest?"

107   He nodded and changed the subject. "I understand that you spent a little time in Paris, Miss Hirschorn?"

108   "Oh, did Mr. Salzman tell you, Rabbi Finkle?" Leo winced but she went on, "It was ages ago and almost forgotten. I remember I had to return for my sister's wedding."

109   And Lily would not be put off. "When," she asked in a trembly voice, "did you become enamored of God?"

110   He stared at her. Then it came to him that she was talking not about Leo Finkle, but of a total stranger, some mystical figure, perhaps even passionate prophet that Salzman had dreamed up for her—no relation to the living or dead. Leo trembled with rage and weakness. The trickster had obviously sold

---

au courant (par. 96): knowledgeable

cloven-hoofed Pan (par. 96): In Greek mythology, Pan was the god of woods and fields and had the body of a man and the ears, horns, and legs of a goat. A goat's hoof is cloven, or divided into two parts.

piping nuptial ditties (par. 96): playing marriage songs

the Law (par. 105): that is, the Law of God

the Highest (par. 106): God

winced (par. 108): flinched

become enamored of (par. 109): begin loving

mystical (par. 110): spiritual

prophet (par. 110): one to whom God reveals the future

her a bill of goods, just as he had him, who'd expected to become acquainted with a young lady of twenty-nine, only to behold, the moment he laid eyes upon her strained and anxious face, a woman past thirty-five and aging rapidly. Only his self control had kept him this long in her presence.

111   "I am not," he said gravely, "a talented religious person," and in seeking words to go on, found himself possessed by shame and fear. "I think," he said in a strained manner, "that I came to God not because I loved Him, but because I did not."

112   This confession he spoke harshly because its unexpectedness shook him.

113   Lily wilted. Leo saw a profusion of loaves of bread go flying like ducks high over his head, not unlike the winged loaves by which he had counted himself to sleep last night. Mercifully, then, it snowed, which he would not put past Salzman's machinations.

114   He was infuriated with the marriage broker and swore he would throw him out of the room the minute he reappeared. But Salzman did not come that night, and when Leo's anger had subsided, an unaccountable despair grew in its place. At first he thought this was caused by his disappointment in Lily, but before long it became evident that he had involved himself with Salzman without a true knowledge of his own intent. He gradually realized—with an emptiness that seized him with six hands—that he had called in the broker to find him a bride because he was incapable of doing it himself. This terrifying insight he had derived as a result of his meeting and conversation with Lily Hirschorn. Her probing questions had somehow irritated him into revealing—to himself more than her—the true nature of his relationship to God, and from that it had come upon him, with shocking force, that apart from his parents, he had never loved anyone. Or perhaps it went the other way, that he did not love God so well as he might, because he had not loved man. It seemed to Leo that his whole life stood starkly revealed and he saw himself for the first time as he truly was—unloved and loveless. This bitter but somehow not fully unexpected revelation brought him to a point of panic, controlled only by extraordinary effort. He covered his face with his hands and cried.

115   The week that followed was the worst of his life. He did not eat and lost weight. His beard darkened and grew ragged. He stopped attending seminars and almost never opened a book. He seriously considered leaving the Yeshivah, although he was deeply troubled at the thought of the loss of all his years of study—saw them like pages torn from a book, strewn over the city—and at the devastating effect of this decision upon his parents. But he had lived without knowledge of himself, and never in the Five Books and all the Commentaries—mea culpa—had the truth been revealed to him. He did not know where to turn, and in all this desolating loneliness there was no *to whom*, although he often thought of Lily but not once could bring himself to go downstairs and make the call. He became touchy and irritable, especially with his landlady, who asked him all manner of personal questions; on the other hand, sensing his own dis-

profusion (par. 113): great number

machinations (par. 113): tricks

subsided (par. 114): ended

unaccountable (par. 114): mysterious

derived (par. 114): arrived at

Five Books (par. 115): Torah, the first five books of the Old Testament

mea culpa (par. 115): Latin for "I am at fault"

desolating (par. 115): gloomy

agreeableness, he waylaid her on the stairs and apologized abjectly, until mortified, she ran from him. Out of this, however, he drew consolation that he was a Jew and that a Jew suffered. But gradually, as the long and terrible week drew to a close, he regained his composure and some idea of purpose in life: to go on as planned. Although he was imperfect, the idea was not. As for his quest of a bride the thought of continuing afflicted him with anxiety and heartburn, yet perhaps with this new knowledge of himself he would be more successful than in the past. Perhaps love would now come to him and a bride to that love. And for this sanctified seeking who needed a Salzman?

116   The marriage broker, a skeleton with haunted eyes, returned that very night. He looked, withal, the picture of frustrated expectancy—as if he had steadfastly waited the week at Miss Lily Hirschorn's side for a telephone call that never came.

117   Casually coughing, Salzman came immediately to the point: "So how did you like her?"

118   Leo's anger rose and he could not refrain from chiding the matchmaker: "Why did you lie to me, Salzman?"

119   Salzman's pale face went dead white, the world had snowed on him.

120   "Did you not state that she was twenty-nine?" Leo insisted.

121   "I give you my word—"

122   "She was thirty-five, if a day. *At least* thirty-five."

123   "Of this don't be too sure. Her father told me—"

124   "Never mind. The worst of it was that you lied to her."

125   "How did I lie to her, tell me?"

126   "You told her things about me that weren't true. You made me out to be more, consequently less than I am. She had in mind a totally different person, a sort of semimystical Wonder Rabbi."

127   "All I said, you was a religious man."

128   "I can imagine."

129   Salzman sighed. "This is my weakness that I have," he confessed. "My wife says to me I shouldn't be a salesman, but when I have two fine people that they would be wonderful to be married, I am so happy that I talk too much." He smiled wanly. "This is why Salzman is a poor man."

130   Leo's anger left him. "Well, Salzman. I'm afraid that's all."

131   The marriage broker fastened hungry eyes on him.

132   "You don't want any more a bride?"

133   "I do," said Leo, "but I have decided to seek her in a different way. I am no longer interested in an arranged marriage. To be frank, I now admit the necessity of pre-marital love. That is, I want to be in love with the one I marry."

waylaid (par. 115): stopped

abjectly (par. 115): miserably

mortified (par. 115): horrified

consolation (par. 115): comfort

composure (par. 115): calmness

afflicted (par. 115): distressed

sanctified (par. 115): holy

withal (par. 116): in addition

refrain from (par. 118): keep from

chiding (par. 118): scolding

wanly (par. 129): weakly

134   "Love?" said Salzman, astounded. After a moment he remarked, "For us, our love is our life, not for the ladies. In the ghetto they—"

135   "I know, I know," said Leo. "I've thought of it often. Love, I have said to myself, should be a by-product of living and worship rather than its own end. Yet for myself I find it necessary to establish the level of my need and fulfil it."

136   Salzman shrugged but answered, "Listen, rabbi, if you want love, this I can find for you also. I have such beautiful clients that you will love them the minute your eyes will see them."

137   Leo smiled unhappily. "I'm afraid you don't understand."

138   But Salzman hastily unstrapped his portfolio and withdrew a manila packet from it.

139   "Pictures," he said, quickly laying the envelope on the table.

140   Leo called after him to take the pictures away, but as if on the wings of the wind, Salzman had disappeared.

141   March came. Leo had returned to his regular routine. Although he felt not quite himself yet—lacked energy—he was making plans for a more active social life. Of course it would cost something, but he was an expert in cutting corners; and when there were no corners left he would make circles rounder. All the while Salzman's pictures had lain on the table, gathering dust. Occasionally as Leo sat studying, or enjoying a cup of tea, his eyes fell on the manila envelope but he never opened it.

142   The days went by and no social life to speak of developed with a member of the opposite sex—it was difficult, given the circumstances of his situation. One morning Leo toiled up the stairs to his room and stared out of the window at the city. Although the day was bright his view of it was dark. For some time he watched the people in the street below hurrying along and then turned with a heavy heart to his little room. On the table was the packet. With a sudden relentless gesture he tore it open. For a half-hour he stood by the table in a state of excitement, examining the photographs of the ladies Salzman had included. Finally, with a deep sigh he put them down. There were six, of varying degrees of attractiveness, but look at them long enough and they all became Lily Hirschorn: all past their prime, all starved behind bright smiles, not a true personality in the lot. Life, despite their frantic yoohooings, had passed them by; they were pictures in a brief case that stank of fish. After a while, however as Leo attempted to return the photographs into the envelope, he found in it another, a snapshot of the type taken by a machine for a quarter. He gazed at it a moment and let out a cry.

143   Her face deeply moved him. Why, he could at first not say. It gave him the impression of youth—spring flowers, yet age—a sense of having been used to the bone, wasted; this came from the eyes which were hauntingly familiar, yet absolutely strange. He had a vivid impression that he had met her before, but try as he might he could not place her although he could almost recall her name, as if he had read it in her own handwriting. No, this couldn't be; he would have remembered her. It was not he affirmed, that she had an extraordinary beauty— no, though her face was attractive enough; it was that *something* about her moved him. Feature for feature, even some of the ladies of the photographs could do better; but she leaped forth to his heart—had *lived*, or wanted to— more than just wanted, perhaps regretted how she had lived—had somehow

ghetto (par. 134): area in European cities where Jews were required to remain

relentless (par. 142): unyielding

vivid (par. 143): very strong

affirmed (par. 143): declared

deeply suffered: it could be seen in the depths of those reluctant eyes, and from the way the light enclosed and shone from her, and within her, opening realms of possibility: this was her own. Her he desired. His head ached and eyes narrowed with the intensity of his gazing, then as if an obscure fog had blown up in the mind, he experienced fear of her and was aware that he had received an impression, somehow, of evil. He shuddered, saying softly, it is thus with us all. Leo brewed some tea in a small pot and sat sipping it without sugar, to calm himself. But before he had finished drinking, again with excitement he examined the face and found it good: good for Leo Finkle. Only such a one could understand him and help him seek whatever he was seeking. She might, perhaps, love him. How she had happened to be among the discards in Salzman's barrel he could never guess, but he knew he must urgently go find her.

144   Leo rushed downstairs, grabbed up the Bronx telephone book, and searched for Salzman's home address. He was not listed, nor was his office. Neither was he in the Manhattan book. But Leo remembered having written down the address on a slip of paper after he had read Salzman's advertisement in the "personals" column of the *Forward*. He ran up to his room and tore through his papers, without luck. It was exasperating. Just when he needed the matchmaker he was nowhere to be found. Fortunately Leo remembered to look in his wallet. There on a card he found his name written and a Bronx address. No phone number was listed, the reason—Leo now recalled—he had originally communicated with Salzman by letter. He got on his coat, put a hat on over his skull cap and hurried to the subway station. All the way to the far end of the Bronx he sat on the edge of his seat. He was more than once tempted to take out the picture and see if the girl's face was as he remembered it but he refrained, allowing the snapshot to remain in his inside coat pocket, content to have her so close. When the train pulled into the station he was waiting at the door and bolted out. He quickly located the street Salzman had advertised.

145   The building he sought was less than a block from the subway, but it was not an office building, not even a loft, nor a store in which one could rent office space. It was a very old tenement house. Leo found Salzman's name in pencil on a soiled tag under the bell and climbed three dark flights to his apartment. When he knocked, the door was opened by a thin, asthmatic, gray-haired woman, in felt slippers.

146   "Yes?" she said, expecting nothing. She listened without listening. He could have sworn he had seen her, too, before but knew it was an illusion.

147   "Salzman—does he live here? Pinye Salzman," he said, "the matchmaker?"

148   She stared at him a long minute. "Of course."

149   He felt embarrassed. "Is he in?"

150   "No." Her mouth, though left open, offered nothing more.

151   "The matter is urgent. Can you tell me where his office is?"

152   "In the air." She pointed upward.

153   "You mean he has no office?" Leo asked.

154   "In his socks."

155   He peered into the apartment. It was sunless and dingy, one large room divided by a half-open curtain, beyond which he could see a sagging metal bed. The near side of a room was crowded with rickety chairs, old bureaus, a three-

---

realms (par. 143): literally, kingdoms

exasperating (par. 144): frustrating

skull cap (par. 144): a cap worn by Jewish men to show their respect for God

tenement house (par. 145): a run-down, low-rental apartment building

legged table, racks of cooking utensils, and all the apparatus of a kitchen. But there was no sign of Salzman or his magic barrel, probably also a figment of the imagination. An odor of frying fish made Leo weak to the knees.

156   "Where is he?" He insisted. "I've got to see your husband."

157   At length she answered. "So who knows where he is? Every time he thinks a new thought he runs to a different place. Go home, he will find you."

158   "Tell him Leo Finkle."

159   She gave no sign she had heard.

160   He walked downstairs, depressed.

161   But Salzman, breathless, stood waiting at his door.

162   Leo was astounded and overjoyed. "How did you get here before me?"

163   "I rushed."

164   "Come inside."

165   They entered. Leo fixed tea, and a sardine sandwich for Salzman. As they were drinking he reached behind him for the packet of pictures and handed them to the marriage broker.

166   Salzman put down his glass and said expectantly, "You found somebody you like?"

167   "Not among these."

168   The marriage broker turned away.

169   "Here is the one I want." Leo held forth the snapshot.

170   Saltzman slipped on his glasses and took the picture into his trembling hand. He turned ghastly and let out a groan.

171   "What's the matter?"

172   "Excuse me. Was an accident this picture. She isn't for you."

173   Salzman frantically shoved the manila packet into his portfolio. He thrust the snapshot into his pocket and fled down the stairs.

174   Leo, after momentary paralysis, gave chase and cornered the marriage broker in the vestibule. The landlady made hysterical outcries but neither of them listened.

175   "Give me back the picture, Salzman."

176   "No." The pain in his eyes was terrible.

177   "Tell me who she is then."

178   "This I can't tell you. Excuse me."

179   He made to depart, but Leo, forgetting himself, seized the matchmaker by his tight coat and shook him frenziedly.

180   "Please," sighed Salzman. *"Please."*

181   Leo ashamedly let him go. "Tell me who she is," he begged. "It's very important for me to know."

182   "She is not for you. She is a wild one—wild, without shame. This is not a bride for a rabbi."

183   "What do you mean wild?"

184   "Like an animal. Like a dog. For her to be poor was a sin. This is why to me she is dead now."

185   "In God's name, what do you mean?"

186   "Her I can't introduce to you," Salzman cried.

ghastly (par. 170): pale

vestibule (par. 174): entry hall

frenziedly (par. 179): frantically

This is why to me she is dead now (par. 184): In Judaism, the family of a person who has done something considered unforgivable can proclaim that person dead. The family sits Shivah, seven days of mourning, and says Kaddish, prayers for the dead. Afterwards, the person is considered literally dead.

187   "Why are you so excited?"

188   "Why, he asks," Salzman said, bursting into tears. "This is my baby, my Stella, she should burn in hell."

189   Leo hurried up to bed and hid under the covers. Under the covers he thought his life through. Although he soon fell asleep he could not sleep her out of his mind. He woke, beating his breast. Though he prayed to be rid of her, his prayers went unanswered. Through days of torment he endlessly struggled not to love her; fearing success, he escaped it. He then concluded to convert her to goodness, himself to God. The idea alternately nauseated and exalted him.

190   He perhaps did not know that he had come to a final decision until he encountered Salzman in a Broadway cafeteria. He was sitting alone at a rear table, sucking the bony remains of a fish. The marriage broker appeared haggard, and transparent to the point of vanishing.

191   Salzman looked up at first without recognizing him. Leo had grown a pointed beard and his eyes were weighted with wisdom.

192   "Salzman," he said, "love has at last come to my heart."

193   "Who can love from a picture?" mocked the marriage broker.

194   "It is not impossible."

195   "If you can love her, then you can love anybody. Let me show you some new clients that they just sent me their photographs. One is a little doll."

196   "Just her I want," Leo murmured.

197   "Don't be a fool, doctor. Don't bother with her."

198   "Put me in touch with her, Salzman," Leo said humbly. "Perhaps I can be of service."

199   Salzman had stopped eating and Leo understood with emotion that it was now arranged.

200   Leaving the cafeteria, he was, however, afflicted by a tormenting suspicion that Salzman had planned it all to happen this way.

201   Leo was informed by letter that she would meet him on a certain corner, and she was there one spring night, waiting under a street lamp. He appeared, carrying a small bouquet of violets and rosebuds. Stella stood by the lamp post, smoking. She wore white with red shoes, which fitted his expectations, although in a troubled moment he had imagined the dress red, and only the shoes white. She waited uneasily and shyly. From afar he saw that her eyes—clearly her father's—were filled with desperate innocence. He pictured, in her, his own redemption. Violins and lit candles revolved in the sky. Leo ran forward with flowers outthrust.

202   Around the corner, Salzman, leaning against a wall, chanted prayers for the dead.

convert (par. 189): change

exalted (par. 189): thrilled

mocked (par. 193): ridiculed

Revelation

Flannery O'Connor

1   The doctor's waiting room, which was very small, was almost full when the Turpins entered and Mrs. Turpin, who was very large, made it look even smaller by her presence. She stood looming at the head of the magazine table set in the center of it, a living demonstration that the room was inadequate and ridiculous. Her little bright black eyes took in all the patients as she sized up the seating situation. There was one vacant chair and a place on the sofa occupied by a blond child in a dirty blue romper who should have been told to move over and make room for the lady. He was five or six, but Mrs. Turpin saw at once that no one was going to tell him to move over. He was slumped down in the seat, his arms idle at his sides and his eyes idle in his head; his nose ran unchecked.

2   Mrs. Turpin put a firm hand on Claud's shoulder and said in a voice that included anyone who wanted to listen, "Claud, you sit in that chair there," and gave him a push down into the vacant one. Claud was florid and bald and sturdy, somewhat shorter than Mrs. Turpin, but he sat down as if he were accustomed to doing what she told him to.

3   Mrs. Turpin remained standing. The only man in the room besides Claud was a lean stringy old fellow with a rusty hand spread out on each knee, whose eyes were closed as if he were asleep or dead or pretending to be so as not to get up and offer her his seat. Her gaze settled agreeably on a well-dressed gray-haired lady whose eyes met hers and whose expression said: if that child belonged to me, he would have some manners and move over—there's plenty of room there for you and him too.

4   Claud looked up with a sigh and made as if to rise.

5   "Sit down," Mrs. Turpin said. "You know you're not supposed to stand on that leg. He has an ulcer on his leg," she explained.

6   Claud lifted his foot onto the magazine table and rolled his trouser leg up to reveal a purple swelling on a plump marble-white calf.

7   "My!" the pleasant lady said. "How did you do that?"

8   "A cow kicked him," Mrs. Turpin said.

9   "Goodness!" said the lady.

10   Claud rolled his trouser leg down.

11   "Maybe the little boy would move over," the lady suggested, but the child did not stir.

12   "Somebody will be leaving in a minute," Mrs. Turpin said. She could not understand why a doctor—with as much money as they made charging five dollars a day to just stick their head in the hospital door and look at you—couldn't afford a decent-sized waiting room. This one was hardly bigger than a garage.

Revelation (title): something that is revealed by God to man

looming (par. 1): impressively

romper (par. 1): one pice outfit for children

idle (par. 1): inactive

unchecked (par. 1): freely

florid (par. 2): ruddy, a red complexion

ulcer (par. 5): infected, festering wound

The table was cluttered with limp-looking magazines and at one end of it there was a big green glass ash tray full of cigarette butts and cotton wads with little blood spots on them. If she had had anything to do with the running of the place, that would have been emptied every so often. There were no chairs against the wall at the head of the room. It had a rectangular-shaped panel in it that permitted a view of the office where the nurse came and went and the secretary listened to the radio. A plastic fern in a gold pot sat in the opening and trailed its fronds down almost to the floor. The radio was softly playing gospel music.

13   Just then the inner door opened and a nurse with the highest stack of yellow hair Mrs. Turpin had ever seen put her face in the crack and called for the next patient. The woman sitting beside Claud grasped the two arms of her chair and hoisted herself up; she pulled her dress free from her legs and lumbered through the door where the nurse had disappeared.

14   Mrs. Turpin eased into the vacant chair, which held her tight as a corset. "I wish I could reduce," she said, and rolled her eyes and gave a comic sigh.

15   "Oh, *you* aren't fat," the stylish lady said.

16   "Ooooo I am too," Mrs. Turpin said. "Claud he eats all he wants to and never weighs over one hundred and seventy-five pounds, but me I just look at something good to eat and I gain some weight," and her stomach and shoulders shook with laughter. "You can eat all you want to, can't you, Claud?" she asked, turning to him.

17   Claud only grinned.

18   "Well, as long as you have such a good disposition," the stylish lady said, "I don't think it makes a bit of difference what size you are. You just can't beat a good disposition."

19   Next to her was a fat girl of eighteen or nineteen, scowling into a thick blue book which Mrs. Turpin saw was entitled *Human Development*. The girl raised her head and directed her scowl at Mrs. Turpin as if she did not like her looks. She appeared annoyed that anyone should speak while she tried to read. The poor girl's face was blue with acne and Mrs. Turpin thought how pitiful it was to have a face like that at that age. She gave the girl a friendly smile but the girl only scowled the harder. Mrs. Turpin herself was fat but she had always had good skin, and though she was forty-seven years old, there was not a wrinkle in her face except around her eyes from laughing too much.

20   Next to the ugly girl was the child, still in exactly the same position, and next to him was a thin leathery old woman in a cotton print dress. She and Claud had three sacks of chicken feed in their pump house that was in the same print. She had seen from the first that the child belonged with the old woman. She could tell by the way they sat—kind of vacant and white-trashy, as if they would sit there until Doomsday if nobody called and told them to get up. And at right angles but next to the well-dressed pleasant lady was a lank-faced woman who was certainly the child's mother. She had on a yellow sweat shirt and wine-colored slacks, both gritty-looking, and the rims of her lips were stained with snuff. Her dirty yellow hair was tied behind with a little piece of red paper

fronds (par. 12): leaves (of ferns)

hoisted (par. 13): raised

corset (par. 14): girdle

disposition (par. 18): temperament, personality

scowling (par. 19): frowning

Doomsday (par. 20): Judgment day: the end of the world

lank-faced (par. 20): thin

snuff (par. 20): ground tobacco that is inhaled or placed inside the lip or cheek

ribbon. Worse than niggers any day, Mrs. Turpin thought.

21   The gospel hymn playing was, "When I looked up and He looked down," and Mrs. Turpin, who knew it, supplied the last line mentally, "And wona these days I know's I'll we-eara crown."

22   Without appearing to, Mrs. Turpin always noticed people's feet. The well-dressed lady had on red and gray suede shoes to match her dress. Mrs. Turpin had on her good black patent leather pumps. The ugly girl had on Girl Scout shoes and heavy socks. The old woman had on tennis shoes and the white-trashy mother had on what appeared to be bedroom slippers, black straw with gold braid threaded through them—exactly what you would have expected her to have on.

23   Sometimes at night when she couldn't go to sleep, Mrs. Turpin would occupy herself with the question of who she would have chosen to be if she couldn't have been herself. If Jesus had said to her before he made her, "There's only two places available for you. You can either be a nigger or white-trash," what would she have said? "Please, Jesus, please," she would have said, "just let me wait until there's another place available," and he would have said, "No, you have to go right now and I have only those two places so make up your mind." She would have wiggled and squirmed and begged and pleaded but it would have been no use and finally she would have said, "All right, make me a nigger then—but that don't mean a trashy one." And he would have made her a neat clean respectable Negro woman, herself but black.

24   Next to the child's mother was a red-headed youngish woman, reading one of the magazines and working a piece of chewing gum, hell for leather, as Claud would say. Mrs. Turpin could not see the woman's feet. She was not white-trash, just common. Sometimes Mrs. Turpin occupied herself at night naming the classes of people. On the bottom of the heap were most colored people, not the kind she would have been if she had been one, but most of them; then next to them—not above, just away from—were the white-trash; then above them were the home-owners, and above them the home-and-land owners, to which she and Claud belonged. Above she and Claud were people with a lot of money and much bigger houses and much more land. But here the complexity of it would begin to bear in on her, for some of the people with a lot of money were common and ought to be below she and Claud and some of the people who had good blood had lost their money and had to rent and then there were colored people who owed their homes and land as well. There was a colored dentist in town who had two red Lincolns and a swimming pool and a farm with registered white-face cattle on it. Usually by the time she had fallen asleep all the classes of people were moiling and roiling around in her head, and she would dream they were all crammed in together in a box car being ridden off to be put in a gas oven.

25   "That's a beautiful clock," she said and nodded to her right. It was a big wall clock, the face encased in a brass sunburst.

26   "Yes, it's very pretty," the stylish lady said agreeably. "And right on the dot too," she added, glancing at her watch.

27   The ugly girl beside her cast an eye upward at the clock, smirked, then looked direclty at Mrs. Turpin and smirked again. Then she returned her eyes to her book. She was obviously the lady's daughter because, although they didn't

pumps (par. 22): a low-heel shoe without straps or laces

hell for leather (par. 24): as fast as possible

moiling and roiling (par. 24): swirling and mixing

encased (par. 25): enclosed

smirked (par. 27): smiled insincerely

look anything alike as to disposition, they both had the same shape of face and the same blue eyes. On the lady they sparkled pleasantly but in the girl's seared face they appeared alternately to smolder and to blaze.

28   What if Jesus had said, "All right, you can be white-trash or a nigger or ugly"!

29   Mrs. Turpin felt an awful pity for the girl, though she thought it was one thing to be ugly and another to act ugly.

30   The woman with the snuff-stained lips turned around in her chair and looked up at the clock. Then she turned back and appeared to look a little to the side of Mrs. Turpin. There was a cast in one of her eyes. "You want to know wher you can get you one of themther clocks?" she asked in a loud voice.

31   "No, I already have a nice clock," Mrs. Turpin said. Once somebody like her got a leg in the conversation, she would be all over it.

32   "You can get you one with green stamps," the woman said. "That's most likely wher he got hisn. Save you up enough, you can get you most anythang. I got me some joo-ry."

33   Ought to have got you a wash rag and some soap, Mrs. Turpin thought.

34   "I get contour sheets with mine," the pleasant lady said.

35   The daughter slammed her book shut. She looked straight in front of her, directly through Mrs. Turpin and on through the yellow curtain and the plate glass window which made the wall behind her. The girl's eyes seemed lit all of a sudden with a peculiar light, an unnatural light like night road signs give. Mrs. Turpin turned her head to see if there was anything going on outside that she should see, but she could not see anything. Figures passing cast only a pale shadow through the curtain. There was no reason the girl should single her out for her ugly looks.

36   "Miss Finley," the nurse said, cracking the door. The gum-chewing woman got up and passed in front of her and Claud and went into the office. She had on red high-heeled shoes.

37   Directly across the table, the ugly girl's eyes were fixed on Mrs. Turpin as if she had some very special reason for disliking her.

38   "This is wonderful weather, isn't it?" the girl's mother said.

39   "It's good weather for cotton if you can get the niggers to pick it," Mrs. Turpin said, "but niggers don't want to pick cotton any more. You can't get the white folks to pick it and now you can't get the niggers—because they got to be right up there with the white folks."

40   "They gonna *try* anyways," the white-trash woman said, leaning forward.

41   "Do you have one of the cotton-picking machines?" the pleasant lady asked.

42   "No," Mrs. Turpin said, "they leave half the cotton in the field. We don't have much cotton anyway. If you want to make it farming now, you have to have a little of everything. We got a couple of acres of cotton and a few hogs and chickens and just enough white-face that Claud can look after them himself."

43   "One thang I don't want," the white-trash woman said, wiping her mouth with the back of her hand. "Hogs. Nasty stinking things, a-gruntin and a-rootin all over the place."

seared (par. 27): scorched

smolder (par. 27): literally, to burn slowly and without flame

green stamps (par. 32): stamps given by stores as a bonus; the shopper collects the stamps and exchanges them for mechandise at the green stamp store.

joo'ry (par. 32): jewelry

contour sheets (par. 34): sheets that fit the shape of a bed

44   Mrs. Turpin gave her the merest edge of her attention. "Our hogs are not dirty and they don't stink," she said. "They're cleaner than some children I've seen. Their feet never touch the ground. We have a pig-parlor—that's where you raise them on concrete," she explained to the pleasant lady, "and Claud scoots them down with the hose every afternoon and washes off the floor." Cleaner by far than that child right there, she thought. Poor nasty little thing. He had not moved except to put the thumb of his dirty hand into his mouth.

45   The woman turned her face away from Mrs. Turpin. "I know I wouldn't scoot down no hog with no hose," she said to the wall.

46   You wouldn't have no hog to scoot down, Mrs. Turpin said to herself.

47   "A-gruntin and a-rootin and a-groanin," the woman muttered.

48   "We got a little of everything," Mrs. Turpin said to the pleasant lady. "It's no use in having more than you can handle yourself with help like it is. We found enough niggers to pick our cotton this year but Claud he has to go after them and take them home again in the evening. They can't walk that half a mile. No they can't. I tell you," she said and laughed merrily, "I sure am tired of buttering up niggers, but you got to love em if you want em to work for you. When they come in the morning, I run out and I say, 'Hi yawl this morning?' and when Claud drives them off to the field I just wave to beat the band and they just wave back." And she waved her had rapidly to illustrate.

49   "Like you read out of the same book," the lady said showing she understood perfectly.

50   "Child, yes," Mrs. Turpin said. "And when they come in from the field, I run out with a bucket of icewater. That's the way it's going to be from now on," she said. "You may as well face it."

51   "One thang I know," the white-trash woman said. "Two things I ain't going to do: love no niggers or scoot down no hog with no hose." And she let out a bark of contempt.

52   The look that Mrs. Turpin and the pleasant lady exchanged indicated they both understood that you had to *have* certain things before you could *know* certain things. But every time Mrs. Turpin exchanged a look with the lady, she was aware that the ugly girl's peculiar eyes were still on her, and she had trouble bringing her attention back to the conversation.

53   "When you got something," she said, "you got to look after it." And when you ain't got a thing but breath and britches, she added to herself, you can afford to come to town every morning and just sit on the Court House coping and spit.

54   A grotesque revolving shadow passed across the curtain behind her and was thrown palely on the opposite wall. Then a bicycle clattered down against the outside of the building. The door opened and a colored boy glided in with a tray from the drugstore. It had two large red and white paper cups on it with tops on them. He was a tall, very black boy in discolored white pants and a green nylon shirt. He was chewing gum slowly, as if to music. He set the tray down in the office opening next to the fern and stuck his head through to look for the secretary. She was not in there. He rested his arms on the ledge and

merest (par. 44): slightest

buttering up (par. 48): flattering

to beat the band (par. 48): as fast and as much as possible

contempt (par. 51): disgust

peculiar (par. 52): strange

coping (par. 53): the top of a short wall

grotesque (par. 54): bizarre, twisted

waited, his narrow bottom stuck out, swaying to the left and right. He raised a hand over his head and scratched the base of his skull.

55   "You see that button there, boy?" Mrs. Turpin said. "You can punch that and she'll come. She's probably in the back somewhere."

56   "Is that right?" the boy said agreeably, as if he had never seen the button before. He leaned to the right and put his finger on it. "She sometime out," he said and twisted around to face his audience, his elbows behind him on the counter. The nurse appeared and he twisted back again. She handed him a dollar and he rooted in his pocket and made the change and counted it out to her. She gave him fifteen cents for a tip and he went out with the empty tray. The heavy door swung to slowly and closed at length with the sound of suction. For a moment no one spoke.

57   "They ought to send all them niggers back to Africa," the white-trash woman said. "That's wher they come from in the first place."

58   "Oh, I couldn't do without my good colored friends," the pleasant lady said.

59   "There's a heap of things worse than a nigger," Mrs. Turpin agreed. "It's all kinds of them just like it's all kinds of us."

60   "Yes, and it takes all kinds to make the world go round," the lady said in her musical voice.

61   As she said it, the raw-complexioned girl snapped her teeth together. Her lower lip turned downwards and inside out, revealing the pale pink inside of her mouth. After a second it rolled back up. It was the ugliest face Mrs. Turpin had ever seen anyone make and for a moment she was certain that the girl had made it at her. She was looking at her as if she had known and disliked her all her life—all of Mrs. Turpin's life, it seemed too, not just all the girl's life. Why, girl, I don't even know you, Mrs. Turpin said silently.

62   She forced her attention back to the discussion. "It wouldn't be practical to send them back to Africa," she said. "They wouldn't want to go. They got it too good here."

63   "Wouldn't be what they wanted—if I had anythang to do with it," the woman said.

64   "It wouldn't be a way in the world you could get all the niggers back over there," Mrs. Turpin said. "They'd be hiding out and lying down and turning sick on you and wailing and hollering and raring and pitching. It wouldn't be a way in the world to get them over there."

65   "They got over here," the trashy woman said. "Get back like they got over."

66   "It wasn't so many of them then," Mrs. Turpin explained.

67   The woman looked at Mrs. Turpin as if here was an idiot indeed but Mrs. Turpin was not bothered by the look, considering where it came from.

68   "Nooo," she said, "they're going to stay here where they can go to New York and marry white folks and improve their color. That's what they all want to do, every one of them, improve their color."

69   "You know what comes of that, don't you?" Claud asked.

70   "No, Claud, what?" Mrs. Turpin said.

71   Claud's eyes twinkled. "White-faced niggers," he said with never a smile.

72   Everybody in the office laughed except the white-trash and the ugly girl. The girl gripped the book in her lap with white fingers. The trashy woman looked around her from face to face as if she thought they were all idiots. The

raw-complexioned (par. 61): red-faced

wailing (par. 64): crying

raring and pitching (par. 64): jumping up and down

old woman in the feed sack dress continued to gaze expressionless across the floor at the high-top shoes of the man opposite her, the one who had been pretending to be asleep when the Turpins came in. He was laughing heartily, his hands still spread out on his knees. The child had fallen to the side and was lying now almost face down in the old woman's lap.

73   While they recovered from their laughter, the nasal chorus on the radio kept the room from silence.

> "You go to blank blank
> And I'll go to mine
> But we'll all blank along
> To-geth-ther,
> And all along the blank
> We'll hep eachother out
> Smile-ling in any kind of
> Weath-ther!"

74   Mrs. Turpin didn't catch every word but she caught enough to agree with the spirit of the song and it turned her thoughts sober. To help anybody out that needed it was her philosophy of life. She never spared herself when she found somebody in need, whether they were white or black, trash or decent. And of all she had to be thankful for, she was most thankful that this was so. If Jesus had said, "You can be high society and have all the money you want and be thin and svelte-like, but you can't be a good woman with it," she would have had to say, "Well don't make me that then. Make me a good woman and it don't matter what else, how fat or how ugly or how poor!" Her heart rose. He had not made her a nigger or white-trash or ugly! He had made her herself and given her a little of everything. Jesus, thank you! she said. Thank you thank you thank you! Whenever she counted her blessings she felt as buoyant as if she weighed one hundred and twenty-five pounds instead of one hundred and eighty.

75   "What's wrong with your little boy?" the pleasant lady asked the white-trashy woman.

76   "He has a ulcer," the woman said proudly. "He ain't give me a minute's peace since he was born. Him and her are just alike," she said, nodding at the old woman, who was running her leathery fingers through the child's pale hair. "Look like I can't get nothing down them two but Co'Cola and candy."

77   That's all you try to get down em, Mrs. Turpin said to herself. Too lazy to light the fire. There was nothing you could tell her about people like them that she didn't know already. And it was not just that they didn't have anything. Because if you gave them everything, in two weeks it would all be broken or filthy or they would have chopped it up for lightwood. She knew all this from her own experience. Help them you must, but help them you couldn't.

78   All at once the ugly girl turned her lips inside out again. Her eyes fixed like two drills on Mrs. Turpin. This time there was no mistaking that there was something urgent behind them.

79   Girl, Mrs. Turpin exclaimed silently, I haven't done a thing to you! The girl might be confusing her with somebody else. There was no need to sit by and let herself be intimidated. "You must be in college," she said boldly, looking directly at the girl. "I see you reading a book there."

feed sack dress (par. 72): a dress made from sacks that contained livestock feed

svelte-like (par. 74): well shaped

buoyant (par. 74): cheerful, light

Co'Cola (par. 76): Coca Cola

intimidated (par. 79): threatened, bullied

80   The girl continued to stare and pointedly did not answer.

81   Her mother blushed at this rudeness. "The lady asked you a question, Mary Grace," she said under her breath.

82   "I have ears," Mary Grace said.

83   The poor mother blushed again. "Mary Grace goes to Wellesley College," she explained. She twisted one of the buttons on her dress. "In Massachusetts," she added with a grimace. "And in the summer she just keeps right on studying. Just reads all the time, a real book worm. She's done real well at Wellesley; she's taking English and Math and History and Psychology and Social Studies," she rattled on, "and I think it's too much. I think she ought get out and have fun."

84   The girl looked as if she would like to hurl them all through the plate glass window.

85   "Way up north," Mrs. Turpin murmured and thought, well, it hasn't done much for her manners.

86   "I'd almost rather to have him sick," the white-trash woman said, wrenching the attention back to herself. "He's so mean when he ain't. Look like some children just take natural to meanness. It's some gets bad when they get sick but he was the opposite. Took sick and turned good. He don't give me no trouble now. It's me waitin to see the doctor," she said.

87   If I was going to send anybody back to Africa, Mrs. Turpin thought, it would be your kind, woman. "Yes, indeed," she said aloud, but looking up at the ceiling, "it's a heap of things worse than a nigger." And dirtier than a hog, she added to herself.

88   "I think people with bad dispositions are more to be pitied than anyone on earth," the pleasant lady said in a voice that was decidedly thin.

89   "I thank the Lord he has blessed me with a good one," Mrs. Turpin said. "The day has never dawned that I couldn't find something to laugh at."

90   "Not since she married me anyways," Claud said with a comical straight face.

91   Everybody laughed except the girl and the white-trash.

92   Mrs. Turpin's stomach shook. "He's such a caution," she said, "that I can't help but laugh at him."

93   The girl made a loud ugly noise through her teeth.

94   Her mother's mouth grew thin and tight. "I think the worst thing in the world," she said, "is an ungrateful person. To have everything and not appreciate it. I know a girl," she said, "who has parents who would give her anything, a little brother who loves her dearly, who is getting a good education, who wears the best clothes, but who can never say a kind word to anyone, who never smiles, who just criticizes and complains all day long."

95   "Is she too old to paddle?" Claud asked.

96   The girl's face was almost purple.

97   "Yes," the lady said, "I'm afraid there's nothing to do but leave her to her folly. Some day she'll wake up and it'll be too late."

98   "It never hurt anyone to smile," Mrs. Turpin said. "It just makes you feel better all over."

99   "Of course," the lady said sadly, "but there are just some people you can't tell anything to. They can't take criticism."

100   "If it's one thing I am," Mrs. Turpin said with feeling, "it's grateful. When I think who all I could have been besides myself and what all I got, a little of everything, and a good disposition besides, I just feel like shouting. 'Thank you, Jesus, for making everything the way it is!' It could have been different!" For one

grimace (par. 83): a facial expression showing disapproval or disbelief

a caution (par. 92): one that does something unexpectedly

folly (par. 97): foolishness

thing, somebody else could have got Claud. At the thought of this, she was flooded with gratitude and a terrible pang of joy ran through her. "Oh thank you, Jesus, Jesus, thank you!" she cried aloud.

101   The book struck her directly over her left eye. It struck almost at the same instant that she realized the girl was about to hurl it. Before she could utter a sound, the raw face came crashing across the table toward her, howling. The girl's fingers sank like clamps into the soft flesh of her neck. She heard the mother cry out and Claud shout, "Whoa!" There was an instant when she was certain that she was about to be in an earthquake.

102   All at once her vision narrowed and she saw everything as if it were happening in a small room far away, or as if she were looking at it through the wrong end of a telescope. Claud's face crumpled and fell out of sight. The nurse ran in, then out, then in again. Then the gangling figure of the doctor rushed out of the inner door. Magazines flew this way and that as the table turned over. The girl fell with a thud and Mrs. Turpin's vision suddenly reversed itself and she saw everything large instead of small. The eyes of the white-trashy woman were staring hugely at the floor. There the girl, held down on one side by the nurse and on the other by her mother, was wrenching and turning in their grasp. The doctor was kneeling astride her, trying to hold her arm down. He managed after a second to sink a long needle into it.

103   Mrs. Turpin felt entirely hollow except for her heart which swung from side to side as if it were agitated in a great empty drum of flesh.

104   "Somebody that's not busy call for the ambulance," the doctor said in the off-hand voice young doctors adopt for terrible occasions.

105   Mrs. Turpin could not have moved a finger. The old man who had been sitting next to her skipped nimbly into the office and made the call, for the secretary still seemed to be gone.

106   "Claud!" Mrs. Turpin called.

107   He was not in his chair. She knew she must jump up and find him but she felt like someone trying to catch a train in a dream, when everything moves in slow motion and the faster you try to run the slower you go.

108   "Here I am," a suffocated voice, very unlike Claud's, said.

109   He was doubled up in the corner on the floor, pale as paper, holding his leg. She wanted to get up and go to him but she could not move. Instead, her gaze was drawn slowly downward to the churning face on the floor, which she could see over the doctor's shoulder.

110   The girl's eyes stopped rolling and focused on her. They seemed a much lighter blue than before, as if a door that had been tightly closed behind them was now open to admit light and air.

111   Mrs. Turpin's head cleared and her power of motion returned. She leaned forward until she was looking directly into the fierce brilliant eyes. There was no doubt in her mind that the girl did know her, knew her in some intense and personal way, beyond time and place and condition. "What you got to say to me?" she asked hoarsely and held her breath, waiting, as for a revelation.

112   The girl raised her head. Her gaze locked with Mrs. Turpin's. "Go back to hell where you came from you old wart hog," she whispered. Her voice was low but clear. Her eyes burned for a moment as if she saw with pleasure that her message had struck its target.

113   Mrs. Turpin sank back in her chair.

114   After a moment the girl's eyes closed and she turned her head wearily to the side.

gangling (par. 102): thin and awkward

astride (par. 102): with one leg on each side

agitated (par. 103): shaking

115   The doctor rose and handed the nurse the empty syringe. He leaned over and put both hands for a moment on the mother's shoulders, which were shaking. She was sitting on the floor, her lips pressed together, holding Mary Grace's hand in her lap. The girl's fingers were gripped like a baby's around her thumb. "Go on to the hospital," he said. "I'll call and make the arrangements."

116   "Now let's see that neck," he said in a jovial voice to Mrs. Turpin. He began to inspect her neck with his first two fingers. Two little moon-shaped lines like pink fish bones were indented over her windpipe. There was the beginning of an angry red swelling above her eye. His fingers passed over this also.

117   "Lea' me be," she said thickly and shook him off. "See about Claud. She kicked him."

118   "I'll see about him in a minute," he said and felt her pulse. He was a thin gray-haired man, given to pleasantries. "Go home and have yourself a vacation the rest of the day," he said and patted her on the shoulder.

119   Quit your pattin me, Mrs. Turpin growled to herself.

120   "And put an ice pack over that eye," he said. Then he went and squatted down beside Claud and looked at his leg. After a moment he pulled him up and Claud limped after him into the office.

121   Until the ambulance came, the only sounds in the room were the tremulous moans of the girl's mother, who continued to sit on the floor. The white-trash woman did not take her eyes off the girl. Mrs. Turpin looked straight ahead at nothing. Presently the ambulance drew up, a long dark shadow, behind the curtain. The attendants came in and set the stretcher down beside the girl and lifted her expertly onto it and carried her out. The nurse helped the mother gather up her things. The shadow of the ambulance moved silently away and the nurse came back in the office.

122   "That ther girl is going to be a lunatic, ain't she?" the white-trash woman asked the nurse, but the nurse kept on to the back and never answered her.

123   "Yes, she's going to be a lunatic," the white-trash woman said to the rest of them.

124   "Po' critter," the old woman murmured. The child's face was still in her lap. His eyes looked idly out over her knees. He had not moved during the disturbance except to draw one leg up under him.

125   "I thank Gawd," the white-trash woman said fervently, "I ain't a lunatic."

126   Claud came limping out and the Turpins went home.

127   As their pick-up truck turned into their own dirt road and made the crest of the hill, Mrs. Turpin gripped the window ledge and looked out suspiciously. The land sloped gracefully down through a field dotted with lavender weeds and at the start of the rise their small yellow frame house with its little flower beds spread out around it like a fancy apron sat primly in its accustomed place between two giant hickory trees. She would not have been startled to see a burnt wound between two blackened chimneys.

128   Neither of them felt like eating so they put on their house clothes and lowered the shade in the bedroom and lay down, Claud with his leg on a pillow and herself with a damp washcloth over her eye. The instant she was flat on her back, the image of a razor-backed hog with warts on its face and horns coming out behind its ears snorted into her head. She moaned, a low quiet moan.

tremulous (par. 121): trembling

a lunatic (par. 122): an insane person

Po' critter (par. 124): poor creature

fervently (par. 125): passionately

the rise (par. 127): the hill

primly (par. 127): neatly

129   "I am not," she said tearfully, "a wart hog. From hell." But the denial had no force. The girl's eyes and her words, even the tone of her voice, low but clear, directed only to her, brooked no repudiation. She had been singled out for the message, though there was trash in the room to whom it might justly have been applied. The full force of this fact struck her only now. There was a woman there who was neglecting her own child but she had been overlooked. The message had been given to Ruby Turpin, a respectable, hard-working, church-going woman. The tears dried. Her eyes began to burn instead with wrath.

130   She rose on her elbow and the washcloth fell into her hand. Claud was lying on his back, snoring. She wanted to tell him what the girl had said. At the same time, she did not wish to put the image of herself as a wart hog from hell into his mind.

131   "Hey, Claud," she muttered and pushed his shoulder.

132   Claud opened one pale baby blue eye.

133   She looked into it warily. He did not think about anything. He just went his way.

134   "Wha, whasit?" he said and closed the eye again.

135   "Nothing," she said. "Does your leg pain you?"

136   "Hurts like hell," Claud said.

137   "It'll quit terreckly," she said and lay back down. In a moment Claud was snoring again. For the rest of the afternoon they lay there. Claud slept. She scowled at the ceiling. Occasionally she raised her fist and made a small stabbing motion over her chest as if she was defending her innocence to invisible guests who were like the comforters of Job, reasonable-seeming but wrong.

138   About five-thirty Claud stirred. "Got to go after those niggers," he sighed, not moving.

139   She was looking straight up as if there were unintelligible handwriting on the ceiling. The protuberance over her eye had turned a greenish-blue. "Listen here," she said.

140   "What?"

141   "Kiss me."

142   Claud leaned over and kissed her loudly on the mouth. He pinched her side and their hands interlocked. Her expression of ferocious concentration did not change. Claud got up, groaning and growling, and limped off. She continued to study the ceiling.

143   She did not get up until she heard the pick-up truck coming back with the Negroes. Then she rose and thrust her feet in her brown oxfords, which she did not bother to lace, and stumped out onto the back porch and got her red plastic bucket. She emptied a tray of ice cubes into it and filled it half full of water and went out into the back yard. Every afternoon after Claud brought the hands in, one of the boys helped him put out hay and the rest waited in the back of the

brooked (par. 129): allowed

repudiation (par. 129): denial

wrath (par. 129): anger

terreckly (par. 137): directly, soon

Job (par. 137): hero of the book of Job in the Old Testament: Job endures many hardships but keeps his faith in God.

handwriting on the ceiling (par. 139): In the Bible, Belshazzar's doom is foretold by mysterious handwriting that appears on the wall of his palace (Daniel 5).

protuberance (par. 139): lump

ferocious (par. 142): intense

truck until he was ready to take them home. The truck was parked in the shade under one of the hickory trees.

144   "Hi yawl this morning?" Mrs. Turpin asked grimly, appearing with the bucket and the dipper. There were three women and a boy in the truck.

145   "Us doin nicely," the oldest woman said. "Hi you doin?" and her gaze struck immediately on the dark lump on Mrs. Turpin's forehead. "You done fell down, ain't you?" she asked in a solicitous voice. The old woman was dark and almost toothless. She had on an old felt hat of Claud's set back on her head. The other two women were younger and lighter and they both had new bright green sunhats. One of them had hers on her head; the other had taken hers off and the boy was grinning beneath it.

146   Mrs. Turpin set the bucket down on the floor of the truck. "Yawl hep yourselves," she said. She looked around to make sure Claud had gone. "No, I didn't fall down," she said, folding her arms. "It was something worse than that."

147   "Ain't nothing bad happen to you!" the old woman said. She said it as if they all knew that Mrs. Turpin was protected in some special way by Divine Providence. "You just had you a little fall."

148   "We were in town at the doctor's office for where the cow kicked Mr. Turpin," Mrs. Turpin said in a flat tone that indicated they could leave off their foolishness. "And there was this girl there. A big fat girl with her face all broke out. I could look at that girl and tell she was peculiar but I couldn't tell how. And me and her mama was just talking and going along and all of a sudden WHAM! She throws this big book she was reading at me and . . ."

149   "Naw!" the old woman cried out.

150   "And then she jumps over the table and commences to choke me."

151   "Naw!" they all exlaimed, "naw!"

152   "Hi come she do that?" the old woman asked. "What ail her?"

153   Mrs. Turpin only glared in front of her.

154   "Somethin ail her," the old woman said.

155   "They carried her off in an ambulance," Mrs. Turpin continued, "but before she went she was rolling on the floor and they were trying to hold her down to give her a shot and she said something to me." She paused. "You know what she said to me?"

156   "What she say?" they asked.

157   "She said," Mrs. Turpin began, and stopped, her face very dark and heavy. The sun was getting whiter and whiter, blanching the sky overhead so that the leaves of the hickory tree were black in the face of it. She could not bring forth the words. "Something real ugly," she muttered.

158   "She sho shouldn't said nothin ugly to you," the old woman said. "You so sweet. You the sweetest lady I know."

159   "She pretty too," the one with the hat on said.

160   "And stout," the other one said. "I never knowed no sweeter white lady."

161   "That's the truth befo' Jesus," the old woman said. "Amen! You des as sweet and pretty as you can be."

162   Mrs. Turpin knew exactly how much Negro flattery was worth and it added to her rage. "She said," she began again and finished this time with a fierce rush of breath, "that I was an old wart hog from hell."

grimly (par. 144): coldly

solicitous (par. 145): concerned

Divine Providence (par. 147): God

ail (par. 152): troubles

163   There was an astounded silence.

164   "Where she at?" the youngest woman cried in a piercing voice.

165   "Lemme see her. I'll kill her!"

166   "I'll kill her with you!" the other one cried.

167   "She b'long in the sylum," the old woman said emphatically. "You the sweetest white lady I know."

168   "She pretty too," the other two said. "Stout as she can be and sweet. Jesus satisfied with her!"

169   "Deed he is," the old woman declared.

170   Idiots! Mrs. Turpin growled to herself. You could never say anything intelligent to a nigger. You could talk at them but not with them. "Yawl ain't drunk your water," she said shortly. "Leave the bucket in the truck when you're finished with it. I got more to do than just stand around and pass the time of day," and she moved off and into the house.

171   She stood for a moment in the middle of the kitchen. The dark protuberance over her eye looked like a miniature tornado cloud which might any moment sweep across the horizon of her brow. Her lower lip protruded dangerously. She squared her massive shoulders. Then she marched into the front of the house and out the side door and started down the road to the pig parlor. She had the look of a woman going single-handed, weaponless, into battle.

172   The sun was deep yellow now like a harvest moon and was riding westward very fast over the far tree line as if it meant to reach the hogs before she did. The road was rutted and she kicked several good-sized stones out of her path as she strode along. The pig parlor was on a little knoll at the end of a lane that ran off from the side of the barn. It was a square of concrete as large as a small room, with a board fence about four feet high around it. The concrete floor sloped slightly so that the hog wash could drain off into a trench where it was carried to the field for fertilizer. Claud was standing on the outside, on the edge of the concrete, hanging onto the top board, hosing down the floor inside. The hose was connected to the faucet of a water trough nearby.

173   Mrs. Turpin climbed up beside him and glowered down at the hogs inside. There were seven long-snouted bristly shoats in it—tan with liver-colored spots—and an old sow a few weeks off from farrowing. She was lying on her side grunting. The shoats were running about shaking themselves like idiot children, their little slit pig eyes searching the floor for anything left. She had read that pigs were the most intelligent animal. She doubted it. They were supposed to be smarter than dogs. There had even been a pig astronaut. He had performed his assignment perfectly but died of a heart attack afterwards because they left him in his electric suit, sitting upright throughout his examination when naturally a hog should be on all fours.

174   A-gruntin and a-rooting and a-groanin.

175   "Gimme that hose," she said, yanking it away from Claud. "Go on and carry them niggers home and then get off that leg."

astounded (par. 163): shocked

sylum (par. 167): asylum, an institution for the care of the insane

emphatically (par. 167): forcefully

protruded (par. 171): stuck out

rutted (par. 172): contained ruts (tracks worn by wheels)

glowered (par. 173): stared angrily

shoats (par. 173): young hogs

farrowing (par. 173): giving birth

176   "You look like you might have swallowed a mad dog," Claud observed, but he got down and limped off. He paid no attention to her humors.

177   Until he was out of earshot, Mrs. Turpin stood on the side of the pen, holding the hose and pointing the stream of water at the hind quarters of any shoat that looked as if it might try to lie down. When he had had time to get over the hill, she turned her head slightly and her wrathful eyes scanned the path. He was nowhere in sight. She turned back again and seemed to gather herself up. Her shoulders rose and she drew in her breath.

178   "What do you send a message like that for?" she said in a low fierce voice, barely above a whisper but with the force of a shout in its concentrated fury. "How am I a hog and me both? How am I saved and from hell too?" Her free fist was knotted and with the other she gripped the hose, blindly pointing the stream of water in and out of the eye of the old sow whose outraged squeal she did not hear.

179   The pig parlor commanded a view of the back pasture where their twenty beef cows were gathered around the hay-bales Claud and the boy had put out. The freshly cut pasture sloped down to the highway. Across it was their cotton field and beyond that a dark green dusty wood which they owned as well. The sun was behind the wood, very red, looking over the paling of the trees like a farmer inspecting his own hogs.

180   "Why me?" she rumbled. "It's no trash around here, black or white, that I haven't given to. And break my back to the bone every day working. And do for the church."

181   She appeared to be the right size woman to command the arena before her. "How am I a hog?" she demanded. "Exactly how am I like them?" and she jabbed the stream of water at the shoats. "There was plenty of trash there. It didn't have to be me.

182   "If you like trash better, go get yourself some trash then," she railed. "You could have made me trash. Or a nigger. If trash is what you wanted why didn't you make me trash?" She shook her fist with the hose in it and a watery snake appeared momentarily in the air. "I could quit working and take it easy and be filthy," she growled. "Lounge about the sidewalks all day drinking root beer. Dip snuff and spit in every puddle and have it all over my face. I could be nasty.

183   "Or you could have made me a nigger. It's too late for me to be a nigger," she said with deep sarcasm, "but I could act like one. Lay down in the middle of the road and stop traffic. Roll on the ground."

184   In the deepening light everything was taking on a mysterious hue. The pasture was growing a peculiar glassy green and the streak of highway had turned lavender. She braced herself for a final assault and this time her voice rolled out over the pasture. "Go on," she yelled, "call me a hog! Call me a hog again. From hell. Call me a wart hog from hell. Put that bottom rail on top. There'll still be a top and bottom!"

185   A garbled echo returned to her.

186   A final surge of fury shook her and she roared, "Who do you think you are?"

187   The color of everything, field and crimson sky, burned for a moment with a transparent intensity. The question carried over the pasture and across the

humors (par. 176): moods

railed (par. 182): said angrily

hue (par. 184): color

garbled (par. 185): confused, jumbled

transparent (par. 187): obvious

highway and the cotton field and returned to her clearly like an answer from beyond the wood.

188   She opened her mouth but no sound came out of it.

189   A tiny truck, Claud's, appeared on the highway, heading rapidly out of sight. Its gears scraped thinly. It looked like a child's toy. At any moment a bigger truck might smash into it and scatter Claud's and the niggers' brains all over the road.

190   Mrs. Turpin stood there, her gaze fixed on the highway, all her muscles rigid, until in five or six minutes the truck reappeared, returning. She waited until it had had time to turn into their own road. Then like a monumental statue coming to life, she bent her head slowly and gazed, as if through the very heart of mystery, down into the pig parlor at the hogs. They had settled all in one corner around the old sow who was grunting softly. A red glow suffused them. They appeared to pant with a secret life.

191   Until the sun slipped finally behind the tree line, Mrs. Turpin remained there with her gaze bent to them as if she were absorbing some abysmal life-giving knowledge. At last she lifted her head. There was only a purple streak in the sky, cutting through a field of crimson and leading, like an extension of the highway, into the descending dusk. She raised her hands from the side of the pan in a gesture hieratic and profound. A visionary light settled in her eyes. She saw the streak as a vast swinging bridge extending upward from the earth through a field of living fire. Upon it a vast horde of souls were rumbling toward heaven. There were whole companies of white-trash, clean for the first time in their lives, and bands of black niggers in white robes, and battalions of freaks and lunatics shouting and clapping and leaping like frogs. And bringing up the end of the procession was a tribe of people whom she recognized at once as those who, like herself and Claud, had always had a little of everything and the God-given wit to use it right. She leaned forward to observe them closer. They were marching behind the others with great dignity, accountable as they had always been for good order and common sense and respectable behvior. They alone were on key. Yet she could see by their shocked and altered faces that even their virtues were being burned away. She lowered her hands and gripped the rail of the hog pen, her eyes small but fixed unblinkingly on what lay ahead. In a moment the vision faded but she remained where she was, immobile.

192   At length she got down and turned off the faucet and made her slow way on the darkening path to the house. In the woods around her the invisible cricket choruses had struck up, but what she heard were the voices of the souls climbing upward into the starry field and shouting hallelujah.

mystery (par. 190): A religious truth that man can know only if God reveals it to him.

suffused (par. 190): spread over

abysmal (par. 191): deep

hieratic (par. 191): priestly

visionary light (par. 191): the light associated with having a vision (a supernatural appearance that reveals a truth)

horde (par. 191): crowd

battalions (par. 191): armies, large groups

altered (par. 191): changed

virtues (par. 191): merits, praiseworthy qualities

hallelujah (par. 192): Hebrew for "praise the Lord"

Good Country People

Flannery O'Connor

1   Besides the neutral expression that she wore when she was alone, Mrs. Freeman had two others, forward and reverse, that she used for all her human dealings. Her forward expression was steady and driving like the advance of a heavy truck. Her eyes never swerved to left or right but turned as the story turned as if they followed a yellow line down the center of it. She seldom used the other expression because it was not often necessary for her to retract a statement, but when she did, her face came to a complete stop, there was an almost imperceptible movement of her black eyes, during which they seemed to be receding, and then the observer would see that Mrs. Freeman, though she might stand there as real as several grain sacks thrown on top of each other, was no longer there in spirit. As for getting anything across to her when this was the case, Mrs. Hopewell had given it up. She might talk her head off. Mrs. Freeman could never be brought to admit herself wrong on any point. She would stand there and if she could be brought to say anything, it was something like, "Well, I wouldn't of said it was and I wouldn't of said it wasn't," or letting her gaze range over the top kitchen shelf where there was an assortment of dusty bottles, she might remark, "I see you ain't ate many of them figs you put up last summer."

2   They carried on their most important business in the kitchen at breakfast. Every morning Mrs. Hopewell got up at seven o'clock and lit her gas heater and Joy's. Joy was her daughter, a large blonde girl who had an artificial leg. Mrs. Hopewell thought of her as a child though she was thirty-two years old and highly educated. Joy would get up while her mother was eating and lumber into the bathroom and slam the door, and before long, Mrs. Freeman would arrive at the back door. Joy would hear her mother call, "Come on in," and then they would talk for a while in low voices that were indistinguishable in the bathroom. By the time Joy came in, they had usually finished the weather report and were on one or the other of Mrs. Freeman's daughters, Glynese or Carramae. Joy called them Glycerin and Caramel. Glynese, a redhead, was eighteen and had many admirers; Carramae, a blonde, was only fifteen but already married and pregnant. She could not keep anything on her stomach. Every morning Mrs. Freeman told Mrs. Hopewell how many times she had vomited since the last report.

3   Mrs. Hopewell liked to tell people that Glynese and Carramae were two of the finest girls she knew and that Mrs. Freeman was a *lady* and that she was never ashamed to take her anywhere or introduce her to anybody they might meet. Then she would tell how she had happened to hire the Freemans in the first place and how they were a godsend to her and how she had had them four

retract (par. 1): take back

imperceptible (par. 1): unnoticeable

receding (par. 1): backing up

put up (par. 1): canned

indistinguishable (par. 2): inseparable

years. The reason for her keeping them so long was that they were not trash. They were good country people. She had telephoned the man whose name they had given as a reference and he had told her that Mr. Freeman was a good farmer but that his wife was the nosiest woman ever to walk the earth. "She's got to be into everything," the man said. "If she don't get there before the dust settles, you can bet she's dead, that's all. She'll want to know all your business. I can stand him real good," he had said, "but me nor my wife neither could have stood that woman one more minute on this place." That had put Mrs. Hopewell off for a few days.

4   She had hired them in the end because there were no other applicants but she had made up her mind beforehand exactly how she would handle the woman. Since she was the type who had to be into everything, then, Mrs. Hopewell had decided, she would not only let her be into everything, she would *see to it* that she was into everything—she would give her the responsibility of everything, she would put her in charge. Mrs. Hopewell had no bad qualities of her own but she was able to use other people's in such a constructive way that she never felt the lack. She had hired the Freemans and she had kept them four years.

5   Nothing is perfect. This was one of Mrs. Hopewell's favorite sayings. Another was: that is life! And still another, the most important, was well, other people have their opinions too. She would make these statements, usually at the table, in a tone of gentle insistence as if no one held them but her, and the large hulking Joy, whose constant outrage had obliterated every expression from her face, would stare just a little to the side of her, her eyes icy blue, with the look of someone who has achieved blindness by an act of will and means to keep it.

6   When Mrs. Hopewell said to Mrs. Freeman that life was like that, Mrs. Freeman would say, "I always said so myself." Nothing had been arrived at by anyone that had not first been arrived at by her. She was quicker than Mr. Freeman. When Mrs. Hopewell said to her after they had been on the place a while, "You know, you're the wheel behind the wheel," and winked, Mrs. Freeman had said, "I know it. I've always been quick. It's some that are quicker than others."

7   "Everybody is different," Mrs. Hopewell said.

8   "Yes, most people is," Mrs. Freeman said.

9   "It takes all kinds to make the world."

10   "I always said it did myself."

11   The girl was used to this kind of dialogue for breakfast and more of it for dinner; sometimes they had it for supper too. When they had no guest they ate in the kitchen because that was easier. Mrs. Freeman always managed to arrive at some point during the meal and to watch them finish it. She would stand in the doorway if it were summer but in the winter she would stand with one elbow on top of the refrigerator and look down on them, or she would stand by the gas heater, lifting the back of her skirt slightly. Occasionally she would stand against the wall and roll her head from side to side. At no time was she in any hurry to leave. All this was very trying on Mrs. Hopewell but she was a woman of great patience. She realized that nothing is perfect and that in the Freemans she had good country people and that if, in this day and age, you get good country people, you had better hang onto them.

12   She had had plenty of experience with trash. Before the Freemans she had averaged one tenant family a year. The wives of these farmers were not the kind

before the dust settles (par. 3): before an event ends

constructive (par. 4): helpful

obliterated (par. 5): wiped out

you would want to be around you for very long. Mrs. Hopewell, who had divorced her husband long ago, needed someone to walk over the fields with her; and when Joy had to be impressed for these services, her remarks were usually so ugly and her face so glum that Mrs. Hopewell would say, "If you can't come pleasantly, I don't want you at all," to which the girl, standing square and rigid-shouldered with her neck thrust slightly forward, would reply, "If you want me, here I am—LIKE I AM."

13   Mrs. Hopewell excused this attitude because of the leg (which had been shot off in a hunting accident when Joy was ten). It was hard for Mrs. Hopewell to realize that her child was thirty-two now and that for more than twenty years she had had only one leg. She thought of her still as a child because it tore her heart to think instead of the poor stout girl in her thirties who had never danced a step or had any *normal* good times. Her name was really Joy but as soon as she was twenty-one and away from home, she had had it legally changed. Mrs. Hopewell was certain that she had thought and thought until she had hit upon the ugliest name in any language. Then she had gone and had the beautiful name, Joy, changed without telling her mother until after she had done it. Her legal name was Hulga.

14   When Mrs. Hopewell thought the name, Hulga, she thought of the broad blank hull of a battleship. She would not use it. She continued to call her Joy to which the girl responded but in a purely mechanical way.

15   Hulga had learned to tolerate Mrs. Freeman, who saved her from taking walks with her mother. Even Glynese and Carramae were useful when they occupied attention that might otherwise have been directed at her. At first she had thought she could not stand Mrs. Freeman for she had found that it was not possible to be rude to her. Mrs. Freeman would take on strange resentments and for days together she would be sullen but the source of her displeasure was always obscure, a direct attack, a positive leer, blatant ugliness to her face—these never touched her. And without warning one day, she began calling her Hulga.

16   She did not call her that in front of Mrs. Hopewell who would have been incensed but when she and the girl happened to be out of the house together, she would say something and add the name Hulga to the end of it, and the big spectacled Joy-Hulga would scowl and redden as if her privacy had been intruded upon. She considered the name her personal affair. She had arrived at it first purely on the basis of its ugly sound and then the full genius of its fitness had struck her. She had a vision of the name working like the ugly sweating Vulcan who stayed in the furnace and to whom, presumably, the goddess had to come when called. She saw it as the name of her highest creative act. One of her major triumphs was that her mother had not been able to turn her dust into Joy, but the greater one was that she had been able to turn it herself into Hulga. However, Mrs. Freeman's relish for using the name only irritated her. It was as if Mrs. Freeman's beady steel-pointed eyes had penetrated far enough behind her face to reach some secret fact. Something about her seemed to fascinate Mrs.

impressed for (par. 12): pressured into

hull (par. 14): body

obscure (par. 15): unclear

leer (par. 15): angry look

blatant (par. 15): obvious

incensed (par. 16): angered

spectacled (par. 16): wearing spectacles (eyeglasses)

scowl (par. 16): frown angrily

Vulcan (par. 16): the Roman god of fire and metalworking

relish (par. 16): pleasure

Freeman and then one day Hulga realized that it was the artificial leg. Mrs. Freeman had a special fondness for the details of secret infections, hidden deformities, assaults upon children. Of diseases, she preferred the lingering or incurable. Hulga had heard Mrs. Hopewell give her the details of the hunting accident, how the leg had been literally blasted off, how she had never lost consciousness. Mrs. Freeman could listen to it any time as if it had happened an hour ago.

17   When Hulga stumped into the kitchen in the morning (she could walk without making the awful noise but she made it—Mrs. Hopewell was certain—because it was ugly-sounding), she glanced at them and did not speak. Mrs. Hopewell would be in her red kimono with her hair tied around her head in rags. She would be sitting at the table, finishing her breakfast and Mrs. Freeman would be hanging by her elbow outward from the refrigerator, looking down at the table. Hulga always put her eggs on the stove to boil and then stood over them with her arms folded, and Mrs. Hopewell would look at her—a kind of indirect gaze divided between her and Mrs. Freeman—and would think that if she would only keep herself up a little, she wouldn't be so bad looking. There was nothing wrong with her face that a pleasant expression wouldn't help. Mrs. Hopewell said that people who looked on the bright side of things would be beautiful even if they were not.

18   Whenever she looked at Joy this way, she could not help but feel that it would have been better if the child had not taken the Ph.D. It had certainly not brought her out any and now that she had it, there was no more excuse for her to go to school again. Mrs. Hopewell thought it was nice for girls to go to school to have a good time but Joy had "gone through." Anyhow, she would not have been strong enough to go again. The doctors had told Mrs. Hopewell that with the best of care, Joy might see forty-five. She had a weak heart. Joy had made it plain that if it had not been for this condition, she would be far from these red hills and good country people. She would be in a university lecturing to people who knew what she was talking about. And Mrs. Hopewell could very well picture her there, looking like a scarecrow and lecturing to more of the same. Here she went about all day in a six-year-old skirt and a yellow sweat shirt with a faded cowboy on a horse embossed on it. She thought this was funny; Mrs. Hopewell thought it was idiotic and showed simply that she was still a child. She was brilliant but she didn't have a grain of sense. It seemed to Mrs. Hopewell that every year she grew less like other people and more like herself—bloated, rude, and squint-eyed. And she said such strange things! To her own mother she had said—without warning, without excuse, standing up in the middle of a meal with her face purple and her mouth half full—"Woman! do you ever look inside? Do you ever look inside and see what you are *not*? God!" she had cried sinking down again and staring at her plate, "Malebranche was right: we are not our own light. We are not our own light!" Mrs. Hopewell had no idea to this day what brought that on. She had only made the remark, hoping Joy would take it in, that a smile never hurt anyone.

19   The girl had taken the Ph.D. in philosophy and this left Mrs. Hopewell at a complete loss. You could say, "My daughter is a nurse," or "My daughter is a schoolteacher," or even, "My daughter is a chemical engineer." You could not say, "My daughter is a philosopher." That was something that had ended with the Greeks and Romans. All day Joy sat on her neck in a deep chair, reading. Sometimes she went for walks but she didn't like dogs or cats or birds or flowers or nature or nice young men. She looked at nice young men as if she could smell their stupidity.

kimono (par. 17): loose Japanese robe

Malebranche (par. 18): Nicolas Malebranche (1638–1715), French philosopher

20   One day Mrs. Hopewell had picked up one of the books the girl had just put down and opening it at random, she read, "Science, on the other hand, has to assert its soberness and seriousness afresh and declare that it is concerned solely with what-is. Nothing—how can it be for science anything but a horror and a phantasm? If science is right, then one thing stands firm: science wishes to know nothing of nothing. Such is after all the strictly scientific approach to Nothing. We know it by wishing to know nothing of Nothing." These words had been underlined with a blue pencil and they worked on Mrs. Hopewell like some evil incantation in gibberish. She shut the book quickly and went out of the room as if she were having a chill.

21   This morning when the girl came in, Mrs. Freeman was on Carramae. "She thrown up four times after supper," she said, "and was up twice in the night after three o'clock. Yesterday she didn't do nothing but ramble in the bureau drawer. All she did. Stand up there and see what she could run up on."

22   "She's got to eat," Mrs. Hopewell muttered, sipping her coffee, while she watched Joy's back at the stove. She was wondering what the child had said to the Bible salesman. She could not imagine what kind of a conversation she could possibly have had with him.

23   He was a tall gaunt hatless youth who had called yesterday to sell them a Bible. He had appeared at the door, carrying a large black suitcase that weighted him so heavily on one side that he had to brace himself against the door facing. He seemed on the point of collapse but he said in a cheerful voice, "Good morning, Mrs. Cedars!" and set the suitcase down on the mat. He was not a bad-looking young man though he had on a bright blue suit and yellow socks that were not pulled up far enough. He had prominent face bones and a streak of sticky-looking brown hair falling across his forehead.

24   "I'm Mrs. Hopewell," she said.

25   "Oh!" he said, pretending to look puzzled but with his eyes sparkling, "I saw it said 'The Cedars' on the mailbox so I thought you was Mrs. Cedars!" and he burst out in a pleasant laugh. He picked up the satchel and under cover of a pant, he fell forward into her hall. It was rather as if the suitcase had moved first, jerking him after it. "Mrs. Hopewell!" he said and grabbed her hand. "I hope you are well!" and he laughed again and then all at once his face sobered completely. He paused and gave her a straight earnest look and said, "Lady, I've come to speak of serious things."

26   "Well, come in," she muttered, none too pleased because her dinner was almost ready. He came into the parlor and sat down on the edge of a straight chair and put the suitcase between his feet and glanced around the room as if he were sizing her up by it. Her silver gleamed on the two sideboards; she decided he had never been in a room as elegant as this.

27   "Mrs. Hopewell," he began, using her name in a way that sounded almost intimate, "I know you believe in Chrustian service."

assert (par. 20): state

phantasm (par. 20): something created by the imagination

incantation (par. 20): a magical chant

gibberish (par. 20): meaningless words

gaunt (par. 23): thin

prominent (par. 23): noticeable

satchel (par. 25): suitcase

pant (par. 25): gasp

earnest (par. 25): sincere

intimate (par. 27): extremely personal

28   "Well, yes," she murmured.

29   "I know," he said and paused, looking very wise with his head cocked on one side, "that you're a good woman. Friends have told me."

30   Mrs. Hopewell never liked to be taken for a fool. "What are you selling?" she asked.

31   "Bibles," the young man said and his eye raced around the room before he added, "I see you have no family Bible in your parlor, I see that is the one lack you got!"

32   Mrs. Hopewell could not say, "My daughter is an atheist and won't let me keep the Bible in the parlor." She said, stiffening slightly, "I keep my Bible by my bedside." This was not the truth. It was in the attic somewhere.

33   "Lady," he said, "the word of God ought to be in the parlor."

34   "Well, I think that's a matter of taste," she began. "I think . . ."

35   "Lady," he said, "for a Chrustian, the word of God ought to be in every room in the house besides in his heart. I know you're a Chrustian because I can see it in every line of your face."

36   She stood up and said, "Well, young man, I don't want to buy a Bible and I smell my dinner burning."

37   He didn't get up. He began to twist his hands and looking down at them, he said softly. "Well, lady, I'll tell you the truth—not many people want to buy one nowadays and beside, I know I'm real simple. I don't know how to say a thing but to say it. I'm just a country boy." He glanced up into her unfriendly face. "People like you don't like to fool with country people like me!"

38   "Why!" she cried, "good country people are the salt of the earth! Besides, we all have different ways of doing, it takes all kinds to make the world go 'round. That's life!"

39   "You said a mouthful," he said.

40   "Why, I think there aren't enough good people in the world!" she said, stirred. "I think that's what's wrong with it!"

41   His face had brightened. "I didn't inraduce myself," he said. I'm Manley Pointer from out in the country around Willohobie, not even from a place, just from near a place."

42   "You wait a minute," she said. "I have to see about my dinner." She went out to the kitchen and found Joy standing near the door where she had been listening.

43   "Get rid of the salt of the earth," she said, "and let's eat."

44   Mrs. Hopewell gave her a pained look and turned the heat down under the vegetables. "I can't be rude to anybody," she murmured and went back into the parlor.

45   He had opened the suitcase and was sitting with a Bible on each knee.

46   "You might as well put those up," she told him. "I don't want one."

47   "I appreciate your honesty," he said. "You don't see any more real honest people unless you go way out in the country."

48   "I know," she said, "real genuine folks!" Through the crack in the door she heard a groan.

49   "I guess a lot of boys come telling you they're working their way through college," he said, "but I'm not going to tell you that. Somehow," he said, "I don't want to go to college. I want to devote my life to Chrustian service. See," he said, lowering his voice, "I got this heart condition. I may not live long. When you know it's something wrong with you and you may not live long, well then, lady . . ." He paused, with his mouth open, and stared at her.

50   He and Joy had the same condition! She knew that her eyes were filling with tears but she collected herself quickly and murmured, "Won't you stay for

atheist (par. 32): one who denies the existence of God

collected (par. 50): calmed

dinner? We'd love to have you!" and was sorry the instant she heard herself say it.

51 "Yes mam," he said in an abashed voice, "I would sher love to do that!"

52 Joy had given him one look on being introduced to him and then throughout the meal had not glanced at him again. He had addressed several remarks to her, which she had pretended not to hear. Mrs. Hopewell could not understand deliberate rudeness, although she lived with it, and she felt she had always to overflow with hospitality to make up for Joy's lack of courtesy. She urged him to talk about himself and he did. He said he was the seventh child of twelve and that his father had been crushed under a tree when he was eight years old. He had been crushed very badly, in fact, almost cut in two and was practically not recognizable. His mother had got along the best she could by hard working and she had always seen that her children went to Sunday School and that they read the Bible every evening. He was now nineteen years old and he had been selling Bibles for four months. In that time he had sold seventy-seven Bibles and had the promise of two more sales. He wanted to become a missionary because he thought that was the way you could do most for people. "He who losest his life shall find it," he said simply and he was so sincere, so genuine and earnest that Mrs. Hopewell would not for the world have smiled. He prevented his peas from sliding onto the table by blocking them with a piece of bread which he later cleaned his plate with. She could see Joy observing sidewise how he handled his knife and fork and she saw too that every few minutes, the boy would dart a keen appraising glance at the girl as if he were trying to attract her attention.

53 After dinner Joy cleared the dishes off the table and disappeared and Mrs. Hopewell was left to talk with him. He told her again about his childhood and his father's accident and about various things that had happened to him. Every five minutes or so she would stifle a yawn. He sat for two hours until finally she told him she must go because she had an appointment in town. He packed his Bibles and thanked her and prepared to leave, but in the doorway he stopped and wrung her hand and said that not on any of his trips had he met a lady as nice as her and he asked if he could come again. She had said she would always be happy to see him.

54 Joy had been standing in the road, apparently looking at something in the distance, when he came down the steps toward her, bent to the side with his heavy valise. He stopped where she was standing and confronted her directly. Mrs. Hopewell could not hear what he said but she trembled to think what Joy would say to him. She could see that after a minute Joy said something and that then the boy began to speak again, making an excited gesture with his free hand. After a minute Joy said something else at which the boy began to speak once more. Then to her amazement, Mrs. Hopewell saw the two of them walk off together, toward the gate. Joy had walked all the way to the gate with him and Mrs. Hopewell could not imagine what they had said to each other, and she had not yet dared to ask.

55 Mrs. Freeman was insisting upon her attention. She had moved from the refrigerator to the heater so that Mrs. Hopewell had to turn and face her in order to seem to be listening. "Glynese gone out with Harvey Hill again last night," she said. "She had this sty."

56 "Hill," Mrs. Hopewell said absently, "is that the one who works in the garage?"

missionary (par. 52): one who is sent to do religious or charitable work

keen (par. 52): sharp, intense

stifle (par. 53): suppress, stop

valise (par. 54): suitcase

confronted (par. 54): faced

57   "Nome, he's the one that goes to chiropracter school," Mrs. Freeman said. "She had this sty. Been had it two days. So she says when he brought her in the other night he says, 'Lemme get rid of that sty for you,' and she says, 'How?' and he says, 'You just lay yourself down across the seat of that car and I'll show you.' So she done it and he popped her neck. Kept on a-popping it several times until she made him quit. This morning," Mrs. Freeman said, "she ain't got no sty. She ain't got no traces of a sty."

58   "I never heard of that before," Mrs. Hopewell said.

59   "He ast her to marry him before the Ordinary," Mrs. Freeman went on, "and she told him she wasn't going to be married in no *office*."

60   "Well, Glynese is a fine girl," Mrs. Hopewell said. "Glynese and Carramae are both fine girls."

61   "Carramae said when her and Lyman was married Lyman said it sure felt sacred to him. She said he said he wouldn't take five hundred dollars for being married by a preacher."

62   "How much would he take?" the girl asked from the stove.

63   "He said he wouldn't take five hundred dollars," Mrs. Freeman repeated.

64   "Well we all have work to do," Mrs. Hopewell said.

65   "Lyman said it just felt more sacred to him," Mrs. Freeman said. "The doctor wants Carramae to eat prunes. Says instead of medicine. Says them cramps is coming from pressure. You know where I think it is?"

66   "She'll be better in a few weeks," Mrs. Hopewell said.

67   "In the tube," Mrs. Freeman said. "Else she wouldn't be as sick as she is."

68   Hulga had cracked her two eggs into a saucer and was bringing them to the table along with a cup of coffee that she had filled too full. She sat down carefully and began to eat, meaning to keep Mrs. Freeman there by questions if for any reason she showed an inclination to leave. She could perceive her mother's eye on her. The first round-about question would be about the Bible salesman and she did not wish to bring it on. "How did he pop her neck?" she asked.

69   Mrs. Freeman went into a description of how he had popped her neck. She said he owned a '55 Mercury but that Glynese said she would rather marry a man with only a '36 Plymouth who would be married by a preacher. The girl asked what if he had a '32 Plymouth and Mrs. Freeman said what Glynese had said was a '36 Plymouth.

70   Mrs. Hopewell said there were not many girls with Glynese's common sense. She said what she admired in those girls was their common sense. She said that reminded her that they had a nice visitor yesterday, a young man selling Bibles. "Lord," she said, "he bored me to death but he was so sincere and genuine I couldn't be rude to him. He was just good country people, you know," she said, "—just the salt of the earth."

71   "I seen him walk up," Mrs. Freeman said, "and then later—I seen him walk off," and Hulga could feel the slight shift in her voice, the slight insinuation, that he had not walked off alone, had he? Her face remained expressionless but the color rose into her neck and she seemed to swallow it down with the next spoonful of egg. Mrs. Freeman was looking at her as if they had a secret together.

72   "Well, it takes all kinds of people to make the world go 'round," Mrs. Hopewell said. "It's very good we aren't all alike."

73   "Some people are more alike than others," Mrs. Freeman said.

Ordinary (par. 59): justice of the peace

inclination (par. 68): desire

perceive (par. 68): sense

insinuation (par. 71): suggestion

74   Hulga got up and stumped, with about twice the noise that was necessary, into her room and locked the door. She was to meet the Bible salesman at ten o'clock at the gate. She had thought about it half the night. She had started thinking of it as a great joke and then she had begun to see profound implications in it. She had lain in bed imagining dialogues for them that were insane on the surface but that reached below to depths that no Bible salesman would be aware of. Their conversation yesterday had been of this kind.

75   He had stopped in front of her and had simply stood there. His face was bony and sweaty and bright, with a little pointed nose in the center of it, and his look was different from what it had been at the dinner table. He was gazing at her with open curiosity, with fascination, like a child watching a new fantastic animal at the zoo, and he was breathing as if he had run a great distance to reach her. His gaze seemed somehow familiar but she could not think where she had been regarded with it before. For almost a minute he didn't say anything. Then on what seemed an insuck of breath, he whispered, "You ever ate a chicken that was two days old?"

76   The girl looked at him stonily. He might have just put this question up for consideration at the meeting of a philosophical association. "Yes," she presently replied as if she had considered it from all angles.

77   "It must have been mighty small!" he said triumphantly and shook all over with little nervous giggles, getting very red to the face, and subsiding finally into his gaze of complete admiration, while the girl's expression remained exactly the same.

78   "How old are you?" he asked softly.

79   She waited some time before she answered. Then in a flat voice she said, "Seventeen."

80   His smiles came in succession like waves breaking on the surface of a little lake. "I see you got a wooden leg," he said. "I think you're brave. I think you're real sweet."

81   The girl stood blank and solid and silent.

82   "Walk to the gate with me," he said, "you're a brave sweet little thing and I liked you the minute I seen you walk in the door."

83   Hulga began to move forward.

84   "What's your name?" he asked, smiling down on the top of her head.

85   "Hulga," she said.

86   "Hulga," he murmured, "Hulga, Hulga. I never heard of anybody name Hulga before. You're shy, aren't you, Hulga?" he asked.

87   She nodded, watching his large red hand on the handle of the giant valise.

88   "I like girls that wear glasses," he said. "I think a lot. I'm not like these people that a serious thought don't ever enter their heads. It's because I may die."

89   "I may die too," she said suddenly and looked up at him. His eyes were very small and brown, glittering feverishly.

90   "Listen," he said, "don't you think some people was meant to meet on account of what all they got in common and all? Like they both think serious thoughts and all?" He shifted the valise to his other hand so that the hand nearest her was free. He caught hold of her elbow and shook it a little. "I don't work on Saturday," he said. "I like to walk in the woods and see what Mother Nature

profound (par. 74): serious

implications (par. 74): possibilities

dialogues (par. 74): conversations

consideration (par. 76): discussion

subsiding (par. 77): settling

is wearing. O'er the hills and far away. Pic-nics and things. Couldn't we go on a pic-nic tomorrow? Say yes, Hulga," he said and gave her a dying look as if he felt his insides about to drop out of him. He had even seemed to sway slightly toward her.

91   During the night she had imagined that she seduced him. She imagined that the two of them walked on the place until they came to the storage barn beyond the two back fields and there, she imagined, that things came to such a pass that she very easily seduced him and that then, of course, she had to reckon with his remorse. True genius can get an idea across even to an inferior mind. She imagined that she took his remorse in hand and changed it into a deeper understanding of life. She took all his shame away and turned it into something useful.

92   She set off for the gate at exactly ten o'clock, escaping without drawing Mrs. Hopewell's attention. She didn't take anything to eat, forgetting that food is usually taken on a picnic. She wore a pair of slacks and a dirty white shirt, and as an afterthought, she had put some Vapex on the collar of it since she did not own any perfume. When she reached the gate no one was there.

93   She looked up and down the empty highway and had the furious feeling that she had been tricked, that he had only meant to make her walk to the gate after the idea of him. Then suddenly he stood up, very tall, from behind a bush on the opposite embankment. Smiling, he lifted his hat which was new and wide-brimmed. He had not worn it yesterday and she wondered if he had bought it for the occasion. It was toast-colored with a red and white band around it and was slightly too large for him. He stepped from behind the bush still carrying the black valise. He had on the same suit and the same yellow socks sucked down in his shoes from walking. He crossed the highway and said, "I knew you'd come!"

94   The girl wondered acidly how he had known this. She pointed to the valise and asked, "Why did you bring your Bibles?"

95   He took her elbow, smiling down on her as if he could not stop. "You can never tell when you'll need the word of God, Hulga," he said. She had a moment in which she doubted that this was actually happening and then they began to climb the embankment. They went down into the pasture toward the woods. The boy walked lightly by her side, bouncing on his toes. The valise did not seem to be heavy today; he even swung it. They crossed half the pasture without saying anything and then, putting his hand easily on the small of her back, he asked softly, "Where does your wooden leg join on?"

96   She turned an ugly red and glared at him and for an instant the boy looked abashed. "I didn't mean you no harm," he said. "I only meant you're so brave and all. I guess God takes care of you."

97   "No," she said, looking forward and walking fast, "I don't even believe in God."

98   At this he stopped and whistled. "No!" he exclaimed as if he were too astonished to say anything else.

99   She walked on and in a second he was bouncing at her side, fanning with his hat. "That's very unusual for a girl," he remarked, watching her out of the corner of his eye. When they reached the edge of the wood, he put his hand on her back again and drew her against him without a word and kissed her heavily.

100   The kiss, which had more pressure than feeling behind it, produced that

remorse (par. 91): guilt

Vapex (par. 92): a brand name for a nasal spray

abashed (par. 96): uneasy

extra surge of adrenaline in the girl that enables one to carry a packed trunk out of a burning house, but in her, the power went at once to the brain. Even before he released her, her mind, clear and detached and ironic anyway, was regarding him from a great distance, with amusement but with pity. She had never been kissed before and she was pleased to discover that it was an unexceptional experience and all a matter of the mind's control. Some people might enjoy drain water if they were told it was vodka. When the boy, looking expectant but uncertain, pushed her gently away, she turned and walked on, saying nothing as if such business, for her, were common enough.

101   He came along panting at her side, trying to help her when he saw a root that she might trip over. He caught and held back the long swaying blades of thorn vine until she had passed beyond them. She led the way and he came breathing heavily behind her. Then they came out on a sunlit hillside, sloping softly into another one a little smaller. Beyond, they could see the rusted top of the old barn where the extra hay was stored.

102   The hill was sprinkled with small pink weeds. "Then you ain't saved?" he asked suddenly, stopping.

103   The girl smiled. It was the first time she had smiled at him at all. "In my economy," she said, "I'm saved and you are damned but I told you I didn't believe in God."

104   Nothing seemed to destroy the boy's look of admiration. He gazed at her now as if the fantastic animal at the zoo had put its paw through the bars and given him a loving poke. She thought he looked as if he wanted to kiss her again and she walked on before he had the chance.

105   "Ain't there somewheres we can sit down sometime?" he murmured, his voice softening toward the end of the sentence.

106   "In that barn," she said.

107   They made for it rapidly as if it might slide away like a train. It was a large two-story barn, cool and dark inside. The boy pointed up the ladder that led into the loft and said, "It's too bad we can't go up there."

108   "Why can't we?" she asked.

109   "Yer leg," he said reverently.

110   The girl gave him a contemptuous look and putting both hands on the ladder, she climbed it while he stood below, apparently awestruck. She pulled herself expertly through the opening and then looked down at him and said, "Well, come on if you're coming," and he began to climb the ladder, awkwardly bringing the suitcase with him.

111   "We won't need the Bible," she observed.

112   "You never can tell," he said, panting. After he had got into the loft, he was a few seconds catching his breath. She had sat down in a pile of straw. A wide sheath of sunlight, filled with dust particles, slanted over her. She lay back against a bale, her face turned away, looking out the front opening of the barn where hay was thrown from a wagon into the loft. The two pink-speckled hillsides lay back against a dark ridge of woods. The sky was cloudless and cold blue. The boy dropped down by her side and put one arm under her and the other over her and began methodically kissing her face, making little noises like a fish. He did not remove his hat but it was pushed far enough back not to inter-

adrenaline (par. 100): a chemical released by the adrenal glands when a person is excited

detached (par. 100): disinterested

economy (par. 103): way of thinking

reverently (par. 109): respectfully

contemptuous (par. 110): hateful

sheath (par. 112): Literally, a sheath is a case for a knife blade.

fere. When her glasses got in his way, he took them off of her and slipped them into his pocket.

113   The girl at first did not return any of the kisses but presently she began to and after she had put several on his cheek, she reached his lips and remained there, kissing him again and again as if she were trying to draw all the breath out of him. His breath was clear and sweet like a child's and the kisses were sticky like a child's. He mumbled about loving her and about knowing when he first seen her that he loved her, but the mumbling was like the sleeping fretting of a child being put to sleep by his mother. Her mind, throughout this, never stopped or lost itself for a second to her feelings. "You ain't said you loved me none," he whispered finally, pulling back from her. "You got to say that."

114   She looked away from him off into the hollow sky and then down at a black ridge and then down farther into what appeared to be two green swelling lakes. She didn't realize he had taken her glasses but this landscape could not seem exceptional to her for she seldom paid any close attention to her surroundings.

115   "You got to say it," he repeated. "You got to say you love me."

116   She was always careful how she committed herself. "In a sense," she began, "if you use the word loosely, you might say that. But it's not a word I use. I don't have illusions. I'm one of those people who see *through* to nothing."

117   The boy was frowning. "You got to say it. I said it and you got to say it," he said.

118   The girl looked at him almost tenderly. "You poor baby," she murmured. "It's just as well you don't understand," and she pulled him by the neck, face-down, against her. "We are all damned," she said, "but some of us have taken off our blindfolds and see that there's nothing to see. It's a kind of salvation."

119   The boy's astonished eyes looked blankly through the ends of her hair. "Okay," he almost whined, "but do you love me or don'tcher?"

120   "Yes," she said and added, "in a sense. But I must tell you something. There mustn't be anything dishonest between us." She lifted his head and looked him in the eye. "I am thirty years old," she said. "I have a number of degrees."

121   The boy's look was irritated but dogged. "I don't care," he said. "I don't care a thing about what all you done. I just want to know if you love me or don'tcher?" and he caught her to him and wildly planted her face with kisses until she said, "Yes, yes."

122   "Okay then," he said, letting her go. "Prove it."

123   She smiled, looking dreamily out on the shifty landscape. She had seduced him without even making up her mind to try. "How?" she asked, feeling that he should be delayed a little.

124   He leaned over and put his lips to her ear. "Show me where your wooden leg joins on," he whispered.

125   The girl uttered a sharp little cry and her face instantly drained of color. The obscenity of the suggestion was not what shocked her. As a child she had sometimes been subject to feelings of shame but education had removed the last traces of that as a good surgeon scrapes for cancer; she would no more have felt it over what he was asking than she would have believed in his Bible. But she was as sensitive about the artificial leg as a peacock about his tail. No one ever touched it but her. She took care of it as someone else would his soul, in private and almost with her own eyes turned away. "No," she said.

fretting (par. 113): fussing

dogged (par. 121): stubborn

obscenity (par. 125): offensiveness

126   "I known it," he muttered, sitting up. "You're just playing me for a sucker."

127   "Oh no no!" she cried. "It joins on at the knee. Only at the knee. Why do you want to see it?"

128   The boy gave her a long penetrating look. "Because," he said, "it's what makes you different. You ain't like anybody else."

129   She sat staring at him. There was nothing about her face or her round freezing-blue eyes to indicate that this had moved her; but she felt as if her heart had stopped and left her mind to pump her blood. She decided that for the first time in her life she was face to face with real innocence. This boy, with an instinct that came from beyond wisdom, had touched the truth about her. When after a minute, she said in a hoarse high voice, "All right," it was like surrendering to him completely. It was like losing her own life and finding it again, miraculously, in his.

130   Very gently he began to roll the slack leg up. The artificial limb, in a white sock and brown flat shoe, was bound in a heavy material like canvas and ended in an ugly jointure where it was attached to the stump. The boy's face and his voice were entirely reverent as he uncovered it and said, "Now show me how to take it off and on."

131   She took it off for him and put it back on again and then he took it off himself, handling it as tenderly as if it were a real one. "See!" he said with a delighted child's face. "Now I can do it myself!"

132   "Put it back on," she said. She was thinking that she would run away with him and that every night he would take the leg off and every morning put it back on again. "Put it back on," she said.

133   "Not yet," he murmured, setting it on its foot out of her reach. "Leave it off for a while. You got me instead."

134   She gave a little cry of alarm but he pushed her down and began to kiss her again. Without the leg she felt entirely dependent on him. Her brain seemed to have stopped thinking altogether and to be about some other function that it was not very good at. Different expressions raced back and forth over her face. Every now and then the boy, his eyes like two steel spikes, would glance behind him where the leg stood. Finally she pushed him off and said, "Put it back on me now."

135   "Wait," he said. He leaned the other way and pulled the valise toward him and opened it. It had a pale blue spotted lining and there were only two Bibles in it. He took one of these out and opened the cover of it. It was hollow and contained a pocket flask of whiskey, a pack of cards, and a small blue box with printing on it. He laid these out in front of her one at a time in an evenly-spaced row, like one presenting offerings at the shrine of a goddess. He put the blue box in her hand. THIS PRODUCT TO BE USED ONLY FOR THE PREVENTION OF DISEASE, she read, and dropped it. The boy was unscrewing the top of the flask. He stopped and pointed, with a smile, to the deck of cards. It was not an ordinary deck but one with an obscene picture on the back of each card. "Take a swig," he said, offering her the bottle first. He held it in front of her, but like one mesmerized, she did not move.

136   Her voice when she spoke had an almost pleading sound. "Aren't you," she murmured, "aren't you just good country people?"

137   The boy cocked his head. He looked as if he were just beginning to understand that she might be trying to insult him. "Yeah," he said, curling his lip slightly, "but it ain't held me back none. I'm as good as you any day in the week."

shrine (par. 135): place of worship

mesmerized (par. 135): hypnotized

138   "Give me my leg," she said.

139   He pushed it farther away with his foot. "Come on now, let's begin to have us a good time," he said coaxingly. "We ain't got to know one another good yet."

140   "Give me my leg!" she screamed and tried to lunge for it but he pushed her down easily.

141   "What's the matter with you all of a sudden?" he asked, frowning as he screwed the top on the flask and put it quickly back inside the Bible. "You just a while ago said you didn't believe in nothing. I thought you was some girl!"

142   Her face was almost purple. "You're a Christian!" she hissed. "You're a fine Christian! You're just like them all—say one thing and do another. You're a perfect Christian, you're . . ."

143   The boy's mouth was set angrily. "I hope you don't think," he said in a lofty indignant tone, "that I believe in that crap! I may sell Bibles but I know which end is up and I wasn't born yesterday and I know where I'm going!"

144   "Give me my leg!" she screeched. He jumped up so quickly that she barely saw him sweep the cards and the blue box into the Bible and throw the Bible into the valise. She saw him grab the leg and then she saw it for an instant slanted forlornly across the inside of the suitcase with a Bible at either side of its opposite ends. He slammed the lid shut and snatched up the valise and swung it down the hole and then stepped through himself.

145   When all of him had passed but his head, he turned and regarded her with a look that no longer had any admiration in it. "I've gotten a lot of interesting things," he said. "One time I got a woman's glass eye this way. And you needn't to think you'll catch me because Pointer ain't really my name. I use a different name at every house I call at and don't stay nowhere long. And I'll tell you another thing, Hulga," he said, using the name as if he didn't think much of it, "you ain't so smart. I been believing in nothing ever since I was born!" and then the toast-colored hat disappeared down the hole and the girl was left, sitting on the straw in the dusty sunlight. When she turned her churning face toward the opening, she saw his blue figure struggling successfully over the green speckled lake.

146   Mrs. Hopewell and Mrs. Freeman, who were in the back pasture, digging up onions, saw him emerge a little later from the woods and head across the meadow toward the highway. "Why, that looks like that nice dull young man that tried to sell me a Bible yesterday," Mrs. Hopewell said, squinting. "He must have been selling them to the Negroes back in there. He was so simple," she said, "but I guess the world would be better off if we were all that simple."

147   Mrs. Freeman's gaze drove forward and just touched him before he disappeared under the hill. Then she returned her attention to the evil-smelling onion shoot she was lifting from the ground. "Some can't be that simple," she said. "I know I never could."

coaxingly (par. 139): in a persuading manner

lofty (par. 143): proud

indignant (par. 143): angry

forlornly (par. 144): literally, forlorn means deserted or forsaken

emerge (par. 146): come out

3

ESSAYS

A Hanging

George Orwell

1   It was in Burma, a sodden morning of the rains. A sickly light, like yellow tinfoil, was slanting over the high walls into the jail yard. We were waiting outside the condemned cells, a row of sheds fronted with double bars, like small animal cages. Each cell measured about ten feet by ten and was quite bare within except for a plank bed and a pot for drinking water. In some of them brown silent men were squatting at the inner bars, with their blankets draped round them. These were the condemned men, due to be hanged within the next week or two.

2   One prisoner had been brought out of his cell. He was a Hindu, a puny wisp of a man, with a shaven head and vague liquid eyes. He had a thick, sprouting moustache, absurdly too big for his body, rather like the moustache of a comic man of the films. Six tall Indian warders were guarding him and getting him ready for the gallows. Two of them stood by with rifles with fixed bayonets, while the other handcuffed him, passed a chain through his handcuffs and fixed it to their belts, and lashed his arms tight to his sides. They crowded very close about him, with their hands always on him in a careful, caressing grip, as though all the while feeling him to make sure he was there. It was like men handling a fish which is still alive and may jump back into the water. But he stood quite unresisting, yielding his arms limply to the ropes, as though he hardly noticed what was happening.

3   Eight o'clock struck and a bugle call, desolately thin in the wet air, floated from the distant barracks. The superintendent of the jail, who was standing apart from the rest of us, moodily prodding the gravel with his stick, raised his head at the sound. He was an army doctor, with a grey toothbrush moustache and a gruff voice. "For God's sake hurry up, Francis," he said irritably. "The man ought to have been dead by this time. Aren't you ready yet?"

4   Francis, the head jailer, a fat Dravidian in a white drill suit and gold spectacles, waved his black hand. "Yes sir, yes sir," he bubbled. "All iss satisfactorily prepared. The hangman iss waiting. We shall proceed."

5   "Well, quick march, then. The prisoners can't get their breakfast till this job's over."

6   We set out for the gallows. Two warders marched on either side of the prisoner, with their rifles at the slope; two others marched close against him, gripping him by arm and shoulder, as though at once pushing and supporting him. The rest of us, magistrates and the like, followed behind. Suddenly, when we had gone ten yards, the procession stopped short without any order or warning. A dreadful thing had happened—a dog, come goodness knows whence, had appeared in the yard. It came bounding among us with a loud volley of barks, and leapt round us wagging its whole body, wild with glee at finding so many

sodden (par. 1): soaked with water

desolately (par. 3): lonely, gloomy

Dravidian (par. 4): a member of the original native population of Southern India

magistrates (par. 6): officials who have the authority to enforce the law

human beings together. It was a large wooly dog, half Airedale, half pariah. For a moment it pranced round us, and then, before anyone could stop it, it had made a dash for the prisoner, and jumping up, tried to lick his face. Everyone stood aghast, too taken aback even to grab at the dog.

7   "Who let that bloody brute in here?" said the superintendent angrily. "Catch it, someone!"

8   A warder, detached from the escort, charged clumsily after the dog, but it danced and gambolled just out of his reach, taking everything as part of the game. A young Eurasian jailer picked up a handful of gravel and tried to stone the dog away, but it dodged the stones and came after us again. Its yaps echoed from the jail walls. The prisoner, in the grasp of the two warders, looked on incuriously, as though this was another formality of the hanging. It was several minutes before someone managed to catch the dog. Then we put my handkerchief through its collar and moved off once more, with the dog still straining and whimpering.

9   It was about forty yards to the gallows. I watched the bare brown back of the prisoner marching in front of me. He walked clumsily with his bound arms, but quite steadily, with the bobbing gait of the Indian who never straightens his knees. At each step his muscles slid neatly into place, the lock of hair on his scalp danced up and down, his feet printed themselves on the wet gravel. And once, in spite of the men who gripped him by each shoulder, he stepped slightly aside to avoid a puddle on the path.

10   It is curious, but till that moment I had never realized what it means to destroy a healthy, conscious man. When I saw the prisoner step aside to avoid the puddle, I saw the mystery, the unspeakable wrongness, of cutting a life short when it is in full tide. This man was not dying, he was alive just as we are alive. All the organs of his body were working—bowels digesting food, skin renewing itself, nails growing, tissues forming—all toiling away in solemn foolery. His nails would still be growing when he stood on the drop, when he was falling through the air with a tenth-of-a-second to live. His eyes saw the yellow gravel and the grey walls, and his brain still remembered, foresaw, reasoned—reasoned even about puddles. He and we were a party of men walking together, seeing, hearing, feeling, understanding the same world; and in two minutes, with a sudden snap, one of us would be gone—one mind less, one world less.

11   The gallows stood in a small yard, separate from the main grounds of the prison, and overgrown with tall prickly weeds. It was a brick erection like three sides of a shed, with planking on top, and above that two beams and a crossbar with the rope dangling. The hangman, a grey-haired convict in the white uniform of the prison, was waiting beside his machine. He greeted us with a servile crouch as we entered. At a word from Francis the two warders, gripping the prisoner more closely than ever, half led half pushed him to the gallows and helped him clumsily up the ladder. Then the hangman climbed up and fixed the rope round the prisoner's neck.

12   We stood waiting, five yards away. The warders had formed in a rough circle round the gallows. And then, when the noose was fixed, the prisoner began crying out to his god. It was a high, reiterated cry of "Ram! Ram! Ram! Ram!"

pariah (par. 6): an outcast

aghast (par. 6): shocked

gambolled (par. 8): leaped playfully

Eurasian (par. 8): one who is of European and Asian descent

gait (par. 9): walk

servile crouch (par. 11): bending like an obedient servant

reiterated (par. 12): repeated

not urgent and fearful like a prayer or cry for help, but steady, rhythmical, almost like the tolling of a bell. The dog answered the sound with a whine. The hangman, still standing on the gallows, produced a small cotton bag like a flour bag and drew it down over the prisoner's face. But the sound, muffled by the cloth, still persisted, over and over again: "Ram! Ram! Ram! Ram! Ram!"

13   The hangman climbed down and stood ready, holding the lever. Minutes seemed to pass. The steady, muffled crying from the prisoner went on and on "Ram! Ram! Ram!" never faltering for an instant. The superintendent, his head on his chest, was slowly poking the ground with his stick; perhaps he was counting the cries, allowing the prisoner a fixed number—fifty, perhaps, or a hundred. Everyone had changed color. The Indians had gone grey like bad coffee, and one or two of the bayonets were wavering. We looked at the lashed, hooded man on the drop, and listened to his cries—each cry another second of life; the same thought was in all our minds: oh, kill him quickly, get it over, stop that abominable noise!

14   Suddenly the superintendent made up his mind. Throwing up his head he made a swift motion with his stick. "Chalo!" he shouted almost fiercely.

15   There was a clanking noise, and the dead silence. The prisoner had vanished, and the rope was twisted on itself. I let go of the dog, and it galloped immediately to the back of the gallows; but when it got there it stopped short, barked, and then retreated into a corner of the yard, where it stood among the weeds, looking timorously out at us. We went round the gallows to inspect the prisoner's body. He was dangling with his toes pointed straight downwards, very slowly revolving, as dead as a stone.

16   The superintendent reached out with his stick and poked the bare body; it oscillated, slightly. "*He's* all right," said the superintendent. He backed out from under the gallows, and blew out a deep breath. The moody look had gone out of his face quite suddenly. He glanced at his wrist-watch. "Eight minutes past eight. Well, that's all for this morning, thank God."

17   The warders unfixed bayonets and marched away. The dog, sobered and conscious of having misbehaved itself, slipped after them. We walked out of the gallows yard, past the condemned cells with their waiting prisoners, into the big central yard of the prison. The convicts, under the command of warders armed with lathis, were already receiving their breakfast. They squatted in long rows, each man holding a tin pannikin, while two warders with buckets marched round ladling out rice; it seemed quite a homely, jolly scene, after the hanging. An enormous relief had come upon us now that the job was done. One felt an impulse to sing, to break into a run, to snigger. All at once everyone began chattering gaily.

18   The Eurasian boy walking beside me nodded towards the way we had come, with a knowing smile: "Do you know, sir, our friend (he meant the dead man), when he heard his appeal had been dismissed, he pissed on the floor of his cell. From fright. Kindly take one of my cigarettes, sir. Do you not admire my new silver case, sir? From the boxwallah, two rupees eight annas. Classy European style."

abominable (par. 13): awful

"Chalo" (par. 14): start

timorously (par. 15): timidly, shyly

oscillated (par. 16): moved back and forth

lathis (par. 17): clubs

pannikin (par. 17): cup

boxwallah (par. 18): peddler

rupees and *annas* (par. 18): rupees are the basic monetary unit of India; annas are equal to one-sixteenth of a rupee.

19   Several people laughed—at what, nobody seemed certain.

20   Francis was walking by the superintendent, talking garrulously: "Well, sir, all hass passed off with the utmost satisfactoriness. It wass all finished—flick! like that. It iss not always so—oah, no! I have known cases where the doctor wass obliged to go beneath the gallows and pull the prissoner's legs to ensure decease. Most disagreeable!"

21   "Wriggling about, eh? That's bad," said the superintendent.

22   "Ach, sir, it iss worse when they become refractory! One man, I recall, clung to the bars of hiss cage when we went to take him out. You will scarely credit, sir, that it took six warders to dislodge him, three pulling at each leg. We reasoned with him. 'My dear fellow,' we said, 'think of all the pain and trouble you are causing to us!' But no, he would not listen! Ach, he was very troublesome!"

23   I found that I was laughing quite loudly. Everyone was laughing. Even the superintendent grinned in a tolerant way. "You'd better all come out and have a drink," he said quite genially. "I've got a bottle of whisky in the car. We could do with it."

24   We went through the big double gates of the prison, into the road. "Pulling at his legs!" exclaimed a Burmese magistrate suddenly, and burst into a loud chuckling. We all began laughing again. At that moment Francis's anecdote seemed extraordinarily funny. We all had a drink together, native and European alike, quite amicably. The dead man was a hundred yards away.

talking garrulously (par. 20): talking in a rambling manner, babbling

refractory (par. 22): stubborn

genially (par. 23): pleasantly

amicably (par. 24): friendly

Death and Justice

Edward Koch

1   Last December a man named Robert Lee Willie, who had been convicted of raping and murdering an 18-year-old woman, was executed in a Louisiana state prison. In a statement issued several minutes before his death, Mr. Willie said: "Killing people is wrong. . . . It makes no difference whether it's citizens, countries, or governments. Killing is wrong." Two weeks later in South Carolina, an admitted killer named Joseph Carl Shaw was put to death for murdering two teenagers. In an appeal to the governor for clemency, Mr. Shaw wrote: "Killing was wrong when I did it. Killing is wrong when you do it. I hope you have the courage and the moral strength to stop the killing."

2   It is a curiosity of modern life that we find ourselves being lectured on morality by cold-blooded killers. Mr. Willie previously had been convicted of aggravated rape, aggravated kidnapping, and the murders of a Louisiana deputy and a man from Missouri. Mr. Shaw committed another murder a week before the two for which he was executed, and admitted mutilating the body of a 14-year-old girl he killed. I can't help wondering what prompted these murderers to speak out against killing as they entered the death-house door. Did their new-

clemency (par. 1): a reduction of the sentence given a criminal found reverence for life stem from the realization that they were about to lose their own?

3   Life is indeed precious, and I believe the death penalty helps to affirm this fact. Had the death penalty been a real possibility in the minds of these murderers, they might well have stayed their hand. They might have shown moral awareness before their victims died, and not after. Consider the tragic death of Rosa Velez, who happened to be home when a man named Luis Vera burglarized her apartment in Brooklyn. "Yeah, I shot her," Vera admitted. "She knew me, and I knew I wouldn't go to the chair."

4   During my 22 years in public service, I have heard the pros and cons of capital punishment expressed with special intensity. As a district leader, councilman, congressman, and mayor, I have represented constituencies generally thought of as liberal. Because I support the death penalty for heinous crimes of murder, I have sometimes been the subject of emotional and outraged attacks by voters who find my position reprehensible or worse. I have listened to their ideas. I have weighed their objections carefully. I still support the death penalty. The reasons I maintain my position can be best understood by examining the arguments most frequently heard in opposition.

5   (1) *The death penalty is "barbaric."* Sometimes opponents of capital punishment horrify with tales of lingering death on the gallows, of faulty electric chairs, or of agony in the gas chamber. Partly in response to such protests, several states such as North Carolina and Texas switched to death by lethal injection. The condemned person is put to death painlessly, without ropes, voltage, bullets, or gas. Did this answer the objections of death penalty opponents? Of course not. On June 22, 1984, *The New York Times* published an editorial that sarcastically attacked the new "hygienic" method of death by injection, and stated that "execution can never be made humane through science." So it's not the method that really troubles opponents. It's the death itself they consider barbaric.

6   Admittedly, capital punishment is not a pleasant topic. However, one does not have to like the death penalty in order to support it any more than one must like radical surgery, radiation, or chemotherapy in order to find necessary these attempts at curing cancer. Ultimately we may learn how to cure cancer with a simple pill. Unfortunately, that day has not yet arrived. Today we are faced with the choice of letting the cancer spread or trying to cure it with the methods available, methods that one day will almost certainly be considered barbaric. But to give up and do nothing would be far more barbaric and would certainly delay the discovery of an eventual cure. The analogy between cancer and murder is

affirm (par. 3): confirm, support

stayed (par. 3): stopped

the chair (par. 3): that is, the electric chair

constituencies (par. 4): groups of voters

liberal (par. 4): one who tends to favor social or political reform; a conservative is one who tends to favor the preservation of existing social or political systems.

heinous (par. 4): horribly evil

reprehensible (par. 4): deserving strong criticism

"barbaric" (par. 5): brutal, uncivilized

lethal (par. 5): deadly

"hygienic" (par. 5): clean, neat

humane (par. 5): compassionate

analogy (par. 6): comparison

imperfect, because murder is not the "disease" we are trying to cure. The disease is injustice. We may not like the death penalty, but it must be available to punish crimes of cold-blooded murder, cases in which any other form of punishment would be inadequate and, therefore, unjust. If we create a society in which injustice is not tolerated, incidents of murder—the most flagrant form of injustice—will diminish.

7   (2) *No other major democracy uses the death penalty.* No other major democracy—in fact, few other countries of any description—are plagued by a murder rate such as that in the United States. Fewer and fewer Americans can remember the days when unlocked doors were the norm and murder was a rare and terrible offense. In America the murder rate climbed 122 percent between 1963 and 1980. During that same period, the murder rate in New York City increased by almost 400 percent, and the statistics are even worse in many other cities. A study at M.I.T. showed that based on 1970 homicide rates a person who lived in a large American city ran a greater risk of being murdered than an American soldier in World War II ran of being killed in combat. It is not surprising that the laws of each country differ according to differing conditions and traditions. If other countries had our murder problem, the cry for capital punishment would be just as loud as it is here. And I dare say that any other major democracy where 75 percent of the people supported the death penalty would soon enact it into law.

8   (3) *An innocent person might be executed by mistake.* Consider the work of Adam Bedau, one of the most implacable foes of capital punishment in this country. According to Mr. Bedau, it is "false sentimentality to argue that the death penalty should be abolished because of the abstract possibility that an innocent person might be executed." He cites a study of the 7,000 executions in this country from 1893 to 1971, and concludes that the record fails to show that such cases occur. The main point, however, is this. If government functioned only when the possibility of error didn't exist, government wouldn't function at all. Human life deserves special protection, and one of the best ways to guarantee that protection is to assure that convicted murderers do not kill again. Only the death penalty can accomplish this end. In a recent case in New Jersey, a man named Richard Biegenwald was freed from prison after serving 18 years for murder; since his release he has been convicted of committing four murders. A prisoner named Lemuel Smith, who, while serving four life sentences for murder (plus two life sentences for kidnapping and robbery) in New York's Green Haven Prison, lured a woman corrections officer into the chaplain's office and strangled her. He then mutilated and dismembered her body. An additional life sentence for Smith is meaningless. Because New York has no death penalty statute, Smith has effectively been given a license to kill.

9   But the problem of multiple murder is not confined to the nation's penitentiaries. In 1981, 91 police officers were killed in the line of duty in this country. Seven percent of those arrested in the cases that have been solved had a previous arrest for murder. In New York City in 1976 and 1977, 85 persons arrested for homicide had a previous arrest for murder. Six of these individuals had two previous arrests for murder, and one had four previous murder arrests. During

---

flagrant (par. 6): obvious

M.I.T. (par. 7): Massachusetts Institute of Technology

implacable (par. 8): unchanging

dismembered (par. 8): cut the limbs off

statute (par. 8): law

those two years the New York police were arresting for murder persons with a previous arrest for murder on the average of one every 8.5 days. This is not surprising when we learn that in 1975, for example, the median time served in Massachusetts for homicide was less than two-and-a-half years. In 1976 a study sponsored by the Twentieth Century Fund found the average time served in the United States for first degree murder is ten years. The median time served may be considerably lower.

10   (4) *Capital punishment cheapens the value of human life.* On the contrary, it can be easily demonstrated that the death penalty strengthens the value of human life. If the penalty for rape were lowered, clearly it would signal a lessened regard for the victims' suffering, humiliation, and personal integrity. It would cheapen their horrible experience, and expose them to an increased danger of recurrence. When we lower the penalty for murder, it signals a lessened regard for the value of the victim's life. Some critics of capital punishment, such as columnist Jimmy Breslin, have suggested that a life sentence is actually a harsher penalty for murder than death. This is sophistic nonsense. A few killers may decide not to appeal a death sentence, but the overwhelming majority make every effort to stay alive. It is by exacting the highest penalty for the taking of human life that we affirm the highest value of human life.

11   (5) *The death penalty is applied in a discriminatory manner.* This factor no longer seems to be the problem it once was. The appeals process for a condemned prisoner is lengthy and painstaking. Every effort is made to see that the verdict and sentence were fairly arrived at. However, assertions of discrimination are not an argument for ending the death penalty but for extending it. It is not justice to exclude everyone from the penalty of the law if a few are found to be so favored. Justice requires that the law be applied equally to all.

12   (6) *Thou Shalt Not Kill.* The Bible is our greatest source of moral inspiration. Opponents of the death penalty frequently cite the sixth of the Ten Commandments in an attempt to prove that capital punishment is divinely proscribed. In the original Hebrew, however, the Sixth Commandment reads, "Thou Shall Not Commit Murder," and the Torah specifies capital punishment for a variety of offenses. The biblical viewpoint has been upheld by philosophers throughout history. The greatest thinkers of the 19th century—Kant, Locke, Hobbes, Rousseau, Montesquieu, and Mill—agreed that natural law properly authorizes the sovereign to take life in order to vindicate justice. Only Jeremy Bentham was ambivalent. Washington, Jefferson, and Franklin endorsed it. Abraham Lincoln authorized executions for deserters in wartime. Alexis de Tocqueville, who expressed profound respect for American institutions, believed that the death penalty was indispensable to the support of social order. The United States Constitution, widely admired as one of the seminal achievements in the history of humanity, condemns cruel and inhuman punishment, but does not condemn capital punishment.

13   (7) *The death penalty is state-sanctioned murder.* This is the defense with

sophistic (par. 10): clever

assertions (par. 11): claims

proscribed (par. 12): forbidden

Torah (par. 12): sacred law of Judaism; first five books of the Old Testament

sovereign (par. 12): ruler

vindicate (par. 12): defend

ambivalent (par. 12): unsure

indispensable (par. 12): necessary

seminal (par. 12): creative

which Messrs. Willie and Shaw hoped to soften the resolve of those who sentenced them to death. By saying in effect, "You're no better than I am," the murderer seeks to bring his accusers down to his own level. It is also a popular argument among opponents of capital punishment, but a transparently false one. Simply put, the state has rights that the private individual does not. In a democracy, those rights are given to the state by the electorate. The execution of a lawfully condemned killer is no more an act of murder than is legal imprisonment an act of kidnapping. If an individual forces a neighbor to pay him money under a threat of punishment, it's called extortion. If the state does it, it's called taxation. Rights and responsibilities surrendered by the individual are what give the state its power to govern. This contract is the foundation of civilization itself.

14   Everyone wants his or her rights, and will defend them zealously. Not everyone, however, wants responsibilities, especially the painful responsibilities that come with law enforcement. Twenty-one years ago a woman named Kitty Genovese was assaulted and murdered on a street in New York. Dozens of neighbors heard her cries for help but did nothing to assist her. They didn't even call the police. In such a climate the criminal understandably grows bolder. In the presence of moral cowardice, he lectures us on our supposed failings and tries to equate his crimes with our quest for justice.

15   The death of anyone—even a convicted killer—diminishes us all. But we are diminished even more by a justice system that fails to function. It is an illusion to let ourselves believe that doing away with capital punishment removes the murderer's deed from our conscience. The rights of society are paramount. When we protect guilty lives, we give up innocent lives in exchange. When opponents of capital punishment say to the state: "I will not let you kill in my name," they are also saying to murderers: "You can kill in your *own* name as long as I have an excuse for not getting involved."

16   It is hard to imagine anything worse than being murdered while neighbors do nothing. But something worse exists. When those neighbors shrink back from justly punishing the murderer, the victim dies twice.

resolve (par. 13): determination

transparently (par. 13): obviously

electorate (par. 13): voters

zealously (par. 14): passionately

diminishes (par. 15): lessens

paramount (par. 15): most important

Shame

Dick Gregory

1   I never learned hate at home, or shame. I had to go to school for that. I was about seven years old when I got my first big lesson. I was in love with a little girl named Helene Tucker, a light-complexioned little girl with pigtails and nice manners. She was always clean and she was smart in school. I think I went to school mostly to look at her. I brushed my hair and even got me a little old handkerchief. It was a lady's handkerchief, but I didn't want Helene to see me wipe my nose on my hand. The pipes were frozen again, there was no water in the

house, but I washed my socks and shirt every night. I'd get a pot, and go over to Mr. Ben's grocery store, and stick my pot down into his soda machine. Scoop out some chopped ice. By evening the ice melted to water for washing. I got sick a lot that winter because the fire would go out at night before the clothes were dry. In the morning I'd put them on, wet or dry, because they were the only clothes I had.

2   Everybody's got a Helene Tucker, a symbol of everything you want. I loved her for her goodness, her cleanness, her popularity. She'd walk down my street and my brothers and sisters would yell, ''Here comes Helene,'' and I'd rub my tennis sneakers on the back of my pants and wish my hair wasn't so nappy and the white folk's shirt fit me better. I'd run out on the street. If I knew my place and didn't come too close, she'd wink at me and say hello. That was a good feeling. Sometimes I'd follow her all the way home, and shovel the snow off her walk and try to make friends with her Momma and her aunts. I'd drop money on her stoop late at night on my way back from shining shoes in the taverns. And she had a Daddy, and he had a good job. He was a paper hanger.

3   I guess I would have gotten over Helene by summertime, but something happened in that classroom that made her face hang in front of me for the next twenty-two years. When I played the drums in high school it was for Helene and when I broke track records in college it was for Helene and when I started standing behind microphones and heard applause I wished Helene could hear it, too. It wasn't until I was twenty-nine years old and married and making money that I really got her out of my system. Helene was sitting in that classroom when I learned to be ashamed of myself.

4   It was on a Thursday. I was sitting in the back of the room, in a seat with a chalk circle drawn around it. The idiot's seat, the troublemaker's seat.

5   The teacher thought I was stupid. Couldn't spell, couldn't read, couldn't do arithmetic. Just stupid. Teachers were never interested in finding out that you couldn't concentrate because you were so hungry, because you hadn't had any breakfast. All you could think about was noontime, would it ever come? Maybe you could sneak in to the cloakroom and steal a bite of some kid's lunch out of a coat pocket. A bite of something. Paste. You can't really make a meal of paste, or put it on bread for a sandwich, but sometimes I'd scoop a few spoonfuls out of the paste jar in the back of the room. Pregnant people get strange tastes. I was pregnant with poverty. Pregnant with dirt and pregnant with smells that made people turn away, pregnant with cold and pregnant with shoes that were never bought for me, pregnant with five other people in my bed and no Daddy in the next room, and pregnant with hunger. Paste doesn't taste too bad when you're hungry.

6   The teacher thought I was a troublemaker. All she saw from the front of the room was a little black boy who squirmed in his idiot's seat and made noises and poked the kids around him. I guess she couldn't see a kid who made noises because he wanted someone to know he was there.

7   It was on a Thursday, the day before the Negro payday. The eagle always flew on Friday. The teacher was asking each student how much his father would give to the Community Chest. On Friday night, each kid would get the money from his father, and on Monday he would bring it to the school. I decided I was going to buy me a Daddy right then. I had money in my pocket from shining shoes and selling papers, and whatever Helene Tucker pledged for her Daddy I was going to top it. And I'd hand the money right in. I wasn't going to wait until Monday to buy me a Daddy.

8   I was shaking, scared to death. The teacher opened her book and started calling out names alphabetically.

The eagle always flew on Friday (par. 7): Friday was payday; the eagle was a gold coin.

9   "Helene Tucker?"

10   "My Daddy said he'd give two dollars and fifty cents."

11   "That's very nice, Helene. Very, very nice indeed."

12   That made me feel pretty good. It wouldn't take too much to top that. I had almost three dollars in dimes and quarters in my pocket. I stuck my hand in my pocket and held onto the money, waiting for her to call my name. But the teacher closed her book after she called everybody else in the class.

13   I stood up and raised my hand.

14   "What is it now?"

15   "You forgot me."

16   She turned toward the blackboard. "I don't have time to be playing with you, Richard."

17   "My Daddy said he'd . . ."

18   "Sit down, Richard, you're disturbing the class."

19   "My Daddy said he'd give . . . fifteen dollars."

20   She turned and looked mad. "We are collecting this money for you and your kind, Richard Gregory. If your Daddy can give fifteen dollars you have no business being on relief."

21   "I got it right now, I got it right now, my Daddy gave it to me to turn in to-day, my Daddy said . . ."

22   "And furthermore," she said, looking right at me, her nostrils getting big and her lips getting thin and her eyes opening wide, "we know you don't have a Daddy."

23   Helene Tucker turned around, her eyes full of tears. She felt sorry for me. Then I couldn't see her too well because I was crying, too.

24   "Sit down, Richard."

25   And I always thought the teacher kind of liked me. She always picked me to wash the blackboard on Friday, after school. That was a big thrill, it made me feel important. If I didn't wash it, come Monday the school might not function right.

26   "Where are you going, Richard?"

27   I walked out of school that day, and for a long time I didn't go back very often. There was shame there.

28   Now there was shame everywhere. It seemed like the whole world had been inside that classroom, everyone had heard what the teacher had said, everyone had turned around and felt sorry for me. There was shame in going to the Worthy Boys Annual Christmas Dinner for you and your kind, because everybody knew what a worthy boy was. Why couldn't they just call it the Boys Annual Dinner, why'd they have to give it a name? There was shame in wearing the brown and orange and white plaid mackinaw the welfare gave to three thousand boys. Why'd it have to be the same for everybody so when you walked down the street the people could see you were on relief? It was a nice warm mackinaw and it had a hood, and my Momma beat me and called me a little rat when she found out I stuffed it in the bottom of a pail full of garbage way over on Cottage Street. There was shame in running over to Mister Ben's at the end of the day and asking for his rotten peaches, there was shame in asking Mrs. Simmons for a spoonful of sugar, there was shame in running out to meet the relief truck. I hated that truck, full of food for you and your kind. I ran into the house and hid when it came. And then I started to sneak through alleys, to take the long way home so the people going into White's Eat Shop wouldn't see me. Yeah, the whole world heard the teacher that day, we all know you don't have a Daddy.

being on relief (par. 20): getting welfare

Daddy Tucked The Blanket

Randall Williams

1   About the time I turned 16, my folks began to wonder why I didn't stay home any more. I always had an excuse for them, but what I didn't say was that I had found my freedom and I was getting out.

2   I went through four years of high school in semi-rural Alabama and became active in clubs and sports; I made a lot of friends and became a regular guy, if you know what I mean. But one thing was irregular about me: I managed those four years without ever having a friend visit at my house.

3   I was ashamed of where I lived. I had been ashamed for as long as I had been conscious of class.

4   We had a big family. There were several of us sleeping in one room, but that's not so bad if you get along, and we always did. As you get older, though, it gets worse.

5   Being poor is a humiliating experience for a young person trying hard to be accepted. Even now—several years removed—it is hard to talk about. And I resent the weakness of these words to make you feel what it was really like.

6   We lived in a lot of old houses. We moved a lot because we were always looking for something just a little better than what we had. You have to understand that my folks worked harder than most people. My mother was always at home, but for her that was a full-time job—and no fun, either. But my father worked his head off from the time I can remember in construction and shops. It was hard, physical work.

7   I tell you this to show that we weren't shiftless. No matter how much money Daddy made, we never made much progress up the social ladder. I got out thanks to a college scholarship and because I was a little more articulate than the average.

8   I have seen my Daddy wrap copper wire through the soles of his boots to keep them together in the wintertime. He couldn't buy new boots because he had used the money for food and shoes for us. We lived like hell, but we went to school well-clothed and with a full stomach.

9   It really is hell to live in a house that was in bad shape 10 years before you moved in. And a big family puts a lot of wear and tear on a new house, too, so you can imagine how one goes downhill if it is teetering when you move in. But we lived in houses that were sweltering in summer and freezing in winter. I woke up every morning for a year and a half with plaster on my face where it had fallen out of the ceiling during the night.

10   This wasn't during the Depression; this was in the late 60's and early 70's.

11   When we boys got old enough to learn trades in school, we would try to fix up the old houses we lived in. But have you ever tried to paint a wall that crumbled when the roller went across it? And bright paint emphasized the holes in the wall. You end up more frustrated than when you began, especially when

shiftless (par. 7): lazy, irresponsible

teetering (par. 9): in poor condition

you know that at best you might come up with only enough money to improve one of the six rooms in the house. And we might move out soon after, anyway.

12   The same goes for keeping a house like that clean. If you have a house full of kids and the house is deteriorating, you'll never keep it clean. Daddy used to yell at Mama about that, but she couldn't do anything. I think Daddy knew it inside, but he had to have an outlet for his rage somewhere, and at least yelling isn't as bad as hitting, which they never did to each other.

13   But you have a kitchen which has no counter space and no hot water, and you will have dirty dishes stacked up. That sounds like an excuse, but try it. You'll go mad from the sheer sense of futility. It's the same thing in a house with no closets. You can't keep clothes clean and rooms in order if they have to be stacked up with things.

14   Living in a bad house is generally worse on girls. For one thing, they traditionally help their mother with the housework. We boys could get outside and work in the field or cut wood or even play ball and forget about living conditions. The sky was still pretty.

15   But the girls got the pressure, and as they got older it became worse. Would they accept dates knowing they had to "receive" the young man in a dirty hallway with broken windows, peeling wallpaper and a cracked ceiling? You have to live it to understand it, but it creates a shame which drives the soul of a young person inward.

16   I'm thankful none of us ever blamed our parents for this, because it would have crippled our relationships. As it worked out, only the relationship between our parents was damaged. And I think the harshness which they expressed to each other was just an outlet to get rid of their anger at the trap their lives were in. It ruined their marriage because they had no one to yell at but each other. I knew other families where the kids got the abuse, but we were too much loved for that.

17   Once I was about 16 and Mama and Daddy had a particularly violent argument about the washing machine, which had broken down. Daddy was on the back porch—that's where the only water faucet was—trying to fix it and Mamma had a washtub out there washing school clothes for the next day and they were screaming at each other.

18   Later that night everyone was in bed and I heard Daddy get up from the couch where he was reading. I looked out from my bed across the hall into their room. He was standing right over Mamma and she was already asleep. He pulled the blanket up and tucked it around her shoulders and just stood there and tears were dropping off his cheeks and I thought I could faintly hear them splashing against the linoleum rug.

19   Now they're divorced.

20   I had courses in college where housing was discussed, but the sociologists never put enough emphasis on the impact living in substandard housing has on a person's psyche. Especially children's.

21   Small children have a hard time understanding poverty. They want the same things children from more affluent families have. They want the same things they see advertised on television, and they don't understand why they can't have them.

22   Other children can be incredibly cruel. I was in elementary school in Geor-

deteriorating (par. 12): decaying, falling apart

futility (par. 13): inability to accomplish something

psyche (par. 20): soul, spirit

affluent (par. 21): wealthy

gia—and this is interesting because it is the only thing I remember about that particular school—when I was about eight or nine.

23   After Christmas vacation had ended, my teacher made each student describe all his or her Christmas presents. I became more and more uncomfortable as the privilege passed around the room towards me. Other children were reciting the names of the dolls they had been given, the kinds of bicycles and the grandeur of their games and toys. Some had lists which seemed to go on and on for hours.

24   It took me only a few seconds to tell the class that I had gotten for Christmas a belt and a pair of gloves. And then I was laughed at—because I cried—by a roomful of children and a teacher. I never forgave them, and that night I made my mother cry when I told her about it.

25   In retrospect, I am grateful for that moment, but I remember wanting to die at the time.

grandeur (par. 23): greatness

Too Big

Dwight MacDonald

1   The trouble is everything is too big. There are too many people, for example, in the city I live in. In walking along the street, one passes scores of other people every minute; any response to them as human beings is impossible; they must be passed by as indifferently as ants pass each other in the corridors of the anthill. A style of behavior which refuses to recognize the human existence of the others has grown up of necessity. Just the scale on which people congregate in such a city breaks down human solidarity, alienates people from each other. There are so many people that there aren't any people; 7,000,000 becomes 0; too big.

2   Some episodes:

3   (1) A friend was going home in the subway at about ten o'clock one night. About half the seats in his car were filled. Opposite him two men were sitting on either side of a third, who was very drunk. Without any attempt at concealment, they were going through the drunk's pockets and taking his watch, money, etc. A dozen people watched the performance from their seats, but no one, including my friend, did anything, and at the next station the two men let the drunk slide to the floor and got off the train.

4   (2) An elderly woman I know slipped going down the stairs in an "El" station and fell all the way to the bottom, where she lay stunned and gasping. A crowd of people—it was the rush hour—were waiting on the platform at the foot of the stairs. Some of them stared at her but no one moved to help her. She told me that she lay there several minutes, too shaken up even to speak; several people remarked "she must be drunk." Finally, a man did come forward and

congregate (par. 1): gather, assemble
solidarity (par. 1): unity, togetherness
alienates (par. 1): separates
"El" station (par. 4): an elevated train station

helped her to her feet. She was frightened by the incident. She had lived in New York all her life without realizing she was living among strangers.

5   (3) I was told a similar story about another person—the friend of a friend. He was knocked down on a mid-town street by a car late at night. The car didn't stop and no one saw the accident. He lay in the gutter, badly hurt and only half conscious, for five or six hours. There must have been scores, probably hundreds of people who passed by, saw him, thought "must be drunk" (the formula by which, in the city, one denies human recognition) and went on their way. Finally, the next morning, a policeman investigated and called an ambulance. (The policeman is the only person in a big city who is professionally required to see people as people, to break the shell of apartness that encases each human being.)

6   (4) The wife of a friend of mine last year became psychotic and is now being treated in an institution. She had been acting "queerly" for some time, but the first big outburst came about ten o'clock one night as they were returning home after visiting friends in Brooklyn. The wife suddenly began to accuse her husband of attempting to poison her; she became increasingly violent and suddenly broke away and began running down the street screaming "Help! Help! He's trying to kill me!" She ran along thus for several blocks, shouting, before he could overtake her and try to calm her. Although most of the houses showed lighted windows, for it was still early, not a door opened, not a window went up, no one paid the slightest attention. When he finally got his wife back to their apartment building, she broke away again as he was unlocking the door, and rushed into the hallway screaming for help. This lasted at least ten minutes, he told me, and again not a door opened, no one appeared although her cries and screams echoed all through the building. Finally a youth came downstairs in his bathrobe and shouted: "Shut up! We're trying to sleep!" He disappeared again immediately. A half hour later, after my friend had persuaded his wife to go inside, he received the first help since the nightmare had begun: Again in the form of a policeman, he had been sent for by some of the neighbors. (When people are forced to see others as human beings, they make contact vicariously through the police. What a "style" of communal relations!)

7   *But he, desiring to justify himself, said unto Jesus: "And who is my neighbor?" Jesus made answer and said: "A certain man was going down from Jerusalem to Jericho; and he fell among robbers, who stripped him and beat him, and departed, leaving him half dead. And by chance a certain priest was going down that way; and when he saw him, he passed by on the other side. And in like manner, a Levite also, when he came to the place and saw him, passed by on the other side. But a certain Samaritan, as he journeyed, came where he was; and when he saw him he was moved with compassion, and came to him, and bound up his wounds, pouring on them oil and wine; and he set him on his own beast and brought him to an inn and took care of him. And on the morrow he took out two shillings, and gave them to the host, and said: 'Take care of him, and whatsoever thou spendest more, I, when I come back again, will repay.' Which of these three, thinkest thou,*

encases (par. 5): surrounds

make contact vicariously (par. 6): to participate by having someone else take action

Par. 7: The closing paragraph is Luke 10: 29–37 and contains the parable (a story used to teach) of the Good Samaritan. Before this passage, it has been said that the second great law of Christianity is to love "thy neighbor as thyself."

Levite (par. 7): a member of the tribe of Levi, one of the twelve tribes of Israel

Samaritan (par. 7): a native of Samaria

the morrow (par. 7): the next day

proved neighbor to him that fell among the robbers?" And he said, "He that showed mercy on him." And Jesus said unto him, "Go, and do thou likewise."

Richard Cory, All Over Again

Roy Meador

1   The same as the rest of us, my friend wanted to be somebody. To make his mark in the world. To have his life count. At the end, he did make his mark in headlines: Deaths Called Murder-Suicide. *Son Finds Bodies.*

2   Carl L. Stinedurf was a good friend. We often lunched together, and our conversations ranged from politics to literature. Carl enjoyed ideas. He knew how to laugh. Face-to-face, most people used his middle name, Larry. But the waitress called him "Frank" because he preferred Sinatra's old records to new stuff. Carl often talked enthusiastically about his family, his son at the university, his daughter in high school. He mentioned his wife, Norma, with special pride. In her 30's, with his help she had finished college and begun teaching. Carl was delighted with his family's accomplishments. But underneath, well-masked, there must have been agonizing terror. Carl carried his pain in silence.

3   My friend worked as an estimator and customer representative for a large printing firm. He was gentle, always soft spoken, exceptionally conscientious. When I gave him work to do for my company, I knew it would be finished with care.

4   Carl tended toward the liberal. He thought more of people than of profits. He deplored cruelty. I considered him one of those who patiently keeps what we call civilization humming along after its fashion.

5   There was just one anomaly I never understood. Carl's hobby was guns. He kept a loaded .38 in his bedroom. There were handguns and rifles throughout his home. Carl used them for target shooting and hunting. A fellow hunter said Carl was an expert marksman, that when he fired at game he made certain of his shot so the animal wouldn't suffer.

6   I couldn't appreciate the gun side of my friend's character. I guess I had seen too much of the gun religion in the Korean war. Carl and I disagreed about guns. He would vote for George McGovern and simultaneously support every argument of the National Rifle Association and the gun lobbies. Yet because he was a peaceful, compassionate man, I considered him one of those who could be trusted to own and use guns responsibly.

Richard Cory (title): central character in the poem "Richard Cory," by E. A. Robinson (p. 4)

liberal (par. 4): one who supports social progress or reform

anomaly (par. 5): something out of the ordinary

George McGovern (par. 6): Democratic candidate for President in 1972; considered a liberal.

National Rifle Association (par. 6): an organization whose members support, among other things, the private citizen's right to own firearms

lobbies (par. 6): groups that work for the passage of laws that they believe in

7   I saw Carl on that last Friday afternoon. We talked about a printing job. He was cheerful, and I think he was already on the other side of his decision. He finished his work that day like someone going on vacation. Like someone not expecting to return on Monday.

8   We had a relaxed talk. Later I learned of the misery he had concealed. "He saw customers and kept control," his employer told me. "When the customer left, he often went in the restroom and vomited. Family trouble."

9   The virus of restlessness. Norma, after 23 years, with a new career and new friends, wanted to leave. She needed to seek that popular, elusive goal, "more out of life." But Carl was an old-fashioned man captive in a time of new fashions. He couldn't handle this threat to the family. He sought medical advice, but every answer seemed to require letting Norma go, with the frail hope she might come back. Carl couldn't live with the uncertainty.

10   It rained that Friday night. Carl went home and in their bedroom he put two bullets through his wife's head, one through his own. He used a .357 magnum handgun. One of Carl's friends told me this proved it was carefully planned. The .357 meant Carl didn't want Norma to suffer. That friend and others were reluctant to credit guns as factors in the event. "Guns are simply tidier than axes," said one. But Carl was a sensitive, orderly man. I doubt he could ever have done the job with less efficient, messier weapons. It had to be over in a moment. So he used the mercy weapon, the no-pain gun, the .357 magnum. It was handy in a house of guns.

11   Endless postmortems began among those who knew Carl and Norma. Why in his torment couldn't he wait? Why couldn't he give time a chance? Why?

12   No one I listened to blamed the guns, questioned their proximity, their easy availability. It will probably be a long time before Carl's small estate is settled for the son who found the bodies, for the daughter in high school. I suppose his guns eventually will be sold and redistributed, including the .357 magnum. Guns are made from enduring metal. They outlive their owners. They go on about their business.

13   News accounts carried the standard facts: Description of Carl's hobby. His age, 39. The comment of a neighbor that Carl and Norma were "very nice." Details of the funeral. There was no indication whether or not gun clubs and the National Rifle Association sent flowers, or assistance for the survivors.

14   The irony department: Carl learned enthusiasm for guns as an adult. His teacher later abandoned guns in favor of photography.

15   I'll miss Carl very much. His last day was Edwin Arlington Robinson's poem translated into tragic fact. "And Richard Cory, one calm summer night, went home and put a bullet through his head." Richard Cory wasn't the sort to use an ice pick. The same with Carl. Only a gun.

16   Damn those guns.

postmortems (par. 11): literally, "after death"; informally, discussions or examinations of a completed event

Hurts Rent-A-Gun

Art Buchwald

1   The Senate recently passed a new gun-control bill, which some observers consider worse than no bill at all. Any serious attempt at handgun registration was gutted, and Senate gun lovers even manged to repeal a 1968 gun law controlling the purchase of .22 rim-fire ammunition.

2   After the Senate got finished with its work on the gun-control bill, I received a telephone call from my friend Bromley Hurts, who told me he had a business proposition to discuss with me. I met him for lunch at a pistol range in Maryland.

3   "I think I've got a fantastic idea," he said, "I want to start a new business called Hurts Rent-A-Gun."

4   "What on earth for?" I asked.

5   "There are a lot of people in this country who only use a handgun once or twice a year, and they don't want to go to all the expense of buying one. So we'll rent them a gun for a day or two. By leasing a firearm from us, they won't have to tie up all their money."

6   "That makes sense," I admitted.

7   "Say a guy is away from home on a trip, and he doesn't want to carry his own gun with him. He can rent a gun from us and then return it when he's finished with his business."

8   "You could set up rent-a-gun counters at gas stations," I said excitedly.

9   "And we could have stores in town where someone could rent a gun to settle a bet," Hurts said.

10   "A lot of people would want to rent a gun for a domestic quarrel," I said.

11   "Right. Say a jealous husband suspects there is someone at home with his wife. He rents a pistol from us and tries to catch them in the act. If he discovers his wife is alone, he isn't out the eighty dollars it would cost him to buy a gun."

12   "Don't forget the kids who want to play Russian roulette. They could pool their allowances and rent a gun for a couple of hours," I said.

13   "Our market surveys indicate," Hurts said, "that there are also a lot of kids who claim their parents don't listen to them. If they could rent a gun, they feel they could arrive at an understanding with their folks in no time."

14   "There's no end to the business," I said. "How would you charge for Hurts Rent-A-Gun?"

15   "There would be hourly rates, day rates, and weekly rates, plus ten cents for each bullet fired. Our guns would be the latest models, and we would guarantee clean barrels and the latest safety devices. If a gun malfunctions through no fault of the user, we will give him another gun absolutely free."

16   "For many Americans it's a dream come true," I said.

17   "We've also made it possible for people to return the gun in another town. For example, if you rent the gun in Chicago and want to use it in Salt Lake City, you can drop it off there at no extra charge."

18   "Why didn't you start this before?"

19   "We wanted to see what happened with the gun-control legislation. We

---

Hurts Rent-a-Gun (title): The name of this company brings to mind Hertz Rent-A-Car.

were pretty sure the Senate and the White House would not do anything about strong gun control, especially during an election year. But we didn't want to invest a lot of money until we were certain they would all chicken out."

20   "I'd like the franchise for Washington's National Airport," I said.

21   "You've got it. It's a great location," Hurts said. "You'll make a fortune in hijackings alone."

Why Gun Control Laws Don't Work

Barry Goldwater

1   Let me say immediately that if I thought more gun-control laws would help diminish the tragic incidence of robberies, muggings, rapes and murders in the United States, I would be the first to vote for them. But I am convinced that making more such laws approaches the problem from the wrong direction.

2   It is clear, I think, that gun legislation simply doesn't work. There are already some 20,000 state and local gun laws on the books, and they are no more effective than was the prohibition of alcoholic beverages in the 1920's. Our most recent attempt at federal gun legislation was the Gun Control Act of 1968, intended to control the interstate sale and transportation of firearms and the importation of uncertified firearms; it has done nothing to check the availability of weapons. It has been bolstered in every nook and cranny of the nation by local gun-control laws, yet the number of shooting homicides per year has climbed steadily since its enactment, while armed robberies have increased 60 percent.

3   Some people, even some law-enforcement officials, contend that "crimes of passion" occur because a gun just happens to be present at the scene. I don't buy that. I can't equate guns with the murder rate, because if a person is angry enough to kill, he will kill with the first thing that comes to hand—a gun, a knife, an ice pick, a baseball bat.

4   I believe our *only* hope of reducing crime in this country is to control not the weapon but the user. We must reverse the trend toward leniency and permissiveness in our courts—the plea bargaining, the pardons, the suspended sentences and unwarranted paroles—and make the law-breaker pay for what he has done by spending time in jail. We have plenty of statutes against killing and maiming and threatening people with weapons. These can be made effective by strong enforcement and firm decisions from the bench. When a man knows that if he uses a potentially deadly object to rob or do harm to another person he is

diminish (par. 1): lessen

uncertified (par. 2): unapproved

bolstered (par. 2): reinforced

plea bargaining (par. 4): a process in which a criminal agrees to plead guilty, thus avoiding a trial, in exchange for a reduced charge or sentence

unwarranted (par. 4): undeserved

statutes (par. 4): laws

maiming (par. 4): injuring

letting himself in for a mandatory, unparolable stretch behind bars, he will think twice about it.

5   Of course, no matter what gun-control laws are enacted—including national registration—the dedicated crook can always get a weapon. So, some people ask, even if national registration of guns isn't completely airtight, isn't it worth trying? Sure, it would cause a little inconvenience to law-abiding gun owners. And it certainly wouldn't stop all criminals from obtaining guns. But it might stop a few, maybe quite a few. What's wrong with that?

6   There are several answers. The first concerns enforcement. How are we going to persuade the bank robber or the street-corner stickup artist to register his means of criminal livelihood? Then there is the matter of expense. A study conducted eight years ago showed a cost to New York City of $72.87 to investigate and process one application for a pistol license. In mid-1970 dollars, the same procedure probably costs over $100. By extrapolation to the national scale, the cost to American taxpayers of investigating and registering the 40 to 50 million handguns might reach $4 billion or $5 billion. On top of that, keeping the process in operation year after year would require taxpayer financing of another sizable federal bureau. We ought to have far better prospects of success before we hobble ourselves with such appalling expenditures.

7   Finally, there are legal aspects based on the much-discussed Second Amendment to the Bill of Rights, which proclaims that "A well regulated Militia, being necessary to the security of a free State, the right of the people to keep and bear Arms, shall not be infringed." The anti-gun faction argues that this right made sense in the days of British oppression but that it has no application today. I contend, on the other hand, that the Founding Fathers conceived of an armed citizenry as a necessary hedge against tyranny from within as well as from without, that they saw the right to keep and bear arms as basic and perpetual, the one thing that could spell the difference between freedom and servitude. Thus, I deem most forms of gun control unconstitutional in intent.

8   Well, then, I'm often asked, what kind of gun laws *are* you for? I reply that I am for laws of common sense. I am for laws that prohibit citizen access to machine guns, bazookas and other military devices. I am for laws that are educational in nature. I believe that before a person is permitted to buy a weapon he should be required to take a course that will teach him how to use it, to handle it safely and keep it safely about the house.

9   Gun education, in fact, can actually reduce lawlessness in a community, as was demonstrated in an experiment conducted in Highland Park, Mich. City police launched a program to instruct merchants in the use of handguns. The idea was to help them protect themselves and their businesses from robbers, and it was given wide publicity. The store-robbery rate dropped from an average of 1.5 a day to none in four months.

mandatory (par. 4): required

extrapolation (par. 6): extension

hobble (par. 6): burden

appalling (par. 6): shocking

Militia (par. 7): part of the military force of a country that is used only emergency

infringed (par. 7): violated

faction (par. 7): group

oppression (par. 7): cruel or unjust rule

hedge (par. 7): protection

perpetual (par. 7): permanent

10   Where do we go from here? My answer to this is based on the firm belief that we have a crime problem in this country, not a gun problem, and that we must meet the enemy on his own terms. We must start by making crime as unprofitable for him as we can. And we have to do this, I believe, by getting tough in the courts and corrections systems.

11   A recent news story in Washington, D. C., reports that, of 184 persons convicted of gun possession in a six-month period, only 14 received a jail sentence. Forty-six other cases involved persons who had previously been convicted of a felony or possession of a gun. Although the maximum penalty for such repeaters in the District of Columbia is ten years in prison, half of these were not jailed at all. A study last year revealed that in New York City, which has about the most prohibitive gun legislation in the country, only one out of six people convicted of crimes involving weapons went to jail.

12   This sorry state of affairs exists because too many judges and magistrates either don't know the law or are unwilling to apply it with appropriate vigor. It's time to demand either that they crack down on these criminals or be removed from office. It may even be time to review the whole system of judicial appointments, to stop weakening the cause of justice by putting men on the bench who may happen to be golfing partners of Congressmen and too often lack the brains and ability for the job. In Arizona today we elect our judges, and the system is working well, in part because we ask the American and local bar associations to consider candidates and make recommendations. In this way, over the last few years, we have replaced many weaklings with good jurists.

13   We have long had all the criminal statutes we need to turn the tide against the crime wave. There is, however, one piece of proposed legislation that I am watching with particular interest. Introduced by Sen. James McClure (R., Idaho), it requires that any person convicted of a federal crime in which a gun is used serve five to ten years in jail automatically on top of whatever penalty he receives for the crime itself. A second conviction would result in an extra ten-year-to-life sentence. These sentences would be mandatory and could not be suspended. It is, in short, a "tough" bill. I think that this bill would serve as an excellent model for state legislation.

14   And so it has in California which, last September, signed into law a similar bill requiring a mandatory jail sentence for any gun-related felony.

15   Finally, it's important to remember that this is an area of great confusion; an area in which statistics can be juggled and distorted to support legislation that is liable to be expensive, counter-productive or useless. The issue touches upon the freedom and safety of all of us, whether we own firearms or not. The debate over gun control is an adjunct to the war against crime, and that war must be fought with all the intelligence and tenacity we can bring to it.

felony (par. 11): serious crime

vigor (par. 12): force

jurists (par. 12): judges

(R., Idaho) (par. 13): that is, a Republican from Idaho

distorted (par. 15): twisted

adjunct (par. 15): additional part

tenacity (par. 15): persistence

No Home in Africa

Annette Dula

1   I have no cultural roots in Africa nor do I want any. I have discovered that Egypt is not black Africa. The skin isn't black enough and the hair isn't kinky enough. An Egyptian merchant put his light brown arm next to my black arm and said, "My skin isn't black but I'm African, too." Sincerity was not in his voice.

2   In Khartoum, the Sudan, a near-riot developed when I appeared to be an African woman walking down the street in a leather miniskirt. I liked melting into the anonymity of hundreds of black faces, but I also wanted the freedom that tourists enjoy.

3   I went to Ethiopia with Kay, who is white. The people were hostile. They pelted me with rotten tomatoes. They did not bother Kay. Didn't they realize that I was black like them?

4   In East Africa, the Africans were too servile toward whites. I got extremely angry when a gnarled little old man would bow down and call my friend "Mensaab." An African woman would not become angry.

5   I hated the mercenary Indians of East Africa more than the Africans hated them. Two years after the incident, I can still taste the bitterness. I wanted to buy material for a blouse. At the time, most shopkeepers in East Africa were Indians. I had walked in ahead of Kay. The shopkeeper continued talking to another Indian. Kay walked in. The shopkeeper rushed up to her.

6   "Can I help you, madam?" he asked, with the proper servility.

7   "My friend wants to buy material," she said

8   "How much does she want to pay for it?" he asked.

9   "Perhaps you'd better talk to her, sir."

10   Completely ignoring her suggestion, he continued explaining to Kay the virtues of expensive imported materials over cheaper native ones. "You know, these Africans are lazy. They just aren't capable of the superior quality you get in Western work!"

11   I walked out. I knew what prejudice was—but not this kind. This was the type my parents had known in North Carolina 25 years ago. I rejoiced when the Indians were kicked out of Uganda.

12   I do have the appearance of a black African. I have even been asked by Africans, "To what tribe do you belong?" And, "From what part of Africa do you come?" When it was to my advantage to be considered African, it pleased me. At other times, embarrassing situations could develop.

13   Once when I was walking from a restaurant at around 9:30 p.m., four or five policemen jumped out of a squad car, surrounded me, and pointed their loaded guns at me. Though they were speaking in Swahili, I soon gathered that I was being arrested on prostitution charges. The more I protested in English, the more incensed they became. I reacted as any American woman would.

anonymity (par. 2): being unknown

servile (par. 4): assuming a role of social inferiority

gnarled (par. 4): twisted

mercenary (par. 5): greedy

"Who do you think you are? Get those guns out of my face. I am an American. I want to call the Ambassador." (Later, I learned that Kenya had a new law making it illegal for unescorted African women to be on the street after 9:30 p.m.)

14   More often than not, I resented being treated as an African by Africans. I was truly galled at the customs station between Zaire and the Central African Republic. Tourists usually pass customs by merely showing their passports. Africans are subjected to a thorough search. As I was about to move along with other tourists, I was roughly grabbed from behind and thrust back into the crowd. I had to be freed by other tourists. The mob attitude was: "Who do you think you are? You're not a tourist! You're one of us." Why didn't I protest the preferential treatment that tourists receive? Because I felt as the American tourists do: "We are entitled to these considerations."

15   When I understood that the average African male has little respect for the female intellect, I was surprised. Ngimbus, a close friend of mine, decided that I was a militant feminist when I lectured him on male-female equality!

16   "She looks like an African, but she talks nonsense," he said later.

17   Often, I found myself defending black Americans to nationalist West-Africans. A favorite question was "Why do you call yourselves *Afro*-Americans?" I usually answered in terms of cultural heritage, identity oppression, and other nebulous words that explain nothing. The conversation would continue: "You have forfeited the right to call yourselves *Afro*-Americans. If you were worthy of the name *Afro*-, your people would never have taken all those years of such treatment. We sympathize with you, but you're too docile for us."

18   "What about South Africa and Mozambique?" I would always ask.

19   The question was usually ignored or if answered, the time factor was brought in: "We have accomplished more in eighty years than you have accomplished in 400 years." The conversation always left me with a need to explain our differences. But there never were acceptable explanations.

20   My experiences in Africa typify the reciprocal misunderstanding between black Americans and Africans. Our common color is not enough. Too much time has passed.

21   I am not patriotic, but I am a product of America. I believe in freedom of speech, even if it is only token. I take education for granted though we may not receive it equally. I believe in the working of democracy even though it never seems to work. I am forced to accept that I am an American and that here in America lie my cultural roots—whether I like it or not.

galled (par. 14): insulted, angered

militant feminist (par. 15): one who aggressively demands that women and men be treated equally

nebulous (par. 17): vague

forfeited (par. 17): given up

docile (par. 17): passive, accepting

typify (par. 20): serve as typical examples of

reciprocal (par. 20): applying to both sides

I Want a Wife

Judy Syfers

1   I belong to that classification of people known as wives. I am A Wife. And, not altogether incidentally, I am a mother.

2   Not too long ago a male friend of mine appeared on the scene fresh from a recent divorce. He had one child, who is, of course, with his ex-wife. He is obviously looking for another wife. As I thought about him while I was ironing one evening, it suddenly occurred to me that I, too, would like to have a wife. Why do I want a wife?

3   I would like to go back to school so that I can become economically independent, support myself, and, if need be, support those dependent upon me. I want a wife who will work and send me to school. And while I am going to school I want a wife to take care of my children. I want a wife to keep track of the children's doctor and dentist appointments. And to keep track of mine, too. I want a wife to make sure my children eat properly and are kept clean. I want a wife who will wash the children's clothes and keep them mended. I want a wife who is a good nurturant attendant to my children, arranges for their schooling, makes sure that they have an adequate social life with their peers, takes them to the park, the zoo, etc. I want a wife who takes care of the children when they are sick, a wife who arranges to be around when the children need special care, because, of course, I cannot miss classes at school. My wife must arrange to lose time at work and not lose the job. It may mean a small cut in my wife's income from time to time, but I guess I can tolerate that. Needless to say, my wife will arrange and pay for the care of the children while my wife is working.

4   I want a wife who will take care of *my* physical needs. I want a wife who will keep my house clean. A wife who will pick up after me. I want a wife who will keep my clothes clean, ironed, mended, replaced when need be, and who will see to it that my personal things are kept in their proper place so that I can find what I need the minute I need it. I want a wife who cooks the meals, a wife who is a *good* cook. I want a wife who will plan the menus, do the necessary grocery shopping, prepare the meals, serve them pleasantly, and then do the cleaning up while I do my studying. I want a wife who will care for me when I am sick and sympathize with my pain and loss of time from school. I want a wife to go along when our family takes a vacation so that someone can continue to care for me and my children when I need a rest and change of scene.

5   I want a wife who will not bother me with rambling complaints about a wife's duties. But I want a wife who will listen to me when I feel the need to explain a rather difficult point I have come across in my course of studies. And I want a wife who will type my papers for me when I have written them.

6   I want a wife who will take care of the details of my social life. When my wife and I are invited out by my friends, I want a wife who will take care of the baby-sitting arrangements. When I meet people at school that I like and want to entertain, I want a wife who will have the house clean, will prepare a special meal, serve it to me and my friends, and not interrupt when I talk about the things that interest me and my friends. I want a wife who will have arranged

nurturant attendant (par. 3): one who nourishes or takes care of

peers (par. 3): people who are of equal age, class, rank, etc.

that the children are fed and ready for bed before my guests arrive so that the children do not bother us. I want a wife who takes care of the needs of my guests so that they feel comfortable, who makes sure that they have an ashtray, that they are passed the hors d'oeuvres, that they are offered a second helping of the food, that their wine glasses are replenished when necessary, that their coffee is served to them as they like it. And I want a wife who knows that sometimes I need a night out by myself.

7   I want a wife who is sensitive to my sexual needs, a wife who makes love passionately and eagerly when I feel like it, a wife who makes sure that I am satisfied. And, of course, I want a wife who will not demand sexual attention when I am not in the mood for it. I want a wife who assumes the complete responsibility for birth control, because I do not want more children. I want a wife who will remain sexually faithful to me so that I do not have to clutter up my intellectual life with jealousies. And I want a wife who understands that *my* sexual needs may entail more than strict adherence to monogamy. I must, after all, be able to relate to people as fully as possible.

8   If, by chance, I find another person more suitable as a wife than the wife I already have, I want the liberty to replace my present wife with another one. Naturally, I will expect a fresh, new life; my wife will take the children and be solely responsible for them so that I am left free.

9   When I am through with school and have a job, I want my wife to quit working and remain at home so that my wife can more fully and completely take care of a wife's duties.

10   My God, who *wouldn't* want a wife?

replenished (par. 6): refilled

monogamy (par. 7): a state of having only one mate

How the Superwoman Myth Puts Women Down

Sylvia Rabiner

1   Sunday afternoon. I'm making my usual desultory way through the Sunday *Times* when I come upon Linda Kanner. Ms. Kanner is prominently on display in The National Economic Survey, where she is referred to as a woman "in the vanguard of women taking routes to the executive suite that were formerly traveled by men." A quick run-through of the article reveals that she is a marketing consultant with an M.B.A. degree from Harvard and a degree from The Simmons School of Social Work. She is married to a physician who has an M.B.A., too. Somewhere along the way she had managed to find time to produce two sons, and all his glory is hers at age 31.

2   Well, there goes my Sunday afternoon. After reading about Ms. Kanner, I will be in a muddy slump until nightfall at least. Every time I come across one

desultory (par. 1): aimless

vanguard (par. 1): forefront

M.B.A. (par. 1): Masters of Business Administration

of these proliferating articles about the successful woman of today, I am beset by feelings of self-contempt, loathing, and failure. Moreover, I hate Ms. Kanner, too, and if she were in my living room at the moment, I would set fire to her M.B.A. I am a six-year-old child once again, listening while my mother compares me to one of my flawless cousins.

3   Let me tell you, it's getting harder all the time to be a successful woman. In the old days, a woman was usually judged by the man she had ensnared. If he was a good provider and she kept the house clean, was a good cook, and raised a few decent children, she was well regarded by her peers and most likely by herself as well. Now the mainstream Women's Movement has thrust forth a new role model: the capitalist feminist. The career woman with a twist, she's not your old-time spinster who sacrificed marriage and motherhood for professional advancement, but a new, trickier model who has it all—a terrific career, a husband with a terrific career, and a couple of children as well.

4   We have Isabel Van Devanter Sawhill, successful economist, wife of New York University president John, and mother; or Letty Cottin Pogrebin, successful author, editor, activist, wife of lawyer Bert, and mother. A recent article in *Newsweek* investigated the life-styles of working couples with children. Their random democratic sampling included Kathy Cosgrove, vice-president of a public relations firm, wife of Mark, an advertising executive; Consuelo Marshall, Superior Court commissioner, wife of George, Columbia Pictures executive; Charlotte Curtis, associate editor of the New York Times, wife of William Hunt, neurosurgeon; and Patricia Schroeder, congresswoman, wife of lawyer Jim. Patricia, the article gushed, managed at 35 to "gracefully combine career, marriage, and family." The article was capped by a description of Carla Hills, Secretary of Housing and Urban Development, presidential possibility for the supreme court, wife of Roderick, chairman of the Securities and Exchange Commission, and mother of four. There was a photograph of Mrs. Hill presiding over her impeccable family at the dinner table. The article was swingy and upbeat. If they can do it, how about you? . . . Another afternoon ruined.

5   I turned for instruction to Letty Cottin Pogrebin, embodiment of the success game. Letty is now an editor at Ms. and author of two books—"How to Make It in a Man's World" and "Getting Yours." Those titles reveal Letty's commitment to self-advancement. She doesn't hesitate to tell her readers that she is a woman to emulate. Letty was an executive at 21. She married a man whom she adores and has three "happy, well-behaved, bright, and spirited kids." I gleaned all this from Letty's first book. Since Letty was also gracefully combining career, marriage, and family, I thought I might get some pointers from her.

6   Letty Cottin arrived at Bernard Geis in 1960. After six months she was promoted to the position of director of publicity, advertising, and subsidiary rights. She met her husband at a party and married him a couple of months later. She proceeded to have her first children (twins) as planned "early in marriage but af-

proliferating (par. 2): increasing in number

loathing (par. 2): disgust

capitalist (par. 3): an economic system based on the private or corporate production, distribution, and pricing of goods

spinster (par. 3): an unmarried woman who has passed the usual age for marriage

impeccable (par. 4): flawless

emulate (par. 5): imitate

gleaned (par. 5): gathered, determined

subsidiary rights (par. 6): the right to use published material (such as making a movie from a novel)

ter one full year as unencumbered newlyweds." Their next baby fit in perfectly after the three-year space between children, which they deemed most desirable. She sums up: "It's better to be working than not working; it's better to be married than single; it's better to be a mommy as well as a Mrs. But it's best to be all four at once!"

7   Now, where does that leave me? My thumbnail autobiography follows: I am a child of my times, definitely more the rule than the exception to it. Raised in the '40s and '50s, the words *career* and *goal* were not spoken when I was in the room. I got the standard New York City College Jewish Parental Advice to Daughters. "Take a few education courses. Then if . . . God forbid . . . anything should happen, you can always take care of yourself." Nora Ephron said that she always knew she wanted to write (Dorothy Parker was her idol). When her less motivated college friends went off after graduation and got married, Nora went off and wrote. A few remarkable women like Nora and Letty undoubtedly knew at the age of 18 or younger what profession they wanted to pursue, but most of us at Hunter College, as I recall, were thundering off in a herd to stand under the marriage canopy. A bunch of simpletons, you say? Not so. We had produced the school plays, edited the school newspapers, put together the creative publications, belonged to Arista, and frequently had our names on the honor roll. What was happening, then? Well, let's call it economics. We were the children of immigrant or near immigrant parents. Hard-working, uneducated or self-educated, they didn't know how to guide their bright daughters. The depression had been deeply felt and was well remembered. Their watchword was security. Dorothy Parker was my idol, too, but to my parents, writing was not a job. With encouragement from neither parents nor teachers, most of us sought security in marriage or teaching.

8   Now, I married neither wisely nor well, which to judge by current divorce statistics, proves me to be obstinately average. I worked to put my husband through graduate school, traveled where his career dictated, had two children as a matter of course and in the fall of 1969, although I had felt suffocated by my marriage, I protestingly and hysterically suffered its demise. My child support settlement would have done nicely to keep me in a cozy little tenement on Avenue C and 5th Street. I wanted to remain part of the middle class so I had to work: I had two children under the age of five and couldn't possibly pay a housekeeper. And I didn't really want a day-care center or baby-sitter with my boys eight or nine hours a day while I was at work. I wanted to be with them, so I found a job teaching night classes, and I tended home and sons during the day. A divorced woman with kids has a lot of things to think about. She is usually racing around trying to pay bills, do her job reasonably well, have some kind of social life, and be a loving mother too.

9   After 1969 I noticed that I never walked down a street, I ran. I ate standing up. I screamed at my sons a lot. The astute reader will detect here the subtle differences between Letty's life and mine. I admit I was failing in being a successful woman, I didn't have a terrific career, and I didn't have a husband with a terrific

---

unencumbered (par. 6): unburdened

the marriage canopy (par. 7): the structure under which the bride and groom stand during a Jewish wedding ceremony

obstinately (par. 8): stubbornly

demise (par. 8): end

tenement (par. 8): a run-down apartment building or rooming house

Avenue C and 5th Street (par. 8): at the time this essay was written, a run-down area of Manhattan

astute (par. 9): having keen insight

career. Where were all those dynamic, achieving wonderful men that the women in the news stories found and married? Not in the playgrounds and supermarkets where I spent my days, not in the classrooms where I spent my evenings, and not in any of the other places I checked out with varying degrees of enthusiasm on the weekends when I had a baby-sitter. As for my long-range career goals—well, to tell the truth, I was grateful to have my teaching contract renewed each semester. My concession to getting ahead was to return to graduate school to earn my M.A. degree. I was able to indulge in this luxury only because the university at which I taught offered me free tuition. At $91 a credit, graduate school is hardly a priority of the divorced working mother. It appears that in addition to all my other errors in judgment, I've made the mistake of living in New York City during a recession. Last June I lost the teaching job that was supposed to be my security in case . . . God forbid . . . anything happened. After collecting unemployment insurance for five months, I am now typing, filing, and serving my boss his coffee four times a day.

10   Now, I ask you—do I need to read about the triumphant lives of Helen Gurley Brown or Mary Wells Lawrence? Statistics currently indicate that there are 7.2 million families headed by women. Most of us are clerks, secretaries, waitresses, salesgirls, social workers, nurses, and—if lucky enough to still be working—teachers. For us, the superwoman who knits marriage, career, and motherhood into a satisfying life without dropping a stitch is as oppressive a role model as the airbrushed Bunny in the Playboy centerfold, or That Cosmopolitan Girl. While I struggle to keep my boat afloat in rough waters with prevailing high winds, I am not encouraged to row on by media hypes of ladies who run companies, serve elegant dinners for 30, play tennis with their husbands, earn advanced degrees, and wear a perfect size eight. They exist, I know, a privileged, talented minority, but to encourage me by lauding their achievements is like holding Sammy Davis, Jr., up as a model to a junior high school class in Bed.-Stuy. What does it really have to do with them?

11   Women are self-critical creatures. We can always find reasons to hate ourselves. Single women believe they are failing if they don't have a loving permanent relationship; working mothers are conflicted about leaving their children; divorced women experience guilt over the break-up of their marriages; housewives feel inadequate because they don't have careers; career women are wretched if they aren't advancing, and everyone is convinced she is too fat!

12   It is ironic that feminism, finally respectable, has been made to backfire in this way. The superwoman image is a symbol of the corruption of feminist politics. It places emphasis on a false ideal of individual success. We are led to believe that if we play our cards right, we'll get to the top, but in the present system it won't work; there just isn't that much room up there. And in our class society, those at the top probably were more than halfway up to start with. The superwoman image ignores the reality of the average working woman or housewife. It elevates an elite of upper-class women executives. The media loves it because it is glamorous and false. In the end it threatens nothing in the system. In fact, all it does is give women like me a sense of inferiority.

concession (par. 9): giving in

to indulge (par. 9): to treat oneself to a special pleasure

priority (par. 9): important concern

recession (par. 9): a temporary decline in the economy

oppressive (par. 10): distressing

hypes (par. 10): statements that exaggerate or overrate

lauding (par. 10): praising

Bed.-Stuy. (par. 10): Bedford-Stuyvesant; a poverty-stricken area of Brooklyn, New York

elite (par. 12): select few

Confession of a Female Chauvinist Sow

Anne Richardson Roiphe

1   I once married a man I thought was totally unlike my father and I imagined a whole new world of freedom emerging. Five years later it was clear even to me—floating face down in a wash of despair—that I had simply chosen a replica of my handsome daddy-true. The updated version spoke English like an angel but—good God!—underneath he was my father exactly: wonderful, but not the right man for me.

2   Most people I know have at one time or another been fouled up by their childhood experiences. Patterns tend to sink into the unconscious only to reappear, disguised, unseen, like marionettes' strings, pulling us this way or that. Whatever ails people—keeps them up at night, tossing and turning—also ails movements no matter how historically huge or politically important. The women's movement cannot remake consciousness, or reshape the future, without acknowledging and shedding all the unnecessary and ugly baggage of the past. It's easy enough to recognize the hidden directions that limit Sis to cake-baking and Junior to bridge-building; it's now possible for even Miss America herself to identify what *they* have done to us, and, of course, *they* have and *they* did and *they* are . . . . But along the way we also developed our own hidden prejudices, class assumptions and an anti-male humor and collection of expectations that gave us, like all oppressed groups, *a secret sense of superiority (co-existing with a poor self-image*—it's not news that people can believe two contradictory things at once).

3   Listen to any group that suffers materially and socially. They have a lexicon with which they tease the enemy: ofay, goy, honky, gringo. "Poor pale devils," said Malcolm X loud enough for us to hear, although blacks had joked about that to each other for years. Behind some of the women's liberation thinking lurk the rumors, the prejudices, the defense systems of generations of oppressed women whispering in the kitchen together, presenting one face to their menfolk and another to their card clubs, their mothers and sisters. All this is natural enough but potentially dangerous in a revolutionary situation in which you hope to create *a future that does not mirror the past*. The hidden anti-male feelings, a result of the old system, will foul us up if they are allowed to persist.

4   During my teen years I never left the house on Saturday night dates with-

chauvinist (title): one who believes in the superiority of one's own group

sow (title): female pig

marionettes' (par. 2): puppets'

consciousness (par. 2): awareness of something

baggage of the past (par. 2): theories or practices that are outdated

oppressed (par. 2): mistreated, subjected to prejudice

contradictory (par. 2): opposite

lexicon (par. 3): vocabulary

Malcolm X (par. 3): civil rights activist in the 1960s; assassinated 1965

out my mother slipping me a few extra dollars—mad money, it was called. I'll explain what it was for the benefit of the new generation in which people just sleep with each other: the fellow was supposed to bring me home, *lead me safely through the asphalt jungle, protect me from slithering snakes, rapists and the like*. But my mother and I knew young men were apt to drink too much, to slosh down so many rye-and-gingers that some hero might well lead me in front of an on-coming bus, smash his daddy's car into Tiffany's window or, less gallantly, throw up on my new dress. Mad money was for getting home on your own, no matter what form of insanity your date happened to evidence. Mad money was also a wallflower's rope ladder; if the guy you came with suddenly fancied someone else, well, you didn't have to stay there and suffer, you could go home. Boys were fickle and likely to be unkind; my mother and I knew that, as surely as we knew they tried to make you do things in the dark they wouldn't respect you for afterwards, and in fact would spread the word and spoil your rep. Boys liked to be flattered; if you made them feel important they would eat out of your hand. So talk to them about their interests, don't alarm them with displays of intelligence—we all knew that, we groups of girls talking into the wee hours of the night in a kind of easy companionship we thought impossible with boys. Boys were prone to have a good time, get you pregnant, and then pretend they didn't know your name when you came knocking on their door for finances or comfort. In short, we believed boys were less moral than we were. They appeared to be hypocritical, self-seeking, exploitative, untrustworthy and very likely to be showing off their precious masculinity. I never had a girl friend I thought would be unkind or embarrass me in public. I never expected a girl to lie to me about her marks or sports skill or how good she was in bed. Al-together—without anyone's directly coming out and saying so—I gathered that men were sexy, powerful, very interesting, but not very nice, not very moral, humane and tender, like us. Girls played fairly while men, unfortunately, re-served their honor for the battlefield.

5   Why are there laws insisting on alimony and child support? Well, everyone knows that men don't have an instinct to protect their young and, given half a chance, with the moon in the right phase, they will run off and disappear. Ev-eryone assumes a mother will not let her child starve, yet it is necessary to legis-late that a father must not do so. We are taught to accept the idea that men are less than decent; their charms may be manifold but their characters are riddled with faults. To this day I never blink if I hear that a man has gone to find his for-tune in South America, having left his pregnant wife, his blind mother and taken the family car. I still gasp in horror when I hear of a woman leaving her asthmatic infant for a rock group in Taos because I can't seem to avoid the as-sumption that men are naturally heels and women the ordained carriers of what little is moral in our dubious civilization.

6   My mother never gave me mad money thinking I would ditch a fellow for

Tiffany's (par. 4): famous jewelry store in New York City

gallantly (par. 4): nobly

to evidence (par. 4): to reveal

fancied (par. 4): took a liking to

fickle (par. 4): unreliable

prone (par. 4): inclined

exploitative (par. 4): to exploit is to use or take advantage of someone

manifold (par. 5): many

ordained (par. 5): chosen

dubious (par. 5): of uncertain value or quality

some other guy or that I would pass out drunk on the floor. She knew I would be considerate of my companion because, after all, I was more mature than the boys that gathered about. Why was I more mature? Women just are people-oriented; they learn to be empathetic at an early age. Most English students (students interested in humanity, not artifacts) are women. Men and boys—so the myth goes—conceal their feelings and lose interest in anybody else's. Everyone knows that even little boys can tell the difference between one kind of a car and another—proof that their souls are mechanical, their attention directed to the nonhuman.

7   I remember shivering in the cold vestibule of a famous men's athletic club. Women and girls are not permitted inside the club's door. What are they doing in there? I asked. They're naked, said my mother, they're sweating, jumping up and down a lot, telling each other dirty jokes and bragging about their stock market exploits. Why can't we go in? I asked. Well, my mother told me, they're afraid we'd laugh at them.

8   The prejudices of childhood are hard to outgrow. I confess that every time my business takes me past that club, I shudder. Images of large bellies resting on massage tables and flaccid penises rising and falling with the Dow Jones average flash through my head. There it is, chauvinism waving its cancerous tentacles from the depths of my psyche.

9   Minorities automatically feel superior to the oppressor because, after all, they are not hurting anybody. In fact, they feel morally better. The old canard that women need love, men need sex—believed for too long by both sexes—attributes moral and spiritual superiority to women and makes of men beasts whose urges send them prowling into the night. This false division of good and bad, placing deforming pressure on everyone, doesn't have to contaminate the future. We know that the assumptions we have about each other become a part of the cultural air we breathe and, in fact, become social truths. Women who want equality must be prepared to give it and to believe in it, and in order to do that it is not enough to state that you are as good as any man, but also it must be stated that he is as good as you and both will be humans together. If we want men to share in the care of the family in a new way, we must assume them as capable of consistent loving tenderness as we.

10   I rummage about and find in my thinking all kinds of anti-male prejudices. Some are just jokes and others I will have a hard time abandoning. First, I share an emotional conviction with many sisters that women given power would not create wars. Intellectually I know that's ridiculous; great queens have waged war before; the likes of Lurleen Wallace, Pat Nixon and Mrs. General Lavelle can be

empathetic (par. 6): compassionate

artifacts (par. 6): objects

vestibule (par. 7): entryway

flaccid (par. 8): limp

tentacles (par. 8): literally, a long, flexible growth projecting from the mouth or head of some animals

psyche (par. 8): soul

canard (par. 9): false story

conviction (par. 10): strong belief

Lurleen Wallace (par. 10): governor of Alabama from 1967–1968; wife of George Wallace, governor of Alabama (1963–1967; 1971–1979; 1983–1987)

Pat Nixon (par. 10): wife of Richard M. Nixon, President of the United States (1969–1974, resigned)

Mrs. General Lavelle (par. 10): wife of General Lavelle, one of the early commanders in Vietnam

depended upon in the future to guiltlessly condemn to death other people's children in the name of some ideal of their own. Little girls, of course, don't take toy guns out of their hip pockets and say "Pow, pow" to all their neighbors and friends like the average well-adjusted little boy. However, if we gave little girls the six-shooters, we would soon have double the pretend body count.

11   *Aggression is not, as I secretly think, a male-sex-linked characteristic: brutality is masculine only by virtue of opportunity.* True, there are 1,000 Jack the Rippers for every Lizzie Borden, but that surely is the result of social norms. Women as a group are indeed more masochistic than men. The practical result of this division is that women seem nicer and kinder, but when the world changes, women will have a fuller opportunity to be just as rotten as men and there will be fewer claims of female moral superiority.

12   Now that I am entering early middle age, I hear many women complaining of husbands and ex-husbands who are attracted to younger females. This strikes the older woman as unfair, of course. But I remember a time when I thought all boys around my age and grade were creeps and bores. I wanted to go out with an older man: a senior or, miraculously, a college man. I had a certain contempt for my *coevals*, not realizing that the freshman in college I thought so desirable, was some older girl's creep. Some women never lose that contempt for men of their own age. That isn't fair either and may be one reason why some sensible men of middle years find solace in young women.

13   I remember coming home from school one day to find my mother's card game dissolved in hysterical laughter. The cards were floating in black rivers of running mascara. What was so funny? A woman named Helen was lying on a couch pretending to be her husband with a cold. She was issuing demands for orange juice, aspirin, suggesting a call to a specialist, complaining of neglect, of fate's cruel finger, of heat, of cold, of sharp pains on the bridge of the nose that might indicate brain involvement. What was so funny? The ladies explained to me that all men behave just like that with colds, they are reduced to temper tantrums by simple nasal congestion, men cannot stand any little physical discomfort—on and on the laughter went.

14   The point of this vignette is the nature of the laughter—*us laughing at them, us feeling superior to them, us ridiculing them behind their backs.* If they were doing it to us, we'd call it male chauvinist pigness; if we do it to them, it is inescapably female chauvinist sowness and, whatever its roots, it leads to the same isolation. Boys are messy, boys are mean, boys are rough, boys are stupid and have sloppy handwriting. A cacophony of childhood memories rushes through my head, balanced, of course, by all the well-documented feelings of inferiority and envy. But the important thing, the hard thing, is to wipe the slate clean, to start again without the meanness of the past. That's why it's so important that the women's movement not become anti-male and allow its most prejudiced spokesmen total leadership. The much-chewed-over abortion issue illustrates this. The women's liberation position, insisting on a woman's right to determine her own body's destiny, leads in fanatical extreme to a kind of *emotional immaculate conception in which the father is not judged even half-responsible*—he has no

Jack the Ripper (par. 11): the name used by an unknown mass murdered in nineteenth-century London

Lizzy Borden (par. 11): woman accused and acquitted of murdering her parents with an axe (1892)

masochistic (par. 11): enjoying suffering

coevals (par. 12): of equal age

solace (par. 12): comfort

vignette (par. 14): short description

cacophony (par. 14): literally, harsh sounds

rights, and no consideration is to be given to his concern for either the woman or the fetus.

15   Woman, who once was abandoned and disgraced by an unwanted pregnancy, has recently arrived at a new pride of ownership or disposal. She has traveled in a straight line that still excludes her sexual partner from an equal share in the wanted or unwanted pregnancy. A better style of life may develop from an assumption that men are as human as we. Why not ask the child's father if he would like to bring up the child? Why not share the decisions, when possible, with the male? If we cut them out, assuming an old-style indifference on their part, we perpetrate the ugly divisiveness that has characterized relations between the sexes so far.

16   Hard as it is for many of us to believe, women are not really superior to men in intelligence or humanity—they are only equal.

fanatical (par. 14): unreasonable

immaculate conception (par. 14): Actually, the writer is referring to the virgin birth, the belief that Mary became pregnant with Jesus without having sexual intercourse. The Immaculate Conception is the Roman Catholic belief that Mary herself was kept free from the stain of original sin from the moment of her conception.

perpetrate (par. 15): continue

divisiveness (par. 15): conflict

Friendships Among Men

Marc Feigen Fasteau

1   There is a long-standing myth in our society that the great friendships are between men. Forged through shared experience, male friendship is portrayed as the most unselfish, if not the highest form, of human relationship. The more traditionally masculine the shared experience from which it springs, the stronger and more profound the friendship is supposed to be. Going to war, weathering crises together at school or work, playing on the same athletic team are some of the classic experiences out of which friendships between men are believed to grow.

2   By and large, men do prefer the company of other men, not only in their structured time but in the time they fill with optional, nonobligatory activity. They prefer to play games, drink, and talk, as well as work and fight together. Yet something is missing. Despite the time men spend together, their contact rarely goes beyond the external, a limitation which tends to make their friendships shallow and unsatisfying.

3   My own childhood memories are of doing things with my friends—playing games or sports, building walkie-talkies, going camping. Other people and

myth (par. 1): widely held belief not based on fact

forged (par. 1): formed

profound (par. 1): intense, significant

structured time (par. 2): time that is devoted to necessary activities, such as work

my relationships to them were never legitimate subjects for attention. If someone liked me, it was an opaque, mysterious occurrence that bore no analysis. When I was slighted, I felt hurt. But relationships with people just happened. I certainly had feelings about my friends, but I can't remember a single instance of trying consciously to sort them out until I was well into college.

4   For most men this kind of shying away from the personal continues into adult life. In conversations with each other, we hardly ever use ourselves as reference points. We talk about almost everything except how we ourselves are affected by people and events. Everything is discussed as though it were taking place out there somewhere, as though we had no more felt response to it than to the weather. Topics that can be treated in this detached, objective way become conversational mainstays. The few subjects which are fundamentally personal are shaped into discussions of abstract general questions. Even in an exchange about their reactions to liberated women—a topic of intensely personal interest—the tendency will be to talk in general, theoretical terms. Work, at least its objective aspects, is always a safe subject. Men also spend an incredible amount of time rehashing the great public issues of the day. Until early 1973, Vietnam was the work-horse topic. Then came Watergate. It doesn't seem to matter that we've all had a hundred similar conversations. We plunge in for another round, trying to come up with a new angle as much as to impress the others with what we know as to keep from being bored stiff.

5   Games play a central role in situations organized by men. I remember a weekend some years ago at the country house of a law-school classmate as a blur of softball, football, croquet, poker, and a dice-and-board game called Combat, with swimming thrown in on the side. As soon as one game ended, another began. Taken one at a time, these "activities" were fun, but the impression was inescapable that the host, and most of his guests, would do anything to stave off a lull in which they would be together without some impersonal focus for their attention. A snapshot of almost any men's club would show the same thing, 90 percent of the men engaged in some activity—ranging from backgammon to watching the tube—other than, or at least as an aid to, conversation.*

6   My composite memory of evenings spent with a friend at college and later when we shared an apartment in Washington is of conversations punctuated by silences during which we would internally pass over any personal or emotional thoughts which had arisen and come back to the permitted track. When I couldn't get my mind off personal matters, I said very little. Talks with my father

---

*Women may use games as a reason for getting together—bridge clubs, for example. But the show is more for the rest of the world—to indicate that they are doing *something*—and the games themselves are not the only means of communication.

legitimate (par. 3): acceptable, proper

opaque (par. 3): unclear

detached (par. 4): impersonal

mainstays (par. 4): supports

fundamentally (par. 4): basically

abstract (par. 4): vague, impersonal

theoretical (par. 4): based on theory or speculation, rather than personal feelings

work-horse topic (par. 4): topic used more than any other for conversation

stave off (par. 5): prevent

composite (par. 6): total

punctuated (par. 6): interrupted

have always had the same tone. Respect for privacy was the rationale for our diffidence. His questions to me about how things were going at school or at work were asked as discreetly as he would have asked a friend about someone's commitment to a hospital for the criminally insane. Our conversations, when they touched these matters at all, to say nothing of more sensitive matters, would veer quickly back to safe topics of general interest.

7   In our popular literature, the archetypal male hero embodying this personal muteness is the cowboy. The classic mold for the character was set in 1902 by Owen Wister's novel *The Virginian* where the author spelled out, with an explicitness that was never again necessary, the characteristics of his protagonist. Here's how it goes when two close friends the Virginian hasn't seen in some time take him out for a drink:

> All of them had seen rough days together, and they felt guilty with emotion. "It's hot weather," said Wiggin.
> "Hotter in Box Elder," said McLean. "My kid has started teething." Words ran dry again. They shifted their positions, looked in their glasses, read the labels on the bottles. They dropped a word now and then to the proprietor about his trade, and his ornaments.

One of the Virginian's duties is to assist at the hanging of an old friend as a horse thief. Afterward, for the first time in the book, he is visibly upset. The narrator puts his arm around the hero's shoulders and describes the Virginian's reaction:

> I had the sense to keep silent, and presently he shook my hand, not looking at me as he did so. He was always very shy of demonstration.

And, for explanation of such reticence, "As all men know, he also knew that many things should be done in this world in silence, and that talking about them is a mistake."

8   There are exceptions, but they only prove the rule.

9   One is the drunken confidence: "Bob, ole boy, I gotta tell ya—being divorced isn't so hot . . . . [and see, I'm too drunk to be held responsible for blurting it out]." Here, drink becomes an excuse for exchanging confidences and a device for periodically loosening the restraint against expressing a need for sympathy and support from other men—which may explain its importance as a male ritual. Marijuana fills a similar need.

10   Another exception is talking to a stranger—who may be either someone the speaker doesn't know or someone who isn't in the same social or business world. (Several black friends told me that they have been on the receiving end of personal confidences from white acquaintances that they were sure had not been shared with white friends.) In either case, men are willing to talk about themselves only to other men with whom they do not have to compete or whom they will not have to confront socially later.

11   Finally, there is the way men depend on women to facilitate certain conversations. The women in a mixed group are usually the ones who make the first

rationale (par. 6): reason, excuse

diffidence (par. 6): hesitance

veer (par. 6): turn

archetypal (par. 7): model

protagonist (par. 7): main character

proprietor (par. 7): owner

reticence (par. 7): shyness

confront (par. 10): face, meet

facilitate (par. 11): to make easier

personal reference, about themselves or others present. The men can then join in without having the onus for initiating a discussion of "personalities." Collectively, the men can "blame" the conversation on the women. They can also feel in these conversations that since they are talking "to" the women instead of "to" the men, they can be excused for deviating from the masculine norm. When the women leave, the tone and subject invariably shift away from the personal.

12   The effect of these constraints is to make it extraordinarily difficult for men to really get to know each other. A psychotherapist who has conducted a lengthy series of encounter groups for men summed it up:

> With saddening regularity [the members of these groups] described how much they wanted to have closer, more satisfying relationships with other men: "I'd settle for having one really close man friend. I supposedly have some close men friends now. We play golf or go for a drink. We complain about our jobs and our wives. I care about them and they care about me. We even have some physical contact—I mean we may even give a hug on a big occasion. But it's not enough."

The sources of this stifling ban on self-disclosure, the reasons why men hide from each other, lie in the taboos and imperatives of the masculine stereotype.

13   To begin with, men are supposed to be functional, to spend their time working or otherwise solving or thinking about how to solve problems. Personal reaction, how one feels about something, is considered dysfunctional, at best an irrelevant distraction from the expected objectivity. Only weak men, and women, talk about—i. e., "give in" to—their feelings. "I group my friends in two ways," said a business executive:

> those who have made it and don't complain and those who haven't made it. And only the latter spend time talking to their wives about their problems and how bad their boss is and all that. The ones who concentrate more on communicating . . . and those who have realized that they aren't going to make it and therefore they have changed the focus of attention.

In a world which tells men they have to choose between expressiveness and manly strength, this characterization may be accurate. Most of the men who talk personally to other men *are* those whose problems have gotten the best of them, who simply can't help it. Men not driven to despair don't talk about themselves, so the idea that self-disclosure and expressiveness are associated with problems and weakness becomes a self-fulfilling prophecy.

14   Obsessive competitiveness also limits the range of communication in male friendships. Competition is the principal mode by which men relate to each other—at one level because they don't know how else to make contact, but more basically because it is the way to demonstrate, to themselves and others, the key masculine qualities of unwavering toughness and the ability to dominate

onus (par. 11): responsibility, blame

deviating (par. 11): departing from

stifling (par. 12): restrictive

self-disclosure (par. 12): revealing one's feelings and thoughts

taboos (par. 12): things forbidden by society

imperatives (par. 12): requirements

dysfunctional (par. 13): not functioning properly

self-fulfilling prophecy (par. 13): a prediction that comes true because people unconsciously act in such a way to make it come true

obsessive (par. 14): extreme

mode (par. 14): method

and control. The result is that they inject competition into situations which don't call for it.

15   In conversations, you must show that you know more about the subject than the other man, or at least as much as he does. For example, I have often engaged in a contest that could be called My Theory Tops Yours, disguised as a serious exchange of ideas. The proof that it wasn't serious was that I was willing to participate even when I was sure that the participants, including myself, had nothing fresh to say. Convincing the other person—victory—is the main objective, with control of the floor an important tactic. Men tend to lecture at each other, insist that the discussion follow their train of thought, and are often unwilling to listen. As one member of a men's rap group said,

> When I was talking I used to feel that I had to be driving to a point, that it had to be rational and organized, that I had to persuade at all times, rather than exchange thoughts and ideas.

Even in casual conversation some men hold back unless they are absolutely sure of what they are saying. They don't want to have to change a position once they have taken it. It's "just like a woman" to change your mind, and, more important, it is inconsistent with the approved masculine posture of total independence.

16   Competition was at the heart of one of my closest friendships, now defunct. There was a good deal of mutual liking and respect. We went out of our way to spend time with each other and wanted to work together. We both had "prospects" as "bright young men" and the same "liberal but tough" point of view. We recognized this about each other, and this recognition was the basis of our respect and of our sense of equality. That we saw each other as equals was important—our friendship was confirmed by the reflection of one in the other. But our constant and all-encompassing competition made this equality precarious and fragile. One way or another, everything counted in the measuring process. We fought out our tennis matches as though our lives depended on it. At poker, the two of us would often play on for hours after the others had left. These *mano-a-mano* poker marathons seem in retrospect especially revealing of the competitiveness of the relationship: playing for small stakes, the essence of the game is in outwitting, psychologically beating down the other player—the other skills involved are negligible. Winning is the only pleasure, one that evaporates quickly, a truth that struck me in inchoate form every time our game broke up at four A.M. and I walked out the door with my five-dollar winnings, a headache, and a sense of time wasted. Still, I did the same thing the next time. It was what we did together, and somehow it counted. Losing at tennis could be balanced by winning at poker; at another level, his moving up in the federal government by my getting on the *Harvard Law Review*.

17   This competitiveness feeds the most basic obstacle to openness between

defunct (par. 16): ended

mutual (par. 16): applying to both sides

precarious (par. 16): uncertain

mano-a-mano (par. 16): hand to hand

marathons (par. 16): long and tiring activity

retrospect (par. 16): looking back

essence (par. 16): the essential quality

negligible (par. 16): unimportant, insignificant

evaporates (par. 16): disappears

inchoate (par. 16): vague

men, the inability to admit to being vulnerable. Real men, we learn early, are not supposed to have doubts, hopes and ambitions which may not be realized, things they don't (or even especially do) like about themselves, fears and disappointments. Such feelings and concerns, of course, are part of everyone's inner life, but a man must keep quiet about them. If others know how you really feel you can be hurt, and that in itself is incompatible with manhood. The inhibiting effect of this imperative is not limited to disclosures of major personal problems. Often men do not share even ordinary uncertainties and half-formulated plans of daily life with their friends. And when they do, they are careful to suggest that they already know how to proceed—that they are not really asking for help or understanding but simply for particular bits of information. Either way, any doubts they have are presented as external, carefully characterized as having to do with the issue as distinct from the speaker. They are especially guarded about expressing concern or asking a question that would invite personal comment. It is almost impossible for men to simply exchange thoughts about matters involving them personally in a comfortable, non-crisis atmosphere. If a friend tells you of his concern that he and a colleague are always disagreeing, for example, he is likely to quickly supply his own explanation—something like "different professional backgrounds." The effect is to rule out observations or suggestions that do not fit within this already reconnoitered protective structure. You don't suggest, even if you believe it is true, that in fact the disagreements arise because he presents his ideas in a way which tends to provoke a hostile reaction. It would catch him off guard; it would be something he hadn't already thought of and accepted about himself and, for that reason, no matter how constructive and well-intentioned you might be, it would put you in control for the moment. He doesn't want that; he is afraid of losing your respect. So, sensing he feels that way, because you would yourself, you say something else. There is no real give-and-take.

18   It is hard for men to get angry at each other honestly. Anger between friends often means that one has hurt the other. Since the straightforward expression of anger in these situations involves an admission of vulnerability, it is safer to stew silently or find an "objective" excuse for retaliation. Either way, trust is not fully restored.

19   Men even try not to let it show when they feel good. We may report the reasons for our happiness, if they have to do with concrete accomplishments, but we try to do it with a straight face, as if to say, "Here's what happened, but it hasn't affected my grown-up unemotional equilibrium, and I am not asking for any kind of response." Happiness is a precarious, "childish" feeling, easy to shoot down. Others may find the event that triggers it trivial or incomprehensible, or even threatening to their own self-esteem—in the sense that if one man is up, another man is down. So we tend not to take the risk of expressing it.

20   What is particulary difficult for men is seeking or accepting help from friends. I, for one, learned early that dependence was unacceptable. When I was eight, I went to a summer camp I disliked. My parents visited me in the middle of the summer and, when it was time for them to leave, I wanted to go with

inhibiting (par. 17): restricting

reconnoitered (par. 17): examined, established

retaliation (par. 18): revenge

equilibrium (par. 19): balance

precarious (par. 19): delicate

trivial (par. 19): unimportant

incomprehensible (par. 19): not understandable

self-esteem (par. 19): pride

them. They refused, and I yelled and screamed and was miserably unhappy for the rest of the day. That evening an older camper comforted me, sitting by my bed as I cried, patting me on the back soothingly and saying whatever it is that one says at times like that. He was in some way clumsy or funny-looking, and a few days later I joined a group of kids in cruelly making fun of him, an act which upset me, when I thought about it, for years. I can only explain it in terms of my feeling, as early as the age of eight, that by needing and accepting his help and comfort I had compromised myself, and took it out on him.

21   "You can't express dependence when you feel it," a corporate executive said, "because it's a kind of absolute. If you are loyal 90 percent of the time and disloyal 10 percent, would you be considered loyal? Well, the same happens with independence: you are either dependent or independent; you can't be both." "Feelings of dependence," another explained, "are identified with weakness or 'untoughness' and our culture doesn't accept those things in men." The result is that we either go it alone or "act out certain games or rituals to provoke the desired reaction in the other and have our needs satisfied without having to ask for anything."

22   Somewhat less obviously, the expression of affection also runs into emotional barriers growing out of the masculine stereotype. When I was in college, I was suddenly quite moved while attending a friend's wedding. The surge of feeling made me uncomfortable and self-conscious. There was nothing inherently difficult or, apart from the fact of being moved by a moment of tenderness, "unmasculine" about my reaction. I just did not know how to deal with or communicate what I felt. "I consider myself a sentimentalist," one man said, "and I think I am quite able to express my feelings. But the other day my wife described a friend of mine to some people as my best friend and I felt embarrassed when I heard her say it."

23   A major source of these inhibitions is the fear of being, of being thought, homosexual. Nothing is more frightening to a heterosexual man in our society. It threatens, at one stroke, to take away every vestige of his claim to a masculine identity—something like knocking out the foundations of a building—and to expose him to the ostracism, ranging from polite tolerance to violent revulsion, of his friends and colleagues. A man can be labeled as homosexual not just because of an overt sexual act but because of almost any sign of behavior which does not fit the masculine stereotype. The touching of another man, other than shaking hands or, under emotional stress, an arm around the shoulder, is taboo. Women may kiss each other when they meet; men are uncomfortable when hugged even by close friends. Onlookers might misinterpret what they saw, and more important, what would we think of ourselves if we felt a twinge of sensual pleasure from the embrace.

24   Direct verbal expressions of affection or tenderness are also something that only homosexuals and women engage in. Between "real" men affection has to be disguised in gruff, "you old son-of-a-bitch" style. Paradoxically, in some instances, terms of endearment between men can be used as a ritual badge of

compromised (par. 20): exposed to danger or ridicule

surge (par. 22): flood

inherently (par. 22): basically

vestige (par. 23): trace, part

ostracism (par. 23): disgraceful exclusion

revulsion (par. 23): disgust

overt (par. 23): open to view

paradoxically (par. 24): seemingly contradictory

manhood, dangerous medicine safe only for the strong. The flirting with homosexuality that characterizes the initiation rites of many fraternities and men's clubs serves this purpose. Claude Brown wrote about black life in New York City in the 1950s:

> The term ["baby"] had a hip ring to it. . . . It was like saying, "Man, look at me. I've got masculinity to spare. . . . I can say 'baby' to another cat and he can say 'baby' to me, and we can say it with strength in our voices." If you could say it, this meant that you really had to be sure of yourself, sure of your masculinity.

Fear of homosexuality does more than inhibit the physical display of affection. One of the major recurring themes in the men's groups led by psychotherapist Don Clark was:

> "A large segment of my feelings about other men are unknown or distorted because I am afraid they might have something to do with homosexuality. Now I'm lonely for other men and don't know how to find what I want with them."

As Clark observes, "The specter of homosexuality seems to be the dragon at the gateway to self-awareness, understanding, and acceptance of male-male needs. If a man tries to pretend the dragon is not there by turning a blind eye to erotic feelings for all other males, he also blinds himself to the rich variety of feelings that are related."

25   The few situations in which men do acknowledge strong feelings of affection and dependence toward other men are exceptions which prove the rule. With "cop couples," for example, or combat soldier "buddies," intimacy and dependence are forced on the men by their work—they have to ride in the patrol car or be in the same foxhole with somebody—and the jobs themselves have such highly masculine images that the men can get away with behavior that would be suspect under any other conditions.

26   Furthermore, even these combat-buddy relationships, when looked at closely, turn out not to be particularly intimate or personal. Margaret Mead has written:

> During the last war English observers were confused by the apparent contradiction between American soldiers' emphasis on the buddy, so grievously exemplified in the break-downs that followed a buddy's death, and the results of detailed inquiry which showed how transitory these buddy relationships were. It was found that men actually accepted their buddies as derivatives from their outfit, and from accidents of association, rather than because of any special personality characteristics capable of ripening into friendship.

One effect of the fear of appearing to be homosexual is to reinforce the practice that two men rarely get together alone without a reason. I once called a friend to suggest that we have dinner together. "O.K.," he said. "What's up?" I felt uncomfortable telling him that I just wanted to talk, that there was no other reason for the invitation.

27   Men get together to conduct business, to drink, to play games and sports,

specter (par. 24): literally, a ghost or spirit; here, a fear

grievously (par. 26): sadly

exemplified (par. 26): shown

transitory (par. 26): temporary, short-lived

derivatives from (par. 26): parts of

ripening (par. 26): developing

reinforce (par. 26): strengthen, encourage

to re-establish contact after long absences, to participate in heterosexual social occasions—circumstances in which neither person is responsible for actually wanting to see the other. Men are particularly comfortable seeing each other in groups. The group situation defuses any possible assumptions about the intensity of feeling between particular men and provides the safety of numbers—"All the guys are here." It makes personal communication, which requires a level of trust and mutual understanding not generally shared by all members of a group, more difficult and offers an excuse for avoiding this dangerous territory. And it provides what is most sought after in men's friendships: mutual reassurance of masculinity.

defuses (par. 27): decreases

A Victim

Bruno Bettelheim

1   Many students of discrimination are aware that the victim often reacts in ways as undesirable as the action of the aggressor. Less attention is paid to this because it is easier to excuse a defendant than an offender, and because they assume that once the aggression stops the victim's reactions will stop too. But I doubt if this is of real service to the persecuted. His main interest is that the persecution cease. But that is less apt to happen if he lacks a real understanding of the phenomenon of persecution, in which victim and persecutor are inseparably interlocked.

2   Let me illustrate with the following example: in the winter of 1938 a Polish Jew murdered the German attaché in Paris, vom Rath. The Gestapo used the event to step up anti-Semitic actions, and in the camp new hardships were inflicted on Jewish prisoners. One of these was an order barring them from the medical clinic unless the need for treatment had originated in work accidents.

3   Nearly all prisoners suffered from frostbite which often led to gangrene and then amputation. Whether or not a Jewish prisoner was admitted to the clinic to prevent such a fate depended on the whim of an SS private. On reaching the clinic entrance, the prisoner explained the nature of his ailment to the SS man, who then decided if he should get treatment or not.

4   I too suffered from frostbite. At first I was discouraged from trying to get medical care by the fate of Jewish prisoners whose attempts had ended up in no treatment, only abuse. Finally things got worse and I was afraid that waiting longer would mean amputation. So I decided to make the effort.

5   When I got to the clinic, there were many prisoners lined up as usual, a score of them Jews suffering from severe frostbite. The main topic of discussion was one's chances of being admitted to the clinic. Most Jews had planned their

students of discrimination (par. 1): those who study discrimination

the phenomenon of (par. 1): the real nature of

attaché (par. 2): a member of a government's diplomatic staff

Gestapo (par. 2): German secret-police

anti-Semitic actions (par. 2): persecution of Jews

SS (par. 3): a prestigious branch of the Nazi armed forces, responsible for maintaining and operating concentration camps throughout Europe

procedure in detail. Some thought it best to stress their service in the German army during World War I: wounds received or decorations won. Others planned to stress the severity of their frostbite. A few decided it was best to tell some "tall story," such as that an SS officer had ordered them to report at the clinic.

6   Most of them seemed convinced that the SS man on duty would not see through their schemes. Eventually they asked me about my plans. Having no definite ones, I said I would go by the way the SS man dealt with other Jewish prisoners who had frostbite like me, and proceed accordingly. I doubted how wise it was to follow a preconceived plan, because it was hard to anticipate the reactions of a person you didn't know.

7   The prisoners reacted as they had at other times when I had voiced similar ideas on how to deal with the SS. They insisted that one SS man was like another, all equally vicious and stupid. As usual, any frustration was immediately discharged against the person who caused it, or was nearest at hand. So, in abusive terms they accused me of not wanting to share my plan with them, or of intending to use one of theirs; it angered them that I was ready to meet the enemy unprepared.

8   No Jewish prisoner ahead of me in the line was admitted to the clinic. The more a prisoner pleaded, the more annoyed and violent the SS became. Expressions of pain amused him; stories of previous services rendered to Germany outraged him. He proudly remarked that *he* could not be taken in by Jews, that fortunately the time had passed when Jews could reach their goal by lamentations.

9   When my turn came he asked me in a screeching voice if I knew that work accidents were the only reason for admitting Jews to the clinic, and if I came because of such an accident. I replied that I knew the rules, but that I couldn't work unless my hands were freed of the dead flesh. Since prisoners were not allowed to have knives, I asked to have the dead flesh cut away. I tried to be matter-of-fact, avoiding pleading, deference, or arrogance. He replied: "If that's all you want, I'll tear the flesh off myself." And he started to pull at the festering skin. Because it did not come off as easily as he may have expected, or for some other reason, he waved me into the clinic.

10   Inside, he gave me a malevolent look and pushed me into the treatment room. There he told the prisoner orderly to attend to the wound. While this was being done, the guard watched me closely for signs of pain but I was able to suppress them. As soon as the cutting was over, I started to leave. He showed surprise and asked why I didn't wait for further treatment. I said I had gotten the service I asked for, at which he told the orderly to make an exception and treat my hand. After I had left the room, he called me back and gave me a card entitling me to further treatment, and admittance to the clinic without inspection at the entrance.

*   *   *

11   Because my behavior did not correspond to what he expected of Jewish prisoners on the basis of his projection, he could not use his prepared defenses against being touched by the prisoner's plight. Since I did not act as the danger-

preconceived (par. 6): thought out beforehand

anticipate (par. 6): foresee

discharged against (par. 7): directed toward, aimed at

rendered (par. 8): done for

lamentations (par. 8): expressions of sorrow

deference (par. 9): submission

festering (par. 9): inflamed

malevolent (par. 10): hateful

suppress (par. 10): hide, control

ous Jew was expected to, I did not activate the anxieties that went with his stereotype. Still, he did not altogether trust me, so he continued to watch while I
received treatment.

12   Throughout these dealings, the SS felt uneasy with me, though he did not
unload on me the annoyance his uneasiness aroused. Perhaps he watched me
closely because he expected that sooner or later I would slip up and behave the
way his projected image of the Jew was expected to act. This would have meant
his delusional creation had become real.

projection (par. 11): expectation

activate (par. 11): set in motion

stereotype (par. 11): a preconceived notion of what a member of a group is like

delusional (par. 12): false

The Prisoner's Dilemma

Stephen Chapman

1   "If the punitive laws of Islam were applied for only one year, all the devastating injustices would be uprooted. Misdeeds must be punished by the law of
retaliation: cut off the hands of the thief; kill the murderers; flog the adulterous
woman or man. Your concerns, your 'humanitarian' scruples are more childish
than reasonable. Under the terms of Koranic law, any judge fulfilling the seven
requirements (that he have reached puberty, be a believer, know the Koranic
laws perfectly, be just, and not be affected by amnesia, or be a bastard, or be of
the female sex) is qualified to be a judge in any type of case. He can thus judge
and dispose of twenty trials in a single day, whereas the Occidental justice might
take years to argue them out."

—from *Sayings of the Ayatollah Khomeini* (Bantam Books)

2   One of the amusements of life in the modern West is the opportunity to observe the barbaric rituals of countries that are attached to the customs of the dark
ages. Take Pakistan, for example, our newest ally and client state in Asia. Last
October President Zia, in harmony with the Islamic fervor that is sweeping this
part of the world, revived the traditional Moslem practice of flogging lawbreak-
ers in public. In Pakistan, this qualified as mass entertainment, and no fewer
than 10,000 law-abiding Pakistanis turned out to see justice done to 26 convicts.

punitive laws (par. 1): laws relating to punishment

Islam (par. 1): a religion founded by the prophet Mohammed (570?–632 A.D.)

retaliation (par. 1): revenge

flog (par. 1): whip

Koranic (par. 1): pertaining to the Koran, the sacred book of Islam

Occidental (par. 1): western

barbaric (par. 2): brutal, uncivilized

client state (par. 2): a country dependent on the economic support of another country

To Western sensibilities the spectacle seemed barbaric—both in the sense of cruel and in the sense of pre-civilized. In keeping with Islamic custom each of the unfortunates—who had been caught in prostitution raids the previous night and summarily convicted and sentenced—was stripped down to a pair of white shorts, which were painted with a red stripe across the buttocks (the target). Then he was shackled against an easel, with pads thoughtfully placed over the kidneys to prevent injury. The floggers were muscular, fierce-looking sorts—convicted murderers, as it happens—who paraded around the flogging platform in colorful loincloths. When the time for the ceremony began, one of the floggers took a running start and brought a five-foot stave down across the first victim's buttocks, eliciting screams from the convict and murmurs from the audience. Each of the 26 received from five to 15 lashes. One had to be carried from the stage unconscious.

3   Flogging is one of the punishments stipulated by Koranic law, which has made it a popular penological device in several Moslem countries, including Pakistan, Saudi Arabia, and, most recently, the ayatollah's Iran. Flogging, or *ta'zir*, is the general punishment prescribed for offenses that don't carry an explicit Koranic penalty. Some crimes carry automatic *hadd* punishments—stoning or scourging (a severe whipping) for illicit sex, scourging for drinking alcoholic beverages, amputation of the hands for theft. Other crimes—as varied as murder and abandoning Islam—carry the death penalty (usually carried out in public). Colorful practices like these have given the Islamic world an image in the West, as described by historian G. H. Jansen, "of blood dripping from the stumps of amputated hands and from the striped backs of malefactors, and piles of stones barely concealing the battered bodies of adulterous couples." Jansen, whose book *Militant Islam* is generally effusive in its praise of Islamic practices, grows squeamish when considering devices like flogging, amputation, and stoning. But they are given enthusiastic endorsement by the Koran itself.

4   Such traditions, we all must agree, are no sign of an advanced civilization. In the West, we have replaced these various punishments (including the death penalty in most cases) with a single device. Our custom is to confine criminals in prison for varying lengths of time. In Illinois, a reasonably typical state, grand theft carries a punishment of three to five years; armed robbery can get you from six to 30. The lowest form of felony theft is punishable by one to three years in prison. Most states impose longer sentences on habitual offenders. In Kentucky, for example, habitual offenders can be sentenced to life in prison. Other states are less brazen, preferring the more genteel sounding "indeterminate sentence," which allows parole boards to keep inmates locked up for as long as life.

sensibilities (par. 2): emotions, reasoning

spectacle (par. 2): public display

summarily (par. 2): quickly and without formality

shackled (par. 2): chained

stave (par. 2): stick

eliciting (par. 2): causing

stipulated (par. 3): specified

penological (par. 3): relating to prisoners

malefactors (par. 3): law breakers

effusive (par. 3): unrestrained, excessive

endorsement (par. 3): approval

brazen (par. 4): excessively bold

genteel (par. 4): well-bred

indeterminate (par. 4): indefinite

It was under an indeterminate sentence of one to 14 years that George Jackson served 12 years in California prisons for committing a $70 armed robbery. Under a Texas law imposing an automatic life sentence for a third felony conviction, a man was sent to jail for life last year because of three thefts adding up to less than $300 in property value. Texas also is famous for occasionally imposing extravagantly long sentences, often running into hundreds or thousands of years. This gives Texas a leg up on Maryland, which used to sentence some criminals to life plus a day—a distinctive if superfluous flourish.

5   The punishment *intended* by Western societies in sending their criminals to prison is the loss of freedom. But, as everyone knows, the actual punishment in most American prisons is of a wholly different order. The February 2 [1980] riot at New Mexico's state prison in Santa Fe, one of several bloody prison riots in the nine years since the Attica blood bath, once again dramatized the conditions of life in an American prison. Four hundred prisoners seized control of the prison before dawn. By sunset the next day 33 inmates had died at the hands of other convicts and another 40 people (including five guards) had been seriously hurt. Macabre stories came out of prisoners being hanged, murdered with blowtorches, decapitated, tortured, and mutilated in a variety of gruesome ways by drug-crazed rioters.

6   The Santa Fe penitentiary was typical of most maximum-security facilities, with prisoners subject to overcrowding, filthy conditions, and routine violence. It also housed first-time, non-violent offenders, like check forgers and drug dealers, with murderers serving life sentences. In a recent lawsuit, the American Civil Liberties Union called the prison "totally unfit for human habitation." But the ACLU says New Mexico's penitentiary is far from the nation's worst.

7   That American prisons are a disgrace is taken for granted by experts of every ideological stripe. Conservative James Q. Wilson has criticized our "[c]rowded, antiquated prisons that require men and women to live in fear of one another and to suffer not only deprivation of liberty but a brutalizing regimen." Leftist Jessica Mitford has called our prisons "the ultimate expression of injustice and inhumanity." In 1973 a national commission concluded that "the American correctional system today appears to offer minimum protection to the public and maximum harm to the offender." Federal courts have ruled that confinement in prisons in 16 different states violates the constitutional ban on "cruel and unusual punishment."

8   What are the advantages of being a convicted criminal in an advanced culture? First there is the overcrowding in prisons. One Tennessee prison, for ex-

---

superfluous flourish (par. 4): unnecessary addition

Attica (par. 5): prison in New York

Macabre (par. 5): horror

decapitated (par. 5): beheaded

gruesome (par. 5): horrible, brutal

American Civil Liberties Union (par. 6): an organization that seeks to protect the civil rights of all Americans

habitation (par. 6): occupancy

ideological stripe (par. 7): political or philosophical position

Conservative (par. 7): one who tends to favor the preservation of existing social or political systems: considered a member of "the Right." (See "Leftist" below.)

antiquated (par. 7): outdated

deprivation (par. 7): loss

regimen (par. 7): system

Leftist (par. 7): a liberal, or one who tends to favor social or political reform

ample, has a capacity of 806, according to accepted space standards, but it houses 2300 inmates. One Louisiana facility has confined four and five prisoners in a single six-foot-by-six-foot cell. Then there is the disease caused by over-crowding, unsanitary conditions, and poor or inadequate medical care. A federal appeals court noted that the Tennessee prison had suffered frequent outbreaks of infectious diseases like hepatitis and tuberculosis. But the most distinctive element of American prison life is its constant violence. In his book *Criminal Violence, Criminal Justice,* Charles Silberman noted that in one Louisiana prison, there were 211 stabbings in only three years, 11 of them fatal. There were 15 slayings in a prison in Massachusetts between 1972 and 1975. According to a federal court, in Alabama's penitentiaries (as in many others), "robbery, rape, extortion, theft and assault are everyday occurrences."

9   At least in regard to cruelty, it's not at all clear that the system of punishment that has evolved in the West is less barbaric than the grotesque practices of Islam. Skeptical? Ask yourself: would you rather be subjected to a few minutes of intense pain and considerable public humiliation, or be locked away for two or three years in a prison cell crowded with ill-tempered sociopaths? Would you rather lose a hand or spend 10 years or more in a typical state prison? I have taken my own survey on this matter. I have found no one who does not find the Islamic system hideous. And I have found no one who, given the choices mentioned above, would not prefer its penalties to our own.

10   The great divergence between Western and Islamic fashions in punishment is relatively recent. Until roughly the end of the 18th century, criminals in Western countries rarely were sent to prison. Instead they were subject to an ingenious assortment of penalties. Many perpetrators of a variety of crimes simply were executed, usually by some imaginative and extremely unpleasant method involving prolonged torture, such as breaking on the wheel, burning at the stake, or drawing and quartering. Michael Foucault's book *Discipline and Punish: The Birth of the Prison* notes one form of capital punishment in which the condemned man's "belly was opened up, his entrails quickly ripped out, so that he had time to see them, with his own eyes, being thrown on the fire; in which he was finally decapitated and his body quartered." Some criminals were forced to serve on slave galleys. But in most cases various corporal measures such as pillorying, flogging, and branding sufficed.

11   In time, however, public sentiment recoiled against these measures. They were replaced by imprisonment, which was thought to have two advantages. First, it was considered to be more humane. Second, and more important,

grotesque (par. 9): hideous, horrible

skeptical (par. 9): doubting

sociopaths (par. 9): those who display anti-social behavior

divergence (par. 10): difference

ingenious (par. 10): creative, clever

perpetrators (par. 10): those who are guilty

drawing and quartering (par. 10): the practice of tying each of a person's limbs to a horse and having the four horses run in different directions so that the person was pulled into four pieces, or quartered

entrails (par. 10): intestines

galleys (par. 10): ships

pillorying (par. 10): a type of punishment in which one's hands and head are placed within the holes of a stock or wooden frame

recoiled (par. 11): turned

prison was supposed to hold out the possibility of rehabilitation—purging the criminal of his criminality—something that less civilized punishments did not even aspire to. An 1854 report by inspectors of the Pennsylvania prison system illustrates the hopes nurtured by humanitarian reformers:

> Depraved tendencies, characteristic of the convict, have been restrained by the absence of vicious association, and in the mild teaching of Christianity, the unhappy criminal finds a solace for an involuntary exile from the comforts of social life. If hungry, he is fed; if naked, he is clothed; if destitute of the first rudiments of education, he is taught to read and write; and if he has never been blessed with a means of livelihood, he is schooled in a mechanical art, which in after life may be to him the source of profit and respectability. Employment is not his toil nor labor, weariness. He embraces them with alacrity, as contributing to his moral and mental elevation.

12   Imprisonment is now the universal method of punishing criminals in the United States. It is thought to perform five functions, each of which has been given a label by criminologist. First, there is simple *retribution:* punishing the lawbreaker to serve society's sense of justice and to satisfy the victims' desire for revenge. Second, there is *specific deterrence:* discouraging the offender from misbehaving in the future. Third, *general deterrence:* using the offender as an example to discourage others from turning to crime. Fourth, *prevention:* at least during the time he is kept off the streets, the criminal cannot victimize other members of society. Finally, and most important, there is *rehabilitation:* reforming the criminal so that when he returns to society he will be inclined to obey the laws and able to make an honest living.

13   How satisfactorily do American prisons perform by these criteria? Well, of course, they do punish. But on the other scores they don't do so well. Their effect in discouraging future criminality by the prisoner or others is the subject of much debate, but the soaring rates of the last 20 years suggest that prisons are not a dramatically effective deterrent to criminal behavior. Prisons do isolate convicted criminals, but only to divert crime from ordinary citizens to prison guards and fellow inmates. Almost no one contends any more that prisons rehabilitate their inmates. If anything, they probably impede rehabilitation by forcing inmates into prolonged and almost exclusive association with other criminals. And prisons cost a lot of money. Housing a typical prisoner in a typical prison costs far more than a stint at a top university. This cost would be justified if prisons did the job they were intended for. But it is clear to all that prisons fail on the very grounds—humanity and hope of rehabilitation—that caused them to replace earlier, cheaper forms of punishment.

14   The universal acknowledgment that prisons do not rehabilitate criminals has produced two responses. The first is to retain the hope of rehabilitation but

purging (par. 11): ridding

aspire to (par. 11): attempt

depraved (par. 11): morally corrupt

solace (par. 11): comfort

destitute (par. 11): lacking

rudiments (par. 11): basics

alacrity (par. 11): eagerness

elevation (par. 11): improvement

criteria (par. 13): a set of guidelines

contends (par. 13): argues

impede (par. 13): hinder

stint (par. 13): stay

do away with imprisonment as much as possible and replace it with various forms of "alternative treatment," such as psychotherapy, supervised probation, and vocational training. Psychiatrist Karl Menninger, one of the principal critics of American penology, has suggested even more unconventional approaches, such as "a new job opportunity or a vacation trip, a course of reducing exercises, a cosmetic surgical operation or a herniotomy, some night school courses, a wedding in the family (even one for the patient!), an inspiring sermon." This starry-eyed approach naturally has produced a backlash from critics on the right, who think that it's time to abandon the goal of rehabilitation. They argue that prisons perform an important service just by keeping criminals off the streets, and thus should be used with that purpose alone in mind.

15 So the debate continues to rage in all the same old ruts. No one, of course, would think of copying the medieval practices of Islamic nations and experimenting with punishments such as flogging and amputation. But let us consider them anyway. How do they compare with our American prison system in achieving the ostensible objectives of punishment? First, do they punish? Obviously they do, and in a uniquely painful and memorable way. Of course any sensible person, given the choice, would prefer suffering these punishments to years of incarceration in a typical American prison. But presumably no Western penologist would criticize Islamic Punishments on the grounds that they are not barbaric enough. Do they deter crime? Yes, and probably more effectively than sending convicts off to prison. Now we read about a prison sentence in the newspaper, then think no more about the criminal's payment for his crimes until, perhaps, years later we read a small item reporting his release. By contrast, one can easily imagine the vivid impression it would leave to be wandering through a local shopping center and to stumble onto the scene of some poor wretch being lustily flogged. And the occasional sight of an habitual offender walking around with a bloody stump at the end of his arm no doubt also would serve as a forceful reminder that crime does not pay.

16 Do flogging and amputation discourage recidivism? No one knows whether the scars on his back would dissuade a criminal from risking another crime, but it is hard to imagine that corporal measures could stimulate a higher rate of recidivism than already exists. Islamic forms of punishment do not serve the favorite new right goal of simply isolating criminals from the rest of society, but they may achieve the same purpose of making further crimes impossible. In the movie *Bonnie and Clyde*, Warren Beatty successfully robs a bank with his arm in a sling, but this must be dismissed as artistic license. It must be extraordinarily difficult, at the very least, to perform much violent crime with only one hand.

17 Do these medieval forms of punishment rehabilitate the criminal? Plainly not. But long prison terms do not rehabilitate either. And it is just as plain that typical Islamic punishments are no crueler to the convict than incarceration in the typical American state prison.

18 Of course there are other reasons besides its bizarre forms of punishment that the Islamic system of justice seems uncivilized to the Western mind. One is the absence of due process. Another is the long list of offenses—such as drink-

herniotomy (par. 14): removal of a hernia

ostensible (par. 15): supposed

incarceration (par. 15): imprisonment

vivid (par. 15): sharp, lasting

recidivism (par. 16): return to criminal behavior

dissuade (par. 16): discourage

due process (par. 18): a set of procedures designed to protect the legal rights of citizens

ing, adultery, blasphemy, "profiteering," and so on—that can bring on conviction and punishment. A third is all the ritualistic mumbo-jumbo in pronouncements of Islamic law (like that talk about puberty and amnesia in the ayatollah's quotation at the beginning of this article). Even in these matters, however, a little cultural modesty is called for. The vast majority of American criminals are convicted and sentenced as a result of plea bargaining, in which due process plays almost no role. It has been only half a century since a wave of religious fundamentalism stirred this country to outlaw the consumption of alcoholic beverages. Most states also still have laws imposing austere-constraints on sexual conduct. Only two weeks ago the *Washington Post* reported that the FBI had spent two and a half years and untold amounts of money to break up a nationwide pornography ring. Flogging the clients of prostitutes, as the Pakistanis did, does seem silly. But only a few months ago Mayor Koch of New York was proposing that clients caught in his own city have their names broadcast by radio stations. We are not so far advanced on such matters as we often like to think. Finally, my lawyer friends assure me that the rules of jurisdiction for American courts contain plenty of petty requirements and bizarre distinctions that would sound silly enough to foreign ears.

19   Perhaps it sounds barbaric to talk of flogging and amputation, and perhaps it is. But our system of punishment also is barbaric, and probably more so. Only cultural smugness about their system and willful ignorance about our own make it easy to regard the one as cruel and the other as civilized. We inflict our cruelties away from public view, while nations like Pakistan stage them in front of 10,000 onlookers. Their outrages are visible; ours are not. Most Americans can live their lives for years without having their peace of mind disturbed by the knowledge of what goes on in our prisons. To choose imprisonment over flogging and amputation is not to choose human kindness over cruelty, but merely to prefer that our cruelties be kept out of sight, and out of mind.

20   Public flogging and amputation may be more barbaric forms of punishment than imprisonment, even if they are not more cruel. Society may pay a higher price for them, even if the particular criminal does not. Revulsion against officially sanctioned violence and infliction of pain derives from something deeply ingrained in the Western conscience, and clearly it is something admirable. Grotesque displays of the sort that occur in Islamic countries probably breed a greater tolerance for physical cruelty, for example, which prisons do not do precisely because they conceal their cruelties. In fact it is our admirable intolerance for calculated violence that makes it necessary for us to conceal what we have not been able to do away with. In a way this is a good thing, since it holds

blasphemy (par. 18): expressing lack of respect for God or anything considered sacred

profiteering (par. 18): making excessive profits

ritualistic (par. 18): ceremonial

pronouncements (par. 18): statements, declarations

plea bargaining (par. 18): a process in which a criminal agrees to plead guilty, thus avoiding a trial, in exchange for a reduced charge or sentence

austere (par. 18): severe

petty (par. 18): unimportant

smugness (par. 19): feeling of superiority

revulsion (par. 20): disgust

sanctioned (par. 20): approved

ingrained (par. 20): rooted

calculated (par. 20): planned, intended

out the hope that we may eventually find a way to do away with it. But in another way it is a bad thing, since it permits us to congratulate ourselves on our civilized humanitarianism while violating its norms in this one area of our national life.

humanitarianism (par. 20): respect for the rights and life of human beings

norms (par. 20): standards of behavior

Total Effect and the Eighth Grade

Flannery O'Connor

1   In two recent instances in Georgia, parents have objected to their eighth-and-ninth-grade children's reading assignments in modern fiction. This seems to happen with some regularity in cases throughout the country. The unwitting parent picks up his child's book, glances through it, comes upon passages of erotic detail or profanity, and takes off at once to complain to the school board. Sometimes, as in one of the Georgia cases, the teacher is dismissed and hackles rise in liberal circles everywhere.

2   The two cases in Georgia, which involved Steinbeck's *East of Eden* and John Hersey's *A Bell for Adano,* provoked considerable newspaper comment. One columnist, in commending the enterprise of the teachers, announced that students do not like to read the fusty works of the nineteenth century, that their attention can best be held by novels dealing with the realities of our own time, and that the Bible, too, is full of racy stories.

3   Mr. Hersey himself addressed a letter to the State School Superintendent in behalf of the teacher who had been dismissed. He pointed out that his book is not scandalous, that it attempts to convey an earnest message about the nature of democracy, and that it falls well within the limits of the principle of "total effect," the principle followed in legal cases by which a book is judged not for isolated parts but by the final effect of the whole book upon the general reader.

4   I do not want to comment on the merits of these particular cases. What concerns me is what novels ought to be assigned in the eighth and ninth grades as a matter of course, for if these cases indicate anything, they indicate the haphazard way in which fiction is approached in our high schools. Presumably there is a state reading list which contains "safe" books for teachers to assign; after that it is up to the teacher.

5   English teachers come in Good, Bad, and Indifferent, but too frequently in high schools anyone who can speak English is allowed to teach it. Since several

hackles rise (par. 1): anger develops

provoked (par. 2): caused

commending (par. 2): praising

fusty (par. 2): stuffy, old-fashioned

racy (par. 2): almost indecent

convey (par. 3): communicate

haphazard (par. 4): random, without order or logic

novels can't easily be gathered into one textbook, the fiction that students are assigned depends upon their teacher's knowledge, ability, and taste: variable factors at best. More often than not, the teacher assigns what he thinks will hold the attention and interest of the students. Modern fiction will certainly hold it.

6   Ours is the first age in history which has asked the child what he would tolerate learning, but that is a part of the problem with which I am not equipped to deal. The Devil of Educationism that possesses us is the kind that can be "cast out only by prayer and fasting." No one has yet come along strong enough to do it. In other ages the attention of children was held by Homer and Virgil, among others, but, by the reverse evolutionary process, that is no longer possible; our children are too stupid now to enter the past imaginatively. No one asks the student if algebra pleases him or if he finds it satisfactory that some French verbs are irregular, but if he prefers Hersey to Hawthorne, his taste must prevail.

7   I would like to put forward the proposition, repugnant to most English teachers, that fiction, if it is going to be taught in the high schools, should be taught as a subject and as a subject with a history. The total effect of a novel depends not only on its innate impact, but upon experience, literary and otherwise, with which it is approached. No child needs to be assigned Hersey or Steinbeck until he is familiar with a certain amount of the best work of Cooper, Hawthorne, Melville, the early James, and Crane, and he does not need to be assigned these until he has been introduced to some of the better English novelists of the eighteenth and nineteenth centuries.

8   The fact that these works do not present him with the realities of his own time is all to the good. He is surrounded by the realities of his own time, and he has no perspective whatever from which to view them. Like the college student who wrote in her paper on Lincoln that he went to the movies and got shot, many students go to college unaware that the world was not made yesterday; their studies began with the present and dipped backward occasionally when it seemed necessary or unavoidable.

9   There is much to be enjoyed in the great British novels of the nineteenth century, much that a good teacher can open up in them for the young student. There is no reason why these novels should be either too simple or too difficult

---

The Devil of Educationism that possesses us is the kind that can be "cast out only by prayer and fasting" (par. 6): O'Conner means in this sentence that certain practices in education will be very difficult to change. Her quotation is biblical (Mark 9: 17–29). Jesus was able to rid a child of a "foul spirit," something his disciples were unable to do. The disciples asked Jesus why they had failed, and he replied: "This kind can come forth by nothing but by prayer and fasting."

Homer (par. 6): ancient Greek writer of the *Iliad* and the *Odyssey*

Virgil (par. 6): Roman poet (70–19 B.C.), author of the *Aeneid*

the reverse evolutionary process (par. 6): According to the evolutionary process, each generation should be slightly more intelligent than the generation that came before it. If that process has been reversed, each generation would be slightly less intelligent than the one before it.

Hawthorne (par. 6): American author (1804–1864)

proposition (par. 7): idea, suggestion

repugnant (par. 7): offensive, unacceptable

The total effect of a novel depends not only on its innate impact, but upon experience, literary and otherwise, with which it is approached (par. 7): The way a novel affects a reader depends on both the novel's content and the reader's experience.

Cooper, Hawthorne, Melville, the early James, and Crane (par. 7): nineteenth-century American writers

perspective (par. 8): experience necessary to develop sound judgment

for the eighth grade. For the simple, they offer simple pleasures; for the more precocious, they can be made to yield subtler ones if the teacher is up to it. Let the student discover, after reading the nineteenth-century British novel, that the nineteenth-century American novel is quite different as to its literary characteristics, and he will thereby learn something not only about these individual works but about the sea-change which a new historical situation can effect in a literary form. Let him come to modern fiction with his experience behind him, and he will be better able to see and to deal with the more complicated demands of the best twentieth-century fiction.

10   Modern fiction often looks simpler than the fiction that preceded it, but in reality it is more complex. A natural evolution has taken place. The author has for the most part absented himself from direct participation in the work and has left the reader to make his own way amid experiences dramatically rendered and symbolically ordered. The modern novelist merges the reader in the experience; he tends to raise the passions he touches upon. If he is a good novelist, he raises them to effect by their order and clarity a new experience—the total effect— which is not in itself sensuous or simply of the moment. Unless the child has had some literary experience before, he is not going to be able to resolve the immediate passions the book arouses into any true, total picture.

11   It is here the moral problem will arise. It is one thing for a child to read about adultery in the Bible or in *Anna Karenina,* and quite another for him to read about it in most modern fiction. This is not only because in both the former instances adultery is considered a sin, and in the latter, at most, an inconvenience, but because modern writing involves the reader in the action with a new degree of intensity, and literary mores now permit him to be involved in any action a human being can perform.

12   In our fractured culture, we cannot agree on morals; we cannot even agree that moral matters should come before literary ones when there is a conflict between them. All this is another reason why the high schools would do well to return to their proper business of preparing foundations. Whether in the senior year students should be assigned modern novelists should depend both on their parents' consent and on what they have already read and understood.

13   The high-school English teacher will be fulfilling his responsibility if he furnishes the student a guided opportunity, through the best writing of the past, to come, in time, to an understanding of the best writing of the present. He will teach literature, not social studies or little lessons in democracy or the customs of many lands.

14   And if the student finds that this is not to his taste? Well, that is regrettable. Most regrettable. His taste should not be consulted; it is being formed.

precocious (par. 9): advanced, gifted

subtler (par. 9): more difficult to detect

absented (par. 10): removed

amid (par. 10): among

rendered (par. 10): presented

merges the reader in the experience (par. 10): attempts to make the reader experience what is happening in a novel

to effect (par. 10): to create

clarity (par. 10): clearness

sensuous (par. 10): likely to arouse passion

Anna Karenina (par. 11): novel by Russian author Leo Tolstoy (1828–1910)

mores (par. 11): standards

fractured (par. 12): diverse, divided

4

TEXTBOOK CHAPTERS

Introduction

—Karen Arms and Pamela S. Camp, from

Biology: A Journey Into Life (Saunders College

Publishing, 1988), pages 1–14

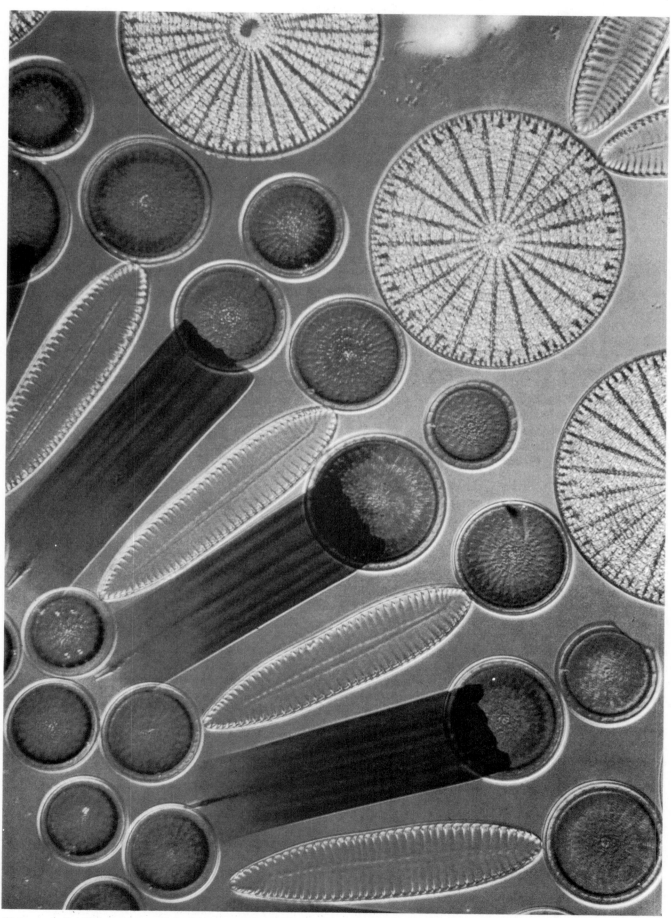

Diatoms, single-celled organisms with intricately patterned cell walls once used to test the ability of microscopes to resolve detail. Victorian microscopists painstakingly arranged diatoms to form designs on microscope slides; this photo shows part of one such arrangement (Biophoto Associates)

CHAPTER   1

INTRODUCTION

L iving things first appeared on earth some 3.5 billion years ago. Their descendants have diversified into the several million kinds of living **organisms** (plants, animals, bacteria, fungi, and the single-celled creatures called protists) alive today.

Human beings have always been interested in the other organisms around them. At first, this was a matter of survival. People needed to know which organisms could be used as food, clothing, medicine, or shelter, and which were dangerous or poisonous. Later came the luxury of scholarly study; people examined organisms more closely, collected them, classified them, and made lists of what lived where. During this time, the study of living things was generally known as natural history, which is not a science. However, natural history was the forerunner of biology, which is a true science. The hallmark of sciences, such as biology, chemistry, or physics, is the use of experiments to answer questions.

In this chapter, we shall consider how scientists go about asking and answering questions. We shall also see that science is just one way of looking at the world. Finally, we shall summarize the most important concepts in biology—which is really a brief synopsis of what is covered in this book.

1-A   SCIENCE AND SOCIETY

Science has assumed enormous importance in modern society. Many decisions affecting our future depend upon scientific discoveries. No one person can learn all that is now known about science and its practical applications. As responsible citizens, however, we can follow some of the important studies that bear on public issues, and we can apply scientific reasoning to arrive at our own positions on these issues.

There is nothing mysterious about scientific reasoning or experiments. They are merely logical ways of trying to solve problems such as are used by business people, historians, and each of us in our everyday lives. We do not need specialized scientific training or knowledge to decide whether conclusions are justified from the data presented. We can request further tests of a theory that does not appear to be well supported by the evidence, and we can agree or disagree with predictions from a theory. We can improve the way we do these things ourselves if we first understand how a scientist arrives at conclusions about natural phenomena through the same kind of process.

1-B   SCIENTIFIC METHOD

You may never have thought about how you solve problems, test theories, or decide upon a plan of action. Let us consider how biologists attack a problem so that we can examine the main types of thinking involved.

The **scientific method** is a formalized way of answering questions about causation in the natural world. In principle, the scientific method has three main steps (although in practice scientists work in many different ways). The first step is to collect **observations,** phenomena which can be detected by the senses (vision, hearing, smell, taste, and touch). Second, the scientist thinks of **hypotheses,** ideas about the cause of what has been observed. The third step is **experimentation,** performing tests designed to show that one or more of the hypotheses is more or less likely to be incorrect. Let us see how this works in practice.

Scientists usually start with observations that stimulate questions. Some years ago, one of your authors was part of a group of biologists discussing the clusters of butterflies that seemed to be everywhere that June (Figure 1–1).

"This evening," said one, "there were about twenty yellow sulfur butter-flies by the stream and some black swallowtails on the manure heap. What are they doing?"

"It's called 'puddling behavior,'" replied another. "You find puddling but-terflies in groups in open places such as the edges of drying puddles, or sand bars. I don't think anyone knows what they are doing. Another odd thing is that in many species only the males puddle."

These observations of puddling lead us to ask what the butterflies are doing and why. To answer these questions, we must think of some hypotheses that would account for the observations. That evening, the hypotheses came thick and fast from our armchair scientists.

"An article I read suggested it was a method of population control. Coming together permits the males to count each other. A newcomer can see if there is likely to be enough land for him to set up a territory in the area. Puddling saves them having to fight over territories."

"That sounds wrong to me," replied one of the company. "How can a butterfly figure out the density of males in the area from a group like that? Besides, I've seen swallowtails fight for territories."

"I think it is more likely they're feeding," another contributed. "It was called 'puddling' in the first place because the butterflies often have their proborces

FIGURE 1–1 Sulphur butterflies pud-dling on a sandbank in Brazil. (Keith Brown)

[tongues] out and seem to be sucking something up from the ground.''

"I wonder if they are feeding on substances that contain nitrogen. All organisms need nitrogen to make amino acids [the building blocks that proteins are made from]. In our lab we've shown that butterfly caterpillars grow faster if you feed them extra nitrogen, and there is lots of nitrogen in a manure pile.''

"But not in sand,'' came the objection. "And if they are after nitrogen, you'd expect females to puddle, not males. The females lay the eggs that turn into caterpillars, and extra nitrogen in the egg might be very useful, but it's not the females that puddle.''

"It sounds to me,'' chipped in another, "as if they're after salts—perhaps those that contain sodium. All the puddling places contain quite a lot of salts: urine in manure piles and concentrations left by evaporation at the edge of puddles. Lots of animals that feed on plants are short of sodium because plants contain so little of it. We put out salt blocks for cows and horses and end up attracting deer and rabbits as well. Animals need lots of sodium because they lose it all the time in their urine. Perhaps male butterflies need more than females.''

We could evaluate these alternate hypotheses only by doing experiments to test them. Some hypotheses are of no use to science because they cannot be tested. For instance, the hypothesis "puddling butterflies decide if there is room for another territory in the neighborhood'' is untestable because we can never know what, or whether, another animal decides. Even a testable hypothesis usually cannot be tested directly. A testable prediction must first be developed from it. From the hypothesis that butterflies sucked up sodium when they puddled we predicted that if we put out trays containing sodium, butterflies would be attracted to puddle on them. The hypothesis that butterflies suck up nitrogen when they puddle generated the prediction that butterflies would puddle on trays of amino acids, which contain nitrogen. Both these predictions can be tested and, in this case, both can be tested at the same time, in the same experiment.

Experiments must be designed so that their results are as unambiguous as human ingenuity can make them. For this reason, experiments have to include **control treatments** as well as **experimental treatments.** The two differ only by the factor(s) in which you are interested. For instance, to test our hypotheses, we had to show that butterflies would puddle on a tray containing amino acids or one containing sodium but would not puddle on control trays that were identical except that they did not contain the amino acids or sodium.

Suppose we put out three trays—one containing sodium, another containing amino acids, and a third containing something butterflies are most unlikely to eat, such as plain sand or sand and water (the controls). We would predict that if butterflies are attracted to puddle on sodium, they would come to puddle on the sodium tray but not on the other two. If they are attracted to amino acids, they would puddle only on that tray. If they are attracted to both, they would puddle on both of these but not on the control tray, and if they are attracted neither to amino acids nor to sodium, they would not puddle on the trays at all. Note that there are dozens of other possible reasons for the last result. If no butterflies turned up to puddle on our trays, we would have learned nothing. Butterflies might not puddle on trays because they won't come near trays for some reason, or because they never see the trays, or because they avoid the human beings watching nearby, or for any one of a number of other reasons.

So that our experiment would not be foiled for lack of butterflies, we put our trays on a sandbank by a lake where tiger swallowtail butterflies often puddled in large numbers. We filled the trays with chemically clean sand for the butterflies to stand on, and in each tray we pinned a dead male tiger swallowtail as a decoy, because we thought butterflies might be attracted to puddling places by the sight of other butterflies. Ten trays of sand were put out and the same volume of solution poured into each one. Different solutions were placed in the trays on different days.

FIGURE 1–2 Arrangement of trays on the second day of the puddling experiment. Each tray contained the same volume of sand. Each of eight trays also contained 1.5 litres of water or solution. Different solutions were placed in different trays on subsequent days. (Sugar was tested because swallowtail butterflies eat sugar-filled nectar from flowers, and therefore we wondered if they might be attracted to puddle on sugar.) The black number on each tray shows the number of "sampling" visits (lasting less than 15 seconds) by butterflies. Colored numbers show the number of butterfly-minutes spent puddling on the tray in visits lasting more than 15 seconds. The numbers make it obvious that the butterflies puddled on the trays containing sodium and those containing amino acids but not on any of the other trays.

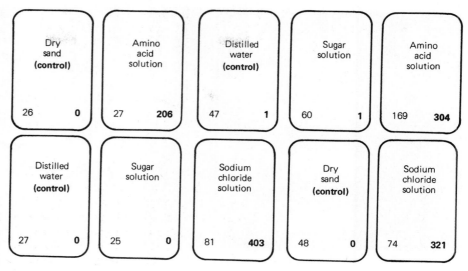

The trays used on one day of the experiment are shown in Figure 1–2. When the trays were ready, we retired behind a nearby bush, with binoculars, notebooks, and watches, to see what would happen (Figure 1–3).

Soon dozens of tiger swallowtails were hovering over the trays. Whenever a butterfly landed on a tray, it stuck its proboscis into the sand. On occasion, as many as thirty butterflies were on a tray together. Most of the butterflies spent a few seconds on every tray, but they puddled (which we defined as staying for more than 15 seconds) on only a few trays: all those containing sodium in any form and those containing amino acids (see Figure 1–2).

We were fairly sure that these results were accurate because we had taken another precaution: the people recording the butterflies' visits did not know which tray contained which solution. Making an experiment "blind" in this way is important. Psychologists have shown that the results achieved, even in a carefully controlled experiment, depend on what the experimenter wants to find.

Those of us who favored the hypothesis that butterflies puddle to obtain sodium were disappointed that they were also attracted to amino acids. But prejudice can sometimes be useful, even in science! Not only were we disappointed by the results, we were inclined to think they were wrong. Back we went to reread the label on the bottle of amino acids we had used. We now noticed that it said, "Prepared in sodium citrate." According to popular myth, scientists are objective and unexcitable, but our hearts were beating fast as a technician determined the sodium content of our amino acids: they were chock full of sodium! There followed frantic phone calls and special deliveries to obtain amino acids free from sodium. Then followed a suspenseful experiment, which showed that butterflies did not puddle on our new, sodium-free amino acids.

We had now conducted a well-controlled scientific experiment. What conclusions could we draw? Had we proved the hypothesis that butterflies puddle so as to obtain sodium? No. We had not even shown that the butterflies actually drank the sodium solution. All we had shown was that male tiger swallowtail butterflies would puddle on sand containing sodium salts but not on sand containing various other solutions. Many more hypotheses and experiments were needed if we were to learn more.

One peculiarity of the scientific method is that a hypothesis can never formally be proved but can only be disproved. A correct hypothesis will generate predictions that are borne out by the experiment, but an incorrect hypothesis may

(a)   (b)

FIGURE 1–3   The puddling experiment. (a) Observers watching puddling trays.
(b) Butterflies visiting the trays. In the middle of each tray is pinned a dead butterfly to
serve as a decoy. (Paul Feeny)

also produce correct predictions (that is, the prediction was right, but for the wrong
reason). Therefore, if the results of an experiment agree with the prediction, we are
still not sure of the validity of the hypothesis. For instance, the hypothesis that
butterflies puddle to obtain sodium for food is not proven by the experimental
finding that butterflies puddle on sodium. They might puddle because wherever
there is sodium in nature there is also nitrogen and they really obtain nitrogen from
puddling. We have not even disproved the hypothesis that puddling is a means for
the butterflies to "count" each other. They might puddle on sodium merely as a
convenient rendezvous (although the fact that butterflies put their probosces into the
sand when they puddle and appear to be feeding makes this hypothesis extremely
unlikely). The more alternative hypotheses we disprove or cast doubt on, however,
the more we increase the likelihood that the hypothesis that remains is correct.

Scientists also hesitate to accept the results of an experiment until they are
assured of its repeatability. Repetition guards against two kinds of errors. First, we
might have inadvertently made a mistake in our technique, such as switching the
solutions, or writing our results in the wrong column of our data notebook, or
alarming the butterflies. (Even in this simple experiment, the possibilities are endless.) Second, any experiment is subject to **sampling error,** error due to the number
of subjects used. Our experiment sampled only a few dozen butterflies on six days,
and it is almost inevitable that these were in some ways inadequate to represent all
tiger swallowtails. We could be more confident of our results if we were to repeat
the experiment, using more butterflies and following precisely the same procedure.
How many butterflies do we need? The more the better, but it would be impractical
to test all the butterflies in the world. In fact, we can use statistical tests to tell how
"sure" we are of our results with a given sample size. If some of the butterflies do
not behave as we expected, we can also use statistical tests to decide whether our
results are so far from our prediction that we should discard our hypothesis.

A hypothesis supported by many different lines of evidence from repeated
experiments is generally regarded as a **theory** and after even further testing comes
to be accepted as a scientific "fact."

FIGURE 1–4 When is a fact not a fact? Nineteenth century doctors were taught that men and women breathed differently: men used their diaphragms (the sheet of muscle below the rib cage) to expand their chests, whereas women raised the ribs near the top of the chest. Finally, a woman doctor found that women breathed in this way because their clothes were so fashionably tight that the diaphragm could not move far enough to admit air into the lungs. Some women, like the one in this drawing of 1870 styles, even had their lower ribs surgically removed so that they could lace their waists more tightly.

1-C IT'S A FACT?

"It's a scientific fact" is often presented as the clincher to an argument. Most scientists, however, would argue that any scientific finding is open to question. As we have just seen, the doubts and uncertainties inherent in scientific method make it impossible to be 100% sure that a scientific discovery is "right."

"The sun rises every morning," or "spiders have eight legs," look like facts at first glance, but they are really predictions about what will happen in the future, based on past experience. "This is a table" may also seem like a fact, but it is really a statement resulting from an agreement or convention: all have agreed to call that sort of object a table.

"Facts" are also less sure than they seem because they depend on our faith in our senses. Suppose several people look at two photographs, one of a table and one of an object floating in a lake. Everyone may agree that the first photo clearly shows a table. When they look at the second one, however, some may say, "That is a Loch Ness monster," but the others may legitimately disagree. When technology, in the form of a camera, microscope, or oscilloscope, intervenes between our senses and an object, as it often must in scientific research, the problem of interpreting what we see or hear or smell becomes even more subject to doubt. Thus, a "fact" is really a piece of information that we believe in strongly or that seems highly likely to be repeated without change.

Although scientific findings are much less reliable than is generally believed, most scientists do believe that their methods discover useful information about objects and events, and that careful study increases the probability that science's generalizations about nature are a close approximation to reality. Public support for science rests on the belief that a better understanding of natural phenomena increases our ability to promote human well-being.

1-D THE LIMITATIONS OF SCIENCE

Science is only one way of exploring the world around us; history, religion, and philosophy are others. Science deals only with things that can be experienced directly or indirectly through the senses (sight and hearing, for example). By definition, science has nothing to say about the supernatural. As biologist George Gaylord Simpson noted, "This is not to say that science necessarily denies the existence of immaterial or supernatural relationships, but only that, whether or not they exist, they are not the business of science." By the same token, many religious leaders argue that religion should not censor science. A Vatican Council report put it this way: "research performed in a truly scientific manner can never be in contrast with faith because both profane and religious realities have their origin in the same God."

Although science does not deal with the supernatural or with the illogical, scientists themselves may be just as emotional, political, or illogical as anyone else, and this may affect their scientific efforts. Furthermore, their social environment strongly influences how scientists think and what projects they undertake. Scientists today do not study the physics of how to build pyramids to last for thousands of years, because we do not wish to build pyramids for the burial of our rulers.

Much public support goes to projects on "applied science," investigating problems of immediate concern such as cancer, alternative energy sources, or food production. However, there is still a great deal of basic, or "pure," research to be done to discover the principles underlying the behavior of objects and organisms in the world around us. Although such research may not benefit humankind immediately, it adds to our understanding of the world and will almost inevitably be put to use sooner or later. And even work that does not find an application may be as intellectually satisfying as painting a picture or writing a play. It is interesting that

FIGURE 1–5 Science often becomes embroiled in political controversy. We have awakened to the fascinating intelligence of whales at a time when many whale species are in danger of extinction because so many of them have been caught by whaling ships like this one. Dead whales are turned into many products, such as pet food and oil, all of which can be obtained easily from other sources. (Biophoto Associates)

people may accept "art for art's sake" but often will not grant the same privilege to science, which must work for its keep.

The history of science is replete with scientific dogmas that turned out to be wrong, although for a time they were widely accepted. This is one reason why the cautious person will not place too much faith or invest heavily in a new scientific discovery until it is fairly clear that the theory will stand the test of time.

Scientists often say that science is neither good nor bad; only the use of science, by scientists or by society, has moral consequences. From a purist's point of view, this is true. The discovery that the atom could be split was merely a scientific discovery with no moral implications. It was the decision to use this knowledge to build an atom bomb that produced the moral dilemma of whether or not it was ever right to use such a weapon.

Despite the traditionally ostrich-like approach of scientists to the moral implications of their work, more and more people now feel that scientists must become involved in society's moral decisions about science. Some scientists now feel that they must take, and that society may force them to take, more moral responsibility for the consequences of their research. However reasonable this attitude, history shows that it can destroy science if carried to extremes. Who would be brave enough to engage in science with the expectation of being held legally and financially responsible for all the unforeseeable consequences? During the Dark Ages, the Western world experienced about 500 years in which very few scientific discoveries were made because particular sorts of research or findings violated religious teachings; few of us want to return to such times.

On the other side of the coin, scientists who discover dangerous situations may be forced to choose between silence and unemployment because the remedy is so expensive. Today many professional scientific societies have adopted guidelines of ethical conduct for their members to follow, and have pledged legal aid to members who "blow the whistle" on employers that make dangerous products or dispose of hazardous materials unsafely.

There is no simple solution to these dilemmas. The peaceful coexistence of science with society depends on citizens who understand what science can and cannot do, and who do not confuse scientific with moral, economic, or political values.

1-E FUNDAMENTAL CONCEPTS OF BIOLOGY

Biology is the branch of science that studies living things: their structure, function, reproduction, and interactions with one another and with the nonliving environment. We can identify several fundamental concepts in biology, which we shall explore in this book:

226

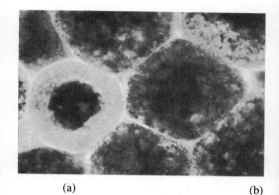

(a)   (b)

FIGURE 1–6 Cells and their characteristics. (a) Cells of *Euglena sanguinea*, seen through the microscope. This organism is classified as a protist because each individual is a single cell with a structure more complex than that of a bacterial cell. These single-celled organisms show all the features of life. They are highly organized, and they obtain and use energy from their environments. The yellowy green structures are chloroplasts, which absorb light energy and use it to make the cell's food. The cells also respond to changes in their environment. In bright light, a red pigment spreads throughout the cell, acting as a sunscreen to protect against damage by the sun's rays. The cells in this photograph have just been illuminated. The one at the middle left has not yet deployed its red pigment throughout the cell, but the cells around it have, so that the green of the chloroplasts is scarcely visible. (b) In the light, a pond with a large population of these cells has patches of blood-red water. (Biophoto Associates)

FIGURE 1–7 Living things develop. This dogfish embryo, lying on top of the yolk sac from which it draws nourishment, will develop into one of the smaller sharks. (Biophoto Associates)

1. Living things are highly ordered. The chemicals that make up a living organism are much more complex and highly ordered on a molecular level than are the chemicals that make up most nonliving systems. This chemical organization is reflected in the organized structure and function of the organism's body. All organisms contain very similar kinds of chemicals, and the chemical makeup of an organism's body differs from that of its nonliving environment.

2. Living things are organized into units called cells. Most cells are so small that we must use a microscope to see them. Many small organisms, such as bacteria and protists, consist of one cell each. Larger organisms, such as grasses and humans, contain up to hundreds of millions of cells.

Each cell is a discrete packet of highly ordered living material, a biochemical factory. It takes in nutrients and energy and uses these to maintain itself, to grow, to respond to changes in the environment, and eventually to reproduce, forming two new cells. Hence, cells are the units of structure, function, and reproduction in organisms.

3. Living things obtain and use energy from their environments to maintain and increase their high degree of orderliness. Most organisms depend, directly or indirectly, on energy from the sun. Green plants use solar energy to make food, which supports the plants themselves. It is also used by all organisms that eat plants, and eventually by those that eat the plant-eaters too. All organisms use energy from their food to maintain their bodies, to grow, and to reproduce.

4. Living organisms respond actively to their environments. Most animals respond rapidly to environmental changes by making some sort of movement—exploring, fleeing, or even rolling into a ball. Plants respond more slowly but still actively: stems and leaves bend toward light, and roots grow downward. The capacity to respond to environmental stimuli is universal among living things.

5. Living things develop. Everything changes with time, but living organisms change in particularly complex ways called development. A nonliving crystal grows by addition of identical or similar units, but a plant or animal develops new structures, such as leaves or teeth, that may differ chemically and structurally from the structures that produced them.

6. Living things reproduce themselves. New organisms—bacteria, protists, animals, plants, and fungi—arise only from the reproduction of other, similar, organisms. New cells arise only from the division of other cells.

7. The information each organism needs to survive, develop, and reproduce is segregated within the organism and passed from each organism to its offspring. This information is contained in the organism's **genetic material**—its chromosomes and genes—which specifies the possible range of the organism's development, structure, function, and response to its environment. An organism passes genetic information to its offspring, and this is why offspring are similar to their parents. Genetic information does vary somewhat, though, so parents and offspring are usually similar but not identical.

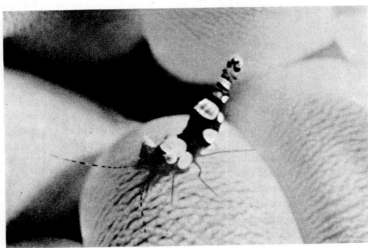

FIGURE 1–8 (*above, left*) Living things reproduce themselves. These flowers are the reproductive structures of pansy plants and will form the seeds that develop into new plants.

FIGURE 1–9 (*above, right*) The information in an organism is passed from each organism to its offspring. These mushrooms look alike because they have all inherited similar genetic information from their parents. (Biophoto Associates, N.H.P.A.)

FIGURE 1–10 (*left*) Living things are adapted to their environments. This delicate shrimp lives on a sea anemone. A sea anemone's tentacles bear stinging structures that kill or damage any other organism that touches them. The shrimp is immune to the stings, adapted to this way of life. (Steven Webster)

8. Living things evolve and are adapted to their environments. Today's organisms have arisen by evolution, the descent and modification of organisms from more ancient forms of life. Evolution proceeds in such a way that living things and their components are well suited to their ways of life. Fish, earthworms, and frogs are all so constructed that we can predict roughly how they live merely by examining them. The adaptation of organisms to their environments is one result of evolution.

1-F EVOLUTION AND NATURAL SELECTION

A living organism is the product of interactions between its genetic information and its environment. This interaction is the basis for the most important generalization in biology, that organisms evolve by means of natural selection. We discuss evolution in more detail in Part Three of this book, but we cannot discuss the material in the next few chapters without a basic understanding of this process.

The theory of evolution states that today's organisms have arisen by descent and modification from more ancient forms of life. For instance, most biologists believe that human beings evolved from now-extinct animals resembling apes, and that this happened through accumulation of changes from generation to generation. In more modern terms, we can say that evolution is the process by which organisms of one generation come to differ from those of preceding generations.

For hundreds of years, scientists have considered the possibility that evolution might occur. Charles Darwin and Alfred Russel Wallace were not the first to suggest the theory of evolution, but their names are linked to it because they were the first to propose an acceptable explanation of *how* it might occur. Like many other great ideas in science, the theory of evolution by means of natural selection presented a simple explanation that made sense of a great many observations of the natural world. Darwin's champion, Thomas Huxley, remarked, "How extremely stupid not to have thought of that!"

Darwin and Wallace started with three familiar observations about living things:

1. Organisms are variable: even the most closely related individuals differ in some respects, and most people, cats, oak trees, or mushrooms are somewhat different from one another.

2. Some of these differences are inherited. Organisms tend to resemble their parents and offspring more closely than they resemble organisms to which they are less closely related genetically.

3. More organisms are produced than live to grow up and reproduce. Fish and birds may produce hundreds of eggs, oak trees thousands of acorns, but only a few of these survive to reproduce in their turn.

Darwin and Wallace suggested that some of the inherited variations between organisms must affect the chances that an individual will live to reproduce. They called this differential survival **natural selection,** which produces evolution. To take an example of natural selection producing evolution, the length and thickness of an animal's hair is largely determined by its genes. A very cold winter may kill many individuals with short, sparse hair. Individuals with longer, thicker fur are more likely to survive the winter and reproduce in the following spring. Because more animals with thicker fur breed and pass on the genetic material that dictates the growth of thick hair, a larger proportion of individuals in the next generation of the population will have genes for thick fur. The genetic makeup of the population has changed somewhat from one generation to the next, and that is evolution. The agent of natural selection in this case is low temperature, which acts as a **selective pressure** against those individuals with short, sparse hair.

The result of natural selection is that populations undergo **adaptation,** or changes appropriate to their environments, over the course of many generations. The selective pressures acting on a population "select" those genetic characteristics that are adapted, or well-suited, to the environment. For instance, through selection, populations living in cold areas will evolve so as to become better adapted to withstand the cold.

When we say that selection causes organisms to become adapted to their environments, we should note that "environment" in this evolutionary context is a

FIGURE 1-11 Genetic variation. All zebras contain similar genetic information, but each has a pattern of stripes as unique as a human fingerprint. In addition, the common zebra (*left*) differs somewhat from the similar Grevy's zebra (*right*), which has more and narrower stripes and larger, more rounded ears. The existence of such similar species suggests that both have descended from a common ancestral species, and that their differences result from somewhat different selective pressures in their respective habitats. Grevy's zebras live in dry savanna and semidesert areas in northern Kenya and parts of Ethiopia. Common zebras inhabit a wider area in eastern and southern Africa, in savanna and open woodlands with slightly more rainfall and vegetation. What might be the selective pressure favoring the striped pattern of the zebras' coats? Why might it be advantageous for the two species to have stripes of different widths?

FIGURE 1–12 (*above, left*) This sheep belongs to a breed with particularly heavy wool. It is adapted to cold, windy winters on high moorland pastures in Europe.

FIGURE 1–13 (*above, right*) A tadpole, which will develop into an adult frog. (Biophoto Associates)

catchall word that means much more than merely whether an organism lives in a forest rather than a desert and whether or not it can obtain enough food. Environment includes all the external factors that can affect whether the organism lives to reproduce.

An organism's environment includes its external environment as an embryo, juvenile, and adult. Let us, for example, consider a frog. Whether it successfully meets the pressure of its environment depends on the speed and normality of its embryonic development, whether bacteria penetrate the jelly coat of the egg and destroy it during development, whether as a tadpole it can find sufficient food for rapid growth and avoid being eaten by a predator, whether the pond in which it lives as a tadpole dries up before it becomes a frog, and whether as a small frog it avoids death by disease and predators. To make things more complicated, environmental pressures are frequently contradictory. For instance, a hot summer is in one way advantageous to our hypothetical frog because frog embryos develop faster at higher temperatures, but a hot summer also increases the chance that the tadpole's pond will dry up before it is ready to live on land (Figure 1–13). Even worse, environmental pressures are subject to frequent change. The frog must have characteristics that allow it to withstand both the heat of summer and the cold of winter; it should remain still to be safe from some predators and move quickly to escape from others; and so forth. Thus the genetic makeup of a frog is a compromise brought about by selection for a number of opposing characteristics.

ADAPTATIONS

We have just defined adaptation as the process by which populations evolve to become better and better suited to their environments as a result of natural selection. Biologists use the word in a second way. An **adaptation** is any genetically determined trait that has been selected for and that occurs in a large part of the population because it increases an individual's chance of reproducing successfully. (Note that this may include the capacity to change depending on environmental conditions, as with the ability to learn.) Much of biology involves the study of the adaptations of organisms.

Adaptations may be broadly classed as anatomical, physiological, or behavioral. **Anatomical** adaptations are those involving the physical structure of the organism. For instance, a penguin's flippers are an anatomical adaptation that permits it to swim. An organism's **physiology** is all of the internal workings of its body: the biochemistry of its cells and the processes that allow it to digest food,

FIGURE 1–14 Always in hot water: the pastel bands of color in the runoff from this geyser are colonies of various species of bacteria.

exchange gases, excrete wastes, reproduce, move, and sense and respond to the outside world. An example of an extreme physiological adaptation to temperature is seen in the ability of some bacteria to live in hot springs at temperatures up to 80°C (175°F), which would destroy all biochemical activity in most other organisms (Figure 1–14). An example of an impressive behavioral adaptation is the ability of a kangaroo rat to eat the leaves of the desert saltbush. No other animal can eat this plant because its leaves contain salt crystals. The kangaroo rat flakes off the salt-filled outer layer of the leaf with its front teeth, and then eats the salt-free inner part. This ability to prepare its food is a behavioral adaptation allowing the kangaroo rat to eat a food that is completely unavailable to other animals.

ENERGY AND NATURAL SELECTION

We have seen that all living things must take in and use energy to maintain their bodies, to grow, to obtain more energy, and to reproduce. The evolutionarily successful individual is one that leaves descendants, bearing its genes, in future generations. Therefore, natural selection favors those individuals that can channel the most energy into producing offspring. The use of energy in other activities such as feeding, fighting, or growing is selectively advantageous only insofar as these activities result in the organism's accumulating more energy to produce offspring.

Each individual has an ''energy income,'' all of the energy that it acquires during its lifetime. It also has an ''energy budget,'' its allotment of different amounts of energy to various activities. The most evolutionarily successful organisms are those most effective in conversion of energy to offspring. This does not mean that organisms use all their energy directly to produce offspring. For example, suppose that a tree converts some of its energy into growing a large root system. The energy thus spent cannot be used to produce offspring. Its large root system may enable the tree to obtain a great deal of water and minerals from the soil and so to produce more leaves, another diversion of energy away from the production of offspring. However, its many leaves may enable the tree to make more food than it would have otherwise and so allow it to recoup some of its previous energy expenditure by producing more offspring in the end. Thus organisms make energy investments that may ultimately yield energy gains that can be reinvested in the production of offspring. Sometimes these investments will turn out to be selectively disadvantageous because they postpone production of offspring. If the organism meets an early death, it will never get a chance to reproduce. So any item in an organism's energy budget must have the potential to confer an ultimate reproductive

(a)

(b)

FIGURE 1–15 Energy conversion. (a) A nasty surprise. A bumblebee, visiting flowers to obtain energy, falls victim to a predaceous bug (green), which uses its tubular mouthparts like a straw to suck up the body fluids of the much larger bee. Plants invest some of their energy in producing showy flowers and nutritious nectar, which attract pollinators such as bees and thereby increase the plants' chances of successful reproduction. The bee would ordinary divert some of the energy she collects from the flowers to produce offspring. In this case, her energy will be used instead to produce the bug's offspring. (b) Fireflies use some of the energy in their food to produce flashes of light to attract mates, a necessary prelude to reproduction. (b, Biophoto Associates, N.H.P.A.)

gain that is commensurate with the risks involved in diverting energy away from the immediate production of offspring.

SUMMARY

Scientific knowledge is developed by subjecting problems to the scientific method. First, scientists make observations. Then they formulate alternative hypotheses that might explain the observations, and they test the hypotheses by experiments designed to disprove one or more of the hypotheses and therefore to strengthen the evidence for those that remain.

Scientific discoveries and theories are useful, but they are always open to question; in science there is no such thing as "proof positive." Time and again in the history of science, widely accepted dogmas have turned out to be wrong, and even today scientists are busily discarding or remodeling some of the cherished "truths" presented in this book. A science editor recently noted that many of his magazine's readers seem to think that what they learned in their science courses was "graven on Sinai." As a science student, you should try to develop a healthy skepticism toward scientific findings, both old and new.

Biology is the science that studies living things. We can group the fundamental concepts of biology under three headings: cellular organization, biological information, and evolution.

All living things consist of one or more cells. Cells take energy from their environments and use it to maintain a high degree of molecular and structural orderliness, and for such activities as maintenance, growth, development, and ultimately, reproduction to produce more cells.

Living things contain information in the form of their genetic material. This information dictates how organisms develop, survive, and reproduce, and determines the characteristics they can pass on to their offspring.

The chief agent of evolution is natural selection, the phenomenon by which individuals with certain traits are more likely to survive and reproduce, thereby increasing the proportion of their own genes in future generations. This ensures that a population of organisms will become increasingly well adapted to its environment. An adaptation that increases the ability to survive and reproduce in the population's environment becomes more common in the population as natural selection eliminates members lacking the adaptation. Natural selection ensures that those individuals most effective in converting energy to offspring will be evolutionarily successful.

In the rest of this book we shall use the theory of evolution by natural selection, and its resulting adaptations, as a framework for the study of biology.

OBJECTIVES

From your study of this chapter, you should be able to:
1. List three steps in the scientific method, and apply them to investigating a sample scientific problem.

2. List eight characteristics of living things.
3. Define evolution, natural selection, selective pressure, adaptation, and energy budget.

QUESTIONS FOR DISCUSSION

1. After every hard rain you find dead earthworms lying on the sidewalk. What experiments would you perform to show the cause of death?
2. Many characteristics of life can be found in some nonliving thing. Can you think of examples of these?
3. To what extent should scientists be held responsible for the social and moral consequences of their discoveries?

4. What might you expect was the selective pressure that resulted in each of the following adaptations?

an elephant's trunk	the scent of honeysuckle
a leopard's spots	the bark of a tree
human language	

REFERENCES AND FURTHER READING

Arms, K., P. Feeny, and R. C. Lederhouse. "Sodium: stimulus for puddling behavior by tiger swallowtail butterflies, *Papilio glaucus*." *Science* 185:372, 1974. The story of the puddling experiments described in this chapter.

Ayala, F. J., and T. Dobzhansky (eds.). *Studies in the Philosophy of Biology*. Berkeley: University of California Press, 1974. An excellent collection of essays on biology, its methods and impact on society.

Mayr, E. *The Growth of Biological Thought*. Boston: Belknap Press of Harvard University Press, 1982. A historical perspective from an eminent evolutionary geneticist.

Roszak, T. *Where the Wasteland Ends*. Garden City, N.Y.: Doubleday, 1973. Critique of modern science by a man who believes science dominates western society and causes much of its malaise.

Stent, G. S. "Prematurity and uniqueness in scientific discovery." *Scientific American*, September 1972. Compares scientific discoveries with artistic creations and discusses what it means to say that a discovery is "ahead of its time."

Wallace, B., and A. M. Srb. *Adaptation*, 2d ed. Englewood Cliffs, N.J.: Prentice-Hall, 1964. A rigorous discussion of adaptation, what it is and how it is brought about, distinguishing an adaptation from the process of adaptation.

The Resurgence of Nationalism

—Richard N. Current, T. Harry Williams,

Frank Freidel, and Alan Brinkley, from

American History: A Survey, Volume 1 (Alfred

A. Knopf, 1987), pages 242–268

Chapter 9   # A Resurgence of Nationalism

Like a "fire bell in the night," as Thomas Jefferson put it, the issue of slavery arose only five years after the end of the War of 1812 to threaten the unity of the nation. The specific question was whether the territory of Missouri should be admitted to the Union as a free or as a slaveholding state. But the larger issue, one that would arise again and again to plague the republic, was the question of whether the vast new Western regions of the United States would ultimately be controlled by the North or by the South.

Yet the Missouri crisis, which was settled by a compromise in 1820, was significant at the time not only because it augured the sectional crises to come but because it stood in such sharp contrast to the rising American nationalism of the 1820s. Whatever forces might be working to pull the nation apart, far stronger ones were acting for the moment to draw it together. The American economy was experiencing revolutionary growth. And while ultimately the industrialization of the North would contribute to sectional tensions, economic progress—which brought with it new systems of transportation and communication—seemed likelier for the moment to link the nation more closely together. The federal government, in the meantime, was acting in both domestic and foreign policy to assert a vigorous nationalism—through the judicial decisions of John Marshall's Supreme Court; through congressional legislation encouraging economic growth; and through James Monroe's foreign policy, which attempted to assert the nation's rising stature in the world.

Above all, perhaps, the United States was held together in the 1820s by a set of shared sentiments and ideals, the "mystic bonds of union," as they were occasionally described. The memory of the Revolution, the veneration of the Constitution and its framers, the widely held sense that America had a special destiny in the world—all combined to obscure sectional differences and arouse a vibrant, even romantic, patriotism. Every year, Fourth of July celebrations reminded Americans of their common struggle for independence, as fife and drum corps and flamboyant orators appealed to patriotism and nationalism. When the Marquis de Lafayette, the French general who had aided the United States during the Revolution, revisited the country in 1824, the glorious past was revived as never before. Everywhere Lafayette traveled, crowds without distinction of section or party cheered him in frenzied celebration.

And on July 4, 1826—the fiftieth anniversary of the adoption of the Declaration of Independence—there occurred an event which seemed to many to confirm that the United States was a nation specially chosen by God. On that special day, Americans were to learn, two of the greatest of the country's founders and former presidents—Thomas Jefferson, author of the Declaration, and John Adams, "its ablest advocate and defender" (as Jefferson had said)—died within hours of each other. Jefferson's last words, those at his bedside reported, were "Is it the Fourth?" And Adams comforted those around him moments before his death by saying, "Thomas Jefferson still survives."

Events would prove that the forces of nationalism were not, in the end, strong enough to overcome the emerging sectional differences. For the time being, however, they permitted the republic to enter an era of unprecedented expansion confident and united.

America's Economic Revolution

There had been signs for many years that the United States was poised for a period of dramatic economic growth. In the 1820s and 1830s, that period finally began. Improvements in transportation and the expanding range of business activity created, for the first time, a national market economy. Each area of the country could concentrate on the production of a certain type of goods, relying on other areas to buy its surplus production and to supply it with those things it no longer produced itself. This regional specialization enabled much of the South, for example, to concentrate on growing its most lucrative crop: cotton. And it enabled the North to develop a new factory system—to begin an industrial revolution that would, in time, become even greater than the one that had begun in England some forty years before. By the mid-1820s, the nation's economy was growing more rapidly than its population.

Many factors combined to produce this dramatic transformation. The American population was growing and spreading across a far greater expanse of territory, providing both a labor supply for the production of goods and a market for the sale of them. A "transportation revolution"—based on the construction of roads, canals, and eventually railroads—was giving merchants and manufacturers access to new markets and raw materials. New entrepreneurial techniques were making a rapid business expansion possible. And technological advances were helping to spur industry to new levels of activity. Equally important, perhaps, Americans in the 1820s embraced an ethic of growth that was based on a commitment to hard work, individual initiative, thrift, and ambition. The results of their efforts seemed, to many people at least, to confirm the value of such a commitment.

The Population, 1820–1840

During the 1820s and 1830s, as during virtually all of American history, three trends of population were clear: rapid increase, migration to the West, and movement to towns and cities.

Americans continued to multiply almost as fast as they had in the colonial period. The population still doubled roughly every twenty-five years. The population had stood at only 4 million in 1790. By 1820, it had reached 10 million; by 1830, nearly 13 million; and by 1840, 17 million. The United States was growing much more rapidly in population than the

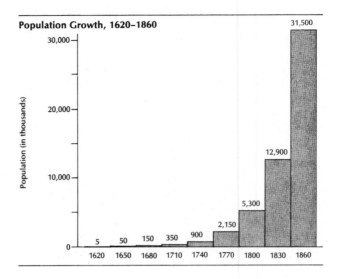

Population Growth, 1620–1860

British Isles or Europe. By 1860 it had moved ahead of the United Kingdom and had nearly overtaken Germany and France.

The black population increased more slowly than the white. After 1808, when the importation of slaves became illegal, the proportion of blacks to whites in the nation as a whole steadily declined. In 1820, there was one black to every four whites; in 1840, one to every five. The slower increase of the black population was a result of its comparatively high death rate, not of a low birth rate. Slave mothers had large families, but life was shorter for both slaves and free blacks than for whites—a result of the enforced poverty in which virtually all blacks lived.

The mortality rate for whites slowly declined, and life expectancy gradually increased. Epidemics continued to take their periodic toll, among them a cholera plague that swept the country in 1832; but public health efforts gradually improved and reduced the number and ferocity of such outbreaks. The population increase was, however, a result less of lengthened life than of the maintenance of a high birth rate.

From the time of independence, immigration had accounted for little of the nation's population growth. The long years of war in Europe, from 1793 to 1815, had kept the number of newcomers to America down to not more than a few thousand a year, and then the Panic of 1819 checked the immigrant tide that had risen after the restoration of peace. During the 1820s, arrivals from abroad averaged about 14,000 annually. Of the total population of nearly 13 million in 1830, the foreign-born numbered fewer than 500,000, most of them naturalized citizens. Soon, however, immi-

The Family at Home, c. 1845

This painting by Henry F. Darby of a minister, his wife, and their six children is an indication of how large American families often were in the early nineteenth century. Unlike in colonial times, a woman in the 1840s could expect not only to bear many children but to see most of them live to maturity. (Museum of Fine Arts, Boston)

gration began to grow once again. It reached a total of 60,000 for 1832 and nearly 80,000 for 1837.

Since the United States exported more goods than it imported, ships returning to America from Europe often had vacant space and took on immigrants to fill it. Competition among shipping lines reduced fares so that, by the 1830s, immigrants could get passage across the Atlantic for as little as $20 or $30. No longer did they need to sell their services to a temporary master in America in order to pay for the voyage. And so the system of indentured servitude, which had dwindled steadily after the Revolution, disappeared entirely after the Panic of 1819.

Until the 1830s, most of the new arrivals came from the same sources as had the bulk of the colonial population—from England and the northern (predominantly Protestant) counties of Ireland. In the 1830s, however, the number of immigrants arriving from the southern (Catholic) counties of Ireland began to grow, the beginning of a tremendous influx of Irish Catholics that was to occur over the next two decades. Generally, the newcomers—Irish as well as others—were welcomed in the United States. They were needed to provide labor for building canals and railroads, manning ships and docks, and performing other heavy work essential to the expanding economic system. But the Irish, as Roman Catholics, excited Protestant prejudices in some communities. In 1834, an anti-Catholic mob set fire to a convent in Charlestown, Massachusetts. The next year, Samuel

Sources of Immigration, 1820–1840

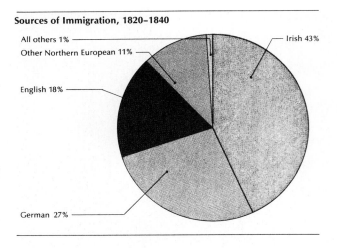

All others 1%
Other Northern European 11%
English 18%
German 27%
Irish 43%

Total Immigration, 1820–1840

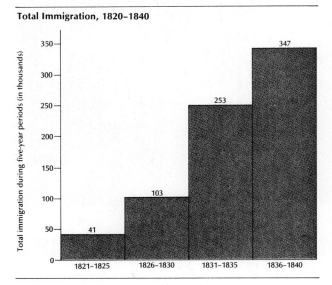

Total immigration during five-year periods (in thousands)

41 1821–1825
103 1826–1830
253 1831–1835
347 1836–1840

F. B. Morse (who is better remembered as a portrait painter and as the inventor of the telegraph) published his *Foreign Conspiracy*, which served thereafter as a textbook for those crusading against what they imagined was a popish plot to gain control of the United States.

The Northwest and the Southwest continued to grow much more rapidly than the rest of the country. By 1830, more than a fourth of the American people lived west of the Appalachians; by 1850, nearly half. As a result, some of the seaboard states suffered a serious loss of human resources (as well as of the material goods that departing migrants took with them). Year after year the Carolinas, for example,

lost nearly as many people through migration as they gained by natural increase, so that their populations remained almost static. The same was true of Vermont and New Hampshire. Many villages in these two states were completely depopulated, their houses and barns left to rot, as their people scattered over the country in search of a better life than the infertile granite hills afforded.

Not all the migrating villagers and farmers sought the unsettled frontier: some moved instead to the increasingly crowded population centers. Cities (defined as communities of 8,000 or more) grew faster than the nation as a whole. In 1820 there were more than twice as many cities, and in 1840 more than seven times as many, as there had been in 1790. While the vast majority of Americans continued to reside in the open country or in small towns, the number of city dwellers increased remarkably. In 1790, one person in thirty lived in a community of 8,000 or more; in 1820, one in twenty; and in 1840, one in twelve.

The rise of New York City was phenomenal. By 1810 it had surpassed Philadelphia as the largest city in America. New York steadily increased its lead in both population and trade. Its growth was based in large part on its superior natural harbor. But it was also a result of several commercial and political decisions, by New Yorkers themselves and by others, following the War of 1812. After the war, the British chose New York as the chief place to "dump" their manufactured goods and thus helped make it the nation's leading center for imports. Liberal state laws regarding auction sales encouraged inland merchants to do their buying in New York. The first packet line, with regularly scheduled monthly sailings between England and the United States, made New York its American terminus in 1816. And the Erie Canal (completed in 1825) gave the city unrivaled access to the interior.

The Canal Age

The so-called turnpike era, which lasted from 1790 to about 1830, saw the construction of an important network of roads that did much to link the nation together and to open access to new markets and sources of materials. Roads alone, however, were not sufficient to provide the system of transportation necessary for a growing industrial society. And so, in the 1820s and 1830s, Americans began to construct other means of transportation as well. As in colonial times, they looked first to water routes.

The Port of New York, 1828
This view of South Street in Manhattan shows the East River lined with docks. Other docks, similarly busy, lined the
Hudson River on the opposite side of the island. The population of New York City was approaching 150,000 by 1828.
(New York Public Library)

The larger rivers, especially the Mississippi and the Ohio, became increasingly useful, as steamboats grew in number and improved in design. A special kind of steamboat evolved to meet the problems of navigation on the Mississippi and its tributaries. These waters were shallow, with strong and difficult currents, shifting bars of sand and mud, and submerged logs and trees. So the boat needed a flat bottom, paddle wheels rather than screw propellers, and a powerful, high-pressure—and thus dangerously explosive—engine. (The river boats were, therefore, prone to deadly, spectacular accidents.) To accommodate as much cargo and as many passengers as possible, the boat was triple-decked, its superstructure rising high in the air. These river boats carried to New Orleans the corn and other crops of Northwestern farmers and the cotton and tobacco of Southwestern planters. From New Orleans, ocean-going ships took the cargoes on to Eastern ports.

But neither the farmers of the West nor the merchants of the East were completely satisfied with this pattern of trade. Farmers knew they would be able to get better prices for their crops if they could ship them directly eastward to market, rather than by the roundabout river-sea route; and merchants knew they would be able to sell larger quantities of their manufactured goods if they could transport them more directly and economically to the West.

The highways across the mountains, such as the Philadelphia-Pittsburgh turnpike and the National Road, provided a partial solution to the problem. But the costs of hauling goods overland, although lower than before the roads were built, were too high for anything except the most compact and valuable merchandise. It took four horses a full day to pull a wagon weight of one ton twelve miles over an ordinary road; on a turnpike, four horses could haul one and a half tons eighteen miles in a day. But the same four horses could draw a boatload of a hundred tons twenty-four miles a day on a canal. Thus interest quickly grew in expanding the nation's water routes.

Canal building was a task too expensive for the existing institutions of private enterprise. Sectional jealousies and constitutional scruples prevented the federal government from financing the projects. So the job of digging extensive canals fell to the various states. New York was the first to act. It had the natural advantage of a comparatively level route be-

tween the Hudson River and Lake Erie through the only break in the Appalachian chain. Yet the engineering tasks were still imposing. The distance from the Hudson to Lake Erie was more than 350 miles, several times as long as any of the existing canals in America. There were high ridges to cross and a wilderness of woods and swamps to penetrate. For many years, New Yorkers debated whether the scheme was practical. The canal advocates finally won the debate after De Witt Clinton, a late but ardent convert to the cause, became governor in 1817. Digging began on July 4, 1817.

The building of the Erie Canal was by far the greatest construction project that Americans had ever

The Erie Canal
In this contemporary pencil sketch, canal boats—loaded with migrants on their way to the West and pulled by horse teams moving along the towpath—arrive at a landing at Little Falls, New York. The boats moved so slowly that passengers often lightened the tedium by going ashore and walking alongside.   (New York Historical Society)

Canals in the Northeast, to 1860

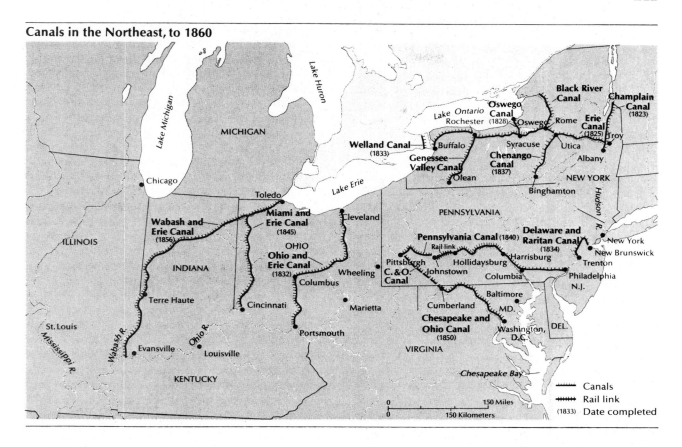

undertaken. It was the work of self-made engineers. One of them had made a careful study of English canals, but he and his associates did more than merely copy what they had seen abroad. They devised ingenious arrangements of cables, pulleys, and gears for bringing down trees and uprooting stumps. Instead of the usual shovels and wheelbarrows, they used specially designed plows and scrapers for moving earth. To make watertight locks they produced cement from native limestone. The canal itself was of simple design: basically a ditch, forty feet wide and four feet deep, with towpaths along the banks for the horses or mules that were to draw the canal boats. (Steamboats were not to be used: the churning of a paddle wheel or propeller would cave in the earthen banks.) Cuts and fills, some of them enormous, enabled the canal to pass through hills and over valleys; stone aqueducts carried it across streams; and eighty-eight locks, of heavy masonry, with great wooden gates, took care of the necessary ascents and descents.

Not only was the Erie Canal an engineering triumph; it quickly proved a financial success as well. It

opened for through traffic in October 1825, amid elaborate ceremonies and celebrations. Governor Clinton headed a parade of canal boats that made the trip from Buffalo to the Hudson and then downriver to New York City, where he emptied a keg of Erie water into the Atlantic to symbolize the wedding of the lake and the ocean. Traffic was soon so heavy that, within about seven years, the tolls had brought in enough money to repay the whole cost of construction.

The profitability of the Erie encouraged the state to enlarge its canal system by building several branches. An important part of the system was the Champlain Canal, begun at about the same time as the Erie and completed in 1822, which connected Lake Champlain with the Hudson River. Some of the branches did not fully pay for themselves, but all provided valuable water connections between New York City and the larger towns of the state. The main line, by providing access to the Great Lakes, led beyond the state's borders, to the West.

The system of water transportation extended farther when the states of Ohio and Indiana, inspired by the success of the Erie Canal, provided water connections between Lake Erie and the Ohio River. In 1825, Ohio began the building of two canals, one between Portsmouth and Cleveland and the other between Cincinnati and Toledo, both of which were in use by 1833. In 1832, Indiana started the construction of a canal to connect Evansville with the Cincinnati-Toledo route. These canals made it possible to ship goods by inland waterways all the way from New York to New Orleans, although it was still necessary to transfer cargoes several times among canal, lake, and river craft. By way of the Great Lakes, it was possible to go by water from New York to Chicago. After the opening of the Erie Canal, shipping on the Great Lakes by sail and steam increased rapidly.

The consequences of the development of this transportation network were far-reaching. One of the immediate results was the stimulation of the settlement of the Northwest, not only because it had become easier for migrants to make the westward journey but also, and more important, because it had become easier for them, after establishing their farms, to ship their produce to markets. Towns boomed along the Erie and other canals. New York City benefited the most of all. Although much of the Western produce, especially corn, continued to go downriver to New Orleans, an increasing proportion of it (including most of the wheat of the Northwest) went to New York. And manufactured goods from throughout the East now moved in growing volume through New York and then via the comparatively direct and economical new routes to the West.

Rival cities along the Atlantic seaboard took alarm at the prospect of New York's acquiring so vast a hinterland, largely at their expense. If they were to hold their own, they knew that they too would have to find ways of tapping the Western market. Boston, its way to the Hudson River blocked by the Berkshire Mountains, did not try to connect itself to the West by canal. Its hinterland would remain confined largely to New England itself. Philadelphia and Baltimore had the still more formidable Allegheny Mountains to contend with, but they nevertheless made a serious effort at canal building. Beginning in 1834, Pennsylvania invested in a complicated and costly system of waterways and railways—with an arrangement of "inclined planes," stationary engines, and cable cars to take canal boats over the mountains—in an effort to connect Philadelphia with Pittsburgh. But the

"Pennsylvania system" was a financial and technological failure. Baltimore planned a canal to ascend the Potomac Valley and tunnel through the mountains to the West. Work began on the grandly conceived Chesapeake and Ohio Canal in 1828, but only the stretch between Washington, D.C., and Cumberland, Maryland, was ever completed. In the South, Richmond and Charleston also aspired to build water routes to the Ohio Valley; Richmond, hoping to link the James and Kanawha rivers, eventually constructed a canal that reached as far as Lynchburg but failed to traverse the Blue Ridge Mountains.

For none of these rivals of New York did canals provide a satisfactory way to the West. Some cities, however, saw their opportunity in a different and newer means of transportation. Even before the canal age had reached its height, the era of the railroad was already beginning.

The Early Railroads

Through most of the 1820s and 1830s, railroads played a relatively secondary role in the nation's transportation system. But the emergence of these first rail lines was of inestimable importance to the future of the American economy. The tentative beginnings of these early years led, by the time of the Civil War, to a great surge of railroad building, linking the nation together as no previous system of transportation had ever done. Railroads eventually became the primary means of transportation for the United States and remained so until the creation of the interstate highway system in the mid-twentieth century.

It is difficult to identify the precise date of the invention of the railroad. It emerged from a combination of innovations, each of which had its own history. One of these innovations was the invention of railroad tracks: rails, wooden or iron, laid on a prepared roadbed to make a fairly straight and level track. Another was the employment of steam-powered locomotives. A third was the operation of trains as public carriers of passengers and freight.

For nearly 200 years before the nineteenth century opened, small railways—wheeled vehicles running along fixed tracks—with cars pulled by men and women or by animals had been used to haul coal from English mines; and in the early 1800s similar railways had appeared in the United States. But it took the development of steam power to make rail-

Racing on the Railroad

Peter Cooper, who in later years was best known as a philanthropist and as the founder of the Cooper Union in New York City, was also a successful iron manufacturer. Cooper designed and built the first steam-powered locomotive in America in 1830 for the Baltimore and Ohio railroad. On August 28 of that year, he raced his locomotive (the "Tom Thumb") against a horse-drawn railroad car. This sketch depicts the moment when Cooper's engine overtook the horsecar. (Museum of the City of New York)

roads viable as a general transportation method. By 1804, both English and American inventors had experimented with steam engines for propelling land vehicles as well as boats. In 1820, John Stevens ran a locomotive and cars around a circular track on his New Jersey estate. Finally, in 1825, the Stockton and Darlington Railroad in England began to operate with steam power over a short length of track. It became the first line to carry general traffic. All earlier rail lines had been operated by particular companies to service only their own needs.

This news quickly aroused the interest of American businessmen, especially in those seaboard cities that sought better communication with the West. The first to organize a railroad company was a group of New Yorkers, who in 1826 obtained a charter for the Mohawk and Hudson, and five years later began running trains along the sixteen miles between Schenectady and Albany. The first company to begin actual operations was the Baltimore and Ohio; the only living signer of the Declaration of Independence, Charles Carroll of Carrollton, dug a spadeful of earth in the ceremonies in Maryland to start the work on July 4, 1828; and a thirteen-mile stretch opened for business in 1830. Not only the seaboard but also the Mississippi Valley became the scene of railroad building. By 1836, a total of more than 1,000 miles of track had been laid in eleven states.

There did not yet exist what could properly be called a railroad system. Even the longest of the lines was comparatively short in the 1830s, and most of them served to connect water routes and otherwise to supplement water transportation. Even when two lines did connect the tracks might differ in gauge (width), so that cars from the one line often could not fit onto the tracks of the other. Schedules were erratic, and since roadbeds and bridges were often of shoddy construction, wrecks were frequent.

In response to these deficiencies, railroad pioneers produced a series of important technological developments in the 1830s. Roadbeds were improved through the introduction of heavier iron rails attached to wooden ties resting on crushed rock—a system that enabled tracks to withstand the shock of use far better than the earlier methods. American manufacturers began to produce steam locomotives more flexible and powerful than the engines of the past, which had usually been imported from Europe. Passenger cars, originally mere stagecoaches, were redesigned after 1840 as elongated boxes with two rows of reversible seats and a center aisle—thus making more room for people.

Railroads and canals were soon competing bitterly with each other. For a time, the Chesapeake and Ohio Canal Company blocked the advance of the Baltimore and Ohio Railroad through the narrow gorge of the upper Potomac, and the state of New York prohibited railroads from hauling freight in competition with the Erie Canal and its branches. But railroads had the advantages of speed and year-round operation (canals had to close for the winter freeze) and could be located almost anywhere, regardless of terrain and the availability of water. Where free competition existed, railroads gradually took over most of the passenger traffic and the light freight. The future, in fact, belonged to the towns and cities along the path of the "iron horse," not to those that continued to depend exclusively on waterways.

The Expansion of Business

The rapid expansion of business activity in the 1820s and 1830s was in part a result of the growth in population and improvements in the means of transportation. It was also, however, the result of daring and imagination on the part of new generations of businessmen and their employees. Two industries, one old and one new, illustrated the capacities of American enterprise. One was the whaling industry, which was reaching its heyday in the 1830s. From New Bedford and other New England ports, bold skippers and their crews, having driven most of the whales from the Atlantic, voyaged far into the Pacific in their hazardous tracking of the source of spermaceti for candles, whale oil for lamps, and whalebone for corset stays and other uses. Another example of Yankee enterprise was the ice industry. For years, Northeastern farmers had harvested winter ice from ponds and stored it for the summer; but the large-scale transportation and sale of ice as a commodity began in the 1830s. The New England ice harvest then found a ready market in Northern cities, on Southern plantations, and halfway around the world in India, where it was carried in fast-sailing ships; a voyage was considered highly successful if no more than half the cargo melted on the way.

Retail distribution of goods, whether of foreign or domestic origin, remained somewhat haphazard by the standards of later times; but it was becoming far more systematic than it had ever been before. Stores specializing in groceries, dry goods, hardware, and other lines appeared in the larger cities. Smaller towns and villages depended on the general store. Storekeepers did much of their business by barter, taking country eggs and other produce in exchange for such things as pins and needles, sugar, and coffee. Many customers, living remote from any store, welcomed the occasional visits of peddlers, who came on foot or by horse.

The organization of business was undergoing a gradual change. Most business continued to be operated by individuals or partnerships operating on a limited scale. The dominating figures were the great merchant capitalists, who controlled much of the big business of the time. They owned their own ships. They organized certain industries on the putting-out system: providing materials to individual craftsmen, directing the work, and selling the finished product.

In larger enterprises, however, the individual merchant capitalist was giving way before the advance of the corporation. Corporations had the advantage of combining the resources of a large number of shareholders, and they began to develop particularly rapidly in the 1830s, when certain legal obstacles to their formation were removed. In the past, a corporation had had to obtain a charter, which at first could be granted only by a special act of the state legislature. By the 1830s, however, states were beginning to pass general incorporation laws. No longer did each corporation need to obtain specific legislative approval. A group could now secure a charter merely by paying a fee. Moreover, the laws began to grant the privilege of limited liability. This meant that individual stockholders risked losing the value of their own investment if a corporation should fail, but they were not liable (as they had been in the past) for the corporation's larger losses.

Corporations made possible the accumulation of larger and larger amounts of capital for manufacturing enterprises as well as for banks, turnpikes, and railroad companies. Some of this capital came from the profits of wealthy merchants who turned from shipping to newer ventures. Some came from the savings of people of only moderate means. Some came from tax collections, since state governments often bought shares in turnpike, canal, and railroad companies. A considerable part was supplied by foreign, especially English, investors.

But these sources provided too little capital to meet the demands of the ambitious schemes of some businesses, and they relied on an expansion of credit—some of it by dangerously unstable means. Credit mechanisms remained highly underdeveloped in the early nineteenth century. The government alone was permitted to issue currency, but it issued no paper—only gold and silver coins—and the amount of official currency in circulation was thus too small to support the demand for credit. Under pressure from corporate promoters, many banks issued large quantities of bank notes to provide capital for expanding business ventures. The notes rested on a bank's promise to redeem them in gold and silver on demand; but many institutions issued notes far in excess of their own reserves. As a result, bank failures were frequent and bank deposits often insecure.

The Rise of the Factory

All of these changes—increasing population, improved transportation, and the expansion of business activity—contributed to perhaps the most profound economic development in mid-nineteenth-century America: the rise of factory manufacturing. Although it was in the 1840s that industry experienced its most spectacular surge of growth in the antebellum period, it was in the 1820s and 1830s that the factory system established itself as an integral part of the national economy.

Before the War of 1812, most of what manufacturing there was in the United States took place within households or in small, individually operated workshops. Most goods were produced by hand; most were sold in local markets. Gradually, however, improved technology and increased opportunities for commerce stimulated the beginnings of a fundamental change. It came first in the New England textile industry. There, even before the war and the Embargo, some farsighted entrepreneurs were beginning to make use of the region's extensive waterpower and of the new machines (some imported from England, some developed at home) to bring textile operations together under a single roof. This factory system, as it was to be called, spread rapidly in the 1820s. Spinning and weaving in the home remained for a time the principal means of producing cloth, but factories were beginning to make serious inroads into the old process of production.

In the shoe industry as well, mass production through the specialization of tasks was expanding and was by the 1830s becoming an important force in the industry. Most of the work in shoe factories continued to be done by hand, but manufacturing in the newer establishments was increasingly divided among men and women who, in a careful division of labor, specialized in one or another of the various tasks involved in production. Private cobblers continued to produce shoes for individual customers; and the artisanal workshops, where groups of shoemakers worked under a single roof but did not divide up the tasks, remained the largest source of shoe manufacturing. But the future of the industry was more clearly suggested by factories producing large numbers of identical shoes in ungraded sizes and without

distinction as to rights and lefts. As with textiles, the new shoe factories emerged first in eastern Massachusetts.

By the 1830s, factory production was spreading from textiles and shoes into other industries as well; and manufacturing was moving beyond Massachusetts and New England to become an important force throughout the American Northeast.

From the beginning, American industry relied heavily on technology for its growth. Because labor was scarce in the United States, at least in comparison to other industrializing countries, there was great incentive for entrepreneurs to improve the efficiency of their productive enterprises by introducing new labor-saving devices. Machine technology advanced more rapidly in the United States in the mid-nineteenth century than in any other country in the world. Change was so rapid, in fact, that some manufacturers built their new machinery out of wood; by the time the wood wore out, they reasoned, improved technology would have made the machine obsolete. By the end of the 1830s, so advanced had American technology—particularly in textile manufacturing—become that industrialists in Britain and Europe were beginning to travel to the United States to learn new techniques, instead of the other way around.

Men and Women at Work

However advanced their technology, manufacturers still relied above all on a supply of labor. In later years, much of that supply would come from great waves of immigration from abroad. In the 1820s and 1830s, however, labor had to come primarily from the native population. Recruitment was not an easy task. Ninety percent of the American people still lived and worked on farms. City residents, although increasing in number, were relatively few, and the potential workers among them even fewer. Many urban laborers were skilled artisans who owned and managed their own shops as small businessmen; they were not likely to flock to factory jobs. The available unskilled workers were not numerous enough to form a reservoir from which the new industries could draw.

What did produce the beginnings of an industrial labor supply was the transformation of American agriculture in the nineteenth century. The opening of vast, fertile new farmlands in the Midwest, the improvement of transportation systems, the development of new farm machinery—all combined to increase food production dramatically. No longer did each region have to feed itself entirely from its own farms; it could import food from other regions. Thus in the Northeast, and especially in New England, where poor land had always placed harsh limits on farm productivity, the agricultural economy began slowly to decline, freeing up rural people to work in the factories.

Two systems of recruitment emerged to bring this new labor supply to the expanding textile mills. One, common in the mid-Atlantic states and in parts of New England, brought whole families from the farm to the mill. Parents and children, even some who were no more than four or five years old, worked together tending the looms. The second system, common in Massachusetts, enlisted young women—mostly the daughters of farmers—in their late teens and early twenties. It was known as the Lowell or Waltham system, after the factory towns in which it first emerged. Most of these women worked for several years in the factories, saved their wages, and ultimately returned home to marry and raise chil-

dren. They did not form a permanent working class.

Labor conditions in these early years of the factory system were significantly better than those in English industry, better too than they would ultimately become in the United States. The employment of young children entailed undeniable hardships. But the evils were fewer than in Europe, since working children in American factories remained under the supervision of their parents. In England, by contrast, asylum authorities often hired out orphans to factory employers who showed little solicitude for their welfare.

Even more distinctive from the European labor system was the lot of working women in the mills in Lowell and factory towns like it. In England, as a parliamentary investigation revealed, woman workers were employed in coal mines in unimaginably wretched conditions. Some had to crawl on their hands and knees, naked and filthy, through cramped, narrow tunnels, pulling heavy coal carts behind them. It was little wonder, then, that English visitors to America considered the Lowell mills a female para-

Specialized Manufacturing Towns: Lowell, Massachusetts, 1832

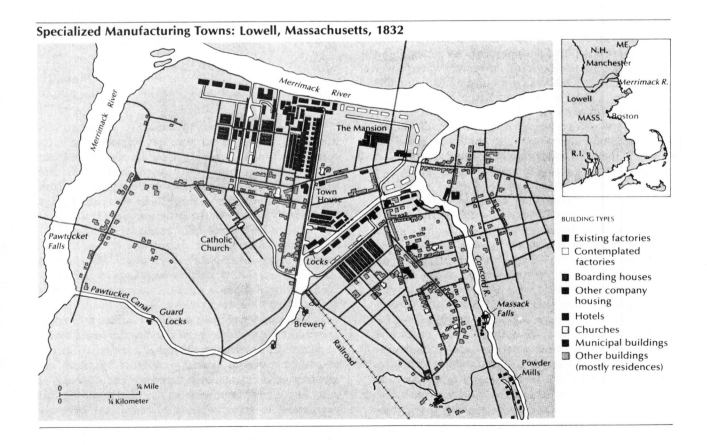

BUILDING TYPES

■ Existing factories
□ Contemplated factories
▦ Boarding houses
■ Other company housing
■ Hotels
□ Churches
■ Municipal buildings
▤ Other buildings (mostly residences)

dise by contrast. The Lowell workers lived in clean boardinghouses and dormitories maintained for them by the factory owners. They were well fed and carefully supervised. Because many New Englanders considered the employment of women to be vaguely immoral, the factory owners placed great emphasis on maintaining an upright environment for their employees, enforcing strict curfews and requiring regular church attendance. Factory girls suspected of immoral conduct were quickly dismissed. Wages for the Lowell workers, modest as they were, were nevertheless generous by the standards of the time. The women even found time to write and publish a monthly magazine, the *Lowell Offering.*

Yet even these relatively well-treated workers often found the transition from farm life to factory work difficult, even traumatic. Uprooted from everything familiar, forced to live among strangers in a regimented environment, many women suffered from loneliness and disorientation. Still more had difficulty adjusting to the nature of factory work—to the repetition of fixed tasks hour after hour, day after day. That the women had to labor from sunrise to sunset was not in itself always a burden; many of them had worked similarly long days on the farm. But that they now had to spend those days performing tedious, unvarying chores, and that their schedules did not change from week to week or season to season, made the adjustment to factory work a painful one.

Female mill workers suffered, moreover, from a special disadvantage. They were, like male workers, generally products of a farm economy in decline and were forced to find nonagricultural work by which to support themselves and contribute to the maintenance of their families. But unlike men, they had very few options. They had no access to construction work; they could not become sailors or dockworkers; it was considered unthinkable for women to travel the country alone, as many men did, in search of opportunities. Work in the mills was in many cases virtually the only option available to them.

The relative powerlessness of woman workers was one reason for the gradual breakdown of the paternalistic factory system. In the competitive textile market as it developed in the 1830s and 1840s—a market prey to the booms and busts that afflicted the American economy as a whole—manufacturers found it difficult to maintain the high living standards and reasonably attractive working conditions with which they had begun. Wages declined; the hours of work lengthened; the conditions of the boardinghouses de-

The *Lowell Offering*
The "factory girls" of the Lowell mills published a small literary magazine, which included poems and stories written by the workers themselves. The cover of this 1845 edition portrays a young mill worker standing in pastoral surroundings, holding a book, with the mill visible in the background. (Massachusetts Historical Society)

teriorated as the buildings decayed and overcrowding increased. In 1834, mill girls in Lowell organized a union—the Factory Girls Association—which staged a strike to protest a 25 percent wage cut. Two years later, the association struck again—against a rent increase in the boardinghouses. Both strikes failed, and a recession in 1837 virtually destroyed the organization. Eight years later, led by the militant Sarah

Bagley, the Lowell women created the Female Labor Reform Association and began agitating for a ten-hour day and for improvements in conditions in the mills. The new association not only made demands of management; it turned to state government and asked for legislative investigation of conditions in the mills. By then, however, the character of the factory work force was changing. Textile manufacturers were turning to a less demanding labor supply: immigrants. The mill girls were gradually moving into other occupations: teaching, domestic service, or marriage.

The increasing supply of immigrant workers was a boon to manufacturers and other entrepreneurs. At last they had access to a cheap and plentiful source of labor. These new workers, because of their growing numbers and because of unfamiliarity with their new country, had even less leverage than the women they at times displaced; and thus they often encountered far worse working conditions. Construction gangs, made up increasingly of Irish immigrants, performed the heavy, unskilled work on turnpikes, canals, and railroads under often intolerable conditions. Because most of these workers had no marketable skills and because of native prejudice against them, they received wages so low—and received them so intermittently, since the work was seasonal and uncertain—that they generally did not earn enough to support their families in even minimal comfort. Many of them lived in flimsy, unhealthy shanties.

By the 1840s, the Irish workers (men and women) predominated in the New England textile mills as well; and their arrival accelerated the deterioration of working conditions there. There was far less social pressure on owners to provide a decent environment for Irish workers than for native women. Employers began paying piece rates rather than a daily wage and employed other devices to speed up production and exploit the labor force more efficiently. By the mid-1840s, the town of Lowell—once a model for foreign visitors of enlightened industrial development—had become a squalid slum. Similarly miserable working-class neighborhoods were emerging in other Northeastern cities.

It was not only the unskilled workers who suffered from the transition to the modern factory system. It was the skilled artisans whose trades the factories were displacing. Threatened with obsolescence, faced with increasing competition from industrial capitalists, craftsmen began early in the nineteenth century to form organizations—the first American labor unions—to protect their endangered

position. As early as the 1790s, printers and cordwainers took the lead. The cordwainers—makers of high-quality boots and shoes—suffered from the competition of merchant capitalists. These artisans sensed a loss of security and status with the development of mass-production methods, and so did members of other skilled trades: carpenters, joiners, masons, plasterers, hatters, and shipbuilders. In such cities as Philadelphia, Baltimore, Boston, and New York, the skilled workers of each craft formed societies for mutual aid. During the 1820s and 1830s, the craft societies began to combine on a city-wide basis and set up central organizations known as trade unions. Since, with the widening of the market, workers of one city competed with those at a distance, the next step was to federate the trade unions or to establish craft unions of national scope. In 1834, delegates from six cities founded the National Trades' Union; and in 1836, the printers and the cordwainers set up their own national craft unions.

This early labor movement soon collapsed. Labor leaders struggled against the handicap of hostile laws and hostile courts. By the common law, as interpreted by judges in the industrial states, a combination among workers was viewed as, in itself, an illegal conspiracy. But adverse court decisions did not alone halt the rising unions. The death blow came from the Panic of 1837 and the ensuing depression.

Sectionalism and Nationalism

For a brief but alarming moment, the increasing differences between the nation's two leading sections threatened in 1819 and 1820 to damage the unity of the United States. But once a sectional crisis was averted with the Missouri Compromise, the forces of nationalism continued to assert themselves; and the federal government began to assume the role of promoter of economic growth.

The Missouri Compromise

When Missouri applied for admission to the Union as a state in 1819, slavery was already well established there. The French and Spanish inhabitants of the Louisiana Territory (including what became Missouri) had owned slaves, and in the Louisiana Purchase treaty of 1803 the American government promised to maintain and protect the inhabitants in the free enjoyment of their property as well as their liberty and religion. By 1819, approximately 60,000 people resided in Missouri Territory, of whom about 10,000 were slaves.

In that year, while Missouri's application for statehood was being considered in Congress, Representative James Tallmadge, Jr., of New York, proposed an amendment that would prohibit the further introduction of slaves into Missouri and provide for the gradual emancipation of those already there. The Tallmadge Amendment provoked a controversy that was to rage for the next two years.

Although the issue arose suddenly, the sectional jealousies that produced it had long been accumulating. Already the concept of a balance of power between the Northern and Southern states was well developed. From the beginning, partly by chance and partly by design, new states had come into the Union more or less in pairs, one from the North, another from the South. With the admission of Alabama in 1819, the Union contained an equal number of free and slave states, eleven of each. If Missouri were to be admitted as a slave state, not only would the existing sectional balance be upset but a precedent would be established that in the future would increase the political power of the South still further.

This concern about the balance of power among the states was not yet accompanied by a widespread or fervent opposition to slavery itself. There were groups, in both the North and the South, opposed to slavery on moral grounds and committed to its destruction. On the eve of the dispute over Missouri, for example, the Manumission Society of New York was busy with attempts to rescue runaway slaves; and Quakers were conducting a campaign to strengthen the laws against the African slave trade and to protect free blacks from kidnappers who sold them into slavery. But most Northern opponents of slavery were affluent philanthropists and reformers associated with the Federalist party; and for many of them, humanitarian concerns were secondary to political ones.

The Missouri controversy provided the opportunity for which Federalist leaders such as Rufus King had long waited: the opportunity to attempt a revival and reinvigoration of their party. By appealing to the Northern people on the issue of slavery extension, the Federalists hoped to win many of the Northern Republicans away from their allegiance to the Republican party's Southern leadership. In New York, the De Witt Clinton faction of the Republicans, who had joined with the Federalists in opposition to the War of 1812 and were outspoken in their hostility to "Virginia influence" and "Southern rule," were more than willing to cooperate with the Federalists again. The cry against slavery in Missouri, Thomas Jefferson wrote, was "a mere party trick." He explained: "King is ready to risk the union for any chance of restoring his party to power and wriggling himself to the head of it, nor is Clinton without his hopes nor scrupulous as to the means of fulfilling them."

The Missouri question was soon complicated by the application of Maine for admission as a state. Massachusetts had earlier consented to the separation of this northern part of the commonwealth, but only on the condition that Maine be granted statehood before March 4, 1820. The Speaker of the House, Henry Clay, now informed Northerners that if they refused to consent to Missouri's becoming a slave state, Southerners would deny the application of Maine. Despite the warning, the Northern majority in the House continued to insist on the principle of the Tallmadge Amendment; but in the Senate, a few Northerners sided with the Southerners and prevented its passage.

The Maine question, however, ultimately produced a way out of the impasse. The Senate finally agreed to combine the Maine and Missouri proposals into a single bill. Maine would be admitted as a free state, Missouri as a slave state. Then, to make the package more acceptable to the House, Senator Jesse B. Thomas of Illinois proposed an amendment prohibiting slavery in all the rest of the Louisiana Purchase territory north of the southern boundary of Missouri (latitude 36° 30'). The Senate adopted the Thomas Amendment, and Speaker Clay, with great difficulty, guided the amended Maine-Missouri bill through the House.

Nationalists in both North and South hailed the Missouri Compromise as a happy resolution of a danger to the Union. Others, however, were less optimistic. Thomas Jefferson, for example, saw in the controversy a "speck on our horizon" which might ultimately "burst on us as a tornado." And he added, "The line of division lately marked out between the different portions of our confederacy is such as will never, I fear, be obliterated." (That was one reason why Jefferson, in his last years, devoted so much attention to the construction of the University of Virginia—an institution that would, he hoped, confirm Southern students in the values of their own region and protect them against the taint of "anti-Missourianism" that he believed pervaded the

The Missouri Compromise, 1820

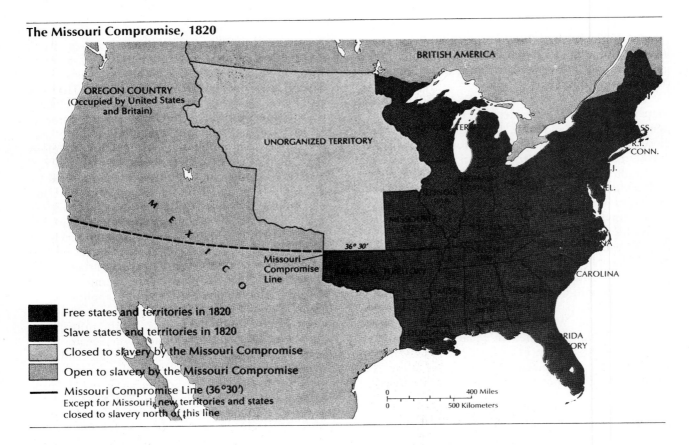

Free states and territories in 1820

Slave states and territories in 1820

Closed to slavery by the Missouri Compromise

Open to slavery by the Missouri Compromise

Missouri Compromise Line (36°30')
Except for Missouri, new territories and states
closed to slavery north of this line

Northern universities.) The Missouri Compromise revealed, in short, a strong undercurrent of sectionalism that competed with—although at the moment failed to derail—the powerful tides of nationalism.

Marshall and the Court

John Marshall served as chief justice of the United States for almost thirty-five years, from 1801 to 1835. He was a man of practical and penetrating mind, of persuasive and winning personality, and of strong will; and he dominated the Court as no one else before or since. During his years as chief justice, Republican presidents filled vacancies with Republican justices, one after another; and yet Marshall continued to carry a majority with him in most of the Court's decisions. The members of the Court boarded together, without their families, during the winter months when the Court was in session, and Marshall had abundant opportunity to influence his younger associates.

But Marshall's achievements went beyond the narrow one of influencing his colleagues. He literally molded the development of the Constitution itself. The net effect of the hundreds of opinions delivered by the Marshall Court was to strengthen the judicial branch at the expense of the other two branches of the government; increase the power of the United States and lessen that of the states themselves; and advance the interests of the propertied classes, especially those engaged in commerce.

No state, the Constitution says, shall pass any law "impairing the obligation of contracts." The first Supreme Court case involving this provision was that of *Fletcher* v. *Peck* (1810), which arose out of the notorious Yazoo land frauds (see p. 201). The Court had to decide whether the Georgia legislature of 1796 could rightfully repeal the act of the previous legislature granting lands under shady circumstances to the Yazoo Land Companies. In the unanimous decision, Marshall held that a land grant was a contract and therefore, regardless of any corruption involved, the repeal was invalid. This was the first time the

Supreme Court had voided a state law on the ground that it conflicted with a provision of the United States Constitution, although the Court had previously declared state laws unconstitutional because they were inconsistent with federal laws or treaties.

Dartmouth College v. *Woodward* (1819) expanded further the meaning of the contract clause. The case had originated in a quarrel between the trustees and the president of the college, and it became a major political issue in New Hampshire when the Republicans championed the president and the Federalists took the side of the trustees. Having gained control of the state government, the Republicans undertook to revise Dartmouth's charter (granted by King George III in 1769) so as to convert the private college into a state university. When the case came before the Supreme Court in Washington, Daniel Webster, a Dartmouth graduate, represented the trustees in opposing the charter revision. The Court, he reminded the judges, had decided in *Fletcher* v. *Peck* that "a *grant* is a contract." The Dartmouth charter, he went on, "is embraced within the very terms of that decision," since "a grant of corporate powers and privileges is as much a *contract* as a grant of land." Then, according to legend, he brought tears to the eyes of the justices with an irrelevant peroration that concluded: "It is, sir, as I have said, a small college. And yet there are those who love it." A year later, the Court gave its decision in favor of Webster and the trustees. The ruling had a significant bearing on the development of business corporations. It proclaimed that corporation charters were contracts and that contracts were inviolable; this doctrine placed important restrictions on the ability of state governments to control corporations.

The *Dartmouth College* case raised another important constitutional question as well. Did the Supreme Court have the power to override the decisions of state courts? The Judiciary Act of 1789 and the *Dartmouth College* decision itself both seemed to have established that the Court did have that right. But some advocates of states' rights, notably in the South, continued to argue otherwise. In *Cohens* v. *Virginia* (1821), Marshall provided a ringing reaffirmation of the constitutionality of federal review of state court decisions. The states no longer were sovereign in all respects, he wrote, since they had given up part of their sovereignty in ratifying the Constitution. The state courts, he insisted, must submit to federal jurisdiction; otherwise the government would be prostrated "at the feet of every state in the Union."

Meanwhile, in *McCulloch* v. *Maryland* (1819),

Marshall had confirmed the "implied powers" of Congress by upholding the constitutionality of the Bank of the United States. The Bank, with headquarters in Philadelphia and branches in various cities throughout the country, had become so unpopular in the South and the West that several of the states tried to drive the branches out of business by outright prohibition or by prohibitory taxes. Maryland, for example, laid a heavy tax on the Baltimore branch of the Bank. This case presented two constitutional questions to the Supreme Court: Could Congress charter a bank? And if so, could one of the states thus tax it? As one of the Bank's attorneys, Webster first repeated the arguments used originally by Hamilton to prove that the establishment of such an institution came within the "necessary and proper" clause. Then, to dispose of the tax issue, Webster added an ingenious argument of his own. The power to tax, he said, involved a "power to destroy," and if the states could tax the Bank at all, they could tax it to death. Since the Bank with its branches was an agency of the federal government, the power to tax it was the power to destroy the United States itself. Marshall adopted Webster's words in deciding for the Bank.

The case of *Gibbons* v. *Ogden* (1824) raised the question of the powers of Congress, as against the powers of the states, in regulating interstate commerce. The state of New York had granted Robert Fulton and Robert Livingston's steamboat company the exclusive right to carry passengers on the Hudson River to New York City. From this monopoly, Aaron Ogden obtained the business of navigation across the river between New York and New Jersey. Thomas Gibbons, with a license granted under an act of Congress, went into competition with Ogden, who brought suit against him and was sustained by the New York courts. When Gibbons appealed to the Supreme Court, the justices faced the twofold question whether "commerce" included navigation and whether Congress alone or Congress and the states together could regulate interstate commerce. Marshall replied that "commerce" was a broad term embracing navigation as well as the buying and selling of goods. Although he did not say that the states had no authority whatever regarding interstate commerce, he asserted that the power of Congress to regulate such commerce was "complete in itself" and might be "exercised to its utmost extent." He concluded that the state-granted monopoly was void.

The decision, the last of Marshall's great pronouncements, was the first conspicuous one in which the Marshall Court appeared to be on the popular

John Marshall
Marshall became Chief Justice of the United States Supreme Court in 1801 after establishing himself as one of the leaders of the Federalist party. He served on the Court for thirty-five years, longer than anyone else in American history. And despite the frequent opposition of a series of Republican presidents, he used his position to make the judiciary a vigorous instrument for asserting and strengthening American nationalism. (Boston Athenaeum)

side. Most people, then as always, hated monopolies, and he had declared this particular monopoly unconstitutional. But the lasting significance of *Gibbons* v. *Ogden* was that it freed internal transportation from restraints by the states and thus prepared the way for the unfettered economic development of the nation by private capitalism.

More immediately, however, the decision had the effect of helping to head off a movement that was under way to weaken the Supreme Court. For some time, such Virginia Republicans as Thomas Jefferson, Spencer Roane, and John Taylor had argued against the views of their fellow Virginian John Marshall. In *Construction Construed and Constitutions Vindicated,* published in 1820, Taylor argued that Marshall and his colleagues were not merely interpreting but were actually changing the nature of the Constitution, which should properly be changed only by the amending process. In Congress some critics of the Court, mostly from the South and the West, proposed various means of curbing what they called judicial tyranny. A Kentucky senator suggested making the Senate, not the Court, the agency to decide the constitutionality of state laws and to settle interstate disputes. Other senators and congressmen introduced bills to increase the membership of the Court (from seven to ten) and to require more than a mere majority to declare a state law unconstitutional.

Still others argued for "codification," that is, for making legislative statutes the basis of the law, rather than the common-law precedents that judges used. Such a reform, codifiers argued, would limit the power of the judiciary and prevent "judge-made" law. The Court reformers did not succeed, however, in passing any of their various panaceas; and after the *Gibbons* v. *Ogden* decision, the hostility to the judicial branch of the government gradually died down.

The decisions of the Marshall Court had a profound cumulative influence on the future development both of American government and of the American economy. They established the primacy of the federal government over the states in exercising control over the economy. They opened the way for an increased federal role in promoting economic growth. And they created or affirmed protection for corporations and other private economic institutions from local government interference, hence facilitating the growth of the new industrial capitalist economy. They were, in short, highly nationalistic decisions, designed to promote the growth of a strong, unified, and economically developed United States.

The Latin American Revolution

Just as the Supreme Court was asserting American nationalism in the shaping of the country's economic life, so the Monroe administration was expressing nationalism in the shaping of foreign policy. As in earlier and later years, the central concern of the United States was its position in relation to Europe. But in defining that position, Americans were forced in the 1820s to develop a policy toward Latin America, which was suddenly winning its independence.

To most citizens of the United States, South and Central America had long seemed to constitute a "dark continent." After the War of 1812, however, they suddenly emerged into the light, and Americans looking southward beheld a gigantic spectacle: the Spanish Empire struggling in its death throes, a whole continent in revolt, new nations in the making with a future no one could foresee.

Already a profitable trade had developed between the ports of the United States and those of the Rio de la Plata (Argentina), Chile, and above all Cuba. Americans exported flour and other staples and received in return sugar, gold, and silver. Great Britain remained the principal trading nation in Latin America, but American commerce was growing steadily. Many believed that trade would increase much faster once the United States established regular diplomatic and commercial relations with the countries in revolt.

In 1815, the United States proclaimed its neutrality in the wars between Spain and its rebellious colonies. This neutrality was in itself advantageous to the rebels, since it implied a partial recognition of their status as nations. It meant, for example, that their warships would be treated as bona-fide belligerent vessels, not as pirate ships. Moreover, even though the neutrality law was revised and strengthened in 1817 and 1818, it still permitted the revolutionists to obtain unarmed ships and supplies from the United States. In short, the United States was not a strict and impartial neutral but a nonbelligerent whose policy, though cautious, was intended to help the insurgents and actually did.

Secretary of State John Quincy Adams and President James Monroe hesitated at first to take the risky step of recognition unless Great Britain would agree to do so at the same time. In 1818 and 1819, the United States made two bids for British cooperation, and both were rejected. Finally, the nationalist impulses so strong in the United States of the 1820s prevailed. In 1822, President Monroe decided to proceed alone. He informed Congress that five nations—La Plata, Chile, Peru, Colombia, and Mexico—were ready for recognition, and he requested an appropriation to send ministers to them. The United States would be the first country formally to recognize the new governments, in defiance of the rest of the world.

The Monroe Doctrine

In 1823, Monroe stood forth as an even bolder champion of America against Europe and an even more forthright champion of American nationalism. Presenting to Congress his annual message on the state of the Union, he announced a policy that would ultimately be known (beginning some thirty years later) as the "Monroe Doctrine." One part of this policy had to do with the role of Europe in America. "The American continents," Monroe declared, ". . . are henceforth not to be considered as subjects for future colonization by any European powers." Further-

James Monroe

This portrait of the fifth president of the United States, by Rembrandt Peale, was painted in the White House during Monroe's presidency. Peale was best known for his idealized portraits of George Washington, painted after Washington's death.

(James Monroe Museum and Memorial Library)

more, "we should consider any attempt on their part to extend their system to any portion of this hemisphere as dangerous to our peace and safety." And the United States would consider any "interposition" against the sovereignty of existing American nations as an unfriendly act. A second aspect of the pronouncement had to do with the role of the United States in Europe. "Our policy in regard to Europe," said Monroe, ". . . is not to interfere in the internal concerns of any of its powers."

How did the president happen to make these statements at the time he did? What specific dangers, if any, did he have in mind? Against what powers in particular was his warning directed? To answer these questions, it is useful to consider first the relations of the United States with the European powers as of 1823, and then the process by which the Monroe administration reached its decision to announce the new "doctrine."

After Napoleon's defeat, the powers of Europe combined in a "concert" to uphold the "legitimacy" of established governments and to prevent the overthrow of existing regimes from within or without. When Great Britain withdrew, the concert became a quadruple alliance, with Russia and France the strongest of its four members. In 1823, after assisting in the suppression of other revolts in Europe, the European allies authorized France to intervene in Spain to restore the Bourbon dynasty that revolutionists had overthrown. Some observers in England and the Americas wondered whether the allies next would back France in an attempt to retake by force the lost Spanish Empire in America. In fact, such concerns were almost certainly groundless. France was still a relatively weak power, not yet recovered from the long and exhausting Napoleonic Wars. It did, to be sure, try to promote the establishment of friendly kingdoms in Latin America by means of intrigue, but it dared not challenge British sea power with an expedition to subvert the new governments by force.

In the minds of most Americans, and certainly in the mind of their secretary of state, Great Britain seemed an even more serious threat to American interests. Adams was much concerned about supposed British designs on Cuba. Like Jefferson and others before him, Adams feared the transfer of Cuba from a weak power such as Spain, its present ruler, to a strong power such as Great Britain. He thought Cuba eventually should belong to the United States; for the "Pearl of the Antilles" had great economic and strategic value and, because of its location, was virtually a part of the American coastline. Adams did not de-

sire to seize the island; he wanted only to keep it in Spanish hands until, by a kind of political gravitation, it should fall naturally to the United States. Despite his worries over the supposed British threat to Cuba, he and other American leaders were pleased to see the rift between Great Britain and the concert of Europe. He was willing to cooperate with Britain, but only to the extent that its policies and his own coincided.

Those policies did not always coincide, however, as the British demonstrated when they rejected the American overtures for joint recognition of Latin American independence in 1818 and 1819. The Americans demonstrated the same thing by their reaction to a British proposal for a joint statement in 1823. That summer, the British secretary for foreign affairs, George Canning, suggested to the American minister in London, Richard Rush, that Great Britain and the United States should combine in announcing to the world their opposition to any European movement against Latin America. But Canning's refusal to join the United States in recognizing the Latin American nations forestalled agreement. And in the fall, after receiving assurances from France that it had no plans to intervene militarily in Latin America, the British abandoned the proposal altogether.

Even before Canning changed his mind about cooperation with the United States, Monroe and Adams were developing grave reservations about a joint pronouncement. Adams, in particular, argued that the American government should act alone instead of following along like a "cock-boat in the wake of a British man-of-war." Canning's loss of interest, therefore, only strengthened an already growing inclination within the administration to make its own pronouncement.

Although Canning's overture led to Monroe's announcement, the message was directed against all the powers of Europe, including Great Britain, which seemed at least as likely as Russia to undertake further colonizing ventures in America. Monroe and Adams hoped the message would rally the people of Latin America to look to their own security. They also hoped it would stir the people of the United States. America was mired in a business depression, divided by sectional politics, and apathetic toward the rather lackluster administration of Monroe. In the rumors of European aggression against the Western Hemisphere lay a chance for the president to arouse and unite the people with an appeal to national pride. The Monroe Doctrine was, then, in one sense a culmination of the growing spirit of unity and nationalism that had been emerging in the United States for over a decade. But it was also an expression of concern about the forces that were already gathering to threaten that spirit.

The Revival of Opposition

For a time during the "era of good feelings," it seemed that the dream of the founders of the republic—of a nation free of party strife—had been realized. After 1816, the Federalist party offered no presidential candidate. Soon it ceased to exist as a national political force. Presidential politics was now conducted wholly within the Republican party, which considered itself not a party at all but an organization representing the whole of the population.

Yet the policies of the federal government during and after the War of 1812, and particularly the nationalizing policies of the 1820s, continued to spark opposition. At first, criticism remained contained within the existing one-party structure. But by the late 1820s, partisan divisions were emerging once again. In some respects, the division mirrored the schism that had produced the first party system in the 1790s. The Republicans had in many ways come to resemble the early Federalist regimes in their promotion of economic growth and centralization. And the opposition, like the opposition in the 1790s, stood opposed to the federal government's expanding role in the economy. There was, however, a crucial difference. At the beginning of the century, the opponents of centralization had also often been opponents of economic growth. Now, in the 1820s, the controversy involved not whether but how the nation should continue to expand.

The "Corrupt Bargain"

From 1796 to 1816, presidential candidates had been nominated by caucuses of the members of each of the two parties in Congress. In 1820, when the Federalists declined to oppose his candidacy, Monroe ran unopposed as the Republican nominee without the necessity of a caucus nomination. If the caucus system had prevailed in 1824, the nominee of the Republicans in Congress would have run unopposed again. But it did not prevail. Several men aspired to the presidency, and they and their followers were

unwilling to let a small group of congressmen and senators determine which one of them was to win the prize.

In 1824, therefore, "King Caucus" was overthrown. Fewer than a third of the Republicans in Congress even bothered to attend the gathering. The caucus did go through the motions of nominating a candidate: William H. Crawford of Georgia, the secretary of the treasury. Other candidates received nominations from state legislatures and endorsements from irregular mass meetings throughout the country.

John Quincy Adams, secretary of state for two terms, had made a distinguished record in the conduct of foreign affairs, and he held the office that had become the traditional stepping stone to the presidency. But as he himself ruefully realized, he was a man of cold and forbidding manners, not a candidate with strong popular appeal. Crawford, in contrast, was an impressive giant of a man who had the backing not only of the congressional caucus but also of the extreme states' rights faction of the Republican party. In midcampaign, however, he was stricken by a paralyzing illness.

Challenging the two cabinet contenders was Henry Clay, the Speaker of the House. The tall, black-haired, genial Kentuckian had a personality that gained him a devoted following. He also stood for a definite and coherent program, which he called the "American System." His plan, attractive to citizens just recovering from a business depression, was to create a great home market for factory and farm producers by raising the tariff to stimulate industry, maintaining the national bank to facilitate credit and exchange, and spending federal funds on internal improvements to provide transportation between the cities and the farms.

Andrew Jackson, the fourth major candidate, offered no such clear-cut program. Although Jackson had served briefly as a representative in Congress and was a member of the United States Senate, he had no significant legislative record. Nevertheless, he had the advantages of a military hero's reputation and a campaign shrewdly managed by the Tennessee politician friends who had put him forward as a candidate. To some of his contemporaries he seemed a crude, hot-tempered frontiersman and Indian fighter. Actually, although he had arisen from a humble background as an orphan in the Carolinas, he had become a well-to-do planter who lived in an elegant mansion ("The Hermitage") near Nashville.

Once the returns were counted, there was no

John Quincy Adams

This photograph of the former president was taken shortly before his death in 1848—almost twenty years after he had left the White House—when he was serving as a congressman from Massachusetts. During his years as president, he was—as he had been throughout his life—an intensely disciplined and hard-working man. He rose at four in the morning and built a fire long before the servants were awake; then, in the predawn hours, he made a long entry in his diary for the previous day. He wrote so much that his right hand at times became paralyzed with writer's cramp, so he taught himself to write with his left hand as well. (Brown Brothers)

doubt that the next vice president was to be John C. Calhoun, of South Carolina, who ran on both the Adams and the Jackson tickets. But there was considerable doubt as to who the next president would be. Jackson received a plurality, although not a majority, of the popular vote. In the electoral college too he came out ahead, with 99 votes to Adams's 84, Crawford's 41, and Clay's 37. Again, however, he lacked a majority. So, in accordance with the Twelfth Amendment, the final decision was left to the House of Representatives, which was to choose among the three candidates with the highest electoral vote. Clay was out of the running.

But while Clay could not be elected president in 1824, he was in a strong position to determine who would be. As Speaker, he had indirect influence throughout the House of Representatives. And as a candidate for the presidency whose electors had won in three states—Kentucky, Ohio, and Missouri—he was in a position to influence those state delegations directly.

Before Congress made its decision, supporters of Jackson, Crawford, and Adams approached Clay on behalf of their respective candidates. Jackson's followers insisted that Jackson, with his popular and electoral pluralities, was really the people's choice and that Congress had no rightful alternative but to ratify the people's will. But Jackson was Clay's most dangerous rival for the political affections of the West; and Jackson, moreover, had demonstrated no support for Clay's nationalistic legislative program. Crawford was out of the question, for he was now a paralytic, incapable of discharging the duties of the presidency. Adams was no friend of Clay and had clashed with him repeatedly when both were peace delegates at Ghent and afterward. But alone among the candidates, Adams was an ardent nationalist and a likely supporter of the American System. Thus Clay finally gave his support to Adams, and the House elected him.

The Jacksonians were angry enough at this, but they became far angrier when the new president announced that Clay was to be his secretary of state. The State Department was the well-established route to the presidency, and Adams thus appeared to be naming Clay as his own successor. To the Jacksonians, it seemed clear that Clay and Adams must have agreed to make each other president—Adams now, Clay next; and they claimed to be horrified by this "corrupt bargain." Very likely there had been some sort of understanding; and though there was nothing corrupt, or even unusual, about it, it proved to be politically costly for both Adams and Clay.

Soon after Adams's inauguration as president, Jackson resigned from the Senate to accept a renomination for the presidency from the Tennessee legislature and to begin a three-year campaign for election in 1828. Politics now overshadowed all else. Throughout his term in the White House, Adams and his policies were to be thoroughly frustrated by the political bitterness arising from the "corrupt bargain."

The Second President Adams

The career of John Quincy Adams divides naturally into three parts. In the first part, as befitted the son of John Adams, he was a brilliant diplomat, serving as the American minister in one foreign capital after another and then as one of the most successful of all secretaries of state. In the second phase of his career, as president from 1825 to 1829, he endured four unhappy and ineffectual years that amounted to a mere interlude between the periods of his greatness. In the third, as a congressman from Massachusetts, he served with high distinction, gaining fame as "Old Man Eloquent," the foremost congressional champion of free speech. His frustration in the White House shows that the presidency demands more than exceptional ability and high-mindedness, for John Quincy Adams possessed both. The presidency also requires political skill and political luck, and these he did not have.

In his inaugural address and in his first message to Congress, Adams gave voice to his own nationalistic vision of the powers and duties of the federal government. He recommended "laws promoting the improvement of agriculture, commerce, and manufactures, the cultivation of the mechanic and of the elegant arts, the advancement of literature, and the progress of the sciences, ornamental and profound." He had no chance of getting an appropriation from Congress for most of these goals. All he actually did get was a few million dollars to improve rivers and harbors and to extend the National Road westward from Wheeling. Still, this was more than Congress had appropriated for internal improvements under all his predecessors together.

Even in the field of diplomacy, where Adams had more experience than any other president before or since, he failed in the major efforts of his administration. Yielding to Secretary of State Clay's wish for

cooperation with the Latin American governments, Adams appointed two delegates to attend an international conference that the Venezuelan liberator, Simón Bolívar, had called to meet at Panama in 1826. Objections arose in Congress for two reasons. One was that Southerners opposed the idea of white Americans mingling in Panama with black delegates from Haiti, a country whose independence the United States refused to recognize. The other reason for obstruction was simply politics—the determination of Jacksonians to discredit the administration. They charged that Adams aimed to sacrifice American interests and involve the nation in an entangling alliance. While the Jacksonians filibustered, Congress delayed the Panama mission so long that by the time it was finally approved it was too late. One of the American delegates died on the way to the conference; the other arrived after it was over. Adams had hoped to offset British influence, which prevailed in Latin America, by having the United States play an active role at the conference. Those hopes were dashed.

Adams was also bested in a contest with the state of Georgia, which wished to remove the remaining Creek and Cherokee Indians from the state so as to gain additional soil for cotton planters. The United States government, in a 1791 treaty, had guaranteed the Creeks possession of the land they occupied. But the Georgians extracted a new treaty from the tribe in 1825, by which the Creeks ceded the land to the state. Adams was convinced that the new treaty had been fraudulently obtained and refused to enforce it, setting up a direct conflict between the president and the leaders of the state. The governor of Georgia defied the president and went ahead with plans for Indian removal. The conflict was finally resolved in 1827, when the Creeks agreed to still another treaty, in which they again yielded their land, thus undercutting Adams's position. The affair was memorable in one sense: Adams became one of the few major American public figures firmly to oppose the continuing displacement of the Indians. But at the time, it served mainly as a political embarrassment.

Even more damaging to the administration was its support for a new tariff on imported goods in 1828. This measure originated in the demands of Massachusetts and Rhode Island woolen manufacturers, who complained that the British were dumping woolens on the American market at prices with which the domestic mill owners could not compete. The New Englanders were frustrated at first by Southern opposition in Congress, but eventually they com-

Choctaws in Louisiana
The Choctaws were among the many Mississippi Valley tribes to experience forced relocation at the hands of the United States in the 1830s. Originally located in central Mississippi, the tribe marched through Louisiana and Arkansas and into Indian Territory (now Oklahoma) beginning in 1830. Some members of the tribe remained behind at various points along the way, living alongside the white community and adopting many of its ways. The French artist Alfred Boisseau painted this scene of a group of them walking along a bayou in Louisiana in 1845.   (New Orleans Museum of Art)

bined with the middle and Western states to create political pressures that could not be resisted.

But the 1828 bill, the result of these efforts, contained provisions attractive to the West that antagonized its original New England supporters. It established high duties not only on woolens, as the New Englanders had wanted, but also on a number of other items, such as flax, hemp, iron, lead, molasses, and raw wool, some of which the West produced and for which they wanted protection from foreign rivals. That distressed New England manufacturers; the benefits of protecting their manufactured goods from foreign competition now had to be weighed against the prospects of having to pay more

for raw materials. Indeed, a story arose that the bill had taken its shape from a Jacksonian plot to embarrass and discredit Adams. The bill related to "manufactures of no sort or kind but the manufacture of a president of the United States," John Randolph said. The bill would present Adams with a dilemma, for he would lose friends whether he signed or vetoed it. To sign the bill would lose him support in both the South and the Northeast. To veto it would lose him support from the farmers and manufacturers of the West.

When Congress considered the bill item by item, Southerners voted against proposals to reduce the tariff rates, in the hope that some of its outrageous duties would so antagonize New Englanders that they would help defeat it. But when it came to a final test, Daniel Webster voted for it despite its duties on raw materials, and he carried with him enough New England votes to enable the bill to pass. Adams signed it. The tactics of the Southerners had backfired, and they were left cursing the bill as the "tariff of abominations."

Jackson Triumphant

By 1828, the schism within the Republican party was complete. Once again, as in 1800, two parties offered candidates in the presidential election. On one side stood the supporters of John Quincy Adams, who called themselves the National Republicans. They supported the economic nationalism of the preceding years. Opposing them were the followers of Andrew Jackson, who took the name Democratic Republicans. They argued for a dispersal of public authority, an assault on privilege, and a widening of opportunity. Adams attracted the support of most of the remaining Federalists (among whose number he had once counted himself); Jackson appealed to a broad coalition that stood opposed to the "economic" aristocracy.

Issues seemed to count for little in the campaign of 1828. There was much talk of the "corrupt bargain" and frequent rhetorical references to the "tariff of abominations." But while Adams's position on the tariff was a matter of record (he had signed the bill), nobody knew where Jackson stood. Again, as in 1824, personalities became a more important factor than policies. Indeed, the tone of the campaign was such as to suggest that two criminals were running for the highest office in the land.

The Jacksonians charged that Adams as president had been guilty of gross waste and extravagance and had used public funds to buy gambling devices (a chess set and a billiard table) for the White House. But that was not the worst of Adams's alleged crimes. While Adams had been minister to Russia, the Jacksonians falsely claimed, he had tried to procure a beautiful American girl for the sinful pleasures of the czar.

Adams's supporters directed even worse accusations at Jackson. He was, they claimed in speeches, handbills, and pamphlets, a murderer and an adulterer. A "coffin handbill" listed, within coffin-shaped

---

SIGNIFICANT EVENTS

1808 Importation of slaves to United States banned	**1828** "Tariff of abominations" passed Andrew Jackson elected president
1817–1825 Erie Canal constructed	**1830** Baltimore & Ohio becomes first American railroad to begin operations
1819 Supreme Court hears *Dartmouth College* and *McCulloch* v. *Maryland*	**1830s** Major immigration from southern (Catholic) Ireland begins
1820 Missouri Compromise enacted Monroe reelected president without opposition	Factory system spreads in textile and shoe industries
1823 Monroe Doctrine is proclaimed	First craft unions founded
1824 John Quincy Adams wins disputed presidential election Supreme Court rules in *Gibbons* v. *Ogden*	**1831** Cyrus McCormick invents mechanical reaper
1826 Thomas Jefferson and John Adams die on July 4	**1832** Cholera plague
	1834 Woman workers at Lowell mills stage strike
1827 Creek Indians cede lands to Georgia	**1837** Commercial panic
	1845 Female Labor Reform Association established at Lowell

Election of 1828   (57.6% of electorate voting)

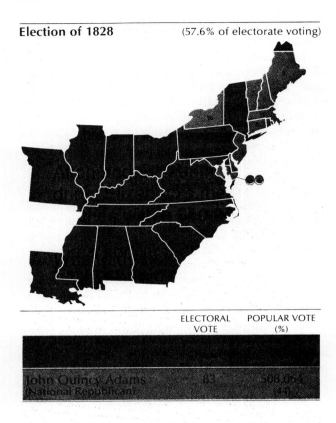

	ELECTORAL VOTE	POPULAR VOTE (%)
John Quincy Adams (National Republican)	83	508,064 (44%)

outlines, the names of militiamen whom Jackson was said to have shot in cold blood during the War of 1812. (The men had been deserters who were executed after due sentence by a court-martial.) It was also rumored that Jackson had knowingly lived in sin with the wife of another man. Actually, he had married the woman, his beloved Rachel, at a time when the pair apparently believed her first husband had divorced her.

Jackson's victory was decisive, if sectional. He won 56 percent of the popular vote and an electoral majority of 178 votes to Adams's 83. But the Jacksonians made few inroads into the National Republican strongholds of the Northeast. Adams swept virtually all of New England, and he showed significant strength in the mid-Atlantic region. Nevertheless, the Jacksonians considered their victory complete, and they hailed it as an event as important as the victory of Jefferson in 1800. Once again, the forces of privilege had been ejected from Washington. Once again, a champion of democracy would occupy the White House and restore liberty to the society and the economy. America had entered, many claimed, the "era of the common man." And Andrew Jackson, the people's champion, departed for Washington determined to transform the federal government.

Conditioning and Desensitization

—**James McConnell,** from *Understanding Human Behavior* (Holt, Rinehart and Winston, Inc., 1986), pages 344–358

STUDY QUESTIONS

As you read through the chapter, see if you can find the answers to the following questions:

1. Why did American psychologists react so negatively to Twitmyer's discovery of the conditioned response?
2. What was Pavlov's first name for conditioned reactions?
3. Why did Pavlov call the musical tone a *conditional* stimulus?
4. According to Pavlov, what is the most important bond that occurs during conditioning?
5. What is an "extinguished response"?
6. What does the term "spontaneous recovery" mean?
7. How did Pavlov train a dog to withstand great pain without flinching?
8. Why is the polygraph *not* really a "lie detector"?
9. What is "counter conditioning"?
10. How does Joseph Wolpe use *systematic desensitization* to reduce phobic reactions?
11. What is "higher order conditioning"?
12. How does "cognitive desensitization" differ from "systematic desensitization"?
13. What is "modeling therapy," and how did Bandura use it to "cure" snake phobias?
14. How did Freud view phobias?
15. What is "symptom substitution"?

Conditioning and Sensitization

"The Leningrad Connection"

THE INNATE REFLEX

Some time about the beginning of this century, a young man named E.B. Twitmyer began work on his doctoral dissertation in psychology at the University of Pennsylvania. Twitmyer was interested in *innate reflexes*—those automatic behavior patterns that are wired into your brain circuits by your genetic blueprint. And most particularly, he was interested in the **patellar reflex**, or knee-jerk.

You can evoke the patellar reflex in either of your legs rather simply (see Fig. 9.1). When you are sitting down, cross one leg on top of the other, leaving your uppermost leg hanging freely. Now, reach down with the edge of your hand and strike this leg smartly just below your kneecap. If you hit just the right place, you will strike your patellar tendon, which runs close to the surface of your skin at this point on your leg. Whenever you tap on this tendon, the lower half of your leg will swing forward involuntarily.

FIG. 9.1 Tapping the patellar tendon with a hammer elicits the "knee-jerk" reflex.

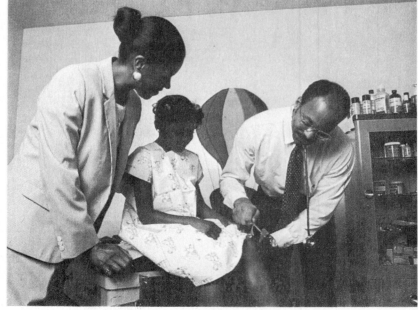

Patellar reflex (pat-TELL-are). The patella is the knee bone. If you strike your leg just below this bone, the lower part of your leg will jerk. This "knee-jerk," or patellar reflex, is an automatic response over which you have little volitional control.

Conditioned reflex (con-DISH-shunned). A learned response pattern in which a stimulus is bonded or connected to a response. The "conditions" for acquiring the reflex usually involve pairing a "neutral" stimulus (such as a bell) with a stimulus that innately sets off a reflexive response (such as striking the patellar tendon). Also called a "conditional reflex."

FIG. 9.2 Ivan Pavlov (white beard) with his students and a dog in a training apparatus.

Twitmyer's Experiment

Twitmyer believed the patellar reflex might be influenced by the *motivational state* a subject was in when the reflex was set off. So he asked fellow graduate students to be his subjects. Then he rigged up a small hammer that would strike the subject's patellar tendon when he let the hammer fall. Twitmyer didn't bother telling his subjects when he was about to stimulate their reflexes—he merely dropped the hammer and measured how far their legs jerked. But his subjects complained the hammer blow often caught them by surprise. Couldn't he ring a bell as a warning? Twitmyer agreed, and began sounding a signal to announce the hammer drop.

One day when Twitmyer was working with a subject whose knee had been hit hundreds of times, he accidentally sounded the warning signal without dropping the hammer. As promptly as clockwork, the subject's knee jerked *despite* the fact that his tendon hadn't been stimulated. Although Twitmyer didn't realize it, he had just discovered the **conditioned reflex**, a response pattern upon which a dozen different psychological theories would later be built.

However, Twitmyer did appreciate the fact that he was on to something important, and he dropped his original research plans in order to investigate his discovery. He established some of the conditions under which this new type of reflex occurred—for example, the fact that much of learning is based on *stimulus-response associations*, and that conditioning is often a matter of making some change in an *innate reflex*. Twitmyer reported his findings at the 1904 meeting of the American Psychological Association. He published his research in a scientific journal the subsequent year (Twitmyer, 1905).

Although the conditioned response is now one of the "basic facts" on which experimental psychology rests, Twitmyer's report excited little or no attention in the US (Dallenbach, 1959). Discouraged by the frosty reception his ideas received, Twitmyer dropped his laboratory research and went on to other things.

About the same time that Twitmyer was working at the University of Pennsylvania, the noted Russian scientist Ivan Pavlov was performing similar studies at his laboratory in Leningrad. Whether Twitmyer or Pavlov was the first to "discover" the conditioned reflex is a matter of some dispute, although it does seem that Twitmyer was the first to publish his findings (Windholz, 1986). Whatever the case, it was Pavlov who ended up making most of the important early discoveries in this area.

PAVLOV'S CONDITIONING STUDIES

Ivan Pavlov, who lived from 1849 to 1936, is perhaps Russia's most famous scientist. After taking his medical degree in 1883, Pavlov traveled in Europe, studying with various other scientists. In 1890, he founded the Institute of Experimental Medicine in Leningrad, which he directed the rest of his life.

Pavlov's early interests were in the biological processes of *digestion*, and he chose dogs for his experimental animals. He trained the dogs to lie quietly on operating tables or in leather harnesses while he studied what went on inside their stomachs before and after the dogs had eaten a meal (see Fig. 9.2). His experiments proved for the first time that the nervous system coordinates *all* digestive responses. Because of the pioneering nature of his work, Pavlov was awarded the Nobel Prize in 1904—the first Russian to be so honored (Wertheimer, 1987).

• *Psychic Stimulations*

Digestion actually begins in the mouth, where *saliva* starts breaking up food particles chemically. So Pavlov began his work by studying the salivary glands. Pavlov soon found a way to measure the amount of saliva the glands produced. While the dog was in a harness, Pavlov would give food to the dog, then count the number of drops of saliva its salivary glands secreted.

Dogs do not have to be trained to salivate when given food—they do so *reflexively*, or automatically. Salivation is therefore an innate *response* (R) or reflex that is elicited by the *stimulus* (S) of food in the mouth.

E.B. Twitmyer

"HE SALIVATES."

Pavlov wanted to determine the neural pathways that *connected* the stimulus receptors in the dog's mouth with its salivary glands. But his research was often interrupted by *peculiar responses* the animals would make. After an animal had gotten accustomed to being fed in the harness, its salivary glands would often "juice up" *before* it got the food. In fact, an experienced dog would usually start salivating if one of Pavlov's assistants merely rattled the food dishes in the sink or walked toward the dog carrying a plate.

Pavlov called these "unusual" reactions *psychic stimulations.* These odd reactions infuriated him because they "got in the way" of his regular research. He did his best to ignore them because he wasn't interested in anything "psychological." However, the psychic stimulations refused to go away. And so, around 1901, Pavlov began to study them systematically, hoping to get rid of these "annoyances." He told his friends this work surely wouldn't take more than a year or two to complete. In fact, Pavlov spent the last 34 years of his life determining the properties of these "psychic stimulations" (Goldenson, 1970).

Unconditional Stimulus-Response Connections

If you blow food powder into a dog's mouth, the animal will salivate reflexively. This response is determined by the dog's genetic blueprint. Pavlov called the food an **unconditional** or **unconditioned stimulus** (UCS) because the food's ability to evoke salivation is not *conditional* upon the dog's having learned the response.

The salivation reaction is also innately determined. Therefore, Pavlov named it the **unconditional** or **unconditioned response** (UCR) since it too is not *conditional* upon learning.

□□ **QUESTION** □□
How would you go about *teaching* a dog to salivate when you gave it food if it didn't do so instinctively?

Conditional Stimulus-Response Connections

One of the first things Pavlov discovered in his research was this: If he sounded a musical tone just before he blew food into the animal's mouth, the dog eventually salivated almost as much to the *tone alone* as it did to the tone plus the food powder. Apparently the animal learned to "associate" the *sound* of the music with the *stimulus* of the food. And thus, each time the tone sounded, the dog *anticipated* it would be fed. So it salivated to the tone just as it did to the food.

This sort of *conditioning* occurs in people as well as in dogs. The smell of bacon frying in the morning is enough to set your mouth to watering, but only because you have *learned to associate* the smell of the meat with how it tastes. In similar fashion, the clang of a dinner bell is often enough to set your stomach rumbling because your stomach muscles have been *conditioned* to expect food shortly after the bell sounds.

• *"Neural S-R Connections"*

According to Pavlov, learning is always a matter of establishing new "connections in the brain" between stimuli (Ss) and responses (Rs).

The neural connection between the unconditional UCS_{food} and the unconditional $UCR_{salivation}$ is innately determined. Therefore, it is an *unlearned* or reflexive S-R connection that we might diagram as follows:

$$UCS_{food} \xrightarrow{\text{(innate S-R connection)}} UCR_{salivation}$$

However, when the previously neutral S_{tone} is presented *just prior* to the unconditioned UCS_{food}, a new "connection" is built up in the animal's brain that links the S_{tone} with the $UCR_{salivation}$.

Pavlov called the tone a **conditional** or **conditioned stimulus** (CS) because its power to call forth the salivation response is *conditional* upon its being paired with the food powder. We can diagram the situation as follows:

$$S_{tone} \xrightarrow{\left(\substack{\text{S-S} \\ \text{association}}\right)} UCS_{food} \xrightarrow{\left(\substack{\text{innate S-R} \\ \text{connection}}\right)} UCR_{salivation}$$

Unconditional (unconditioned) stimulus. Abbreviated UCS. You are born with certain innate responses, such as the patellar reflex. These reflexes are set off (elicited) by innately-determined (unconditioned or unlearned) stimuli. The blow to your patellar tendon is an unconditioned stimulus that elicits the unconditioned response we call the knee-jerk. The term "unconditional" is used to describe these stimuli because their ability to elicit the response are not *conditional* on learning.

Unconditional (unconditioned) response. Abbreviated UCR. Any innately-determined response pattern or reflex that is set off by a UCS. The knee-jerk is a UCR.

Conditional (conditioned) stimulus. Abbreviated CS. The CS is the "neutral" stimulus which, through frequent pairings with an unconditioned stimulus, acquires the ability to elicit an unconditioned response.

Conditional (conditioned) response. Abbreviated CR. Any reaction set off by a CS. A bright light (UCS) flashed in your eye causes your pupil to contract (UCS). If someone frequently rings a bell (CS) just before turning on the bright light (UCS), the sound of the bell (CS) would soon gain the power to make your pupil contract. Once this conditioning has taken place, the UCR (contraction) becomes a CR that can be elicited by the CS. Since pupil contraction can now be set off by *either* the CS or the UCS, the contractive response is *both* a CR and a UCR. In many cases, however, the CR looks slightly different from the UCR. In Pavlov's studies, for example, the CR usually consisted of fewer drops of saliva than did the UCR.

Once the dog has learned the connection between the tone and the food, you can present just the tone alone—without giving the food—and the dog will salivate. In similar fashion, once you have learned to associate the aroma of bacon with its taste, the mere *smell* of the meat will set off your salivary glands even if you don't eat any of the bacon.

□□ **QUESTION** □□
Is the odor of bacon more likely to cause you to salivate when you're hungry or when you've just finished a large meal?

● *The "Conditioned Response"*
But what can we call the salivary response when it is triggered off by the tone alone? Surely it is no longer an *unconditioned* response because there is no innate connection in the brain between a "neutral" musical tone and salivation. Pavlov named this *learned* reaction to the neutral stimulus a **conditional** or **conditioned response** (CR).

Conditioning is the term Pavlov used to describe the process by which the previously neutral stimulus (CS) gains the power to *elicit* the conditioned response (CR) (Pavlov, 1927). The CS gains this power, of course, because of the *new neural connections* that occur in the animal's brain linking the tone (CS) with the salivation (CR).

Once the conditioning process has taken place, we can diagram the situation as follows:

$$CS_{tone} \xrightarrow{\text{(learned S-R connection)}} CR_{partial\ salivation}$$

The type of training developed by Pavlov is called by many names: classical conditioning,

reflex conditioning, Pavlovian conditioning, respondent conditioning, and stimulus-response (S-R) learning.

● *Conditioning: A Definition*
Generally speaking, when psychologists use the term *conditioning,* they refer to some situation in which a *previously neutral stimulus* gains the power to elicit a *response* in a reflexive or mechanical fashion. So when we say that you have been "conditioned" to do something, we mean that you have learned to respond rather automatically to a particular stimulus. We often speak of this sort of conditioning as "bonding" the S to the R.

Technically speaking, conditioning occurs because of the *association* that occurs when the CS and the UCS are "paired" repeatedly. However, from a Pavlovian point of view, this "pairing" merely allows the CS to become "connected" (or bonded) to the UCR. When Pavlov spoke of *conditioning,* he almost always referred to S-R bonds, not to "mental associations" between stimuli.

Perhaps the most important point about Pavlovian conditioning is this: Because the learning is reflexive, *you need not be aware that it has taken place.*

□□ **QUESTION** □□
Can you figure out how you were conditioned to believe that, in our society, men shouldn't wear pantyhose?

Factors Affecting Conditioning
During the many years that Pavlov studied the conditioning process, he discovered several factors that affect this type of learning:

● **1.** The more *frequently* the CS and the UCS are paired, the *stronger* the S-R bond becomes (see Fig. 9.3). For example, up to a

FIG. 9.3 The charts show first the acquisition of conditioned salivation in a trained dog, and then extinction.

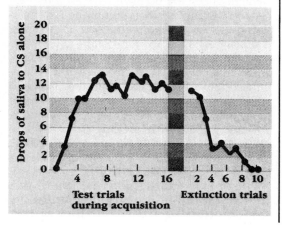

theoretical limit, the more often a tone is associated with food powder, the more drops of saliva the tone will elicit. And the more frequently the CS and UCS are paired, the stronger the S-R bond becomes and the better the animal will remember the learning later on.

- 2. Conditioning typically is fastest when the CS is presented *immediately* before the UCS. For example, the optimum time interval for conditioned salivation in the dog is about half a second. If the tone is presented more than a few seconds *before* the food—or is presented *after* the food—little or no learning usually occurs. However, the optimum time interval does vary from animal to animal, from species to species, and from situation to situation. And there is one notable exception to this rule that we will discuss momentarily.

- 3. Conditioned responses are *unlearned* just as easily as they are learned. Suppose you train a dog to salivate. That is, you establish a CS-CR connection in the animal between a tone and salivation. Now you present the dog with the tone *without* giving it the food. You would find that the animal salivates less and less on each trial. Finally, the response would be **extinguished** completely (see Fig. 9.4). Put another way, the S-R "bond" has been broken.

- 4. An "extinguished response" is not completely *forgotten*. Suppose you condition a dog, then extinguish the response. Then you pair the CS with the UCS for a second round of training trials. The dog now will re-acquire the conditioned response much more quickly than it did the first time around. Apparently the original conditioning has left a "trace" of some kind that makes relearning easier.

- 5. In similar fashion, suppose you *extinguish* a dog's conditioned salivation response and then let the animal sit in its cage for two weeks. Now you bring the dog back to the lab, hook it up in its harness, and again sound the tone. What will happen? As you might guess, the dog will have *forgotten the extinction* and it will again salivate. Psychologists call this *spontaneous recovery* of a previously extinguished S-R bond.

- 6. The mere passage of time can act as a conditioning stimulus. When Pavlov fed his animals regularly each half-hour, they began to salivate a minute or so before the next feeding was due even though there were no *external stimuli* such as dish rattles to give them cues that it was almost time to eat.

□ □ **QUESTION** □ □

Pavlov believed the mere pairing of the CS and the UCS was sufficient for conditioning to occur—whether or not

the subject wished to learn or found the experience rewarding. Look back over the past couple of pages. How many times have the terms "CS" and "conditioned stimulus" been paired? Are the two terms now associated in your mind? Were you conscious that you were learning? And the next time you watch television, look closely at the commercials. Do the advertisers seem to be using Pavlovian techniques to get you to like or remember their products?

- ### Conditioned Taste Aversion

As we mentioned, conditioning usually occurs most quickly when the CS precedes the UCS by less than one second. This "fact" is really just common sense. Suppose you ring a bell, and then a second later give a dog mild shock to its forepaw. The animal will surely whine, and withdraw its paw from the shock plate (if it can do so). After a few such trials, the animal will probably whine and pull back its paw *even if you don't turn on the shock.* However, if you ring a bell, then wait 30 minutes, and *then* give the animal shock, it probably never will associate the bell with the shock. For the *temporal delay* between CS and UCS is just too great in this case.

There is an important exception to this principle, however. If you eat an unusual food for lunch and then, *for any reason whatsoever*, become "sick to your stomach" a few hours later, you are likely to avoid that unusual food in the future. Here, the temporal delay between stimulus (unusual food) and response (illness) is several hours—but the **conditioned taste aversion** is strong, and is established in just one trial (Deems & Garcia, 1986).

The exact physiological mechanisms that control conditioned taste aversion are still a matter of considerable debate. However, it does seem as if this type of learning has high survival value. One reason that wild rats are so difficult to destroy is that, when they first encounter a novel-tasting food, they eat just a tiny amount even if they are extremely hungry. They then wait several hours. If the rats don't become ill, they then ingest more of the novel food. However, if they do become ill, they often return to the food and "mark" it by urinating or defecating on it—apparently as a way of warning other rats not to eat the suspect food (Bhardwaj & Khan, 1979). For obvious reasons, this type of learning is often called "bait shyness."

□ □ **QUESTION** □ □

How might you *overcome* a conditioned taste aversion if you wished to do so?

Extinguished (ex-TING-guished). To "extinguish" a response is to reduce the frequency (or intensity) of a learned response either by withdrawing the reward that was used during training, or by presenting the CS many times without the UCS. In fact, it is the "bond" or "connection" between the CS and the CR that is extinguished.

Conditioned taste aversion. A type of conditioning in which the unconditioned stimulus (internal cues associated with nausea or vomiting) usually occurs several hours after the conditioning stimulus (a novel food), but a strong CS-UCS association is built up in just one trial. Also called "bait shyness."

Masochists (MASS-oh-kists). Masochism (MASS-oh-kiss-em) is a sexual deviation in which pleasure is derived from pain. The pain may be psychological or physical, and may be self-inflicted or inflicted by others. The term comes from the name of the Austrian novelist Leopold V. Sacher-Masoch, whose stories frequently featured scenes in which sexual pleasure was associated with painful stimulus inputs.

Discrimination training. Teaching an animal to discriminate—that is, to react differently to fairly similar stimuli. If you can tell the difference between two things, you know how to discriminate between them.

Generalization (jen-er-al-eye-ZAY-shun). Stimulus generalization is the tendency to make the same response to two similar stimuli. If a monkey has been trained to lift its right paw when you turn on an orange light, it may also lift its paw when you turn on a yellow or a red light. Response generalization is the tendency to make a slightly different reaction to the same stimulus. If you hold down the monkey's right paw when you turn on the orange light, the response may generalize to the left paw instead.

Pavlov's Masochistic Dog

Pavlov believed "conditioning" could account for most types of human behavior. One way to prove his point, he reasoned, would be to produce in *animals* various abnormal behaviors some people thought could only occur in *humans*.

For instance, Pavlov wondered why a few individuals—called **masochists**—seemed to enjoy or seek out pain. Many psychologists believed *masochism* was the result of some "flaw" in the individual's personality. Pavlov suspected this "love of painful inputs" might be learned. To settle the matter—at least, in his own mind—Pavlov trained a dog to withstand extremely painful stimuli by using a "step-by-step" conditioning technique.

First, Pavlov marked off an area of skin on the dog's front leg. Then he stimulated this area with a weakly painful CS—and immediately gave the dog some food. The dog salivated to the food, but didn't flinch at the pain. Apparently the strong unconditioned salivation response *inhibited* the normal pain reflex.

Then, day after day, Pavlov slowly increased the intensity of the painful CS, each time pairing it with food. At no time did the animal respond as if it were being hurt. Indeed, the dog seemed more than willing to be put in the training harness and given the pain—since the pain soon *became a conditioned signal* that the dog would soon receive food.

Once the dog was fully trained, it would passively withstand incredible amounts of painful stimulation delivered to its front leg. However, if Pavlov applied the painful CS to any other part of the dog's body, the animal would instantly set up a great howl and attempt to escape from its training harness.

Pavlov concluded that when he touched the CS to the dog's front leg, the animal did not in fact *feel* any pain. Why not? Because the salivation response was so strong it *suppressed* all other responses to the *same stimulus*, Pavlov said. Apparently in dogs, as well as in humans, "You can't do more than one thing at a time." And whatever response is strongest tends to repress most other reactions that could be made to the same stimulus (Pavlov, 1927).

The parallel between Pavlov's masochistic dogs and those humans who seek out pain or humiliation in order to gain pleasure (often sexual) is rather remarkable. But as important as these experiments might have been to the discovery of a "cure" for masochism in humans, this research was regarded with considerable distaste by most other scientists.

□ □ **QUESTION** □ □

What similarities do you see between Pavlov's "step-by-step" conditioning procedure and the techniques for coping with stress discussed in the previous chapter?

Discrimination and Generalization

Perhaps the most interesting "mental health" experiment Pavlov conducted had to do with **discrimination training**. Pavlov began by showing a dog a drawing of a circle, then giving it food immediately. Very soon the dog became conditioned to salivate whenever it saw a circle.

Pavlov then tested the animal by showing it drawings of figures such as an ellipse, a pentagon, a square, a rectangle, a triangle, and a star. He found that the salivary response *generalized* to stimulus inputs other than the original CS (the circle). As you might suspect, this **generalization** followed a specific pattern—the more similar the other figure was to a circle, the more the animal salivated.

Pavlov then trained the dog to *discriminate* between the two stimuli by always giving food to the dog when the circle appeared, but never giving it a reward when he showed it the ellipse. Soon the dog learned to salivate *only* when the circle was shown.

After Pavlov had established that the dog could discriminate between a circle and an ellipse, he tried to fool the animal. On subsequent trials, he presented the dog with ellipses that were closer and closer to being completely round. Eventually the animal's "cognitive system" was strained to the breaking point, for the animal could not perceive the difference between the positive CS (the circle) and the negative CS (the ellipse). Therefore, Pavlov said, the animal did not know *which response to make*—

the response to the circle, or the response to the ellipse.

Overcome by stress, the animal broke down, snapped at Pavlov and his assistants, barked loudly, urinated and defecated, and tried very hard to get out of the restraining harness (Pavlov, 1927). If a human being had displayed the same behavior patterns, we probably would say the person was **neurotic** or "unable to cope."

How different Pavlov's two "mental health" experiments were! In the first case, an animal learned to give a *normal* response to a very abnormal stimulus input. In the second study— even though the dog received no painful stimulation at all—the animal gave an *abnormal* response to a very "normal" set of stimuli.

These two studies convinced Pavlov that "mental illness" was learned and was mostly a matter of mixed-up "connections in the brain." (Pavlov took a purely biological view toward the causes of mental illness. As we will see in later chapters, there are intra-psychic and environmental influences that are at least as important.)

□ □ **QUESTION** □ □
Pavlov believed his dog became "masochistic" because it had learned that a food reward would always follow the pain. How could you use "extinction procedures" and "retraining" to bring about normal behavior patterns in the animal?

CONDITIONED EMOTIONAL RESPONSES

Once Pavlov had shown the way, a number of other psychologists began experimenting with conditioning procedures using humans rather than animals. John B. Watson, the father of behaviorism, was perhaps the first to study how emotional responses (such as fear) get established in children.

Watson and Little Albert

In one of Watson's most famous experiments, he and his second wife (Rosalie Rayner) conditioned a boy named Albert to fear a white rat. At the beginning of the study, Albert was unafraid of the animal and played with it freely. While Albert was doing so one day, Watson deliberately frightened the child by sounding a terrifying noise behind him. Albert was startled and began to cry. Thereafter, he avoided the rat and cried if it was brought close to him (Watson & Rayner, 1920). (This sort of experimentation is now forbidden by the American Psychological Association's Code of Ethics.)

In Pavlovian terms, Watson and Rayner had set up a *bond* or "connection" between the

The *generalization* of a fear response to objects that are similar in appearance is shown in this archival photo of Little Albert with John Watson and his assistant. Watson is wearing a furry white mask, which frightens Little Albert much as a furry white rat would have. (Courtesy Dr. Ben Harris, University of Wisconsin–Parkside)

sight of the rat (CS) and an arousal response in Albert's autonomic nervous system (CR). Once this S-R bond was fixed, the fear response could also be elicited by showing Albert almost any furry object. Put another way, fears often *generalize* to stimuli similar to the CS. The burnt child dreads not only the fire, but often comes to fear stoves, pots and pans, ovens, pictures of flames, and even stories about the great Chicago fire.

We will have more to say about conditioned fears (and how to treat them) in just a moment. First, let's look at how emotional responses such as fears are often measured in the laboratory.

Measuring Emotional Responses

Words are *stimuli*, just like bells and musical tones. If you were chased by a bull when you were a child, you probably experienced great fear. And you would still show some conditioned *autonomic arousal* even now if you read the word "bull," saw a picture of one, or were asked to think about one.

● *The Polygraph*

We could *measure* your fear reaction to "bulls" by attaching you to a **polygraph**, a machine often (incorrectly) called a "lie-detector." The polygraph would record your pulse, blood pressure, breathing rate, and the amount of sweat produced on the palms of your hands. These are all measures of *autonomic arousal*. And as you know from reading Chapter 8, auto-

Neurotic (new-ROT-tick). Abnormal or unusual behavior patterns are sometimes referred to as being "neurotic." A neurosis (new-ROW-sis) is a relatively mild form of mental disorder. As we will see in Chapter 19, however, psychologists do not agree on the causes and cures of neurotic behaviors. Although the term is widely used in psychology, it has recently fallen out of favor in psychiatry and is no longer an "accepted diagnosis" for any type of mental problem.

Polygraph (PAHL-ee-graff). *Poly* means "many." A polygraph is a machine that makes a graph of many different responses simultaneously. Sometimes called a "lie-detector," but it records emotional responses, not "lies."

Emits. To "emit" a response is to give forth, or produce that response. Technically speaking, conditioned responses are *elicited*, which is to say they are "pulled" out of the organism reflexively because of the association between the S and the R. However, voluntary responses are usually said to be "emitted."

David Lykken

The polygraph measures body responses such as pulse, blood pressure, breathing rate, and the amount of sweat on the palms. Its effectiveness as a "lie detector" has been questioned.

nomic arousal is often—*but not always*—associated with the subjective experience of emotionality.

If we showed you an emotionally "neutral" stimulus while you were hooked up to the polygraph, your record presumably would remain calm and regular. If we then presented you with a picture of a large bull, or said the word aloud, the graph would note a sudden, sharp *change* in your autonomic activity. We would then assume you had experienced some emotional arousal, such as that associated with fear, anxiety, or guilt.

The polygraph *can* detect lying at an above-chance level. However, when tested with actual criminal suspects in real-life conditions, its "success rate" in detecting lying is only about 70 percent (where chance expectancy is 50 percent). And, as Minnesota psychiatrist David Lykken points out, "the polygraph test is biased against the truthful respondent. . . . [Almost 50 percent] of the truthful suspects in these studies were erroneously classified as 'deceptive'" (Lykken, 1983).

In a recent survey of the scientific literature on "lie detection," Benjamin Kleinmuntz and Julian Szucko note that use of the polygraph "assumes that liars are aware of their lying, which in turn causes measurable emotional reactions. . . . The polygraphic technique based on this assumption yields unacceptably high error rates that have had ruinous effects on the lives of many misclassified truthful persons" (Kleinmuntz & Szucko, 1984).

□ □ **QUESTION** □ □

The ancient Chinese often gave criminal suspects rice to eat. If the suspect could swallow the rice easily, he or she was presumed to be innocent. What have you learned about the effects of autonomic arousal on salivation that might support the use of the "rice guilt detector"?

● ***"Beating" the Lie Detector***

David Lykken has, for years, crusaded against the *misuse* of the polygraph. According to Lyk-

ken, "There is no such thing as a lie detector. . . . There is no specific response that everyone **emits** when lying but never when telling the truth. When we lie about something serious, most of us experience some sort of inner turmoil, what Daniel Defoe described 250 years ago as 'a tremor in the blood.' . . . What we forget is that a false accusation can elicit an inner turmoil also—and the lie detector cannot tell the difference!" (Lykken, 1980).

To show what he means, Lykken notes that you can "confuse the experts" during a polygraph test by biting your tongue (to cause pain) and pressing your toes against the floor (to create strong muscle tension). And recent studies do tend to support Lykken's views. For example, University of Wisconsin psychologists Charles Honts, Robert Hodes, and David Raskin trained students to use both the "tongue-biting" and the "toe-pressing" techniques, and then challenged expert polygraph examiners to discover which students were lying and which ones weren't. The students were able to fool the examiners almost 50 percent of the time (Honts, Hodes, & Raskin, 1985).

□ □ **QUESTION** □ □

How would it affect your responses if you took a tranquilizer just before being given a polygraph examination?

● ***Uses and Abuses of Polygraphs***

David Lykken is not opposed to the *proper* use of polygraph tests, particularly in two situations: First, the polygraph is of considerable value in many scientific studies of autonomic responses. Second, the polygraph can be of great help in police investigations. Wisely employed, polygraph tests can help screen out innocent suspects. The police can then spend their time investigating just the people who "flunk" the exams. And, as Lykken notes, many criminals who "believe" in the polygraph often confess when threatened with a test.

But Lykken believes no person should ever be convicted just on the basis of a lie detector test. The chances the test will be wrong are simply too great, which is one reason few courts admit polygraph records as evidence. Nor, Lykken says, should corporations or government organizations use lie detector tests as "routine screening devices." Again, the odds are too large that people will be denied employment on the basis of some "expert's intuition," and not on the basis of their real skills and talents (Lykken, 1980). And David Raskin puts it this way: "There is not a single scientific study which demonstrates any reasonable degree of accuracy for [the use of the lie detector] for general employment screen tests" (cited in Holden, 1986).

• Conditioned Emotional Responses: A Summary

As we saw in Chapter 8, emotionality is a powerful force in human affairs. And it does appear that many (if not all) emotional reactions are acquired by Pavlovian conditioning. However, if most emotional reactions are *learned*, then we might assume most of them can be *unlearned*, or extinguished. That particular insight has led to the development of a new type of psychotherapy called *counter conditioning*.

COUNTER CONDITIONING

In a recent article, Kansas State psychologist Franz Samelson describes the difficulties John B. Watson and Rosalie Rayner had trying to "condition fear" in Little Albert. At first they attempted to make the boy afraid of a flash of light (rather than a rat). They failed, in part because whenever they tried to frighten the child, he would pop his thumb into his mouth. Then he would sit peacefully thumb-sucking, instead of showing the normal "fear" response. According to Samelson, Watson and Rayner could get the fear reaction only when they kept Albert's thumb out of his mouth (Samelson, 1980).

It seems likely the problems Watson and Rayner had *conditioning* fear in Albert gave them the idea of how to *decondition* similar responses. For if thumb-sucking "overwhelmed" the fear response, perhaps they could "counter condition" other children to recover from fear by teaching them a "relaxing" reaction like thumb-sucking. In 1924, a student of Watson's named Mary Cover Jones tried just that.

To appreciate how "counter conditioning" works, imagine that at some time in the future, your own 2-year-old son accidentally learned to fear small furry animals. You might try to cure the boy the way Mary Cover Jones did—by attempting to attach a *strongly positive* response to the fear-arousing stimulus.

The *sight* of a white rat would presumably upset your son—but the sight of food when he was hungry would surely make him happy and eager to eat. If you could somehow *bond* the "rat" stimulus to the "positive" eating response, you could "decondition" the child by making him like the rat rather than fear it.

You might begin the counter-conditioning procedure by bringing a white rat into the same room with your son while you were feeding him. At first, you would want to keep the animal so far away that your son could barely see it out of the corner of his eye. Since the animal wouldn't be close enough to bother him, he probably would keep right on eating. Then, step by step, you might bring the rat closer.

Children do not generally fear small furry animals, such as rabbits, unless one or more unpleasant experiences have "taught" them to feel fearful. Teaching children to overcome such learned fears has been done quite successfully using counter-conditioning techniques.

Since your son could not cry and eat *at the same time*, the CS-CR fear response would gradually *extinguish*. And while the strength of the fear reaction was decreasing, the strength of the CS-CR "pleasure of eating" bond would increase. Eventually, your son would be conditioned to give a new response to the animal that was *counter* to his previous reaction. When Mary Cover Jones followed this procedure (actually using a white rabbit instead of a rat), she found that children soon learned to play with animals that had previously terrified them (Jones, 1924).

The important point about counter conditioning is this—the technique almost always involves *breaking* an inappropriate S-R bond by attaching the *old* "S" to a *new* and more appropriate "R" (Catania, 1984).

□ □ **QUESTION** □ □
For most people, the sight of a big, hairy spider is a stimulus that evokes a very strong avoidance reaction. How might you try to "treat this fear" by counter counditioning the spider stimulus to a new response?

Phobias

In a sense, Watson and Rayner created a **phobia** about rats in little Albert. Phobias are intense, irrational fears about people, places, things, or situations. Usually these fears are so strong that the person with the phobia cannot control her or his reactions even when the person clearly realizes the terror is illogical and unreasonable.

Specific phobias—such as fear of snakes— are often created from a single emotion-charged encounter with the object dreaded.

Mary Cover Jones

Phobia (FOE-bee-uh). From the Greek word for "fear." A phobia is a strong and often unusual fear of something.

Desensitization (DEE-sen-suh-tie-ZAY-shun). When you acquire a conditioned fear of cats, you have become *sensitized* to cats and thus become anxious or afraid each time you see one. Systematic *de*-sensitization, as developed by Joseph Wolpe (WOHL-pee), involves training you to relax whenever you see a cat. Once this form of counter conditioning is complete, your fear of cats will have been "desensitized."

Hierarchy (HIGH-er-ARK-key). To make up a hierarchy is to list things (or people) in order of their importance. A hierarchy of fears, as used in desensitization therapy, is a list of dreaded stimuli running from the most feared to the least feared.

Just as likely, they can come about because of a series of highly unpleasant interactions. In Pavlovian terms, the phobia is said to be caused by the *association* of a previously neutral stimulus (the snake) with those stimuli associated with pain, fear, or great autonomic arousal. The snake stimulus therefore automatically becomes connected to the fear reaction.

The belief that phobias are *learned by association* led psychiatrists and psychologists to attempt to "cure" these irrational fears by using the same sort of *counter-conditioning* techniques pioneered by Mary Cover Jones. The technical term used to describe these techniques is **desensitization**.

Put simply, *desensitization* always involves *breaking* an old S-R bond by associating a *new response* with the *old stimulus*. In treating a snake phobia, for example, you could break the "snake-fear" S-R bond by attaching a *relaxation response* to the *snake stimulus*.

● *A Hierarchy of Fears*

Joseph Wolpe, a psychiatrist now working at Temple University in Philadelphia, is usually given credit for having popularized the use of "counter conditioning" in treating simple phobias. Wolpe's type of therapy is usually called *systematic* desensitization.

Let's suppose that, like a number of students, you have somehow acquired an "exam phobia." That is, every time you try to take an exam, you break out in a cold sweat and your mind "goes blank" no matter how hard you have studied. If you sought Wolpe's help, he would begin treatment by asking you to make a list or **hierarchy** of what frightened you about exam situations. Your hierarchy would range from the least-feared stimulus to the most feared. Wolpe would then try to pair *muscular relaxation* with each stimulus on your list, starting with the least-frightening item on the hierarchy.

Let's say that the lowest item on your list is thinking about an exam some time before it occurs. Wolpe would ask you to relax ("go limp") as you contemplated taking a test some time in the future. If the desensitization technique worked, the relaxation *response* would soon become "connected" to the internal *stimulus* of "thinking about taking an exam."

Then Wolpe would move up the hierarchy, step by step, trying to pair relaxation with each item on your list. At any point, if you tended to panic, Wolpe would stop immediately, get you to calm down, and then start over with an item lower on the list that you had already learned to handle successfully. Eventually, you'd know how to "go limp" as you sat in the classroom waiting for the teacher to pass out the tests on exam day.

Wolpe believes that, during treatment, the phobic reaction must never be allowed to get so strong that it cannot be counteracted by voluntary muscular relaxation (Wolpe, 1981b).

Thousands of patients have been treated with apparent success using one form of desensitization or another. However, there is still considerable debate as to whether "systematic" desensitization occurs for the reasons Wolpe says it does and whether the technique is actually the best type of therapy to use with phobic patients.

□ □ **QUESTION** □ □
Do you think it might help you to overcome your "exam phobia" if you learned better study habits after the phobic reaction itself had been desensitized?

Systematic Desensitization: Pro and Con

Joseph Wolpe is a psychiatrist who, like Pavlov, believes that the "body controls the mind." And, like Pavlov, Wolpe sees the "important" association that occurs during learning as being that which connects Ss to Rs. Therefore, therapy must consist of breaking S-R bonds.

Put another way, as far as Wolpe is concerned, it is your *autonomic arousal* to a fearful object or situation that must be "desensitized," not your "inner feelings" or "thoughts." As you can imagine, psychologists who take an intra-psychic view of things tend to disagree with Wolpe.

For example, is learning *primarily* an association between Ss and Rs? Can't strong bonds also be built up between two different Ss? In fact, there can be. Suppose we take an untrained dog and, for a dozen trials, present it with a white light (S_{light}) followed immediately by a musical tone (S_{tone}). Does the animal salivate? Of course not, since we haven't yet "paired" either stimulus with food powder. But perhaps this "pairing" of S_{light} and S_{tone} brought about a strong "mental association" linking the two stimuli. To test for this possibility, we next condition the animal to salivate to the tone using Pavlovian techniques. Once the CS_{tone}-$CR_{salivation}$ bond is firmly established, we

Joseph Wolpe

then present the dog with the S_{light} stimulus. Although the light has never been "paired" with the food powder, the S_{light} still elicits a few drops of saliva.

Pavlov called this type of training **higher order conditioning** and stoutly maintained it was "mediated" by S-R learning. However, a number of experiments suggest that *higher order conditioning* is better explained in terms of S-S associations (Rescorla, 1984, 1987).

□□ QUESTION □□
How could you explain an "exam phobia" in terms of S-S associations rather than S-R conditioning? (Hint: Could the student *misperceive* either the exam situation or his or her own abilities?) What type of treatment could you use to break inappropriate S-S associations?

● *Cognitive Desensitization*

Perceptual, attitudinal, and other cognitive changes often occur during desensitization training. That is, the patient frequently reports perceiving the once-feared situation in a new and less frightening light. When Wolpe first began his work, he appeared to believe that these perceptual changes were *caused* by changes in autonomic arousal.

However, D.H. Meichenbaum (and many other therapists) soon insisted Wolpe had put the cart before the horse. For instance, Meichenbaum noted that, during therapy, cognitive changes often occurred *first*. Once the patients had changed the *manner in which they perceived the situation,* they could relax more in the presence of the dreaded stimulus (Meichenbaum, 1974).

Furthermore, many studies show that purely mental relaxation can be as powerful in helping to cure phobias as is muscular relaxation (Berman, Miller, & Massman, 1985). The use of *mental* rather than *muscular* relaxation is sometimes called **cognitive desensitization** (Beck, 1986).

□□ QUESTION □□
How could you use a polygraph to measure the *decrease in fear* that occurs in either systematic or cognitive desensitization?

● *"Modeling Therapy"*

Stanford psychologist Albert Bandura believes that treatment shouldn't stop when the phobic response is desensitized. Next, Bandura says, the therapist should help the client learn an *appropriate* response to replace the "inappropriate" fear reaction. And the most efficient way to learn new response patterns, Bandura believes, is to "imitate the behaviors of an appropriate *model*." Then the client can learn a new

response *merely by observing* what the model does.

In a frequently-cited experiment, Bandura and his colleagues used an *observational learning* technique to help subjects overcome their phobic reactions to snakes. The subjects began by watching a "model"—a trained snake handler—who was playing with a reptile several feet from where the clients were standing. Then the clients were encouraged slowly to approach the model (and the snake, of course). Next the clients were urged to touch the reptile, then to hold it briefly. The "final exam" consisted of having the clients sit quietly in a chair while the snake crawled all over them. Bandura and his associates report that "modeling therapy" was significantly more effective at breaking the snake phobia than was systematic desensitization alone (Bandura, Blanchard, & Ritter, 1969).

□□ QUESTION □□
Suppose you watched a woman pick up a strange object, then drop the object in obvious pain. Could you develop a strong fear of the strange object even though you had never touched it yourself? Would this be S-S learning or S-R learning?

● *Wolpe's Response to His Critics*

In a recent article, Wolpe comments on the many criticisms of his approach. He now differentiates between "cognitively-based anxiety" and "conditioned anxiety." According to Wolpe, *cognitive anxiety* is brought about by mental "errors or misinformation." *Conditioned anxiety*, though, is "based on autonomic conditioning" and is acquired in just the manner that Pavlov described. Conditioned anxiety occurs primarily in such simple situations as specific phobias, Wolpe says. Both types of anxiety are likely to be present in more complex cases, such as non-specific phobias.

Wolpe urges the use of desensitization therapy to treat conditioned anxiety. However, he does not make any specific recommendations about how to treat purely "cognitive" anxiety (Wolpe, 1981a).

● *Desensitization or "Natural Extinction"?*

A survey of the literature suggests that any technique which keeps the patient in the "presence" of the feared object (or situation) for an extended period of time will help extinguish the fear. Desensitization may be effective, therefore, simply because it is an elegant way of getting patients to remain near the things they are afraid of until a sort of "natural extinction" takes place. And the more "cognitive" forms of counter-conditioning may work because they require the patient to think about

One step in Bandura's snake phobia therapy is holding a snake in one's hands. The person suffering from the phobia would not be asked to perform this activity until she could perform a less fearful activity — just touching the snake with her fingers, for example — without feeling fear.

Higher order conditioning. A training technique that involves "pairing" two neutral stimuli, then "connecting" one of the Ss to a response using Pavlovian conditioning. When the other neutral S is now presented, it usually can elicit a weak conditioned response even though it has never been directly "paired" with that response.

Cognitive desensitization. Pavlov and the early behavioral psychologists dealt entirely with external stimuli and observable responses. During the 1960's, psychologists discovered that Pavlovian techniques could be used to condition (or decondition) inner processes, such as thoughts and feelings. Desensitization seems to occur just as rapidly if the patient thinks relaxing thoughts (a cognitive process) as if the patient actually relaxes (an observable response).

Whatever method of treating phobias we think is best, we should remember that the goal of all therapies is to help the person engage in normal activities — such as flying in an airplane — without undue anxiety.

the feared objects or situations until the same sort of natural extinction occurs.

Which Position Is Correct?

In fact, there's little sense in fighting over which form of therapy is best, since all types of treatment have their uses. And, as we will see in a later chapter, most types of therapy yield similar results.

In fact, this battle (like many others in psychology) boils down to a matter of *definitions* and *theoretical viewpoints.* Many behavioral psychologists define learning entirely in terms of "stimuli" and "responses." Cognitive psychologists, on the other hand, see learning primarily in terms of *associations between thoughts or ideas.* In truth, however, the *same laws of learning* seem to hold—roughly speaking—whether you deal with behaviors or cognitions.

From a holistic point of view, a person with a snake phobia has *both* disordered behaviors *and* disordered thoughts and feelings. Treating just one part of the problem seldom is as helpful as treating *all aspects* of the phobic condition.

Sometimes, in the heat of defending our theoretical positions, we all lose sight of the prime goal—namely, to get the patient back to normal as quickly and as surely as possible. And to do that, we surely should make use of any type of treatment that "works." We will raise this issue again at the end of the next chapter, after we have looked at a different form of learning called *operant conditioning.*

SUMMARY

1. The American psychologist E.B. Twitmyer was probably the first to publish research on the **conditioned reflex**, but Ivan Pavlov developed most of the conditioning techniques and terminology still in use.
2. Conditioning involves pairing a **neutral stimulus** (the CS) with an **unconditioned stimulus** or *unconditional stimulus* (the UCS). The UCS already has the power to elicit the **unconditioned response** (the UCR). If the CS is associated with the UCS enough times, it conditionally takes on the power to evoke a reaction similar to the UCR. This "similar" reaction is called the **conditioned response** or *conditional response* (the CR).
3. Pavlov paired a tone (CS) with food powder blown into a dog's mouth (the UCS). The food naturally evoked salivation (the UCR). Once the tone had been paired with the food for several trials, sounding the tone without food caused the dog to salivate (the CR).
4. Psychologists often use the term **conditioning** to mean **learning**.
5. According to Pavlov, all learning or conditioning is built on—or is an adaption of—**innately determined stimulus-response connections**, the UCS-UCR bond.
6. Conditioning is sometimes referred to as strengthening S-R bonds or **stimulus-response bonds**. The stronger the bond, the more likely it is the conditioned stimulus will elicit the desired conditioned response.
7. The more often the CS and the UCS are paired, the stronger the **S-R bond** becomes.
8. Conditioning typically proceeds fastest when the CS is presented immediately **before** the UCS. The exception to this rule is a **conditioned taste aversion**. If you become ill several hours after eating some particular food, you may avoid that food in the future.
9. Conditioned responses are unlearned just as easily as they are learned. Unlearning proceeds fastest when the CS is presented several times without being followed by the UCS. Once the S-R bond is broken, the response is said to be **extinguished**.
10. An extinguished response is not totally forgotten. If the CS is again paired with the UCS, **relearning** usually takes fewer trials than did the original learning. Furthermore, extinguished responses often show **spontaneous recovery** after some time has passed.
11. **Internal stimuli** (such as muscle tension) can serve as a CS just as well as can bells or musical tones. The passage of time can also serve as a conditional stimulus.
12. Pavlov conditioned dogs to withstand pain by pairing a weak painful stimulus with a strong UCS, such as food. The food evoked salivation. Soon the **painful stimulus** also evoked salivation rather than escape.
13. If an animal is trained to respond to an orange light, this response may **generalize** to other similar stimuli, such as a red or yellow light. However, with the proper train-

ing, the animal can usually learn to **discriminate** among similar stimuli and give different responses to each.

14. If this discrimination becomes too difficult, the animal may show such **neurotic** responses as biting, barking, and defecation.

15. Watson and Rayner conditioned a boy called Little Albert to fear a rat by pairing the sight of the rat with a frightening noise. Mary Cover Jones reduced this sort of **conditioned emotional response** by pairing the sight of the animal with food using a technique called **counter-conditioning**.

16. The **polygraph** or "lie detector" measures **conditioned emotional responses**, not "lies" or "guilt."

17. Many psychologists believe that most human **phobic reactions** are conditioned in the same manner that Watson and Rayner created a fear response in Little Albert.

18. Joseph Wolpe showed that conditioned fears can be lessened through the use of **systematic desensitization**, a counter-conditioning technique that involves pairing the feared stimulus with relaxation. The patient makes a **hierarchy of fears** ranging from the least feared to the most feared. The patient learns to relax in the presence of stimuli low on the hierarchy of fears first, then **step by step** moves up the hierarchy.

19. **Higher order conditioning** involves first pairing two neutral stimuli, then bonding one of the stimuli to a conditioned response. When the other neutral stimulus is then presented, the animal often gives the conditioned response even though that stimulus has never been associated with the CR.

20. **Cognitive desensitization** involves the use of mental rather than physical relaxation, and seems to be more effective with complex fears than is *systematic desensitization*.

21. **Modeling therapy** encourages the phobic patient to observe and then imitate "appropriate" responses toward the feared object made by someone who doesn't fear the object. Bandura believes it is more important to give the phobic patient new ways of handling fears than it is merely to break S-R bonds.

22. There is some evidence that desensitization (and other therapies) are effective because they keep the patient in the presence of the feared stimulus long enough so that **natural extinction** of the fear can occur.

23. Perhaps the best form of therapy is one that treats all of the patient's problems, whether the problems are biological, psychological, or social.

Glossary of Important Literary Terms

action: the events that take place in a story. "Action" covers everything that happens in a story, from a character's thoughts to his or her interactions with other characters. The arrangement of the action is called plot.

allusion: a reference to a person, place, event, literary work, etc. Writers generally use allusions to make their own meaning clearer or to prove a point. For example, Auden, in "Musee des Beaux Arts," makes an allusion to the painting "Landscape with the Fall of Icarus" in order to support his point.

ambiguity: a word, line, event, etc. that can be interpreted in more than one way. The title of Faulkner's story, "A Rose for Emily," can be interpreted in different ways and is thus ambiguous.

analogy: a comparison in which one thing is compared to another in order to clarify meaning or defend a point. In "Death and Justice," Koch makes an analogy between the death penalty and treatments for cancer. His point is that the death penalty may seem harsh as, say, chemotherapy is harsh, but both are necessary to correct problems.

anecdote: a brief story told to illustrate a point or for humor. In "Too Big," Mac-Donald uses anecdotes as examples to prove his point.

climax: in a story or play, the point at which a major change occurs in a character or in the action. This change affects the remainder of the story or play. In "The Magic Barrel," the climax occurs when Leo sees Stella's picture; this experience changes him, and he begins to behave differently.

conflict: in literature, a struggle between forces: character against character; character against nature; character against society; or character against internal forces. In Welty's "Why I Live at the P.O.," the conflict is between characters; in Piercy's "Barbie Doll," the main character is in conflict with the expectations of the society in which she lives.

connotation: the meaning associated with a word that goes beyond a dictionary definition. The words "woman," "lady," and "dame" all literally refer to a female, but they have different connotations.

denotation: the dictionary definition of a word.

elegy: a poem written in honor of someone who has died. Ransom's "Bells for John Whiteside's Daughter" is an elegy.

foil: a character who stands in direct contrast to another character. Through this contrast, the qualities of both characters are easier to see. In Walker's "Everyday Use," Maggie and Dee are foils to each other.

foreshadowing: a hint of something that will follow. In O'Connor's "Revelation," Mary Grace's angry looks at Mrs. Turpin foreshadow the violence that occurs later

genre: "kind" or "type"; some genres of literature are poetry, fiction, and essay.

hyperbole: an exaggeration intended to emphasize. Hyperboles are common in everyday speech, such as, "I have a million things to do."

image: a mental picture or an association created by a word or group of words. In Thurber's "The Catbird Seat," it is said that Mr. Martin "squirmed slightly." The word "squirmed" reminds us of a worm. In one sense, Mr. Martin is a "worm."

imagery: a group of related images. There are many images of decay in Faulkner's "A Rose for Emily." Thus one speaks of the "decay imagery" in the story.

irony: a conflict between what seems to be and what is, or between what should be and what is. Three types of irony are verbal, situational, and dramatic. Verbal irony is created when one says the opposite of what one means. Situational irony is created when something happens that is the opposite of what one would expect to happen. Dramatic irony is created when the reader knows more than a character knows. In Piercy's "Barbie Doll," the statement is made, "To every woman a happy ending," an example of verbal irony. (The ending has not been happy.) Situational irony is seen in Robinson's "Richard Cory." The character Richard Cory seems to have everything, yet he kills himself. An example of dramatic irony is seen in O'Connor's "Good Country People" when Mrs. Hopewell says of Manley Pointer: "He was so simple." The reader knows that Pointer is not simple.

metaphor: a literary comparison. Metaphor involves calling one thing another: "he was a lion in battle." In this example, "he" is called a "lion"; however, the comparison is between the qualities of this person and the qualities of a lion. We think of such qualities as courage, strength, determination; thus the person was strong and brave in battle and stuck with the fight. A metaphor may be considered in terms of its two parts, the vehicle and tenor. The vehicle is the concrete image that is presented to the reader; the tenor is the idea or concept that is represented by the vehicle. In Hughes' "Mother to Son," the concrete image presented is that of a stairway (the vehicle); the stairway represents life (the tenor).

motivation: why a character behaves a certain way. In some stories, character motivation is the central issue. In Brush's "Birthday Party," the central question is "Why does the husband behave the way he does?"

narrative: the name given to a piece of writing that tells a story; the word also refers to the story itself.

narrator: the person telling a story. A narrator who is involved in the action of the story should be treated as a character, and his or her attitudes and traits should be examined.

parable: a brief story told to illustrate a point or to teach a lesson. MacDonald ends his essay "Too Big" by quoting the parable of the Good Samaritan from the Bible.

personification: a literary device in which human characteristics are given to a thing or an animal. In Kennedy's "In a Prominent Bar in Secaucus One Day," time is personified: "When time takes you out for a spin in his car, . . ."

plot: the structure of the events of a story. The writer may arrange the events in the order that they occurred (as in "The Lottery"), or the writer may move back and forth in time (as in "A Rose for Emily"). The reader should distinguish between plot and theme.

poetic justice: justice that is especially appropriate considering the character's behavior. In O'Connor's "Good Country People," it is poetic justice that Manley Pointer outsmarts Hulga because she has thought herself superior to everyone else.

point of view: the vantage point from which a story is told. A story may be told from a first-person point of view in which someone who is personally involved in the story tells it (as in "I Stand Here Ironing" and "Everyday Use"). A story may be told from third-person point of view. This point of view may be *objective*, in which case the reader is given only those events that are observable ("The Lottery"); or *limited*, in which case the reader is allowed into the mind of one central character ("He"); or *omniscient*, in which case the reader is allowed into the minds of all or several of the characters.

satire: a form of writing that ridicules or makes fun of some situation, person, or human weakness. Some satiric writing only gently ridicules its subject; other satiric writing is harsh or bitter. Satire frequently uses verbal irony. See Auden's "The Unknown Citizen" for an example of satire.

setting: the time and place of the action of a story. "Time" may be as specific as a particular hour of a particular day, or it may be as vague as, say, the nineteenth century or "sometime in the fifties." "Place" may be as specific as a particular room in a house or a particular house in a town, or it may be as vague as the United States or "somewhere in the West." In some pieces, setting plays a more important role than in others. Setting in "The Lottery" and "A Rose for Emily" is very important in shaping the meaning of the story. In other pieces, such as "The Catbird Seat" and "I Stand Here Ironing," setting is relatively unimportant in shaping the meaning of the story. The reader should consider the effects of setting on such things as character, action, and tone.

simile: a literary comparison using "like" or "as." Thus "He was like a lion in battle" is considered a simile, whereas "He was a lion in battle" is considered a metaphor. The function of a simile, as with a metaphor, is to explain something by comparing it to something else. The reader's job is to see what is being said about something through the use of simile. See Hughes' "Harlem," a poem developed chiefly through the use of similes.

symbol: something that represents something else. Like a metaphor, a symbol involves a comparison: what is used as a symbol has something in common with the thing it represents. Thus a lamb may be a symbol for human qualities such as meekness, since lambs are generally meek creatures. Characters in a piece of writing may be symbols or may be considered symbolic of certain human qualities or conditions. An elderly character such as Old Man Warner in "The Lottery," for example, is a symbol for all people who resist change. (Usually elderly people are more resistent to change.) Action also may be symbolic. In "Shiloh," Norma Jean is concerned with improving her body through exercise; this is symbolic of her desire to be emotionally and intellectually stronger.

theme: the main idea or the "point" of a poem, short story, play, etc. A piece of literature may have more than one theme, or the theme may be seen differently by different readers. With some pieces of literature, one can make a neat statement of theme; with other more complex pieces, it is better to talk about the main issues or questions raised, since the meaning is likely, as Flannery O'Connor notes, to "go on expanding for the reader the more he thinks about it." Theme should be distinguished from plot. In "The Lottery," for example, the plot consists of townspeople gathering together and holding a lottery. The theme, however, is not about lotteries or what happens in them. The theme is a statement about people in general or about human nature.

thesis: the main idea or the point that the writer is arguing. The term *thesis* may be applied to any type of writing but is always used to describe the main idea of essays.

tone: an expression of the writer's attitude. In speech, our attitudes are frequently shown by our "tone of voice"; in writing, tone is shown by such features as descriptions of people, places, and events. Some words that describe tone in writing are "approving," "cheerful," "sarcastic," "angry," and "bitter." The tone of "Dulce et Decorum Est" could be described as "bitter," reflecting the poet's resentment toward those who glorify war.

understatement: language that expresses less than one feels or thinks. See "Bells for John Whiteside's Daughter" for an example of understatement.

Name Index

Literary Acknowledgments

p. 3—Kristine Batey, "Lot's Wife" copyright © 1978 by *Jam To-Day*. Reprinted with permission.

p. 4—From *The New English Bible*. Copyright © The Delegates of the Oxford University Press and The Syndics of the Cambridge Uinversity Press 1961, 1970. Reprinted by permission.

p. 5—Robert Frost, "The Road Not Taken" copyright 1916, 1930 by Holt, Rinehart and Winston and renewed 1944, 1958 by Robert Frost. Reprinted from *The Poetry of Robert Frost* edited by Edward Connery Lathem, by permission of Henry Holt and Company, Inc.

p. 6—From *Selected Poems of Langston Hughes*. Copyright © 1959 by Langston Hughes. Reprinted by permission of Alfred A. Knopf, Inc.

p. 6—Robert Hayden, "Those Winter Sundays" is reprinted from *Angle of Ascent, New and Selected Poems* by Robert Hayden, by permission of Liveright Publishing Corporation. Copyright © 1975, 1972, 1970, 1966 by Robert Hayden.

p. 7—From *Selected Poems of Langston Hughes*. Copyright © 1959 by Langston Hughes. Reprinted by permission of Alfred A. Knopf.

p. 9—Wilfred Owen, "Dulce et Decorum Est" from *Collected Poems of Wilfred Owen*. Copyright © 1963 by Chatto and Windus, Ltd. Reprinted by permission of New Directions Publishing Corporation, the Estate of Wilfred Owen, and The Hogarth Press.

p. 11—Emily Dickinson, "Hope Is a Strange Invention" and "Hope Is a Subtle Glutton" reprinted by permission of Harvard University Press and The Trustees of Amherst College from *The Poems of Emily Dickinson*, Thomas H. Johnson, ed., Cambridge, Mass.; The Belknap Press of Harvard University Press. Copyright 1951, © 1955, 1979, 1983 by the President and Fellows of Harvard College.

p. 12—From *Spoon River Anthology* by Edgar Lee Masters, published by the Macmillan Company. Reprinted by permission of Ellen C. Masters.

p. 14—From *W. H. Auden: Collected Poems*, edited by Edward Mendelson. Copyright © 1976 by Edward Mendelson, William Meredith and Monroe K. Spears, Executors of the Estate of W. H. Auden. Reprinted by permission of Random House, Inc. and Faber and Baber, Ltd.

p. 16—Willie Morris, "The Accident" reprinted by permission of Joan Daves.

p. 16—Edwin Arlington Robinson, "Mr. Flood's Party" reprinted with permission of Macmillan Publishing Company from *Collected Poems* by Edwin Arlington Robinson. Copyright 1921 by Edwin Arlington Robinson, renewed 1949 by Ruth Nivison.

p. 18—From *Collected Poems 1930-1986* by Richard Eberhart. Copyright © 1960, 1976, 1988 by Richard Eberhart. Reprinted by permission of Oxford University Press, Inc.

p. 21—From *New and Collected Poems 1917-1982* by Archibald MacLeish. Copyright © 1985 by The Estate of Archibald MacLeish. Reprinted by permission of Houghton Mifflin Company.

p. 175—Randall Williams, "Daddy Tucked the Blanket" copyright © 1975 by the New York Times Company. Reprinted by permission.

p. 179—Roy Meador, "Richard Cory, All Over Again" copyright © 1976 by The New York Times Company. Reprinted by permission.

p. 181—Art Buchwald, "Hurts Rent-A-Gun" reprinted by permission of the Putnam Publishing Group from *I Never Danced at the White House* by Art Buchwald. Copyright © 1973 by Art Buchwald.

p. 182—Barry Goldwater, "Why Gun Control Laws Don't Work" reprinted with permission from the December 1975 *Reader's Digest*. Copyright © 1975 by The Reader's Digest Assn., Inc.

p. 185—Annette Dula, "No Home in Africa" copyright © 1975 by The New York Times Company. Reprinted by permission.

p. 187—Judy Syfers, "I Want a Wife" from *MS*, December, 1971. Copyright © 1971 by Judy Syfers. Reprinted by permission of the author.

p. 188—Sylvia Rabiner, "How the Superwoman Myth Puts Women Down" reprinted by permission of the author and *The Village Voice*.

p. 192—Anne Roiphe, "Confession of a Female Chauvinist Sow" published in *New York Magazine*. Copyright © 1972 by Anne Roiphe. Reprinted by permission of Brandt & Brandt Literary Agents, Inc.

p. 196—From *The Male Machine* by Marc Feigen Fasteau. Copyright © 1974. Reprinted by permission of McGraw-Hill Publishing Company.

p. 204—From *The Informed Heart* by Bruno Bettelheim, reprinted with permission of The Free Press, a division of Macmillan, Inc. Copyright © 1960 by The Free Press, renewed 1988 by Bruno Bettelheim.

p. 206—Stephen Chapman, "The Prisoner's Dilemma," from *The New Republic* March 8, 1980. Reprinted by permission of The New Republic, © 1980, The New Republic, Inc.

p. 213—Flannery O'Connor, "Total Effect and the Eighth Grade" from *Mystery and Manners* by Flannery O'Connor. Copyright © 1957, 1961, 1963, 1964, 1966, 1967, 1969 by the Estate of Mary Flannery O'Connor. Reprinted by permission of Farrar, Straus and Giroux, Inc.

p. 218—From *Biology*, third edition by Karen Arms and Pamela S. Camp. Copyright © 1987 by Saunders College Publishing, a division of Holt, Rinehart and Winston, Inc.; reprinted by permission of the publisher.

p. 234—From *American History*, Volume 1 by Richard N. Current, T. Harry Williams, Frank Freidel, and Alan Brinkley. Copyright © 1987 by Alfred A. Knopf, Inc. Reprinted by permission.

p. 261—Excerpt from *Understanding Human Behavior* by James V. McConnell. Copyright © 1986 by Holt, Rinehart and Winston, Inc. Reprinted by permission of the publisher.